The media's watching Vault.com!
Here's a sampling of our coverage.

"It's the next best thing to taking a job out for a test drive."
— *New York Magazine*

"Vault's research...is sure to be snapped up on Wall Street.""
— *The Daily Deal*

"Vault.com has become a de facto Internet outsourcer of the corporate grapevine."
— *Fortune*

"The well-written profiles make Vault.com the next best thing to camping out in a company rest room."
—*Yahoo! Internet Life*

"For those hoping to climb the ladder of success, [Vault.com's] insights are priceless."
— *Money.com*

"Vault.com is indispensible for locating insider information."
— *Metropolitan Corporate Counsel*

"The granddaddy of worker sites."
— *U.S. News and World Report*

"Vault.com is another killer app for the Internet."
— *New York Times*

VAULT.COM
> the insider career network™

VAULT.COM CAREER GUIDE TO INVESTMENT BANKING

> the insider career network™

VAULT.COM CAREER GUIDE TO INVESTMENT BANKING

ANITA KAPADIA, CHRIS PRIOR, AND TOM LOTT

For information about permission to reproduce selections from this book, contact Vault.com Inc., P.O. Box 1772, New York, New York 10011-1772, (212) 366-4212.

Library of Congress CIP Data is available.

ISBN 1-58131-115-X

Printed in the United States of America

ACKNOWLEDGEMENTS

Vault.com would like to acknowledge the assistance and support of Geoff Baum, Ken Cron, Matt Doull, Glenn Fischer, Mark Hernandez, Ravi Mhatre, Tom Phillips, Jay Oyakawa, Carter Weiss, the folks at Hollinger Ventures, Ingram, and Globix, and our families and friends.

This book is the result of the extraordinary efforts of Doug Cantor, Catherine Cugell, Rebekah Curry, Marcy Lerner, Clarissa Londis, Sumiya Nowshin, Kathleen Pierce, Rob Schipano, and Ed Shen.

Special thanks to all of the investment banking firm recruiting coordinators, corporate communications representatives, and partners who helped with this book. We appreciate your patience with our repeated requests for information and ever-tightening deadlines.

We dedicate the *Vault.com Career Guide to Investment Banking* to the hundreds of investment bankers who took time out of their busy schedules to be interviewed or complete our survey.

unlimited

OVERVIEW OF INVESTMENT BANKING

THE INDUSTRY

THE JOBS

Hungry for more inside scoop? Join Vault.com's popular online
community for finance and banking — www.vault.com

VAULT.com   xi

LEADING EMPLOYERS

Hungry for more inside scoop? Join Vault.com's popular online
community for finance and banking — www.vault.com

V/\ULT.com   xiii

technology
& healthcare

Investment Banking

The Organization

SG Cowen provides investment banking services to emerging growth companies in the technology, healthcare, and utilities industries. Driven by a strong research-based tradition, our focus has allowed us to develop a unique perspective of these sectors and the forces affecting them. By combining this sophisticated industry knowledge with innovative banking products and services, we have created a strong foundation from which to serve our clients.

A collaborative organizational structure allows us to merge our resources more efficiently, and to create better and more comprehensive solutions to our clients' rapidly changing needs. From private placements, venture financing and equity underwriting, to mergers and acquisitions advisory, leveraged lending, convertible debt offerings and syndicated loans, we are dedicated to providing integrated solutions tailored to each client.

The Profile

We have opportunities for 40 analysts and 20 associates in our New York, San Francisco, Boston, Chicago, Washington, D.C., and London investment banking offices. An excellent academic record, exceptional interpersonal skills and superior analytical, computer and communication skills are essential. We value individuals who are highly motivated, demonstrated team players who can interact with all levels of the organization in a collegial and constructive manner. Initiative, integrity, and creativity distinguish successful candidates.

To apply, please send your cover letter and resume to Chip Rae, Director, SG Cowen, 1221 Avenue of the Americas, New York, New York 10020.

SG Cowen is an Equal Opportunity Employer.

OVERVIEW OF INVESTMENT BANKING

THE INDUSTRY

What is an Investment Bank?

CHAPTER 1

What is investment banking? Is it investing? Is it banking? Really, it is neither. Investment banking, or I-banking, as it is often called, is the term used to describe the business of raising capital for companies. Capital essentially means money. Companies need cash in order to grow and expand their businesses; investment banks sell securities to public investors in order to raise this cash. These securities can come in the form of stocks or bonds, which we will discuss in depth later.

The Players

The biggest investment banks include Goldman Sachs, Merrill Lynch, Morgan Stanley Dean Witter, Salomon Smith Barney, Donaldson, Lufkin & Jenrette, J.P. Morgan and Lehman Brothers, among others. Of course, the complete list of I-banks is more extensive, but the firms listed above compete for the biggest deals both in the U.S. and worldwide.

You have probably heard of many of these firms, and perhaps have a brokerage account with one of them. While brokers from these firms cover every city in the U.S., the headquarters of every one of these firms is in New York City, the epicenter of the I-banking universe. It is important to realize that investment banking and brokerage go hand-in-hand, but that brokers are one small cog in the investment banking wheel. As we will cover in detail later, brokers sell securities that a firm underwrites and manage the portfolios of retail investors.

Many an I-banking interviewee asks, "Which firm is the best?" The answer, like many things in life, is unclear. Each firm listed above certainly can produce reams of paper and data attesting to its dominance, and most have several strengths. But no single firm rules in every aspect of banking. Merrill leads in total underwriting volume, but trails DLJ in high-yield. Goldman Sachs' reputation in equity underwriting and M&A advisory is stellar, but it lags the competition in the asset-backed debt business. The following pages contain the rankings of investment banks (commonly called league tables) in several categories. All in all, every firm has its own pros and cons, and choosing one based on reputation alone would be foolhardy. In general, the people you work with are the most important part of choosing a firm

Hungry for more inside scoop? Join Vault.com's popular online community for finance and banking — www.vault.com

VAULT.com   5

— no one ever reported loving their job because their firm ranked number one in the industry.

All Debt and Equity in the Public and Rule 144A U.S. Market

Full credit to lead manager (equal if joint)

1999 RANK	MANAGERS	TRANSACTION VALUE ($MILS)	1998 RANK	MKT SHARE	# OF ISSUES
1	Merrill Lynch	333,564.6	1	15.7	2,049
2	Salomon Smith Barney	262,908.8	2	12.3	1,521
3	Morgan Stanley Dean Witter	217,852.7	3	10.2	2,281
4	Goldman Sachs	196,593.0	4	9.2	1,087
5	Credit Suisse First Boston	181,255.7	6	8.5	1,167
6	Lehman Brothers	164,267.8	5	7.7	951
7	Chase Manhattan	123,784.3	9	5.8	1,111
8	JP Morgan	89,934.7	7	4.2	517
9	Bear Stearns	80,384.1	8	3.8	633
10	Banc of America Securities	77,581.4	12	3.6	661
	Top 10 Totals	1,728,127.0		81.1	11,978
	Industry Totals	2,130,640.6		100.0	17,431

Source: Thomson Financial Securities Data

IPOs in the Public U.S. Market (Excludes Closed End Funds)

Full credit to lead manager (equal if joint)

1999 RANK	MANAGERS	TRANSACTION VALUE ($MILS)	1998 RANK	MKT SHARE	# OF ISSUES
1	Goldman Sachs	14,547.0	3	21.1	54
2	Morgan Stanley Dean Witter	13,967.5	1	20.3	49
3	Merrill Lynch	7,721.5	2	11.2	41
4	Credit Suisse First Boston	5,913.0	5	8.6	59
5	Donaldson, Lufkin & Jenrette	3,892.1		5.7	39
6	Lehman Brothers	2,905.5	13	4.2	32
7	JP Morgan	2,785.5	10	4.1	10
	Fleet Boston	2,683.8	15	3.9	45
9	Salomon Smith Barney	2,530.8	4	3.7	22
10	Deutsche Bank	2,128.2	7	3.1	28
	Top 10 Totals	59,074.9		85.8	379
	Industry Totals	68,825.2		100.0	543

Source: Thomson Financial Securities Data

Hungry for more inside scoop? Join Vault.com's popular online
community for finance and banking — www.vault.com

VAULT.COM   7

Common Stock in the Public and Rule 144A U.S. Market (Excludes Closed End Funds)

Full credit to lead manager (equal if joint)

1999 RANK	MANAGERS	PROCEEDS ($MILS)	1998 RANK	MKT SHARE	# OF ISSUES
1	Goldman Sachs	33,722.8	2	19.3	123
2	Morgan Stanley Dean Witter	32,741.7	1	18.7	99
3	Merrill Lynch	17,436.3	3	10.0	112
4	Credit Suisse First Boston	15,084.9	8	8.6	113
5	Salomon Smith Barney	13,208.0	4	7.6	73
6	Donaldson, Lufkin & Jenrette	10,359.9	5	5.9	73
7	JP Morgan	9,563.1	6	5.5	27
8	Lehman Brothers	6,642.0	9	3.8	54
9	Deutsche Bank	5,548.8	7	3.2	68
10	Bear Stearns	5,100.1	10	2.9	47
	Top 10 Totals	149,407.4		85.4	789
	Industry Totals	174,956.4		100.0	1070

Source: Thomson Financial Securities Data

Announced U.S. M&A

Credit to Target & Acquirer Advisors

1999 RANK	ADVISOR	TRANSACTION VALUE ($MILS)	1998 RANK	MKT SHARE	# OF DEALS
1	Goldman Sachs	662,787.6	1	38.8	249
2	Morgan Stanley Dean Witter	503,750.2	3	29.5	234
3	Merrill Lynch	483,153.0	2	28.3	178
4	Salomon Smith Barney	363,375.7	4	21.3	212
5	Credit Suisse First Boston	246,962.0	5	14.4	154
6	Donaldson, Lufkin & Jenrette	209,757.9	7	12.3	240
7	Lehman Brothers	197,302.2		11.5	125
	Lazard	179,323.6	13	10.5	64
9	UBS Warburg	178,738.6	10	10.5	77
10	Bear Stearns	168,903.8	9	9.9	77
	Deals with Advisor	1,541,276.3		90.1	2,599
	Deals w/o Advisor	168,862.2		9.9	8,528
	Industry Totals	1,710,138.0		100.0	11,125

Source: Thomson Financial Securities Data

Hungry for more inside scoop? Join Vault.com's popular online
community for finance and banking — www.vault.com

VAULT.com   9

Completed Worldwide M&A

Credit to Target & Acquirer Advisors

1999 RANK	ADVISOR	TRANSACTION VALUE ($MILS)	1998 RANK	MKT SHARE	# OF DEALS
1	Goldman Sachs	915,332.7	1	38.5	1369
2	Morgan Stanley Dean Witter	630,263.8	3	26.5	377
3	Merrill Lynch	521,475.7	2	21.9	342
4	Credit Suisse First Boston	386,687.9	5	16.3	306
5	JP Morgan	364,192.0	7	15.3	235
6	Salomon Smith Barney	355,148.7	4	14.9	400
7	Donaldson, Lufkin & Jenrette	325,548.2	12	13.7	317
8	Lehman Brothers	181,982.7	6	7.7	184
9	Lazard	168,159.0	8	7.1	158
10	UBS Warburg	146,251.7	9	6.2	268
	Deals with Advisor	2,158,012.7	-	90.8	6,074
	Deals w/o Advisor	218,594.0	-	9.2	18,975
	Industry Totals	2,376,606.7	-	100.0	25,046

Source: Thomson Financial Securities Data

Corporate Investment Grade Non-Convertible Debt in the Public and Rule 144A U.S. Market

Full credit to lead manager (equal if joint)

1999 RANK	MANAGERS	TRANSACTION VALUE ($MILS)	1998 RANK	MKT SHARE	# OF ISSUES
1	Merrill Lynch	168,895.7	1	22.3	1,250
2	Salomon Smith Barney	111,801.0	2	14.8	773
3	Chase Manhattan	88,663.6	6	11.7	800
4	Goldman Sachs	71,176.4	3	9.4	474
5	Morgan Stanley Dean Witter	66,631.7	4	8.8	1,422
6	Credit Suisse First Boston	50,701.9	5	6.7	478
7	Lehman Brothers	45,012.7		5.9	304
	Banc of America Securities	42,470.9	10	5.6	361
9	JP Morgan	31,762.8	7	4.2	238
10	Bear Stearns	16,830.5	9	2.2	171
	Top 10 Totals	693,947.2		91.6	6,271
	Industry Totals	757,998.1		100.0	7,165

Source: Thomson Financial Securities Data

Hungry for more inside scoop? Join Vault.com's popular online
community for finance and banking — www.vault.com

VAULT.COM   11

Corporate High Yield Non-Convertible Debt in the Public and Rule 144A U.S. Market (Excludes Split High Yield Rated Issues)

Full credit to lead manager (equal if joint)

1999 RANK	MANAGERS	PROCEEDS ($MILS)	1998 RANK	MKT SHARE	# OF ISSUES
1	Donaldson, Lufkin & Jenrette	17,476.9	1	18.4	74
2	Salomon Smith Barney	13,432.1	3	14.1	62
3	Goldman Sachs	10,724.6	7	11.3	52
4	Chase Manhattan	10,277.5	6	10.8	48
5	Morgan Stanley Dean Witter	8,734.8	2	9.2	121
6	Merrill Lynch	5,699.1	4	6.0	26
7	Credit Suisse First Boston	5,255.3	8	5.5	30
8	Lehman Brothers	4,309.6	9	4.5	27
9	Bear Stearns	4,136.5	10	4.4	24
10	Banc of America Securities	2,949.9	12	3.1	20
	Top 10 Totals	82,996.2		87.3	484
	Industry Totals	95,107.3		100.0	530

Source: Thomson Financial Securities Data

Asset-Backed Debt in the Public and Rule 144A U.S. Market

Full credit to lead manager (equal if joint)

1999 RANK	MANAGERS	TRANSACTION VALUE ($MILS)	1998 RANK	MKT SHARE	# OF ISSUES
1	Credit Suisse First Boston	38,410.2	1	14.0	190
2	Lehman Brothers	36,110.0	5	13.2	179
3	Salomon Smith Barney	35,383.0	4	12.9	177
4	Merrill Lynch	21,513.7	3	7.9	125
5	Morgan Stanley Dean Witter	20,602.0	2	7.5	133
6	JP Morgan	16,895.7	10	6.2	51
7	Bear Stearns	14,532.0	7	5.3	128
	Prudential Securities Inc	14,496.6	9	5.3	161
9	Banc of America Securities	13,282.7	11	4.9	78
10	Goldman Sachs	12,232.2	6	4.5	53
	Top 10 Totals	223,458.0		81.6	1,275
	Industry Totals	273,976.3		100.0	1,590

Source: Thomson Financial Securities Data

Hungry for more inside scoop? Join Vault.com's popular online
community for finance and banking — www.vault.com

VAULT.COM   13

The Game

Generally, the breakdown of an investment bank includes the following areas:

Corporate Finance

The bread and butter of a traditional investment bank, corporate finance generally performs two different functions: 1) Mergers and acquisitions advisory and 2) Underwriting. On the mergers and acquisitions (M&A) advising side of corporate finance, bankers assist in negotiating and structuring a merger between two companies. If, for example, a company wants to buy another firm, then an investment bank will help finalize the purchase price, structure the deal, and generally ensure a smooth transaction. The underwriting function within corporate finance involves shepherding the process of raising capital for a company. In the investment banking world, capital can be raised by selling either stocks or bonds to investors.

Sales

Sales is another core component of any investment bank. Salespeople take the form of: 1) the classic retail broker, 2) the institutional salesperson, or 3) the private client service representative. Brokers develop relationships with individual investors and sell stocks and stock advice to the average Joe. Institutional salespeople develop business relationships with large institutional investors. Institutional investors are those who manage large groups of assets, for example pension funds or mutual funds. Private Client Service (PCS) representatives lie somewhere between retail brokers and institutional salespeople, providing brokerage and money management services for extremely wealthy individuals. Salespeople make money through commissions on trades made through their firms.

Trading

Traders also provide a vital role for the investment bank. Traders facilitate the buying and selling of stock, bonds, or other securities such as currencies, either by carrying an inventory of securities for sale or by executing a given trade for a client. Traders deal with transactions large and small and provide liquidity (the ability to buy and sell securities) for the market. (This is often called making a market.) Traders make money by purchasing securities and selling them at a slightly higher price. This price differential is called the "bid-ask spread."

Research

Research analysts follow stocks and bonds and make recommendations on whether to buy, sell, or hold those securities. Stock analysts (known as equity analysts) typically focus on one industry and will cover up to 20 companies' stocks at any given time. Some research analysts work on the fixed income side and will cover a particular segment, such as high yield bonds or U.S. Treasury bonds. Salespeople within the I-bank utilize research published by analysts to convince their clients to buy or sell securities through their firm. Corporate finance bankers rely on research analysts to be experts in the industry in which they are working. Reputable research analysts can generate substantial corporate finance business as well as substantial trading activity, and thus are an integral part of any investment bank.

Syndicate

The hub of the investment banking wheel, syndicate provides a vital link between salespeople and corporate finance. Syndicate exists to facilitate the placing of securities in a public offering, a knock-down drag-out affair between and among buyers of offerings and the investment banks managing the process. In a corporate or municipal debt deal, syndicate also determines the allocation of bonds. The breakdown of these fundamental areas differs slightly from firm to firm, but typically an investment bank will have the following areas:

Corporate Finance (equity)
Corporate Finance (debt)
Mergers & Acquisitions (M&A)
Equity Sales
Fixed Income Sales
Syndicate (equity)
Syndicate (debt)
Equity Trading
Fixed Income Trading
Equity Research
Fixed Income Research

Hungry for more inside scoop? Join Vault.com's popular online
community for finance and banking — www.vault.com

VAULT.com   **15**

The functions of all of these areas will be discussed in much more detail later in the book. In this overview section, we will cover the nuts and bolts of the business, providing an overview of the stock and bond markets, and how an I-bank operates within them.

Commercial Banking, Investment Banking, and Asset Management

Before describing how an investment bank operates, let's back up and start by describing traditional commercial banking. Commercial and investment banking share many aspects, but also have many fundamental differences. After a quick overview of commercial banking, we will build up to a full discussion of what I-banking entails.

Although the barriers between investment and commercial banks have essentially been removed by the recent passage of the Gramm-Leach-Bliley Financial Services Modernization Act of 1999, we will for now examine the traditional model of the commercial banking industry and compare it to investment banking. We will then investigate how the new legislation affects commercial and investment banking organizations. Also, we will distinguish between the buy-side and the sell-side of the securities industry.

Commercial banking vs. investment banking

While regulation has changed the businesses in which commercial and investment banks may now participate, the core aspects of these different businesses remain intact. In other words, the difference between how a typical investment bank and a typical commercial operate bank is simple: A commercial bank takes deposits for checking and savings accounts from consumers while an investment bank does not. We'll begin examining what this means by taking a look at what commercial banks do.

Commercial banks

A commercial bank may legally take deposits for checking and savings accounts from consumers. The federal government provides insurance guarantees on these deposits through the Federal Deposit Insurance Corporation (the FDIC), on amounts up to $100,000. To get FDIC guarantees, commercial banks must follow a myriad of regulations

Hungry for more inside scoop? Join Vault.com's popular online community for finance and banking — www.vault.com

VAULT.COM 17

The typical commercial banking process is fairly straightforward. You deposit money into your bank, and the bank loans that money to consumers and companies in need of capital (cash). You borrow to buy a house, finance a car, or finance an addition to your home. Companies borrow to finance the growth of their company or meet immediate cash needs. Companies that borrow from commercial banks can range in size from the dry cleaner on the corner to a multinational conglomerate.

Private contracts

Importantly, loans from commercial banks are structured as private legally binding contracts between two parties — the bank and you (or the bank and a company). Banks work with their clients to individually determine the terms of the loans, including the time to maturity and the interest rate charged. Your individual credit history (or credit risk profile) determines the amount you can borrow and how much interest you are charged. Perhaps you need to borrow $200,000 over 15 years to finance the purchase of your home, or maybe you need $30,000 over five years to finance the purchase of a car. Maybe for the first loan, you and the bank will agree that you pay an interest rate of 7.5 percent; perhaps for the car loan, the interest rate will be 11 percent. The same process applies to loans to companies as well — the rates are determined through a negotiation between the bank and the company.

Let's take a minute to understand how a bank makes its money. On most loans, commercial banks in the U.S. earn interest anywhere from 5 to 14 percent. Ask yourself how much your bank pays you on your deposits — the money that it uses to make loans. You probably earn a paltry 1 percent on a checking account, if anything, and maybe 2 to 3 percent on a savings account. Commercial banks thus make gobs of money, taking advantage of the large spread between their cost of funds (1 percent, for example) and their return on funds loaned (ranging from 5 to 14 percent).

Investment banks

An investment bank operates differently. An investment bank does not have an inventory of cash deposits to lend as a commercial bank does. In essence, an investment bank acts as an intermediary, and matches sellers of stocks and bonds with buyers of stocks and bonds.

Note, however, that companies use investment banks toward the same end as they use commercial banks. If a company needs capital, it may get a loan from a bank, or it may ask an investment bank to sell equity or debt (stocks or bonds). Because commercial banks already have funds available from their depositors and an investment bank does not, an I-bank must spend considerable time finding investors in order to obtain capital for its client.

Public securities

Investment banks typically sell public securities (as opposed private loan agreements). Technically, securities such as Microsoft stock or Ford AAA bonds, represent government-approved stocks or bonds that are traded either on a public exchange or through an approved dealer. The dealer is the investment bank.

Private Debt vs. Bonds — An Example

Let's look at an example to illustrate the difference between private debt and bonds. Suppose Acme Company needs capital, and estimates its need to be $200 million. (Acme is bigger than your corner dry cleaner.) Acme could obtain a commercial bank loan from Bank of New York for the entire $200 million, and pay interest on that loan just like you would pay on a $2,000 loan from Bank of New York. Alternately, it could sell bonds publicly using an investment bank such as Merrill Lynch. The $200 million bond issue raised by Merrill would be broken into many bonds and then sold to the public. (For example, the issue could be broken into 200,000 bonds, each worth $1,000.) Once sold, the company receives its $200 million and investors receive bonds worth a total of the same amount.

Over time, the investors in the bond offering receive coupon payments (the interest), and ultimately the principal (the original $1,000) at the end of the life of the loan, when Acme Corp buys back the bonds (retires the bonds). Thus, we see that in a bond offering, while the money is still loaned to Acme, it is actually loaned by numerous investors, rather than a bank.

Because the investment bank involved in the offering does not own the bonds but merely placed them with investors at the outset, it earns no interest — the bondholders earn this interest in the form of regular coupon payments. The investment bank makes money by charging the client (in this case, Acme) a small percentage of the transaction upon its completion. Investment banks call this upfront fee the "underwriting discount." In contrast, a commercial bank making a loan actually receives the interest and simultaneously owns the debt.

Hungry for more inside scoop? Join Vault.com's popular online
community for finance and banking — www.vault.com

VAULT.com   **19**

Later, we will cover the steps involved in underwriting a public bond deal. Legally, bonds must first be approved by the Securities and Exchange Commission (SEC). (The SEC is a government entity that regulates the sale of all public securities.) The investment bankers guide the company through the SEC approval process, and then market the offering utilizing a written prospectus, its sales force and a roadshow to find investors.

The question of equity

Investment banks underwrite stock offerings just as they do bond offerings. In the stock offering process, companies sell a portion of the equity (or ownership) of itself to the investing public. The very first time a company chooses to sell equity, this offering of equity is transacted through a process called an initial public offering of stock (commonly known as an IPO). Through the IPO process, stock in a company is created and sold to the public. After the deal, stock sold in the U.S. is traded on a stock exchange such as the New York Stock Exchange (NYSE) or the Nasdaq. We will cover the equity offering process in greater detail in Chapter 6. The equity underwriting process is another major way in which investment banking differs from commercial banking.

Commercial banks (even before Glass-Steagall repeal) were able to legally underwrite debt, and some of the largest commercial banks have developed substantial expertise in underwriting public bond deals. So, not only do these banks make loans utilizing their deposits, they also underwrite bonds through a corporate finance department. When it comes to underwriting bond offerings, commercial banks have long competed for this business directly with investment banks. However, only the biggest tier of commercial banks are able to do so, mostly because the size of most public bond issues is large and Wall Street competition for such deals is quite fierce.

Glass-Steagall Reform

Previously, we briefly discussed that much has changed in the investment banking industry, driven primarily by the breakdown of the Glass-Steagall Act. This section will cover why the Act was originally put into place, why it was criticized, and how recent legislation will impact the securities industry.

The history of Glass-Steagall

The famous Glass-Steagall Act, enacted in 1934, erected barriers between commercial banking and the securities industry. A piece of Depression-Era legislation, Glass-Steagall was created in the aftermath of the stock market crash of 1929 and the subsequent collapse of many commercial banks. At the time, many blamed the securities activities of commercial banks for their instability. Dealings in securities, critics claimed, upset the soundness of the banking community, caused banks to fail, and crippled the stock markets. Therefore, separating securities businesses and commercial banking seemed the best solution to provide solidity to the U.S. banking and securities' system.

In later years, a different truth seemed evident. The framers of Glass-Steagall argued that a conflict of interest existed between commercial and investment banks. The conflict of interest argument ran something like this: 1) A bank that made a bad loan might try to reduce its risk of defaulting by underwriting a public offering and selling stock in that company; 2) The proceeds from the IPO would be used to pay off the bad loan; and 3) Essentially, the bank would shift risk from its own balance sheet to new investors via the initial public offering. Academic research and common sense, however, has convinced many that this conflict of interest isn't valid. A bank that consistently sells ill-fated stock would quickly lose its reputation and ability to sell IPOs to new investors.

Glass-Steagall's fall in the late 1990s

In the late 1990s, before legislation officially eradicated the Glass-Steagall Act's restrictions, the investment and commercial banking industries witnessed an abundance of commercial banking firms making forays into the I-banking world. The mania reached a height in the spring of 1998. In 1998, NationsBank bought Montgomery Securities, Societe Generale bought Cowen & Co., First Union bought Wheat First and Bowles Hollowell Connor, Bank of America bought

Hungry for more inside scoop? Join Vault.com's popular online community for finance and banking — www.vault.com

VAULT.COM   21

Robertson Stephens (and then sold it to BankBoston), Deutsche Bank bought Bankers Trust (which had bought Alex. Brown months before), and Citigroup was created in a merger of Travelers Insurance and Citibank. While some commercial banks have chosen to add I-banking capabilities through acquisitions, some have tried to build their own investment banking business. J.P. Morgan stands as the best example of a commercial bank that has entered the I-banking world through internal growth. Interestingly, J.P. Morgan actually used to be both a securities firm and a commercial bank until federal regulators forced the company to separate the divisions. The split resulted in J.P. Morgan, the commercial bank, and Morgan Stanley, the investment bank. Today, J.P. Morgan has slowly and steadily clawed its way back into the securities business, and Morgan Stanley has merged with Dean Witter to create one of the biggest I-banks on the Street.

What took so long?

So why did it take so long to enact a repeal of Glass-Steagall? There were several logistical and political issues to address in undoing Glass-Steagall. For example, the FDIC and the Federal Reserve regulate commercial banks, while the SEC regulates securities firms. A debate emerged as to who would regulate the new "universal" financial services firms. The Fed eventually won with Alan Greenspan defining his office's role as that of an "umbrella supervisor." A second stalling factor involved the Community Reinvestment Act of 1977 — an act that requires commercial banks to re-invest a portion of their earnings back into their community. Senator Phil Gramm (R-TX), Chairman of the Senate Banking Committee was a strong opponent of this legislation while President Clinton was in favor of keeping and even expanding CRA. The two sides agreed on a compromise in which CRA requirements were lessened for small banks.

In November 1999, President Clinton signed the Gramm-Leach Bliley Act, which repealed restrictions contained in Glass-Steagall that prevent banks from affiliating with securities firms. The new law allows banks, securities firms, and insurance companies to affiliate within a financial holding company ("FHC") structure. Under the new system, insurance, banking, and securities activities are "functionally regulated."

The Buy-side vs. the Sell-side

The traditional investment banking world is considered the sell-side of the securities industry. Why? Investment banks create stocks and bonds, and sell these to investors. Sell is the key word, as I-banks continually sell their firms' capabilities to generate corporate finance business, and salespeople sell securities to generate commission revenue.

Who are the buyers of public stocks and bonds? They are individual investors (you and me) and institutional investors, firms like Fidelity and Vanguard. The universe of institutional investors is appropriately called the buy-side of the securities industry.

Fidelity, T. Rowe Price, Janus and other mutual fund companies all represent a portion of the buy-side business. These are mutual fund money managers. Insurance companies like Prudential, Northwestern Mutual, and Allstate also manage large blocks of assets and are another segment of the buy-side. Yet another class of buy-side firms manage pension fund assets — frequently, a company's pension assets will be given to a specialty buy-side firm that can better manage the funds and hopefully generate higher returns than the company itself could have. There is substantial overlap among these money managers — some, such as Putnam and T. Rowe, manage both mutual funds for individuals as well as pension fund assets of large corporations.

Hedge Funds: What Exactly Are They?

Hedge funds are one sexy component of the buy side. Since the mid-1990s, hedge funds' popularity has grown tremendously. Hedge funds pool together money from large investors (usually wealthy individuals) with the goal of making outsized gains. Historically, hedge funds bought individual stocks, and shorted (or borrowed against) the S&P 500 or another market index, as a hedge against the stock. (The funds bet against the S&P in order to reduce their risk.) As long as the individual stocks outperformed the S&P, the fund made money.

Nowadays, hedge funds have evolved into a myriad of high-risk money managers who essentially borrow money to invest in a multitude of stocks, bonds and derivative instruments (these funds with borrowed money are said to be leveraged). Essentially, a hedge fund uses its equity base to borrow substantially more capital, and therefore multiply its returns through this risky leveraging. Buying derivatives is a common way to automatically leverage a portfolio.

Hungry for more inside scoop? Join Vault.com's popular online community for finance and banking — www.vault.com

VAULT.com   **23**

The Equity Markets

"The Dow Jones Industrial Average finished up 80.61 points, or 0.8%, to 10727.19, off its highs for the day, after rising 10.60 points the previous session," *The Wall Street Journal* reported on July 11, 2000. The *Journal* also reported an increase in blue chips, a result of positive quarterly earnings reports and statements from Federal Reserve Chairman Alan Greenspan that did not yield concerns about interest rates. The Nasdaq Composite Index, however, ended lower.

You may be wondering exactly what all of these headlines mean and how to interpret them. The next two chapters are intended to provide a quick overview of the financial markets and what drives them, and introduce you to some market lingo as well. For reference, many definitions and explanations of many common types of securities can be found in the glossary at the end of this book.

Bears vs. bulls

Everyone loves a bull market, and an investor seemingly cannot go wrong when the market continues to reach new highs. At Goldman Sachs, a bull market is said to occur when stocks exhibit expanding multiples — we will give you a simpler definition. Essentially, a bull market occurs when stock prices (as measured by an index like the Dow Jones Industrial or the S&P 500) move up. A bear market occurs when stocks fall. Simple. More specifically, bear markets occur when the market has fallen by greater than 20 percent from its highs, and a correction occurs when the market has fallen by more than 10 percent but less than 20 percent. The most widely publicized, most widely traded, and most widely tracked stock index in the world is the Dow Jones Industrial Average. The Dow was created in 1896 as a yardstick to measure the performance of the U.S. stock market in general. Initially composed of only 12 stocks, the Dow began trading at a mere 41 points. Today the Dow is made up of 30 large companies in a variety of industries and tops 10,000 points. In November 1999, the Dow Jones updated its composite, adding and removing companies to better reflect the current economy. Union Carbide, Goodyear Tire & Rubber, Sears, Roebuck & Co., and Chevron were removed. Microsoft, Intel, SBC Communications, and Home Depot were added. The stocks in the following chart comprise the index.

Hungry for more inside scoop? Join Vault.com's popular online community for finance and banking — www.vault.com

VAULT.com   25

Components of the Dow Jones Industrial Average

AT&T	Eastman Kodak	McDonald's
Alcoa	Exxon Mobil	Merck
AlliedSignal	General Electric	Microsoft
American Express	General Motors	3M
Boeing	Hewlett-Packard	J.P. Morgan
Caterpillar	Home Depot	Philip Morris
Citigroup	IBM	Procter & Gamble
The Coca-Cola Co.	Intel	SBC Communications
Walt Disney	International Paper	United Technologies
DuPont	Johnson & Johnson	Wal-Mart
Source: Dow Jones & Co.		

The Dow and Nasdaq

The Dow has historically performed remarkably well, particularly in the late 1990s. In 2000 the Dow soared above 11,000 points. Propelling the Dow upward was a combination of the success of U.S. businesses in capturing productivity/efficiency gains, the continuing economic expansion, rapidly growing market share in world markets, and the U.S.'s global dominance in the expanding technology sectors. Although the Dow is widely watched and cited because it's comprised of select, large companies, the Dow cannot gauge fluctuations and movements in smaller companies.

The Nasdaq Composite has garnered significant interest in recent years. The Nasdaq stock market is an electronic market on which the stocks of many well-know technology companies (including Microsoft and Intel) trade. In early 2000, the Nasdaq stock market became the first to stock market to trade two billion shares in a single day.

In 2000 both the Nasdaq composite and the Dow reached all time-highs. As the markets soared, critics warned that a bull market could not continue indefinitely. In April 2000, the markets suffered a serious hit which some optimistically called a correction that would eliminate companies which couldn't compete. More pessimistic observers called the down shift in the markets a "burst of the Internet bubble."

A Word of Caution

While the Dow may dominate news and conversation, investors should take care to know it has limitations as a market barometer. For one, the Dow can be swiftly moved by changes in only one stock. Roughly speaking, for every dollar that a Dow component stock moves, the Dow Index will move by approximately three points. Therefore, a $10 move in IBM in one day will cause a change in the Dow of 30 points! Also, the Dow is only composed of immense companies, and will only reflect movements in big-cap stocks.

Other benchmarks

Besides the Dow Jones and the Nasdaq Composite, investors follow many other important benchmarks. The NYSE Composite Index, which measures the performance of every stock traded on the New York Stock Exchange, represents an excellent broad market measure. The S&P 500 Index, composed of the 500 largest publicly traded companies in the U.S., also presents a nice broad market measure, but, like the Dow is limited to large companies. The Russell 2000 compiles 2000 small-cap stocks, and measures stock performance in that segment of companies.

Big-cap and small-cap

At a basic level, market capitalization or market cap, represents the company's value according to the market," and is calculated by multiplying the total number of shares by share price. (This is the equity value of the company.) Companies and their stocks tend to be categorized into three categories: big-cap, mid-cap and small-cap.

While there are no hard and fast rules, generally speaking, a company with a market cap greater than $5 billion will be classified as a big-cap stock. These companies tend to be established, mature companies, although with the haywire market valuation of some Internet companies, this is not necessarily the case. Sometimes huge companies with $25 billion and greater market caps, for example, GE, Microsoft and Mobil, are called mega-cap stocks. Small-cap stocks tend to be riskier, but are also often the faster growing companies. Roughly speaking, a small-cap stock includes those companies with market caps less than $1 billion. And as one might expect, the stocks in between $1 billion and $5 billion are referred to as mid-cap stocks.

Hungry for more inside scoop? Join Vault.com's popular
online community for consulting — www.vault.com

VAULT.com   **27**

What moves the stock market?

Not surprisingly, the factors that most influence the broader stock market are economic in nature. Among equities, Gross Domestic Product (GDP) and the Consumer Price Index (CPI) are king.

When GDP slows substantially, market investors fear a recession. And if economic conditions worsen and the market enters a recession, many companies will face reduced demand for their products, company earnings will be hurt, and hence equity (stock) prices will decline. Thus, when the GDP suffers, so does the stock market.

When the CPI heats up, investors fear inflation. Inflation fears trigger a different chain of events than fears of recession. First, inflation will cause interest rates to rise. Companies with debt will be forced to pay higher interest rates on existing debt, thereby reducing earnings (and earnings per share). And compounding the problem, because inflation fears cause interest rates to rise, higher rates will make investments other than stocks more attractive from the investor's perspective. Why would an investor purchase a stock that may only earn 8 percent (and carries substantial risk), when lower risk CD's and government bonds offer similar yields with less risk? These inflation fears are known as capital allocations in the market (whether investors are putting money into stocks vs. bonds), which can substantially impact stock and bond prices. Investors typically re-allocate funds from stocks to low-risk bonds when the economy experiences a slowdown and vice versa when the opposite occurs.

What moves *individual* stocks?

When it comes to individual stocks, it's all about earnings, earnings, earnings. No other measure even compares to earnings per share (EPS) when it comes to an individual stock's price. Every quarter, companies must report EPS figures, and stockholders wait with bated breath, ready to compare the actual EPS figure with the EPS estimates. For instance, if a company reports $1.00 EPS for a quarter, but the market had anticipated EPS of $1.20, then the stock will be dramatically hit in the market that day. Conversely, a company that beats its estimates will rally in the markets.

It is important to note at this point, that in the frenzied Internet stock market of 1999, investors did not show the traditional focus on near-term earnings. It was acceptable for these companies to operate at a loss for a year or more, because these companies, investors hoped, would achieve long term future earnings. However, when the markets turned in the spring of 2000, many industry insiders believed investors would expect even "new economy" companies to demonstrate more substantial earnings capacity.

The market does not care about last year's earnings. Investors maintain a tough, "what have you done for me lately" attitude, and forgive slowly a company that "misses its numbers."

Stock valuation measures and ratios

As far as stocks go, it is important to realize that absolute stock prices mean nothing. A $100 stock could be "cheaper" than a $10 stock. To clarify how this works, consider the following ratios and what they mean. Keep in mind that these are only a few of the major ratios, and that literally hundreds of financial and accounting ratios have been invented to compare dissimilar companies. Again, it is important to note that most of these ratios were not as applicable in the market's recent evaluation of certain Internet and technology stocks.

P/E Ratio

You can't go far into a discussion about the stock market without hearing about the all-important price to earnings ratio, or P/E ratio. By definition, a P/E ratio equals the stock price divided by the earnings per share. In usage, investors use the P/E ratio to indicate how cheap or expensive a stock is.

Consider the following example. Two similar firms each have $1.50 in EPS. Company A's stock price is $15.00 per share, and Company B's stock price is $30.00 per share.

Company	Stock Price	Earnings Per Share	P/E Ratio
A	$ 15.00	$1.50	10x
B	$ 30.00	$1.50	20x

Clearly, Company A is cheaper than Company B with regard to the P/E ratio because both firms exhibit the same level of earnings, but A's stock trades at a higher price. That is, Company A's P/E ratio of 10 (15/1.5) is lower than Company B's P/E ratio of 20 (30/1.5). Hence, Company A's stock is cheaper. The terminology one hears in the market is, "Company A is trading at 10 times earnings, while Company B is trading at 20 times earnings." Twenty times is a higher multiple.

Hungry for more inside scoop? Join Vault.com's popular
online community for consulting — www.vault.com

VAULT.com   29

However, the true measure of cheapness vs. richness cannot be summed up by the P/E ratio. Some firms simply deserve higher P/E ratios than others, and some deserve lower P/Es. Importantly, the distinguishing factor is the anticipated growth in earnings per share.

PEG ratio

Because companies grow at different rates, another comparison investors often make is between the P/E ratio and the stock's expected growth rate in EPS. Returning to our previous example, let's say Company A has an expected EPS growth rate of 10 percent, while Company B's expected growth rate is 20 percent.

Company	Stock Price	Earnings Per Share	P/E Ratio	Estimated Growth Rate in EPS
A	$ 15.00	$1.50	10x	10x
B	$ 30.00	$1.50	20x	20x

We might propose that the market values Company A at 10 times earnings because it anticipates 10 percent annual growth in EPS over the next five years. Company B is growing faster — at a 20 percent rate — and therefore justifies the 20 times earnings stock price. To determine true cheapness, market analysts have developed a ratio that compares the P/E to the growth rate — the PEG ratio. In this example, one could argue that both companies are valued similarly (both have PEG ratios of 1).

Sophisticated market investors therefore utilize this PEG ratio. Roughly speaking, the average company has a PEG ratio of 1:1 or 1 (i.e., the P/E ratio matches the anticipated growth rate). By convention, expensive firms have a PEG ratio greater than one, and cheap stocks have a PEG ratio less than one.

Cash Flow Multiples

For companies with no earnings and therefore no EPS, one cannot calculate the P/E ratio — it is a meaningless number. The quick fix then is to compute the firm's cash flow and compare that to the market value of the firm. The following example illustrates how a typical cash flow multiple like Enterprise Value/EBITDA ratio is calculated.

EBITDA: A proxy for cash flow, EBITDA stands for Earnings before interest, taxes, depreciation and amortization. To calculate EBITDA, work your way up the Income Statement, adding back the appropriate items to net income. Adding together depreciation and amortization to operating earnings, a common subtotal on the income statement, can serve as a shortcut to calculating EBITDA.

Enterprise Value (EV) = market value of equity + net debt. To compute market value of equity, simply multiply the current stock price times the number of shares outstanding. Net debt is simply the firm's total debt (as found on the balance sheet) minus cash.

Enterprise Value to Revenue Multiple (EV/Revenue)

If you follow Internet stocks and their valuations, you have probably heard the multiple of revenue lingo. Sometimes it is called the price-sales ratio (though this technically is not correct). Why use this ratio? For one, many firms not only have negative earnings, but also negative cash flow. That means any cash flow or P/E multiple must be thrown out the window, leaving revenue as the last positive income statement number left to compare to the firm's enterprise value. Specifically one calculates this ratio by dividing EV by the last 12 months revenue figure.

Return on Equity (ROE)

Net income divided by total shareholders equity. An important measure that evaluates the income return that a firm earned in any given year. Return on equity is expressed as a percent. Many firms' financial goal is to achieve a certain level of ROE per year, say 20 percent or more.

Value stocks, growth stocks and momentum investors

It is important to know that investors typically classify stocks into one of two categories — growth and value stocks. Momentum investors buy a subset of the stocks in the growth category.

Value stocks are those that have been battered by investors. Typically, a stock that trades at low P/E ratios after having once traded at high P/E's, or a stock with declining sales or earnings fits into the value category. Investors choose value stocks with to the hope that their businesses will turn around and profits will return. Or, investors perhaps realize that a stock is trading close to break-up value, and hence have little downside.

Growth stocks are just the opposite. High P/E's, high growth rates, and often hot stocks fit the growth category. Internet stocks, with astoundingly high P/E's, may be classified as growth stocks, based on

Hungry for more inside scoop? Join Vault.com's popular
online community for consulting — www.vault.com

VAULT.com   **31**

their high growth rates. Keep in mind that a P/E ratio often serves as a proxy for a firm's average expected growth rate.

Momentum investors buy growth stocks that have exhibited strong upward price appreciation. Usually trading at 52-week highs, momentum investors cause these stocks to trade up and down with extreme volatility. Momentum investors, who typically don't care about the firm's business or valuation ratios, will dump their stocks the moment they show price weakness. Thus, a stock run-up by momentum investors can crash dramatically as they bail out at the first sign of trouble.

EQUITY DEFINITIONS

Common stock — Also called common equity, common stock represents an ownership interest in a company. The vast majority of stock traded in the markets today is common. Common stock enables investors to vote on company matters. An individual with 51 percent or more of a company's shares owned controls a company's decisions and can appoint anyone he/she wishes to the board of directors or to the management team.

Convertible preferred stock — This is a relatively uncommon type of equity issued by a company, often when it cannot successfully sell either straight common stock or straight debt. Preferred stock pays a dividend, in a manner similar to the way a bond pays coupon payments. However, preferred stock ultimately converts to common stock after a period of time. Preferred stock can be viewed as a mix of debt and equity, and is most often used as a way for a risky company to obtain capital when neither debt nor equity works.

Non-convertible preferred stock — Sometimes companies issue non-convertible preferred stock, which remains outstanding in perpetuity and trades similar to stocks. Utilities represent the best example of non-convertible preferred stock issuers.

The Fixed Income Markets

CHAPTER 4

What is the bond market?

What is the bond market? The average person doesn't follow it and often doesn't even hear about it. Because of the bond market's low profile, it's surprising to many people that the bond markets are approximately the same size as the equity markets.

Until the late 1970s and early 80s, bonds were considered unsexy investments, bought by retired grandparents and insurance companies. They traded infrequently, and provided safe, steady returns. Beginning in the early 1980s, however, Michael Milken essentially created the tremendous junk bond world, making a killing at the same time. And with the development of mortgage-backed securities, Salomon Brothers also transformed bonds into something exciting and extremely profitable.

To begin our discussion of the fixed income markets, we'll identify the main types of securities that make it up. We'll discuss some of these more in-depth throughout the chapter. Also, definitions of each of these can be found at the end of this chapter.

- U.S. Government Treasury securities
- Agency bonds
- High grade corporate bonds
- High yield (junk) bonds
- Municipal bonds
- Mortgage-backed bonds
- Asset-backed securities
- Emerging market bonds

Bond market indicators

The Yield Curve

A primary measure of importance to fixed income investors is the yield curve. The yield curve (also called the "term structure of interest rates") depicts graphically the yields on different maturity U.S. government securities. To construct a simple yield curve, investors typically look at the yield on a 90-day U.S. T-bill and then the yield on the 30-year U.S.

Hungry for more inside scoop? Join Vault.com's popular online community for finance and banking — www.vault.com

VAULT.com   33

government bond (called the Long Bond). Typically, the yields of
shorter-term government T-bill are lower than Long Bond's yield,
indicating what is called an upward sloping yield curve.

Bond Indices

As with the stock market, the bond market has some widely watched
indexes. One prominent example is the Lehman Government Corporate
Bond Index. The LGC index measures the returns on mostly
government securities, but also blends in a portion of corporate bonds.
The index is adjusted to reflect the percentage of assets in government
and in corporate bonds in the market. Mortgage bonds are excluded
entirely from the LGC index.

U.S. government bonds

Particularly important in the universe of fixed income products are U.S.
government bonds. These bonds are the most reliable in the world, as
the U.S. government is unlikely to default on its loans (and if it ever did,
the world financial market would essentially be in shambles). Because
they are virtually risk-free, U.S. government bonds, also called
Treasuries, offer low yields (a low rate of interest), and are standards by
which other bonds are measured.

Spreads

In the bond world, investors track spreads as carefully as any single
index of bond prices or any single bond. The spread is essentially the
difference between a bond's yield (the amount of interest, measured in
percent, paid to bondholders), and the yield on a U.S. Treasury bond of
the same time to maturity. For instance, an investor investigating the
20-year Acme Company bond would compare it to a U.S. Treasury
bond that has 20 years remaining until maturity.

Bond ratings for corporate and municipal bonds

A bond's risk level, or the risk that the bond issuer will default on
payments to bondholders, is measured by bond rating agencies. Several
companies rate credit, but Standard & Poor's and Moody's are the two
largest. The riskier a bond, the larger the spread: low-risk bonds trade
at a small spread to Treasuries, while below-investment grade bonds
trade at tremendous spreads to Treasuries. Investors refer to company
specific risk as credit risk.

Triple A ratings represents the highest possible corporate bond designation, and are reserved for the best-managed, largest blue-chip companies. Triple A bonds trade at a yield close to the yield on a risk-free government Treasury. Junk bonds, or bonds with a rating of BB or below, currently trade at yields ranging from 10 to 15 percent, depending on the precise rating, the company's situation, and the economic conditions at the time.

Companies continue to be monitored by the rating agencies as long as bonds trade in the markets. If a company is put on credit watch, it is possible that the rating agencies are considering raising or lowering the rating on the company. When a bond is actually downgraded by Moody's or S&P, the bond's price drops dramatically (and therefore its yield increases).

The following table summarizes rating symbols of the two major rating agencies and provides a brief definition of each.

Bond Rating Codes

Rating	S&P	Moody's
Highest quality	AAA	Aaa
High quality	AA	Aa
Upper medium quality	A	A
Medium grade	BBB	Baa
Somewhat speculative	BB	Ba
Low grade, speculative	B	B
Low grade, default possible	CCC	Caa
Low grade, partial recovery possible	CC	Ca
Default expected	C	C

Source: Moody's Investor's Service and Standard and Poor's

Hungry for more inside scoop? Join Vault.com's popular
online community for consulting — www.vault.com

VAULT.COM   35

Factors affecting the bond market

What factors affect the bond market? In short, interest rates. The general level of interest rates, as measured by many different barometers (see inset) moves bond prices up and down, in dramatic inverse fashion. In other words, if interest rates rise, the bond markets suffer.

Think of it this way. Say you own a bond that is paying you a fixed rate of 8 percent today, and that this rate represents a 1.5 percent spread over Treasuries. An increase in rates of 1 percent means that this same bond purchased now (as opposed to when you purchased the bond) will now yield 9 percent. And as the yield goes up, the price declines. So, your bond loses value and you are only earning 8 percent when the rest of the market is earning 9 percent.

You could have waited, purchased the bond after the rate increase, and earned a greater yield. The opposite occurs when rates go down. If you lock in a fixed rate of 8 percent and rates plunge by 1 percent, you now earn more than those who purchase the bond after the rate decrease.

Which Interest Rate Are You Talking About?

Investors often discuss interest rates in general terms. But what are they really talking about? So many rates are tossed about that they may be difficult to track. To clarify, we will take a brief look at the key rates worth tracking. We have ranked them in ascending order: the discount rate usually is the lowest rate; the yield on junk bonds is usually the highest.

The Discount Rate — The discount rate is the rate that the Federal Reserve charges on overnight loans to banks. Today, the discount rate can be directly moved by the Fed, but maintains a largely symbolic role.

Federal Funds Rate — The rate domestic banks charge one another on overnight loans to meet Federal Reserve requirements.

T-Bill Yields — The yield or internal rate of return an investor would receive at any given moment on a 90- to 120-day Treasury bill.

LIBOR (London Interbank Offered Rate) — The rate banks in England charge one another on overnight loans or loans up to five years. Often used by banks to quote floating rate loan interest rates. Typically the benchmark LIBOR is the three-month rate.

The Long Bond (30-Year Treasury) Yield — The yield or internal rate of return an investor would receive at any given moment on the 30-year U.S. Treasury bond.

Municipal Bond Yields — The yield or internal rate of return an investor would receive at any given moment by investing in municipal bonds. We should note that the interest on municipal bonds typically is free from federal government taxes and therefore has a lower yield than other bonds of similar risk. These yields, however, can vary substantially depending on their rating, so could be higher or lower than presented here.

High Grade Corporate Bond Yield — The yield or internal rate of return an investor would receive by purchasing a corporate bond with a rating above BB.

Prime Rate — The average rate that U.S. banks charge to companies for loans.

High Yield Bonds — The yield or internal rate of return an investor would receive by purchasing a corporate bond with a rating below BBB (also called junk bonds).

Why do interest rates move?

Interest rates react mostly to inflation expectations. If it is believed that inflation will be high, interest rates rise. Think of it this way. Say inflation is 5 percent a year. In order to make money on a loan, a bank would have to at least charge more than 5 percent — otherwise it would essentially be losing money on the loan. The same is true with bonds and other fixed income products.

In the late 1970s, interest rates topped 20 percent, as inflation began to spiral out of control (and the market expected continued high inflation). Today, many believe that the Federal Reserve has successfully slayed inflation and has all but eliminated market concerns of future inflation. This is certainly debatable, but clearly, the sound monetary policies and remarkable price stability in the U.S. have made it the envy of the world.

Hungry for more inside scoop? Join Vault.com's popular
online community for consulting — www.vault.com

VAULT.com **37**

A Note About the Federal Reserve

The Federal Reserve Bank, called the Fed and headed by Alan Greenspan, monitors the U.S. money supply and regulates banking institutions. While this role may not sound too significant, in fact the Fed's role is crucial to the U.S. economy and stock market.

Academic studies of economic history have shown that a country's inflation rate tends to track that country's increase in its money supply. Therefore, if the Fed increases the money supply by 2 percent this year, inflation can best be predicted to increase by 2 percent as well. And since inflation so dramatically impacts the stock and bond markets, the markets scrutinize the week-to-week activities of the Fed and hang onto every word uttered by Greenspan.

The Fed can manage consumption patterns and hence the GDP by raising or lowering interest rates.

The chain of events when the Fed raises rates is as follows:

> The Fed raises interest rates. This interest rate increase triggers banks to raise interest rates, which leads to consumers borrowing less and spending less. This decrease in consumption tends to slow down GDP, thereby reducing earnings at companies. Since consumers borrow less, they have left their money in the bank and hence the money supply does not expand. Note also that companies tend to borrow less when rates go up, and therefore invest less in capital equipment, which discourages productivity gains. Any economist will tell you that the key to a growing economy on a per capita basis is improving productivity in the workplace.

The following glossary may be useful for defining securities that trade in the markets as well as talking about the factors that influence them. Note that this is just a list of the most common types of fixed income products and economic indicators. Thousands of fixed income products actually trade in the markets.

Fixed Income Definitions

Types of Securities	
Treasury securities	United States government-issued securities. Categorized as Treasury bills (maturity of up to two years), Treasury notes (from two years to 10 years maturity), and Treasury bonds (10 years to 30 years). As they are government-guaranteed, Treasuries are considered "risk-free." In fact, U.S. Treasuries have no default risk, but do have interest rate risk — if rates increase, then the price of UST's will decrease.
Agency bonds	Agencies represent all bonds issued by the federal government, but excluding those issued by the Treasury (i.e. bonds issued by other agencies of the federal government). Examples of agencies that issue bonds include Federal National Mortgage Association (FNMA), Guaranteed National Mortgage Association (GNMA).
High grade corporate bonds (a.k.a. investment grade)	Bonds with a Standard & Poor's rating of at least a BBB-. Typically big, blue-chip companies issue highly rated bonds.
High yield (junk) bonds	Bonds with a Standard & Poor's rating lower than BBB-. Typically smaller, riskier companies issue high yield bonds.
Municipal bonds	Bonds issued by local and state governments, a.k.a. municipalities. Municipal bonds are tax-free for the investor, which means investors in "muni's" earn interest payments without having to pay federal taxes. Sometimes investors are exempt from state and local taxes too. Consequently, municipalities can pay lower interest rates on muni bonds than other bonds of similar risk.

Hungry for more inside scoop? Join Vault.com's popular
online community for consulting — www.vault.com

VAULT.com   **39**

Money market securities	The market for securities maturing within one year, including short-term CDs, Repurchase Agreements, and Commercial Paper (low-risk corporate issues), among others. These are low-risk, short-term securities that have yields similar to Treasuries.
Mortgage-backed bonds	Bonds collateralized by a pool of mortgages. Interest and principal payments are based on the individual homeowners making their mortgage payments. The more diverse the pool of mortgages backing the bond, the less risky they are.
Economic Indicators	
Gross Domestic Product	GDP measures the total domestic output of goods and services in the United States. Generally, when the GDP grows at a rate of less than 2%, the economy is considered to be in a recession.
Consumer Price Index	The CPI measures the percentage increase in the price for goods and services. Essentially, the CPI measures inflation affecting consumers.
Producer Price Index	The PPI measures the percentage increase in the price of a standard basket of goods and services. PPI is a measure of inflation for producers and manufacturers
Unemployment Rate and Wages	In 1999 through early 2000, U.S. unemployment was at record lows. Clearly, this is a positive sign for the U.S. economy because jobs are plentiful. The markets sometimes react negatively to extremely low levels of unemployment, however, as a tight labor market means that firms may have to raise wages (called wage pressure). Substantial wage pressure may force firms to raise prices, and hence may cause inflation to flare up.

Trends In I-Banking

CHAPTER 5

International mergers and acquisitions

Another important trend in the financial services industry has been increased global presence through acquisitions. As banks place increasing priority on size, international mergers and acquisitions in the financial services industry became more and more common. In recent years, Deutsche Bank bought Bankers Trust (who had previously acquired Alex. Brown), ING bought Barings, Merrill Lynch bought a significant stake in Yamaichi Securities in Japan, Citigroup purchased the investment banking operations of Schroders, and UBS announced it would acquire PaineWebber.

Most industry observers say that merger mania took hold for two reasons. One, financial institutions want to become global, and two, they want to establish one-stop-shopping for consumers and investors. A good example of the second rationale is the Travelers-Smith Barney-Salomon combination. Travelers provides insurance products; Smith Barney provides an I-banking operation with historical strengths in equity; and Salomon provides an I-banking operation with historical strengths in debt. (Travelers then merged with Citibank, which provides commercial banking operations, to form Citigroup.) These types of combinations can be enormously profitable if the firms' cultures can be successfully combined.

Adding fuel to the consolidation fire is the recent frenzy to snap up mutual fund companies, or buy-side firms that manage huge sums of money. Many major investment banks have made major asset management acquisitions in recent years: Merrill Lynch bought Britain's Mercury Asset Management, Morgan Stanley Dean Witter bought Van Kampen American Capital, Credit Suisse First Boston bought Warburg Pincus Asset Management, and J.P. Morgan bought a significant stake in American Century Investments. One of the reasons for this trend is the same consolidating force that is driving combinations of investment banks and commercial banks — institutions want to be able to offer more products to sell to existing customers. (In this case, mutual funds.) Perhaps as importantly, investment management fee income is much more stable in nature than trading and underwriting business, which can exhibit huge swings in volatility and also depend significantly on bull markets.

Hungry for more inside scoop? Join Vault.com's popular online community for finance and banking — www.vault.com

VAULT.COM   41

Interestingly, the traditional Wall Street firms have been unable to grow money management businesses internally. Firms such as Merrill Lynch, Smith Barney and Morgan Stanley have all offered mutual funds, but have underperformed the market and the rest of the fund industry. Thus the race to acquire good money management firms is a race to acquire people and expertise that the investment banks have not been able to build organically. As more and more individual investors become knowledgeable about financial markets, and depend less on hand-holding from full-service brokers, they are looking to make decisions on their own and perform trades on their own — at the least cost possible. This has made possible the success of discount brokerages like Charles Schwab, and most recently, do-it-yourself online brokerages such as E*Trade and Ameritrade.

A larger and larger portion of stock market trades is being enacted online daily, and Wall Street is finally joining the game. In 1999 and 2000 brokerage leader Merrill Lynch and many other firms such as Morgan Stanley Dean Witter, DLJ and Salomon Smith Barney began offering online brokerage services. Because the businesses of these firms were for years based on their armies of financial advisors (brokers), these firms were initially hesitant to go online, but have responded to the market's demands. At one point in 1999, for example, the market capitalization of Charles Schwab was greater than that of Merrill, primarily because of the success of its online brokerage business. It should be noted that online brokerages are at the same time beginning to offer more full-service advice.

Not only is the brokerage business moving online, but so is investment banking. Online I-banking firms such as Wit SoundView, and W.R. Hambrecht (founded by the former chairman of high-tech boutique Hambrecht & Quist). While these on-line firms promised to change the shape of investment banking, they have not experienced the same large-scale success as the on-line brokerage firms. The existing client relationships and large-scale distribution abilities of the larger investment banks make the firms exceptionally challenging foes for smaller, on-line I-banks.

The dot-com craze

In addition to the advent of online investment bank and investment banking services, the rise of the Internet and technology-related businesses had other notable effects on the investment banking industry.

The number of Internet related investment banking deals has surpassed many industry expectations. In 1999, 544 companies completed IPOs, and approximately 40 percent of these companies were Internet firms, according to ABC News.

The effects of the boom in Internet-related companies yielded yet another result for investment bankers. With an increasing number of Internet companies and increasing reports of Internet millionaires, more and more junior professionals (both undergraduates from top universities and graduates of top business schools) opted out of the investment banking lifestyle in exchange for the excitement of Internet start-ups.

As a result, investment banking positions, once considered among the most competitively sought jobs in the country, were not as eagerly sought. In 1999, *Investment Dealers' Digest* reported that for the first time ever, more graduates of Harvard Business School pursued careers in high-tech than careers on Wall Street. Those favoring a dot-com future were certainly motivated by entrepreneurial challenges, less hierarchy than large corporations, the excitement of a new industry, and dreams of lucrative stock options — but lifestyle also emerged as a critical factor. Casual dress and rock music playing in the offices of dot-coms were also appealing to young professionals. Investment banks were facing a brand new challenger in the arena for talent. Mary Taylor, senior vp of human resources at Merrill Lynch told *IDD*: "The war for talent definitely includes some non-traditional competitors now." The investment banks struck back with salary increases, business casual dress policies, more flexible reimbursement procedures and numerous other perks. The firms also had to expand the search for talent — recruiting at universities, colleges and business schools that previously did not hit the radar screen of I-bank recruiters. In an unprecedented move, Donaldson Lufkin and Jenrette offered junior bankers salary guarantees provided they signed a contract with various stipulations (see the DLJ profile).

Stock and Bond Offerings

In this chapter, we will take you through the basics of three types of public offerings: the IPO, the follow-on equity offering, and the bond offering.

Initial public offerings

An initial public offering (IPO) is the process by which a private company transforms itself into a public company. The company offers, for the first time, shares of its equity (ownership) to the investing public. These shares subsequently trade on a public stock exchange like the New York Stock Exchange (NYSE) or the Nasdaq.

The first question you may ask is why a company would want to go public. Many private companies succeed remarkably well as privately owned enterprises. One privately held company, Cargill, tops $50 billion in revenue each year. And until recently, Wall Street's leading investment bank, Goldman Sachs, was a private company. However, for many private companies, a day of reckoning comes for the owners when they decide to sell a portion of their ownership in their firm.

The primary reason for going through the rigors of an IPO is to raise cash to fund the growth of a company. For example, industry observers believe that Goldman Sachs' partners wished to at least have available a publicly traded currency (the stock in the company) with which to acquire other financial services firms.

While obtaining growth capital is the main reason for going public, it is not the only reason. Often, the owners of a company may simply wish to cash out either partially or entirely by selling their ownership in the firm in the offering. Thus, the owners will sell shares in the IPO and get cash for their equity in the firm. Or, sometimes a company's CEO may own a majority or all of the equity, and will offer a few shares in an IPO, in order to diversify his/her net worth or to gain some liquidity. To return to the example of Goldman Sachs, some felt that another driving force behind the partners' decision to go public was the feeling that financial markets were at their peak, and that they could get a good price for their equity in their firm. It should be noted that going public is not a slam dunk. Firms that are too small, too stagnant or have poor growth prospects will — in general — fail to find an investment bank willing to underwrite their IPOs.

Hungry for more inside scoop? Join Vault.com's popular online community for finance and banking — www.vault.com

VAULT.com 45

From an investment banking perspective, the IPO process consists of these three major phases: hiring the mangers, due diligence, and marketing.

Hiring the Managers. The first step for a company wishing to go public is to hire managers for its offering. This choosing of an investment bank is often referred to as a "beauty contest." Typically, this process involves meeting with and interviewing investment bankers from different firms, discussing the firm's reasons for going public, and ultimately nailing down a valuation. In making a valuation, I-bankers, through a mix of art and science, pitch to the company wishing to go public what they believe the firm is worth, and therefore how much stock it can realistically sell. Perhaps understandably, companies often choose the bank that provides the highest valuation during this beauty contest phase instead of the best-qualified manager. Almost all IPO candidates select two or more investment banks to manage the IPO process.

Due Diligence and Drafting. Once managers are selected, the second phase of the process begins. For investment bankers on the deal, this phase involves understanding the company's business as well as possible scenarios (called due diligence), and then filing the legal documents as required by the SEC. The SEC legal form used by a company issuing new public securities is called the S-1 (or prospectus) and requires quite a bit of effort to draft. Lawyers, accountants, I-bankers, and of course company management must all toil for countless hours to complete the S-1 in a timely manner.

Marketing. The third phase of an IPO is the marketing phase. Once the SEC has approved the prospectus, the company embarks on a roadshow to sell the deal. A roadshow involves flying the company's management coast to coast (and often to Europe) to visit institutional investors potentially interested in buying shares in the offering. Typical roadshows last from two to three weeks, and involve meeting literally hundreds of investors, who listen to the company's canned presentation, and then ask scrutinizing questions. Often, money managers decide whether or not to invest thousands of dollars in a company within just a few minutes of a presentation.

The marketing phase ends abruptly with the placement of the stock, which results in a new security trading in the market. Successful IPOs trade up on their first day (increase in share price), and tend to succeed over the course of the next few quarters. Young public companies that miss their numbers are dealt with harshly by institutional investors, who not only sell the stock, causing it to drop precipitously, but also blame management and lose faith in the management team.

Follow-on offering of stock

A company that is already publicly traded will sometimes sell stock to the public again. This type of offering is called a follow-on offering, or a secondary offering. One reason for a follow-on offering is the same as a major reason for the initial offering: a company may be growing rapidly, either by making acquisitions or by internal growth, and may simply require additional capital.

Another reason that a company would issue a follow-on offering is similar to the cashing out scenario in the IPO. In a secondary offering, a large existing shareholder (usually the largest shareholder, say, the CEO) may wish to sell a large block of stock in one fell swoop. The reason for this is that this must be done through an additional offering (rather than through a simple sale on the stock market through a broker), is that a company may have shareholders with unregistered stock who wish to sell large blocks of their shares. By SEC decree, all stock must first be registered by filing an S-1 (or S-2) document before it can trade on a public stock exchange. Thus, pre-IPO shareholders who do not sell shares in the initial offering hold what is called unregistered stock, and are restricted from selling large blocks unless the company files an S-2 form. (The equity owners who hold the shares sold in an offering, whether it be an IPO or a follow-on, are called the selling shareholders.)

An Example of a Follow-on Offering: "New" and "Old" Shares

There are two types of shares that are sold in secondary offerings. When a company requires additional growth capital, it sells "new" shares to the public. When an existing shareholder wishes to sell a huge block of stock, "old" shares are sold to the public. Follow-on offerings often include both types of shares.

Let's look at an example. Suppose Acme Company wished to raise $100 million to fund certain growth prospects. Suppose that at the same time, its biggest shareholder, a venture capital firm, was looking to "cash out," or sell its stock.

(next page...)

Hungry for more inside scoop? Join Vault.com's popular online community for finance and banking — www.vault.com

VAULT.com   **47**

Assume the firm already had 100 million shares of stock trading in the market. Let's also say that Acme's stock price traded most recently at $10 per share. The current market value of the firm's equity is:

$10 x 100,000,000 shares = $1,000,000,000 ($1 billion)

Say XYZ Venture Capitalists owned 10 million shares (comprising 10 percent of the firm's equity pre-deal). They want to sell all of their equity in the firm, or the entire 10 million shares. And to raise $100 million of new capital, Acme would have to sell 10 million additional (or new) shares of stock to the public. These shares would be newly created during the offering process. In fact, the prospectus for the follow-on, called an S-2 (as opposed to the S-1 for the IPO), legally "registers" the stock with the SEC, authorizing the sale of stock to investors.

The total size of the deal would thus be 20 million shares, 10 million of which are "new" and 10 million of which are coming from the selling shareholders, the VC firm. Interestingly, because of the additional shares and what is called "dilution of earnings" or "dilution of EPS," stock prices typically trade down upon a follow-on offering announcement. (Of course, this only happens if the stock to be issued in the deal is "new" stock.)

After this secondary offering is completed, Acme would have 110 million shares outstanding, and its market value will be $1.1 billion if the stock remains at $10 per share. And, the shares sold by XYZ Venture Capitalists will now be in the hands of new investors in the form of freely tradable securities.

Market Reaction. What happens when a company announces a secondary offering indicates the market's tolerance for additional equity. Because more shares of stock "dilute" the old shareholders, the stock price usually drops on the announcement of a follow-on offering. Dilution occurs because earnings per share (EPS) in the future will decline, simply based on the fact that more shares will exist post-deal. And since EPS drives stock prices, the share price generally drops.

The Process. The follow-on offering process changes little from that of an IPO, and actually is far less complicated. Since underwriters have already represented the company in an IPO, a company often chooses the same managers, thus making the hiring the manager or beauty contest phase much simpler. Also, no valuation is required (the market now values the firm's stock), a prospectus has already been written, and a roadshow presentation already prepared. Modifications to the prospectus and the roadshow demand the most time in a follow-on offering, but still can usually be completed with a fraction of the effort required for an initial offering.

Bond offerings

When a company requires capital, it sometimes chooses to issue public debt instead of equity. Almost always, however, a firm undergoing a public bond deal will already have stock trading in the market. (It is very rare for a private company to issue bonds before its IPO.)

The reasons for issuing bonds rather than stock are various. Perhaps the stock price of the issuer is down, and thus a bond issue is a better alternative. Or perhaps the firm does not wish to dilute its existing shareholders by issuing more equity. These are both valid reasons for issuing bonds rather than equity. Sometimes in down markets, investor appetite for public offerings dwindles to the point where an equity deal just could not get done (investors would not buy the issue).

The bond offering process resembles the IPO process. The primary difference lies in: (1) the focus of the prospectus (a prospectus for a bond offering will emphasize the company's stability and steady cash flow, whereas a stock prospectus will usually play up the company's growth and expansion opportunities), and (2) the importance of the bond's credit rating (the company will want to obtain a favorable credit rating from a debt rating agency like S&P or Moody's, with the help of the credit department of the investment bank issuing the bond; the bank's credit department will negotiate with the rating agencies to obtain the best possible rating). As covered in Chapter 5, the better the credit rating — and therefore, the safer the bonds — the lower the interest rate the company must pay on the bonds to entice investors debt rating on the issue. Clearly, a firm issuing debt will want to have the highest possible bond rating, and hence pay a low interest rate (or yield).

Hungry for more inside scoop? Join Vault.com's popular online
community for finance and banking — www.vault.com

VAULT.com   **49**

M&A, Private Placements, and Reorgs

CHAPTER 7

Mergers & acquisitions

In the 1980s, hostile takeovers and LBO acquisitions were all the rage. Companies sought to acquire others through aggressive stock purchases and cared little about the target company's concerns. The 1990s were the decade of friendly mergers, dominated by a few sectors in the economy. Mergers in the telecommunications, financial services, and technology industries have been commanding headlines as these sectors go through dramatic change, both regulatory and financial. But giant mergers have been occurring in virtually every industry (witness the biggest of them all, the merger between Exxon and Mobil). M&A business has been consistently brisk, as demands to go global, to keep pace with the competition, and to expand earnings by any possible means have been foremost in the minds of CEOs.

After a slow period, LBOs have experienced a resurgence in recent years. According to *The Daily Deal*, LBO funds raised over $120 billion from 1997-2000. "If the public markets won't validate a strong business model, the private markets usually will," J.P. Morgan market strategist Doug Cliggott told TheStreet.com in March 2000. "As some very well-run companies start to trade at three or four times earnings, I don't see how we won't see a groundswell of leveraged buyouts." As boom markets suffered "corrections" in the spring of 2000 many industry analysts predict that sinking stock prices would yield leverage buyouts.

When a public company acquires another public company, the target company's stock often shoots through the roof while the acquiring company's stock often declines. Why? One must realize that existing shareholders must be convinced to sell their stock. Few shareholders are willing to sell their stock to an acquirer without first being paid a premium on the current stock price. In addition, shareholders must also capture a takeover premium to relinquish control over the stock. The large shareholders of the target company typically demand such an extraction. For example, the management of the selling company may require a substantial premium to give up control of their firm.

M&A transactions can be roughly divided into either mergers or acquisitions. These terms are often used interchangeably in the press,

Hungry for more inside scoop? Join Vault.com's popular online community for finance and banking — www.vault.com

VAULT.com   **51**

and the actual legal difference between the two involves arcana of accounting procedures, but we can still draw a rough difference between the two.

Acquisition — When a larger company takes over another (smaller firm) and clearly becomes the new owner, the purchase is called an acquisition. Typically, the target company ceases to exist post-transaction (from a legal corporation point of view) and the acquiring corporation swallows the business. The stock of the acquiring company continues to be traded.

Merger — A merger occurs when two companies, often roughly of the same size, combine to create a new company. Such a situation is often called a merger of equals. Both companies' stocks are tendered (or given up), and new company stock is issued in its place. For example, both Chrysler and Daimler-Benz ceased to exist when their firms merged, and a new combined company, DaimlerChrysler was created.

M&A advisory services

For an I-bank, M&A advising is highly profitable, and there are many possibilities for types of transactions. Perhaps a small private company's owner/manager wishes to sell out for cash and retire. Or perhaps a big public firm aims to buy a competitor through a stock swap. Whatever the case, M&A advisors come directly from the corporate finance departments of investment banks. Unlike public offerings, merger transactions do not directly involve salespeople, traders or research analysts. In particular, M&A advisory falls onto the laps of M&A specialists and fits into one of either two buckets: seller representation or buyer representation (also called target representation and acquirer representation).

Representing the target

An I-bank that represents a potential seller has a much greater likelihood of completing a transaction (and therefore being paid) than an I-bank that represents a potential acquirer. Also known as sell-side work, this type of advisory assignment is generated by a company that approaches an investment bank and asks the bank to find a buyer of either the entire company or a division. Often, sell-side representation comes when a company asks an investment bank to help it sell a division, plant or subsidiary operation.

Generally speaking, the work involved in finding a buyer includes writing a Selling Memorandum and then contacting potential strategic or financial buyers of the client. If the client hopes to sell a semiconductor plant, for instance, the I-bankers will contact firms in that industry, as well as buyout firms that focus on purchasing technology or high-tech manufacturing operations.

Buyout Firms and LBOs

Buyout firms, which are also called financial sponsors, acquire companies by borrowing substantial cash. These buyout firms (also called LBO firms) implement a management team they trust, and ultimately seek an exit strategy (usually a sale or IPO) for their investment within a few years. These firms are driven to achieve a high return on investment (ROI), and focus their efforts toward streamlining the acquired business and preparing the company for a future IPO or sale. It is quite common that a buyout firm will be the selling shareholder in an IPO or follow-on offering.

Representing the acquirer

In advising sellers, the I-bank's work is complete once another party purchases the business up for sale, i.e., once another party buys your client's company or division or assets. Buy-side work is an entirely different animal. The advisory work itself is straightforward: the investment bank contacts the firm their client wishes to purchase, attempts to structure a palatable offer for all parties, and make the deal a reality. However, most of these proposals do not work out; few firms or owners are willing to readily sell their business. And because the I-banks primarily collect fees based on completed transactions, their work often goes unpaid.

Consequently, when advising clients looking to buy a business, an I-bank's work often drags on for months. Often a firm will pay a non-refundable retainer fee to hire a bank and say, "Find us a target company to buy." These acquisition searches can last for months and produce nothing except associate and analyst fatigue as they repeatedly build merger models and work all-nighters. Deals that do get done, though, are a boon for the I-bank representing the buyer because of their enormous profitability. Typical fees depend on the size of the deal, but

Hungry for more inside scoop? Join Vault.com's popular online
community for finance and banking — www.vault.com

VAULT.com **53**

generally fall in the 1 percent range. For a $100 million deal, an investment bank takes home $1 million. Not bad for a few months' work.

Private Placements

A private placement, which involves the selling of debt or equity to private investors, resembles both a public offering and a merger. A private placement differs little from a public offering aside from the fact that a private placement involves a firm selling stock or equity to private investors rather than to public investors. Also, a typical private placement deal is smaller than a public transaction. Despite these differences, the primary reason for a private placement — to raise capital — is fundamentally the same as a public offering.

Why private placements?

As mentioned previously, firms wishing to raise capital often discover that they are unable to go public for a number of reasons. The company may not be big enough; the markets may not have an appetite for IPOs, or the company may simply prefer not to have its stock be publicly traded. Such firms with solidly growing businesses make excellent private placement candidates. Often, firms wishing to go public may be advised by investment bankers to first do a private placement, as they need to gain critical mass or size to justify an IPO.

Private placements, then, are usually the province of small companies aiming ultimately to go public. The process of raising private equity or debt changes only slightly from a public deal. One difference is that private placements do not require any securities to be registered with the SEC, nor do they involve a roadshow. In place of the prospectus, I-banks draft a detailed Private Placement Memorandum (PPM for short) which divulges information similar to a prospectus. Instead of a roadshow, companies looking to sell private stock or debt will host potential investors as interest arises, and give presentations detailing how they will be the greatest thing since sliced bread.

Often, one firm will be the sole investor in a private placement. In other words, if a company sells stock through a private placement, often only one venture capital firm will buy the stock offered. Conversely, in an IPO, shares of stock fall into the hands of literally thousands of buyers immediately after the deal is completed.

The I-bank's role in private placements

The investment banker's work involved in a private placement is quite similar to sell-side M&A representation. The bankers attempt to find a buyer by writing the PPM and then contacting potential strategic or financial buyers of the client.

In the case of private placements, however, financial buyers are venture capitalists rather than buyout firms, which is an important distinction. A VC firm invests in less than 50 percent of a company's equity, whereas a buyout firm purchases greater than 50 percent of a company's equity, thereby gaining control of the firm. Note that the same difference applies to private placements on the sell-side. A sale occurs when a firm sells greater than 50 percent of its equity (giving up control), but a private placement occurs when less than 50 percent of its equity is sold.

Because private placements involve selling equity and debt to a single buyer, the investor and the seller (the company) typically negotiate the terms of the deal. Investment bankers function as negotiators for the company, helping to convince the investor of the value of the firm.

Fees involved in private placements work like those in public offerings. Usually they are a fixed percentage of the size of the transaction. (Of course, the fees depend on whether a deal is consummated or not.) A common private placement fee is 5 percent of the size of the equity/debt sold.

Financial Restructurings

When a company cannot pay its cash obligations — for example, when it cannot meet its bond payments or its payments to other creditors (such as vendors) — it goes bankrupt. In this situation, a company can, of course, choose to simply shut down operations and walk away. On the other hand, if it can also restructure and remain in business.

What does it mean to restructure? The process can be thought of as two-fold: financial restructuring and organizational restructuring. Restructuring from a financial viewpoint involves renegotiating payment terms on debt obligations, issuing new debt, and restructuring payables to vendors. Bankers provide guidance to the firm by recommending the sale of assets, the issuing of special securities such as convertible stock and bonds, or even selling the company entirely.

Hungry for more inside scoop? Join Vault.com's popular online community for finance and banking — www.vault.com

VAULT.com   **55**

From an organizational viewpoint, a restructuring can involve a change in management, strategy and focus. I-bankers with expertise in "reorgs" can facilitate and ease the transition from bankruptcy to viability.

Fees in restructuring work

Typical fees in a restructuring depend on whatever retainer fee is paid upfront and what new securities are issued post-bankruptcy. When a bank represents a bankrupt company, the brunt of the work is focused on analyzing and recommending financing alternatives. Thus, the fee structure resembles that of a private placement. How does the work differ from that of a private placement? I-bankers not only work in securing financing, but may assist in building projections for the client (which serve to illustrate to potential financiers what the firm's prospects may be), in renegotiating credit terms with lenders, and in helping to re-establish the business as a going concern.

Because a firm in bankruptcy already has substantial cash flow problems, investment banks often charge minimal monthly retainers, hoping to cash in on the spread from issuing new securities. Like other public offerings, this can be a highly lucrative and steady business.

THE JOBS

Corporate Finance

CHAPTER 8

Stuffy bankers?

The stereotype of the corporate finance department is stuffy, arrogant (white and male) MBAs who frequent golf courses and talk on cellphones nonstop. While this is increasingly less true, corporate finance remains the most white-shoe department in the typical investment bank. The atmosphere in corporate finance is, unlike that in sales and trading, often quiet and reserved. Junior bankers sit separated by cubicles, quietly crunching numbers.

Depending on the firm, corporate finance can also be a tough place to work, with unforgiving bankers and expectations through the roof. Stories of analyst abuse abound, and some bankers come down hard on new analysts to scare and intimidate them. The lifestyle for corporate finance professionals can be a killer. In fact, many corporate finance workers find that they literally dedicate their lives to the job. Social life suffers, free time disappears, and stress multiplies. It is not uncommon to find analysts and associates wearing rumpled pants and wrinkled shirts, exhibiting the wear and tear of all-nighters. Fortunately, these long hours pay remarkable dividends in the form of six-figure salaries and huge year-end bonuses.

Personality-wise, bankers tend to be highly intelligent, motivated, and not lacking in confidence. Money is important to the bankers, and many anticipate working for just a few years to earn as much as possible, before finding less demanding work. Analysts and associates tend also to be ambitious, intelligent and pedigreed. If you happen to be going into an analyst or associate position, make sure to check your ego at the door but don't be afraid to ask penetrating questions about deals and what is required of you.

The deal team

Investment bankers generally work in deal teams which, depending on the size of a deal, vary somewhat in makeup. In this chapter we will provide an overview of the roles and lifestyles of the positions in corporate finance, from analyst to managing director. (Often, a person in corporate finance is called an I-banker.) Because the titles and roles really do not change between underwriting to M&A, we have included

Hungry for more inside scoop? Join Vault.com's popular online community for finance and banking — www.vault.com

VAULT.com 59

both in this explanation. In fact, at most smaller firms, underwriting and transaction advisory are not separated, and bankers typically pitch whatever business they can scout out within their industry sector.

Section One: The Players

Analysts

Analysts are the grunts in the corporate finance world. They often toil endlessly with little thanks, little pay (when figured on an hourly basis), and barely enough free time to sleep four hours a night. Typically hired directly out of top undergraduate universities, this crop of bright, highly motivated kids does the financial modeling and basic entry-level duties associated with any corporate finance deal.

Modeling every night until 2 a.m. and not having much of a social life proves to be unbearable for many an analyst and after two years many analysts leave the industry. Unfortunately, many bankers recognize the transient nature of analysts, and work them hard to get the most out of them they can. The unfortunate analyst that screws up or talks back too much may never get real work, spending his days bored until 10 p.m. waiting for work to come, stressing even more than the busy analyst. These are the analysts that do not get called to work on live transactions, and do menial work or just put together pitchbooks all the time.

When it comes to analyst pay, much depends on whether the analyst is in New York or not. In the City, pay often begins for first-year analysts at $45,000 to $55,000 per year, with an annual bonus of approximately $30,000. While this seems to be a lot for a 22-year-old with just an undergrad degree, it's not a great deal if you consider per-hour compensation. At most firms, analysts also get dinner every night for free if they work late, and have little time to spend their income, often meaning fat checking and savings accounts and ample fodder to fund business school down the road. At regional firms, pay typically is 20 percent less than that of their New York counterparts. Worth noting, though, is the fact that at regional firms 1) hours are often less, and 2) the cost of living is much lower. Be wary, however, of the small regional firm that pays at the low end of the scale and still shackles analysts to their cubicles. While the salary generally does not improve much for second-year analysts, the bonus can double for those second-years who demonstrate high performance. At this level, bonuses depend mostly on an analyst's contribution, attitude, and work ethic, as opposed to the volume of business generated by the bankers with whom he or she works.

Hungry for more inside scoop? Join Vault.com's popular online
community for finance and banking — www.vault.com

VAULT.com   **61**

Associates

Much like analysts, associates hit the grindstone hard. Working 80- to 100-hour weeks, associates stress over pitchbooks and models all night, become experts with financial modeling on Excel, and sometimes shake their heads wondering what the point is. Unlike analysts, however, associates more quickly become involved with clients and, most importantly, are not at the bottom of the totem pole. Associates quickly learn to play quarterback and hand-off menial modeling work and research projects to analysts. However, treatment from vice presidents and managing directors doesn't necessarily improve for associates versus analysts, as bankers sometimes care more about the work getting done, and not about the guy working away all night to complete it.

Hailing directly from top business schools, associates often possess only a summer's worth of experience in corporate finance, so they must start almost from the beginning. The overall level of business awareness and knowledge a bright MBA has, however, makes a tremendous difference, and associates quickly earn the luxury of more complicated work and better bonuses.

Associates are at least much better paid than analysts. A $80,000 salary generally starts them off, and usually bonuses hit $25,000 in the first six months. (At most firms, associates start in August and get their first bonus in January.) Newly minted MBAs cash in on signing bonuses and forgivable loans as well, especially on Wall Street. These can amount to another $25,000 to $30,000, depending on the firm, providing total compensation of up to $130,000 for top firms. Associates beyond their first year begin to rake it in.

Vice Presidents

Upon attaining the position of vice president, those in corporate finance enter the realm of real bankers. The lifestyle becomes much more manageable once the associate moves up to VP. On the plus side, weekends free up, all-nighters drop off, and the general level of responsibility increases — VPs are the ones telling analysts to stay late on Friday nights. In the office, VPs manage the financial modeling/ pitchbook production process in the office. On the negative side, the wear and tear of traveling that accompanies banker responsibilities can be difficult. As a VP, one begins to handle client relationships, and thus spends much more time on the road than analysts or associates. You can look forward to being on the road at least three to four days per week, usually visiting clients and potential clients. Don't forget about closing dinners (to celebrate completed deals), industry conferences (to drum up potential business and build a solid network within their industry), and, of course, roadshows. VPs are perfect candidates to baby-sit company management on roadshows.

The formula for paying bankers varies dramatically from firm to firm. Some adhere to rigid formulas based on how much business a banker brought in, while others pay based on a subjective allocation of corporate finance profits. No matter how compensation is structured, however, when business is slow, bonuses taper off rapidly. For most bankers, typical salaries may range from $100,000 to $200,000 per year, but bonuses can be significantly greater. Total packages for VPs on Wall Street often hit over $500,000 level in the first year — and pay can skyrocket from there.

Directors/Managing Directors

Directors and managing directors are the major players in corporate finance. Typically, MDs work their own hours, deal with clients at the highest level, and disappear whenever a drafting session takes place, leaving this grueling work to others. (We will examine these drafting sessions in depth later.) MDs mostly develop and cultivate relationships with various companies in order to generate corporate finance business for the firm. MDs typically focus on one industry, develop relationships among management teams of companies in the industry and visit these companies on a regular basis. These visits are aptly called sales calls.

Top bankers at the MD level might be pulling in bonuses of up to $1 million or more a year, but slow markets (and hence slow business) can cut that number dramatically. It is important to realize that for the most part, MDs act as relationship managers, and are essentially paid on commission. For top performers compensation can be almost inconceivable. For example, in 1999, Warburg Dillon Read (now UBS Warburg) hired health care banker Benjamin Lorello away from Salomon Smith Barney with a reported package of $70 million over five years.

Hungry for more inside scoop? Join Vault.com's popular online
community for finance and banking — www.vault.com

VAULT.com   **63**

Section Two: The Role of the Players

What do corp fin professionals actually do on a day-to-day basis to underwrite an offering? The process, though not simple, can easily be broken up into the same three phases that we described previously. We will illustrate the role of the bankers by walking through the IPO process.

Hiring the managers

This phase in the process can vary in length substantially, lasting for many months or just a few short weeks. The length of the hiring phase depends on how many I-banks the company wishes to meet, when they want to go public, and how market conditions fare. Remember that several investment banks are usually tapped to manage a single equity or debt deal, complicating the hiring decisions that companies face.

MDs and Sales Calls

Often when a large IPO candidate is preparing for an offering, word gets out on the Street that the company is looking to go public. MDs all over Wall Street scramble to create pitchbooks (see inset) and set up meetings in order to convince the company to hire them as the lead manager. I-bankers who have previously established a good relationship with the company have a distinct advantage. What is surprising to many people unfamiliar with I-banking is that MDs are essentially traveling salespeople who pay visits to the CEOs and CFOs of companies, with the goal of building investment banking relationships.

Typically, MDs meet informally with the company several times. In an initial meeting with a firm's management, the MD will have an analyst and an associate put together a general pitchbook, which is left with the company to illustrate the I-bank's capabilities.

A Word About Pitchbooks

Pitchbooks come in two flavors: the general pitchbook and the deal-specific pitchbook. Bankers use the general pitchbook to guide their introductions and presentations during sales calls. These pitchbooks contain general information and include a wide variety of selling points bankers make to potential clients. Usually, general pitchbooks include an overview of the I-bank and detail its specific capabilities in research, corporate finance, sales and trading.

The second flavor of pitchbooks is the deal-specific pitch. While a general pitchbook does not differ much from deal to deal, bankers prepare offering pitchbooks specifically for the transactions (for example, an IPO) they are proposing to a company's top managers. Deal-specific pitchbooks are highly customized and usually require at least one analyst or associate all-nighter to put together (although MDs, VPs, associates, and analysts all work closely together to create the book). The most difficult aspect to creating this type of pitchbook is the financial modeling involved. In an IPO pitchbook, valuations, comparable company analyses, and industry analyses are but a few of the many specific topics covered in detail.

Apart from the numbers, these pitchbooks also include the bank's customized selling points. The most common of these include:

- the bank's reputation, which can lend the offering an aura of respectability

- the performance of other IPOs managed by the bank

- the prominence of a bank's research analyst in the industry, which can tacitly guarantee that the new public stock will receive favorable coverage by a listened-to stock expert

- the bank's expertise as an underwriter in the industry

Once an MD knows a company plans to go public, he or she will first discuss the IPO with the company's top management and gather data regarding past financial performance and future expected results. This data, farmed out to a VP or associate and crucial to the valuation, is then used in the preparation of the pitchbook.

Pitchbook Preparation

After substantial effort and probably a few all-nighters on the part of analysts and associates, the deal-specific pitchbook is complete. The

Hungry for more inside scoop? Join Vault.com's popular online
community for finance and banking — www.vault.com

VAULT.com   **65**

most important piece of information in this kind of pitchbook is the valuation of the company going public. (Remember that this is the same company to which the bank is presenting the pitchbook.) Prior to its initial public offering, a company has no public equity and therefore no market value of common stock. So, the investment bankers, through a mix of financial and industry expertise, develop a suitable offering size range and hence a marketable valuation range for the company. Of course, the higher the valuation, the happier the potential client. At the same time, though, I-bankers must not be too aggressive in their valuation — if the market does not support the valuation and the IPO fails, the bank loses credibility.

The Pitch

While analysts and associates are the members of the deal team who spend the most time working on the pitchbook, the MD is the one who actually visits the company with the books under his or her arm to make the pitch. The pitchbook serves as a guide for the presentation (led by the MD) to the company. This presentation generally concludes with the valuation. Companies invite many I-banks to present their pitches at separate meetings. These multiple rounds of presentations comprise what is often called the beauty contest.

The pitch comes from the managing director in charge of the deal. The MD's supporting cast typically consists of a VP from corporate finance, as well as the research analyst who will cover the company's stock once the IPO is complete. For especially important pitches, an I-bank will send other top representatives from either its corporate finance, research or syndicate departments. (We will cover the syndicate and research departments later.) Some companies opt to have their board of directors sit in on the pitch — the MD might face the added pressure of tough questions from the board during the presentation.

Selecting the Managers

After a company has seen all of the pitches in a beauty contest, it selects one firm as the lead manager, while some of the other firms are chosen as the co-managers. The number of firms chosen to manage a deal runs the gamut. Sometimes a firm will sole manage a deal, and sometimes, especially on large global deals, four to six firms might be selected as managers. An average-sized offering will generally have three to four managers underwriting the offering — one lead manager and two or three co-managers.

Due diligence and drafting

Organizational Meeting

Once the I-bank has been selected as a manager in the IPO, the next step is an organizational meeting at the company's headquarters. All parties in the working group involved in the deal meet for the first time, shake hands and get down to business. The attendees and their roles are summarized in the table below.

Group	Typical Participants
The Company	Management, namely the CEO and CFO, division heads, and heads of major departments or lines of business.
The Company's lawyers	Partner plus one associate.
The Company's accountants	Partner, plus one or two associates.
The lead manager	I-banking team, with up to four corporate finance professionals. A research analyst may come for due diligence meetings.
The co-manager(s), or I-bank(s) selected behind the lead	I-banking team with typically two or three members instead of four.
Underwriters' counsel, or the lawyers representing the managers	Partner plus one associate.

At the initial organizational meeting, the MD from the lead manager guides and moderates the meeting. Details discussed at the meeting include the exact size of the offering, the timetable for completing the deal, and other concerns the group may have. Usually a two- or three-month schedule is established as a beacon toward the completion of the offering. Often, the organizational meeting wraps up in an hour or two and leads directly to due diligence.

Due Diligence

Due diligence involves studying the company going public in as much detail as possible. Much of this process involves interviewing top

Hungry for more inside scoop? Join Vault.com's popular online community for finance and banking — www.vault.com

V/\ULT.com **67**

management at the firm. Due diligence usually entails a plant tour (if relevant), and explanations of the company's business, how the company operates, how management plans to grow the company, and how the company will perform over the next few quarters.

As with the organizational meeting, the moderator and lead questioner throughout the due diligence sessions is the top banker in attendance from the lead manager. Research analysts from the I-banks attend the due diligence meetings during the IPO process in order to probe the business, ask tough questions and generally better understand how to project the company's financials. While bankers tend to focus on the relevant operational, financial, and strategic issues at the firm, lawyers involved in the deal explore mostly legal issues, such as pending litigation.

Drafting the Prospectus

Once due diligence wraps up, the IPO process moves quickly into the drafting stage. Drafting refers to the process by which the working group writes the S-1 registration statement, or prospectus. This prospectus is used to shop the offering to potential investors.

Generally, the client company's lawyers compile the first draft of the prospectus, but thereafter the drafting process includes the entire working group. Unfortunately, writing by committee means a multitude of style clashes, disagreements, and tangential discussions, but the end result usually is a prospectus that most team members can live with. On average, the drafting stage takes anywhere from four to seven drafting sessions, spread over a six- to 10-week period. Initially, all of the top corp fin representatives from each of the managers attends, but these meetings thin out to fewer and fewer members as they continue. The lead manager will always have at least a VP to represent the firm, but co-managers often settle on VPs, associates, and sometimes even analysts to represent their firms.

Drafting sessions are initially exciting to attend as an analyst or associate, as they offer client exposure, learning about a business, and getting out of the office. However, these sessions can quickly grow tiring and annoying. Drafting sessions at the printer can mean more all-nighters, as the group scrambles to finish the prospectus in order to file on time with the SEC.

Going to the Printer

When a prospectus is near completion, lawyers, bankers and the company all go to the printer, which is sort of like going to a country club prison. These printers, where prospectuses are actually printed, are equipped with showers, all the food you can eat, and other amenities to accommodate locked-in-until-you're-done sessions.

Printers are employed by companies to print and distribute prospectuses. A typical public deal requires anywhere from 10,000 to 20,000 copies of the preliminary prospectus (called the red herring or red) and 5,000 to 10,000 copies of the final prospectus. Printers receive the final edited version from the working group, literally print the thousands of copies in-house and then mail them to potential investors in a deal. (The list of investors comes from the managers.) Printers also file the document electronically with the SEC. As the last meeting before the prospectus is completed, printer meetings can last anywhere from a day to a week or even more. Why is this significant? Because printers are extraordinarily expensive and companies are eager to move onto the next phase of the deal. This amounts to loads of pressure on the working group to finish the prospectus.

For those in the working group, perfecting the prospectus means wrangling over commas, legal language, and grammar until the document is error-free. Nothing is allowed to interrupt a printer meeting, meaning one or two all-nighters in a row is not unheard of for working groups.

On the plus side, printers stock anything and everything that a person could want to eat or drink. The best restaurants cater to printers, and M&M's always seem to appear on the table just when you want a handful. And food isn't all: Many printers have pool tables and stocked bars for those half-hour breaks at 2:00 a.m. Needless to say, an abundance of coffee and fattening food keeps the group going during late hours.

Marketing

Designing Marketing Material
Once a deal is filed with the SEC, the prospectus (or S-1) becomes public domain. The information and details of the upcoming IPO are publicly known. After the SEC approves the prospectus, the printer spits out thousands of copies, which are mailed to literally the entire universe of potential institutional investors.

Hungry for more inside scoop? Join Vault.com's popular online
community for finance and banking — www.vault.com

VAULT.com **69**

In the meantime, the MD and VP of the lead manager work closely with the CEO and CFO of the company to develop a roadshow presentation, which consists of essentially 20 to 40 slides for use during meetings with investors. Junior team members in corporate finance help edit the roadshow slides and begin working on other marketing documents. For example, associates and analysts develop a summary rehash of the prospectus in a brief selling memo, which is distributed to the bank's salesforce.

The Roadshow (Baby Sitting)

The actual roadshow begins soon after the reds are printed. The preliminary prospectus, called a red herring or red, helps salespeople and investors alike understand the IPO candidate's business, historical financial performance, growth opportunities and risk factors. Using the prospectus and the selling memo as references, the salespeople of the investment banks managing the deal contact the institutional investors they cover and set up roadshow meetings. The syndicate department, the facilitators between the salesperson and corporate finance, finalizes the morass of meetings and communicates the agenda to corporate finance and sales. And, on the roadshow itself, VPs or associates generally escort the company. Despite the seemingly glamorous nature of a roadshow (traveling all over the country in limos with your client, the CEO), the corporate finance professional acts as little more than a babysitter on the roadshow. The most important duties of the corporate finance professionals often include making sure luggage gets from point A to point B, ensuring that hotel rooms are booked, and finding the limousine driver at the airport terminal.

After a grueling two to three weeks and hundreds of presentations, the roadshow ends and the group flies home for much needed rest. During the roadshow, sales and syndicate departments compile orders for the company's stock and develop what is called the book. The book details how investors have responded, how much stock they want (if any), and at what price they are willing to buy into the offering.

The End in Sight — Pricing the Deal

IPO prospectuses list a range of stock prices on the cover (usually something like $16 to $18 per share). This range is preset by the underwriting team before the roadshow and meant to tell investors what the company is worth and hence where it will price. Highly sought-after offerings will price at the top of the range and those in less demand will price at the bottom of the range.

Hot IPOs with tremendous demand end up above the range and often trade up significantly on the first day in the market. The hottest offerings close two to three times higher than the initial offering price. Memorable examples include Apple Computer in the 1980s, Boston Chicken in the mid-90s, and Netscape Communications and a slew of Internet stocks in the past two years. The process of going public is summarized on pages 72-73.

Follow-on public offerings and bond offerings

Bond deals and follow-on offerings are less complex in nature than IPOs for many reasons. The biggest reason is that they have an already agreed-upon and approved prospectus from prior publicly filed documents. The language, content, and style of the prospectus usually stay updated year to year, as the company either files for additional offerings or files its annual report (officially called the 10K). Also, the fact that the legal hurdles involved in registering a company's securities have already been leaped makes life significantly easier for everyone involved in a follow-on or bond offering.

If a follow-on offering involves the I-banks that handled a company's IPO (and they often do), the MDs that worked on the deal are already familiar with the company. They may not even have to develop a pitchbook to formally pitch the follow-on if the relationship is sound. Because the banking relationship is usually between individual bankers and individual executives at client companies, bankers can often take clients with them if they switch banks.

Because of their relative simplicity, follow-ons and bond deals quickly jump from the manager-choosing phase to the due diligence and drafting phase, which also progresses more quickly than it would for an IPO. The roadshow proceeds as before, with the company and a corp fin VP or associate accompanying management to ensure that the logistics work out.

Hungry for more inside scoop? Join Vault.com's popular online
community for finance and banking — www.vault.com

VAULT.com   **71**

Going Public

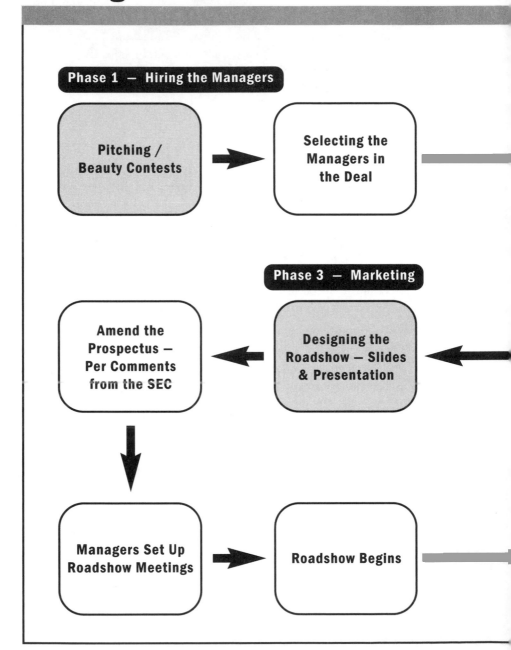

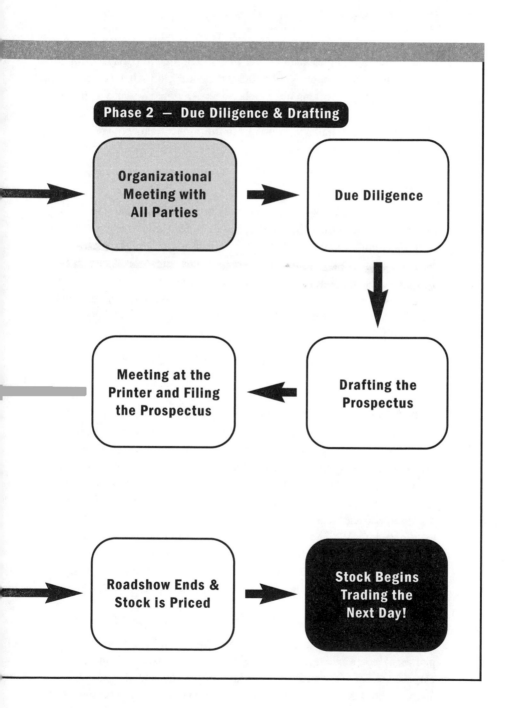

Phase 2 — Due Diligence & Drafting

Organizational Meeting with All Parties

Due Diligence

Meeting at the Printer and Filing the Prospectus

Drafting the Prospectus

Roadshow Ends & Stock is Priced

Stock Begins Trading the Next Day!

Hungry for more inside scoop? Join Vault.com's popular
online community for consulting — www.vault.com

V/\ULT.com   73

Section Three:
The Typical Week in Corporate Finance

One of the most common questions an interviewee asks is "What is the typical day for an investment banker like?" Truth be told, days spent in investment banking often vary widely, depending on what aspect of a deal you might be working on. But because deals are similar, you might be able to conjure up a typical week in the life of an analyst, associate, vice president, or managing director in corporate finance. We'll start with analysts.

Analysts

For I-banking analysts, it's all about the computer screen. Analysts, especially those in their first year, spend countless hours staring at their computer monitors and working until midnight or all night. Building models, creating "comps," (see sidebar) and editing pitchbooks fills the majority of their time. Many analysts do nothing but put together pitchbooks, and never see the light of day. Hard working and talented analysts, however, tend to find their way out of the office and becoming involved in meetings related to live transactions.

A typical week for an analyst might involve the following:

Monday

Up at 8:30 a.m. Monday morning, the analyst makes it into the office by 9:15. Mornings often move at a snail's pace, so the analyst builds a set of comparable company analysis (a.k.a. comps, see sidebar) and then updates the latest league table data, which track how many deals I-banks have completed. Lunch is a leisurely forty-five minutes spent with other analysts at a deli a few blocks away. The afternoon includes a conference call with a company considering an IPO, and at 5, a meeting with a VP who drops a big model on the analyst's lap. Dinner is delivered at 8 and paid for by the firm, but this is no great joy — it is going to be a late night because of the model. At midnight, the analyst has reached a stopping point and calls a car to give him a free ride home.

Tuesday

The next day is similar, but the analyst spends all day working on a pitchbook for a meeting on Wednesday that a banker has set up. Of course, the banker waited until the day before the meeting to tell the analyst about it. After working all night and into the morning, the analyst finally gets home at 5 a.m., which gives him enough time for a two-hour nap, a shower, and a change of clothes.

Wednesday

Unfortunately, there is a scheduled drafting session out of town on Wednesday relating to another transaction, and the flight is at 8 a.m. Having slept only two hours, the analyst reads his draft of the prospectus on the plane, and arrives with a VP at the lawyer's office at 11 a.m., armed with some comments to point out to the group. Many hours and coffees later, the VP and analyst get back on the plane, where the analyst falls dead asleep. After the flight touches down, the analyst returns to the office at 8 p.m. — and continues modeling for a few hours. At midnight, the analyst heads home.

Thursday

The analyst is roped into doing another pitchbook, this one for a merger deal. He frantically works to complete a merger model: gathering information, keying in data, and working with an associate looking over his shoulder. By the time he and the associate have finished the analysis, it is 1 a.m.

Friday

Friday is even worse. The merger model is delivered to the hands of the senior VP overseeing the work, but returned covered in red ink. Changes take the better part of the day, and progress is slow. Projections have to be rejiggered, more research found, and new companies added to the list of comps. At 7 p.m. on Friday, the analyst calls his friends to tell them he won't make it out tonight — again. At 11 p.m., he heads home.

Saturday

Even Saturday requires nearly 10 hours of work, but much of the afternoon the analyst waits by the phone to hear from the VP who is looking at the latest version of the models.

Sunday

No rest on Sunday. This day involves checking some numbers, but the afternoon, thankfully, is completely free for some napping and downtime.

Hungry for more inside scoop? Join Vault.com's popular online
community for finance and banking — www.vault.com

VAULT.COM   **75**

The analyst adds up a total of maybe 90 hours this week. It could have been much worse: at some firms, analysts typically work more than 100 hours per week.

COMPS, ILLUSTRATED

What exactly are comps? You may have heard of comps, or comparable company analysis — and the fact that after two years, analysts never want to do comp analysis ever again.

In short, comps summarize financial market measures of companies within an industry group. For example, suppose we wanted to compare a software company (our client, Company C) to other software companies, Companies A and B. Comps usually are many pages long, but often begin with something like the following.

Last 12 Months Data ($ in millions)

Company	Sales	EBITDA	Net Income	EPS	Stock Price
A	2,800	500	200	$ 2.00	$ 75.00
B	900	200	50	$ 0.65	$ 18.00
C	3,000	600	195	$ 1.15	$ 48.75

Valuation Measures

Company	Shares (millions)	Market Value	Net Debt	Enterprise Value
A	100	7,500	1,450	8,950
B	77	1,385	600	1,985
C	170	8,266	190	8,456

Ratios and Multiples

Company	Ent Value/ Revenue	Ent Value/ EBITDA	Price/ Earning
A	3	18	38
B	2	10	28
C	3	14	42

Here we begin to summarize income statement data, including sales and EPS and build up to market valuation measures and, finally, a few ratios. From this illustration, we could interpret the numbers above as: "Our client (Company C) is the biggest firm in terms of sales, has the most cash flow, and the highest P/E ratio. The high P/E ratio makes Company C the most "expensive" stock, trading at 42 times earnings. Note that EBITDA is often used as a proxy for cash flow.

Such analyses help bankers interpret how firms are trading in the market, how they compare to their peers, and what valuations seem typical. Comps are useful for valuing companies going public as well as valuing companies that are acquisition targets. Keep in mind that this is a very simplified version of what true comps look like.

Associates

With a role similar to analysts, associates are primarily responsible for financial models and pitchbooks. A week for an associate (especially a first-year associate) might resemble closely the scenario painted above, with oversight duties over analysts working on models for the associate. In addition, the associate may be more involved in dealing with the MDs and in checking pitchbooks before they are sent out.

A more experienced associate will sit down more frequently with an MD, going over details of potential deals or discussing numbers. In contrast to analysts, who work as generalists, associates typically focus on one specific industry. One week for an analyst might include deals for a steel company, a high-tech company, and a restaurant company; an associate will focus on an industry like high tech or health care. However, like analysts, associates must work carefully and thoughtfully and put in long hours to gain the respect of their supervisors.

Day in the Life: Associate, Corporate Finance (Goldman Sachs)

We've asked insiders at leading investment banks to offer us insight into a day in the life of their position. Here's a look at a day of an associate I-banker at Goldman Sachs.

8:15   Arrive at 85 Broad Street. (Show Goldman ID card to get past the surly elevator guards).

8:25   Arrive on 17th Floor. Use "blue card" to get past floor lobby. ("Don't ever forget your blue card. Goldman has tight security and you won't be able to get around the building all day.")

Hungry for more inside scoop? Join Vault.com's popular online community for finance and banking — www.vault.com

VΛULT.com   **77**

8:45   Pick up work from Word Processing, review it, make changes.

9:00   Check voice mail, return phone calls.

9:30   Eat breakfast; read *The Wall Street Journal*. ("But don't let a supervisor see you with your paper sprawled across your desk.")

10:00   Prepare pitchbooks, discuss analysis with members of deal team.

12:00   Conference call with members of IPO team, including lawyers and client.

1:00   Eat lunch at desk. ("The Wall Street McDonald's delivers, but it's the most expensive McDonald's in New York City; Goldman's cafeteria is cheaper, but you have to endure the shop talk.")

2:00   Work on restructuring case studies; make several document requests from company library.

3:00   Start to prepare analysis; order additional data from DRG (Data Resources Group).

5:00   Check in with vice presidents and heads of deal teams on status of work.

6:00   Go to gym for an abbreviated workout.

6:45   Dinner. ("Dinner is free in the IBD cafeteria, but avoid it. Wall Street has pretty limited food options, so for a quick meal it's the Indian place across the street that's open 24 hours.")

8:00   Meet with VP again. ("You'll probably get more work thrown at you.")

9:45   Try to make FedEx cutoff. Drop off pitchbook to Document Processing on 20th Floor. ("You have to call ahead and warn them if you have a last-minute job or you're screwed.")

10:00   Order in food again. ("It's unlikely that there will be any room left in your $20 meal allowance — but we usually order in a group and add extra names to bypass the limit.")

10:30   Leave for home. ("Call for a car service. Enjoy your nightly 'meal on wheels' on the way home.")

Vice Presidents and MDs (a.k.a. "Bankers")

As one becomes a banker, one begins to shift from modeling and number crunching to relationship building. This gradual transition happens during the senior associate phase as the associate begins with interfacing with existing clients. Ultimately, VPs and MDs spend most of their time and energy finding new clients and servicing existing clients. VPs spend more time managing associates and analysts and the pitchbook creation process than MDs, but their responsibilities begin to resemble those of MDs at the SVP level. The typical week for a banker, then, looks quite different than that of an analyst or associate.

Monday

The banker gets a courier package delivered at 6 a.m. at her house, and carries this with her to the airport. The package contains several copies of an M&A pitch that she intends to make that day. Her team put the finishing touches on the analysis just a few hours before, while she slept at home. Her schedule that day includes three meetings in Houston and one important pitch in the afternoon. As an oil and gas banker, the banker finds she spend two-thirds of her time flying to Texas and Louisiana, where her clients are clustered. In her morning sales calls, the banker visits with a couple CEOs of different companies, gives them an updated general pitchbook and discusses their businesses. The third meeting of the day is a lunch meeting with a CFO from a company she did a deal for last year.

The banker's cell phone seems glued to her head as she drives from meeting to meeting, but she turns it off for her final meeting — an M&A pitch to a CEO of an oilfield service company. Afterward, the banker grabs dinner with another top manager at the company, and finds her way to her hotel around 9 p.m.

Tuesday

The next day the banker heads to a drafting session at the offices of a law firm downtown. She had gotten up early to read through and review the draft of the prospectus, and made comments in the margins. As her firm is only the co-manager on the deal, she merely brings up issues for the group to consider, and does not lead the discussion. After the drafting session, the banker catches an early afternoon flight home, leaving a VP to cover for her.

Hungry for more inside scoop? Join Vault.com's popular online community for finance and banking — www.vault.com

VAULT.com   79

Wednesday

Back in the office, the banker spends all day on the phone. Flooded with calls, the banker has no time to look at any of the models dropped off in her in-box. Finally, around 6 p.m., she calls the associate and analyst team building an IPO model into her office. For an hour, they go through the numbers, with the banker pointing out problems and missing data items. The associate and analyst leave with a full plate of work ahead. The banker heads home at 8 p.m.

Thursday

The banker is back in the office in the morning to review more models and take some phone calls, but she leaves around noon to catch a flight to make it to a "closing dinner." It is time to celebrate one of her successfully managed transactions (it was a follow-on) with the working group. As the lead manager, the banker makes sure that she has plenty of gag gifts for the management team and jokes to tell the group.

Friday

The banker plans on staying in town to make a few sales visits in the morning. Armed again with pitchbooks, the banker spends a few hours wooing potential clients by discussing merger ideas, financing alternatives and any other relevant transaction that could lead to a fee. Heading home, the banker touches base with her favorite associate to discuss a few models that need work, and what she needs for Monday.

Weekend

Over the weekend, the banker has models couriered to her home, where she goes over the numbers and calls her comments and changes in to the associate.

Section 4: Formulas For Success

For analysts and associates

The formula for succeeding in banking depends on your role, but some generalizations can be made. The expected qualities of hard work, confidence and dedication ring true in every job, but corporate finance takes these expectations to the nth degree.

Analysts

For the analyst, it is all about keeping your head in the computer, working long hours, and double-checking your work before showing it to bankers. Nothing angers a time-constrained VP more than a young naive analyst who puts together subpar work. Quality of work is key to establishing respect early on, and bankers respect number crunchers who make few mistakes and are not afraid to ask smart, to-the-point questions pertaining to a particular assignment. And, while face time is officially rejected at every bank, bankers tend to frown upon analysts gone before dinner time. A new analyst's best move is to ease into a stressful environment by working hard, learning the ropes as quickly as possible, and representing oneself as eager and willing to put in the effort required of them.

Generally, analyst programs last two years. Then, graduating analysts often leave to attend graduate school or to find another job. The experience is not all gloom and doom, as analysts receive a fast-track learning experience on Wall Street, top bonuses, and admission to some of the best business schools in the country. Depending on the firm, Wall Street analysts either join a specific industry or product group, or fall into a category called generalists, which means that they work on deals and pitchbooks for a variety of industry groups and hence learn about a variety of companies in a range of industries. An increased number of business school graduates opting out of investment banking careers has added another improvement to the analyst's life. In 2000 several firms including DLJ, Lehman Brothers, and Morgan Stanley began promoting a larger number of well-regarded analysts directly to the associate level after just two years. Previously, only a small handful of the brightest analysts were promoted to the associate level without an MBA.

Hungry for more inside scoop? Join Vault.com's popular online community for finance and banking — www.vault.com

VAULT.com   **81**

Associates

The associate excels by demonstrating an aptitude to learn quickly, work hard, and establish himself or herself early on as a dedicated group member. At the associate level, placement into an industry group typically occurs soon after the training program ends, although some firms such as Salomon Smith Barney offer generalist programs for an extended period. Impressions can form quickly, and a new group member who shows willingness to work hard and late for a group will create a positive impression. Associates are more involved than analysts in client meetings, due diligence meetings, drafting sessions and roadshows. So, associates must be able to socialize with clients well.

Over time, associates spend more time on the road, and supervisors keep an eye on their manner and carriage in front of clients. Sharp comments, confidence and poise in front of clients will at this point do more for an associate than all-nighters and face time. Like analysts, associates have also benefited from the recent dearth of talented candidates at investment banks. The promotion time from associate to vice president has recently been shorted at many firms. Several I-banks have also started to offer private equity investment opportunities to associates — opportunities which were previously available only to officers of the firm (vice presidents or higher). Typically, associates move up to vice president level within three to four years.

Vice Presidents

Depending on the firm, VPs often succeed by showing good managerial skills over deals and transactions, as well as over analysts and associates. VPs ultimately are responsible for pitchbooks, transaction details and therefore become managers both in and out of the office. Organization, attention to detail, and strong motivational skills lead to big-sized bonuses. Most important however, is a demonstration of leadership. VPs must win business, convince clients to go ahead with certain deals, handle meetings effectively, and cover for MDs at all times. At regional I-banks, the ability to generate business reigns supreme over other characteristics, whereas Wall Street VPs tend to be transaction processors, who complete deals handed to them.

Managing Directors

Success for an MD comes with industry knowledge, an ability to handle clients, and an ability to find new ones. The MD's most important task includes schmoozing in the industry, finding potential deals, and pitching them with confidence and poise. Public speaking skills, industry awareness, demonstrated experience and an ability to sell combine to create the best bankers. Importantly however, MDs must still be able to grasp the numbers side of the business and be able to explain them to clients. The progression from associate to MD is typically an eight- to 10-year track.

Hungry for more inside scoop? Join Vault.com's popular online
community for finance and banking — www.vault.com

V∧ULT.com   83

Institutional Sales and Trading (S&T)

CHAPTER 9

The war zone

If you've ever been to an investment banking trading floor, you've witnessed the chaos. It's usually a lot of swearing, yelling and shouting: a pressure cooker of stress. Sometimes the floor is a quiet rumble of activity, but when the market takes a nosedive, panic ensues and the volume kicks up a notch. Traders must rely on their market instincts, and salespeople yell for bids when the market tumbles. Deciding what to buy or sell, and at what price to buy and sell, is difficult with millions of dollars are at stake.

However, salespeople and traders work much more reasonable hours than research analysts or corporate finance bankers. Rarely does a salesperson or trader venture into the office on a Saturday or Sunday, making the trading floor completely void of life on weekends. Any corporate finance analyst who has crossed a trading floor on a Saturday will tell you that the only noise to be heard on the floor is the clocks clicking every minute and the whir of the air conditioner.

Shop Talk

Here's a quick example of how a salesperson and a trader interact on an emerging market bond trade.

SALESPERSON: Receives a call from a buy-side firm. The buy-side firm wishes to sell $10 million of a particular Mexican Par government-issued bond (denominated in U.S. dollars). The emerging markets bond salesperson, seated next to the emerging markets traders, stands up in his chair and yells to the relevant trader, "Give me a bid on $10 million Mex Par, six and a quarter, nineteens."

TRADER: "I got 'em at 73 and an eighth."

Translation: I am willing to buy them at a price of $73.125 per $100 of face value. As mentioned, the $10 million represents amount of par value the client wanted to sell, meaning the trader will buy the bonds, paying 73.125 percent of $10 million plus accrued interest (to factor in interest earned between interest payments).

SALESPERSON: "Can't you do any better than that?"

Translation: Please buy at a higher price, as I will get a higher commission.

Hungry for more inside scoop? Join Vault.com's popular online community for finance and banking — www.vault.com

VAULT.com 85

> **TRADER**: "That's the best I can do. The market is falling right now. You want to sell?"
>
> **SALESPERSON**: "Done. $10 million."

S&T: A symbiotic relationship?

Institutional sales and trading are highly dependent on one another. The propaganda that you read in glossy firm brochures portrays those in sales and trading as a shiny, happy integrated team environment of professionals working for the client's interests. While often that is true, salespeople and traders frequently clash, disagree, and bicker.

Simply put, salespeople provide the clients for traders, and traders provide the products for sales. Traders would have nobody to trade for without sales, but sales would have nothing to sell without traders. Understanding how a trader makes money and how a salesperson makes money should explain how conflicts can arise.

Traders make money by selling high and buying low (this difference is called the spread). They are buying stocks or bonds for clients, and these clients filter in through sales. A trader faced with a buy order for a buy-side firm could care less about the performance of the securities once they are sold. He or she just cares about making the spread. In a sell trade, this means selling at the highest price possible. In a buy trade, this means buying at the lowest price possible.

The salesperson, however, has a different incentive. The total return on the trade often determines the money a salesperson makes, so he wants the trader to sell at a low price. This of course leads to many interesting situations, and at the extreme, salespeople and traders who eye one another suspiciously.

The personalities

Salespeople possess remarkable communication skills, including outgoing personalities and a smoothness not often seen in traders. Traders sometimes call them bullshit artists while salespeople counter by calling traders quant guys with no personality. Traders are tough, quick, and often consider themselves smarter than salespeople. The salespeople probably know better how to have fun, but the traders win the prize for mental sharpness and the ability to handle stress.

Section One: Trading — The Basics

Trading can make or break an investment bank. Without traders to execute buy and sell transactions, no public deal would get done, no liquidity would exist for securities, and no commissions or spreads would accrue to the bank. Traders carry a "book" accounting for the daily revenue that they generate for the firm — down to the dollar.

Liquidity

Liquidity is the ability to find tradeable securities in the market. When a large number of buyers and sellers co-exist in the market, a stock or bond is said to be highly liquid. Let's take a look at the liquidity of various types of securities.

- **Common Stock.** For stock, liquidity depends on the stock's float in the market. Float is the number of shares available for trade in the market (not the total number of shares, which may include unregistered stock) times the stock price. Usually over time, as a company grows and issues more stock, its float and liquidity increase.

- **Debt.** Debt, or bonds, is another story however. For debt issues, corporate bonds typically have the most liquidity immediately following the placement of the bonds. After a few months, most bonds trade infrequently, ending up in a few big money manager's portfolios for good. If buyers and sellers want to trade corporate debt, the lack of liquidity will mean that buyers will be forced to pay a liquidity premium, or sellers will be forced to accept a liquidity discount.

- **Government Issues.** Government bonds are yet another story. Muni's, treasuries, agencies, and other government bonds form an active market with better liquidity than corporate bonds enjoy. In fact, the largest single traded security in the world is the 30-year U.S. Government bond (known as the Long Bond).

Floor brokers vs. traders

Often when people talk about traders, they imagine frenzied men and women on the floor of a major stock exchange waving a ticket, trying to buy stock. The NYSE is the classic example of a stock exchange bustling with activity as stocks and bonds are traded and auctioned back and forth by floor traders. In fact, these traders are really floor brokers, who follow through with the execution of a stock or bond transaction.

Hungry for more inside scoop? Join Vault.com's popular online
community for finance and banking — www.vault.com

VAULT.com   **87**

Floor brokers receive their orders from actual traders working for investment banks.

As opposed to floor brokers, traders work at the offices of brokerage firms, handling orders via phone from salespeople and investors. Traders either call in orders to floor brokers on the exchange floor or sell stock they actually own in inventory, through a computerized system called an over-the-counter (OTC) system. Floor brokers represent buyers and sellers and gather near a trading post on the exchange floor to literally place buy and sell orders on behalf of their clients. On the floor of the NYSE, these mini-auctions are handled by a specialist, whose job is to ensure the efficiency and fairness of the trades taking place. We will cover the mechanics of a trade later. First, let's discuss the basics of how a trader makes money and carries inventory.

How the trader makes money

Understanding how traders make money is simple. Traders buy stocks and bonds at a low price, then sell them for a slightly higher price. This difference is called the bid-ask spread, or, simply, the spread. For example, a bond may be quoted at 99 1/2 bid, 99 5/8 ask. Money managers who wish to buy this bond would have to pay the ask price to the trader, or 99 5/8. It is likely that the trader purchased the bond earlier at 99 1/2, from an investor looking to sell his securities. Therefore, the trader earns the bid-ask spread on a buy/sell transaction. The bid-ask spread here is 1/8 of a dollar, or $0.125, per $1 of bonds. If the trader bought and sold 10,000 bonds (which each have $1,000 face value for a total value of $100 million), the spread earned would amount to $1,250,000 for the trader. Not bad for a couple of trades.

Spreads vary depending on the security sold. Generally speaking, the more liquidity a stock or bond has, the narrower the spread. Government bonds, the most liquid of all securities, typically trade at spreads of a mere 1/128th of a dollar. That is, a $100 trade nets only 78 cents for the trader. However, government bonds (called govies for short) trade in huge volumes. So, a $100 million govie trade nets $781,250 to the investment bank — not a bad trade.

Inventory

While the concept of how a trader makes money (the bid-ask spread) is eminently simple, actually executing this strategy is a different story. Traders are subject to market movements — bond and stock prices fluctuate constantly. Because the trader's ultimate responsibility is simply to buy low and sell high, this means anticipating and reacting appropriately to dynamic market conditions that often catch even the most experienced people off guard. A trader who has bought securities but has not sold them is said to be carrying inventory.

Suppose, for instance, that a trader purchased stock at $52 7/8, the market bid price, from a money manager selling his stock. The ask was $53 when the trade was executed. Now the trader looks to unload the stock. The trader has committed the firm's money to purchase stock, and therefore has what is called price movement risk. What happens if the stock price falls before she can unload at the current ask price of $53? Obviously, the trader and the firm lose money. Because of this risk, traders attempt to ensure that the bid-ask spread has enough cushion so that when a stock falls, they do not lose money.

The problem with carrying inventory is that security prices can move dramatically. A company announcing bad news may cause such a rush of sell orders that the price may drop significantly. Remember, every trade has two sides, a buyer and a seller. If the price of a stock or bond is falling, the only buyers in the market may be the traders making a market in that security (as opposed to individual investors). These market makers have to judge by instinct and market savvy where to offer to buy the stock back from investors. If they buy at too high a price (a price higher than the trader can sell the stock back for), they can lose big. Banks will lose even more if a stock falls while a trader holds that stock in inventory.

So what happens in a widespread free-falling market? Well, you can just imagine the pandemonium on the trading floor as investors rush to sell their securities however possible. Traders and investors carrying inventory all lose money. At that point, no one knows where the market will bottom out.

On the flip side, in a booming market, carrying inventory consistently leads to making money. In fact, it is almost impossible not to. Any stock or bond held on the books overnight appreciates in value the next day in a strong bull market. This can foster an environment in which poor decisions become overlooked because of the steady upward climb of the markets. Traders buy and sell securities as investors demand. Usually, a trader owns a stock or bond, ready to sell when asked. When a trader owns the security, he is said to be long the security (what we previously called carrying inventory). This is easy enough to understand.

Hungry for more inside scoop? Join Vault.com's popular online community for finance and banking — www.vault.com

VAULT.com   89

Being long or short

Consider the following, though. Suppose an investor wished to buy a security and called a trader who at the time did not have the security in inventory. In this case, the trader can do one of two things — 1) not execute the trade or 2) sell the security, despite the fact that he or she does not own it.

How does the second scenario work? The trader goes short the security by selling it to the investor without owning it. Where does he get the security? By borrowing the security from someone else.

Let's look at an example. Suppose a client wished to buy 10,000 shares of Microsoft (MSFT) stock, but the trader did not have any MSFT stock to sell. The trader likely would sell shares to the client by borrowing them from elsewhere and doing what is called short-selling, or shorting. In such a short transaction, the trader must eventually buy 10,000 shares back of MSFT to replace the shares he borrowed. The trader will then look for sellers of MSFT in the broker-dealer market, and will often indicate to salespeople of his need to buy MSFT shares. (Salespeople may even seek out their clients who own MSFT, checking to see if they would be willing to sell the stock.)

The problems with shorting or short-selling stock are the opposite of those that one faces by owning the stock. In a long position, traders worry about big price drops — as the value of your inventory declines, you lose money. In a short position, a trader worries that the stock increases in price. He has locked in his selling price upfront, but has not locked in his purchase price. If the price of the stock moves up, then the purchase price moves up as well.

Tracking the trades

Traders keep track of the exact details of every trade they make. Trading assistants often perform this function, detailing the transaction (buy or sell), the amount (number of shares or bonds), the price, the buyer/seller, and the time of the trade. At the end of the day, the compilation of the dollars made/lost for that day is called a profit and loss statement, or P&L. The P&L statement is all-important to a trader: daily, weekly, monthly, quarterly — traders know the status of their P&L's for these periods at any given time.

Types of Trades

Unbeknownst to most people, traders actually work in two different markets, that is, they buy and sell securities for two different types of customers.

- One is the inside market which is a monopoly market made up only of broker-dealers. Traders actually utilize a special broker screen that posts the prices broker-dealers are willing to buy and sell to each other. This works as an important source of liquidity when a trader needs to buy or sell securities.

- The other is outside market, composed of outside customers an investment bank transacts with. These include a diverse range of money managers and investors, or the firm's outside clients. Traders earn the bulk of their profits in the outside market.

Not only do traders at investment banks work in two different markets, but they can make two different types of trades. These include:

- **Client trades.** These are simply trades done on the behest of outside customers. Most traders' jobs are to make a market in a security for the firm's clients. They buy and sell as market forces dictate and pocket the bid-ask spread along the way. The vast majority of traders trade for clients.

- **Proprietary Trades.** Sometimes traders are given leeway in terms of what securities they may buy and sell for the firm. Using firm capital, proprietary traders, or prop traders as they are often called, actually trade not to fulfill client demand for stocks and bonds, but to make bets on the market. Some prop traders trade such obscure things as the curve or the yield curve, making bets as the direction that the yield curve will move. Other are arbitragers, who follow the markets and lock in arbitrage profit when market inefficiencies develop. (In a simple example, a market inefficiency would occur if a security, say U.S. government bonds, are trading for different prices in different locales, say in the U.S. vs. the U.K. Actual market inefficiencies these days often involve derivatives and currency exchange rates.)

Hungry for more inside scoop? Join Vault.com's popular online community for finance and banking — www.vault.com

VAULT.com   **91**

A Trader's Cockpit

You may have wondered about the pile of computer gear a trader uses. This impressive mess of technology, which includes half a dozen blinking monitors, represents more technology per square inch than that used by any other professional on Wall Street. Each trader utilizes different information sources, and so has different computer screens spouting out data and news. Typically, though, a trader has the following:

• **Bloomberg machine:** Bloombergs were invented originally only as bond calculators. (The company that makes them was founded by a former Salomon Brothers trader, Mike Bloomberg, who now owns a media empire.) Today, however, they perform so many intricate and complex functions that they've become ubiquitous on any equity or debt trading floor. In a few quick keystrokes, a trader can access a bond's price, yield, rating, duration, convexity, and literally thousands of other tidbits. Market news, stock information and even e-mail reside real-time on the Bloomberg.

• **Phone monitor:** Traders' phone systems are almost as complex as the Bloombergs. The phones consist of a touch-screen monitor with a cluster of phone lines. There are multiple screens that a trader can flip to, with direct dialing and secured lines designed to ensure a foolproof means of communicating with investors, floor brokers, salespeople and the like. For example, one Morgan Stanley associate tells of a direct phone line to billionaire George Soros. Associates and interns are always doomed to goof up a call with these phones, leading to quite a few choice curse words from a nearby trader.

• **Small broker screens:** These include monitors posting market prices from other broker-dealers, or investment banks. Traders deal with each other to facilitate client needs and provide a forum for the flow of securities.

• **Large Sun Microsystems monitor:** Typically divided into numerous sections, the Sun monitor can be tailored to the trader's needs. Popular pages include U.S. Treasury markets, bond market data, news pages and equity prices.

Section Two: Executing a Trade

If you are a retail investor, and call your broker to place an order, how is the trade actually executed? Now that we know the basics of the trading business, we will cover the mechanics of how stocks or bonds are actually traded. We will begin with what is called small lots trading, or the trading of relatively small amounts of a security.

Small lots trading

Surprising to many people, the process of completing a small lot transaction differs depending on where the security is traded and what type of security it is.

- For an NYSE-traded stock, the transaction begins with an investor placing the order and ends with the actual transaction being executed on the floor of the New York Stock Exchange. Here, the trade is a physical, as opposed to an electronic one.

- For Nasdaq-traded stocks, the transaction typically originates with an investor placing an order with a broker and ends with that broker selling stock from his current inventory of securities (stocks the broker actually owns). An excellent analogy of this type of market, called an Over-the-Counter (OTC) Market, is that a trader acts like a pawn shop, selling an inventory of securities when a buyer desires, just like the pawn shop owner sells a watch to a store visitor. And, when an investor wishes to sell securities, he or she contacts a trader who willingly purchases them at a price dictated by the trader, just like the pawn shop owner gives prices at which he will buy watches. (As in a pawn shop, the trader makes money through the difference between the buying and selling price, the bid-ask spread.) In the OTC scenario, the actual storage of the securities is electronic, residing inside the trader's computer.

- For bonds, transactions rarely occur in small lots. By convention, most bonds have a face value of $1,000, and orders for one or even 10 bonds are not common. However, the execution of the trade is similar to Nasdaq stocks. Traders carry inventory on their computer and buy and sell on the spot without the need for an NYSE-style trading pit.

Hungry for more inside scoop? Join Vault.com's popular online
community for finance and banking — www.vault.com

VAULT.com **93**

The following pages illustrate the execution of a trade on both the Nasdaq and the NYSE stock exchanges. A bond transaction works similarly to a Nasdaq trade.

Here's a look at the actions that take place during a trade of a Nasdaq-listed stock.

Nasdaq

ORDER. You call in an order of 1,000 shares of ABCD stock to your retail broker. For small orders, you agree on a trade placed at the market. That is, you say you are willing to pay the ask price as it is currently trading in the market.

EXECUTION. First, the retail broker calls the appropriate trader to handle the transaction. The Nasdaq trader, called a market maker, carries an inventory of stocks available for purchase.

TRANSACTION. The market maker checks his inventory of stock. If he carries the security, he simply makes the trade, selling the 1,000 shares of ABCD from his account (the market maker's account) to you. If he does not already own the stock, then he will buy 1,000 shares directly from another market maker and then sell them immediately to you.

Here's a look at a trade of a stock listed on the New York Stock Exchange.

NYSE

ORDER You decide to buy 1,000 shares of XYZ. You contact your broker and give the information to buy 1,000 shares. The broker tells you that the last trade price (65 1/2) and the current quote (65 3/8 bid, 65 5/8 ask) and takes your order to buy 1,000 shares at the market. The broker also notes the volume of stock available for buy and sell, currently 500 X 500 (i.e. 500 shares of XYZ in demand at the bid and 500 shares of XYZ available for sale at the ask).

TRANSMITTAL TO THE FLOOR. The order is transmitted from the broker at the I-bank through the NYSE's computer systems directly to what are called NYSE specialists (see sidebar) handling the stock.

THE TRADE. The specialist's book displays a new order to buy 1,000 shares of XYZ at the market. At this point, the specialist can fill the order himself from his own account at the last trade price of 65 1/2, or alternatively, he can transact the 1,000 shares trade at 65 5/8. In the latter case, 500 shares would come from the public customer (who had 500 shares of stock available at the bid price) and 500 shares would come from the specialist selling from his own account.

THE TRADE FINALIZED. If the floor specialist elects to trade at 65 5/8, he sends the details of the trade to his back office via the Exchange's computer system and also electronically to the brokerage firm. This officially records the transaction.

Hungry for more inside scoop? Join Vault.com's popular online community for finance and banking — www.vault.com

V/\ULT.com   **95**

The New York Stock Exchange

The NYSE, the largest exchange in the world, is comprised of more than 3,000 listed stocks with a total market capitalization of more than 12 trillion dollars as of June 1999. The NYSE is often referred to as the Big Board. We have all seen the videos of frantic floor brokers scrambling to execute trades in a mass of bodies and seeming confusion. To establish order amidst the chaos, trading in a particular stock occurs at a specific location on the floor (the trading post), so that all buy and sell interests can meet in one place to determine a fair price.

The NYSE hires what are called specialists to oversee the auctioning or trading of particular securities. Specialists match buyers and sellers, but sometimes there is insufficient public interest on one side of a trade (i.e. there is a seller but no buyer, or a buyer and no seller). Since the specialist cannot match the other side of the trade, the Exchange requires the specialist to act as a dealer to buy (or sell) the stock to fill in the gap. According to the NYSE, specialists are directly involved in approximately 10 percent of trades executed on the floor, while they act as the auctioneer the other 90 percent of the time.

Note that while the NYSE is a physical trading floor, the Nasdaq is actually a virtual trading arena. Approved Nasdaq dealers make a market in particular stocks by buying and selling shares through a computerized trading system. This is called an over-the-counter system or OTC system, with a network of linked computers acting as the auctioneer.

According to the NYSE's web site, "To buy and sell securities on the Trading Floor, a person must first meet rigorous personal and financial standards and be accepted for membership in the NYSE." Members are said to have a seat on the NYSE, but they rarely find time to sit down. Members, like everyone else at the NYSE, are on their feet most of the working day. A seat is simply the traditional term for the right to trade on the NYSE's Trading Floor.

According to the exchange, "The number of seats is limited to 1,366, and the price of a seat, like a stock, depends on supply and demand. The price of a seat dipped to as low as $35,000 during the 1977 recession. Today, a seat can cost more than $1 million. It takes more than money to become a member, though. Each prospective member must pass a thorough test covering NYSE rules and regulations."

Source: www.nyse.com

Block trades

Small trades placed through brokers (often called retail trades) require a few simple entries into a computer. In these cases, traders record the exchange of a few hundred shares or a few thousand shares, and the trade happens with a few swift keystrokes.

However, when a large institutional investor seeks to buy or sell a large chunk of stock, or a block of stock, the sheer size of the order involves additional facilitation. A buy order for 200,000 shares of IBM stock, for instance, would not easily be accomplished without a block trader. At any given moment, only so much stock is available for sale, and to buy a large quantity would drive the price up in the market (to entice more sellers into the market to sell).

For a NYSE stock, the process of block trading is similar to that of any small buy or sell order. The difference is that a small trade arrives electronically to the specialist on the floor of the exchange, while a block trade runs through a floor broker, who then hand-delivers the order to the specialist. The style of a block trade also differs, depending on the client's wishes. Some block trades are done at the market and some block trades involve working the order.

- **At the market.** Say Fidelity wishes to buy 200,000 shares of IBM, and they first contact the block trader at an investment bank. If Fidelity believed that IBM stock was moving up, they would indicate that the purchase of the shares should occur at the market. In this case, the trader would call the floor broker (in reality, he contacts the floor broker's clerk), to tell him or her to buy the next available 200,000 shares of IBM. The clerk delivers the ticket to the floor broker, who then takes it to the specialist dealing in IBM stock. Again, the specialist acts as an auctioneer, matching sellers to the IBM buyer. Once the floor broker accumulates the entire amount of stock, likely from many sellers, his or her clerk is sent back to the phones to call back the trader. The final trading price is a weighted average of all of the purchase prices from the individual sellers.

- **Working the order.** Alternately, if Fidelity believes that IBM was going to bounce around in price, they might ask the trader to work the order in order to hopefully get a better price than what is currently in the market. The trader then would call the floor broker and indicate that he or she should work at finding as low a price as possible. In this case, the floor broker might linger at the IBM

Hungry for more inside scoop? Join Vault.com's popular online community for finance and banking — www.vault.com

VAULT.com   **97**

trading post, watching for sell orders to come in, hoping to accumulate the shares at as low a price as possible.

Trading bonds

Bond trading takes place in OTC fashion, just as stocks do on the Nasdaq. That is, there is no physical trading floor for bonds, merely a collection of linked computers and market makers around the world (literally). As such, there is no central open outcry market floor for bonds, as there is for NYSE stocks. Therefore, for bond orders, the transaction flow is similar to that of an OTC stock. A buyer calls a broker-dealer, indicates the bonds he wishes to buy, and the trader sells the securities with a phone call and a few keystrokes on his computer.

Section Three: Trading — The Players

Each desk on a trading floor carries its own sub-culture. Some are tougher than others, some work late, and some socialize outside of work on a regular basis. While some new associates in trading maintain ambitions of working on a particular desk because of the product (say, equity or high yield debt), most find themselves in an environment where they most enjoy the people. After all, salespeople and traders sit side-by-side for 10 hours a day. Liking the guy in the next chair takes precedence when placing an associate full-time on a desk, especially considering the levels of stress, noise and pressure on a trading floor.

The desk

Different areas on the trading floor at an I-bank typically are divided into desks. Common desks include OTC equity trading, big board (NYSE) equity trading, convertibles (called converts), municipal bonds, high yield, and Treasuries. This list is far from complete — some of the bigger firms have 50 or more distinct trading desks on the floor (depending how they are defined). Investment banks usually separate the equity trading floor from the fixed income trading floor. In fact, equity traders and debt traders rarely interact. Conversely, sales and trading within one of these departments are combined and integrated as much as possible. For example, treasury salespeople and treasury traders work next to one another on the same desk. Sales will be covered in following sections.

The players

The players in the trading game depend on the firm. There are no hard and fast rules regarding whether or not one needs an MBA. The degree itself, though less applicable directly to the trading position, tends to matter beyond the trader level. Managers (heads of desks) and higher-ups are often selected from the MBA ranks.

Generally, regional I-banks hire clerks and/or trading assistants (non-MBAs) who are sometimes able to advance to a full-fledged trading job within a few years. Other banks, like Merrill Lynch and others on Wall Street, hire analysts and associates just as they do in investment banking. Thus an analyst job on Wall Street in trading includes a two- to three-year stint before the expectation of going back to business school, and the associate position begins after one earns his or her MBA. The ultimate job in trading is to become a full-fledged trader or

Hungry for more inside scoop? Join Vault.com's popular online community for finance and banking — www.vault.com

VAULT.com   **99**

a manager over a trading desk. Here we break out the early positions into those more common at regional I-banks and those more common on Wall Street.

Entry-level positions

Regional Frameworks — Traditional Programs

Clerks. The bottom rung of the ladder in trading in regional firms, clerks generally balance the books, tracking a desk or a particular trader's buy and sell transactions throughout the day. A starting point for an undergrad aiming to move up to an assistant trader role, clerks gain exposure to the trading floor environment, the traders themselves and the markets. However, clerks take messages, make copies, go get coffee, and are hardly respected by traders. And at bigger firms, this position can be a dead-end job: clerks may remain in these roles indefinitely, while new MBAs move into full-time trading positions or top undergrads move into real analyst jobs.

Trading Assistants. Typically filled by recent graduates of undergraduate universities, the trading assistant position is more involved in trades than the clerk position. Trading assistants move beyond staring at the computer and balancing the books to become more involved with the actual traders. Backing up accounts, relaying messages and reports to and from the floor of the NYSE, and actually speaking with some accounts occasionally — these responsibilities bring trading assistants much closer to understanding how the whole biz works. Depending on the firm, some undergrads immediately move into a trading assistant position with the hope of moving into a full-time trading job.

Note: Clerks and trading assistants at some firms are hired with the possibility of upward advancement, although promoting non-MBAs to full-time trading jobs is becoming more and more uncommon, even at regional firms.

Wall Street Analyst and Associate Programs

Analysts. Similar to corporate finance analysts, trading analysts at Wall Street firms typically are smart undergraduates with the desire to either become a trader or learn about the trading environment. Quantitative skills are a must for analysts, as much of their time is spent dealing with books of trades and numbers. The ability to crunch numbers in a short time is especially important on the fixed income side. Traders often demand bond price or yield calculations with only a moment's notice, and analysts must be able to produce. After a two- to three-year stint, analysts move on to business school or go to another firm, although promotion to the associate level is much more common in trading than it is in corporate finance. (Salaries mirror those paid to corporate finance analysts.)

Associates. Trading associates, typically recent business school graduates, begin in either rotational programs or are hired directly to a desk. Rotations can last anywhere from a month to a year, and are designed to both educate new MBAs on various desks and to ensure a good fit prior to placement. As in other areas of investment banks, new MBAs begin at about $80,000 salary with an about $25,000 bonus at major Wall Street banks. Second-year associate compensation also tracks closely to that of the second-year corporate finance associate. Associates move to full-fledged trading positions generally in about two to three years, but can move more quickly if they perform well and there are openings (turnover) on the desk.

Full-fledged trading positions

The Block Trader. These are the folks you see sitting on a desk with dozens of phone lines ringing simultaneously and four or more computer monitors blinking, with orders coming in like machine-gun fire. Typically, traders deal in active, mature markets, such as government securities, stocks, currencies and corporate bonds. Sometimes hailing from top MBA schools, and sometimes tough guys named Vinny from the mailroom, traders historically are hired based on work ethic, attitude and street-smarts.

The Sales-trader. A hybrid between sales and trading, sales-traders essentially operate in a dual role as both salesperson and block trader. While block traders deal with huge trades and often massive inventories of stocks or bonds, salestraders act somewhat as a go-between for salespeople and block traders and trade somewhat smaller blocks of securities. Different from the pure block trader, the sales-trader actually initiates calls to clients, pitches investment ideas and gives market commentary. The sales-trader keeps abreast of market conditions and research commentaries, but, unlike the salesperson, does not need to know the ins and outs of every company when pitching products to clients. Salespeople must be thoroughly versed in the companies they

Hungry for more inside scoop? Join Vault.com's popular online
community for finance and banking — www.vault.com

VAULT.com **101**

are pitching to clients, whereas sales-traders typically cover the highlights and the big picture. When specific questions arise, a sales-trader will often refer a client to the research analyst.

The Structured Product Trader. At some of the biggest Wall Street firms, structured product traders deal with derivatives, a.k.a. structured products. (Derivatives are complex securities that derive their value out of, or have their value contingent on the values of other assets like stocks, bonds, commodity prices, or market index values.) Because of their complexity, derivatives typically require substantial time to price and structure, so foster an entirely different environment than that of a block trader who deals with heavy trading flows and intense on-the-spot pressure. Note, however, that common stock options (calls and puts) and even Treasury options trade much like any other liquid security. The pricing is fairly transparent, the securities standardized and the volume high. Low-volume, complex derivatives such as interest rate swaps, structured repurchase agreements, and credit derivatives require pricing and typically more legwork prior to trading.

Note that in Trading, job titles can range from Associate to VP to Managing Director. But, the roles as a trader change little. The difference is that MDs typically manage the desks, spending their time dealing with desk issues, risk management issues, personnel issues, etc.

Trader's Compensation: The Bonus Pool

In trading, most firms pay a fixed salary plus a bonus based on the profits the trader brings to the group. Once associates have moved into full-fledged trading roles after two or three years, they begin to be judged by their profit contributions. How much can a trader make? Typically, each desk on the trading floor has a P&L statement for the group. As the group does well, so do the primary contributors. In a down year, everyone suffers. In up years, everyone is happy.

Exactly how the bonuses are determined can be a mystery. Office politics, profits brought into the firm, and tenure all contribute to the final distribution. Often, the MDs on the desk or the top two or three traders on the desk get together and hash out how the bonus pool will be allocated to each person. Then, each trader is told what his or her bonus is. If he or she is unhappy, it is not uncommon for traders (as well as any other employee at an I-bank) to jump ship and leave the firm the second that his or her bonus check clears the bank. Top traders can pull in well over $1 million per year.

Section Four: Trading — The Routine

The compressed day

Instead of working long hours, traders pack more work into an abbreviated day — a sprint instead of the slow marathon that corporate finance bankers endure. Stress, caffeine, and adrenaline keep traders wired to the markets, their screens and the trades they are in the midst. While traders typically arrive by 7 a.m., it is not unheard of to make phone calls to overseas markets in the middle of the night or wake up at 4 a.m. to check on the latest market news form Asia. The link among markets worldwide has never been so apparent as in the past several years, and traders, perhaps more so than any other finance professional, must take care to know the implications of a wide variety of global economic and market events.

Traders consider themselves smarter than the salespeople, who they believe don't understand the products they sell, and bankers, who they believe are slaves with no lives whatsoever. Traders take pride in having free weekends and the option of leaving early on a Friday afternoon. Typically, a trader's day tracks closely to those of the market, and includes an additional two or more hours.

Mornings start usually between 6 a.m. and 7 a.m., and the day ends shortly after the market close.

Traders typically start the day by checking news, reviewing markets that trade overnight (i.e. Asian markets), and examining their inventory. At 7:30, the morning meeting is held to cover a multitude of issues (see inset).

The Morning Meeting

Every morning of every trading day, each I-banking firm (both on and off Wall Street) holds a morning meeting. What happens at these meetings? Besides coffee all around and a few yawns, morning meetings generally are a way to brief sales, trading and research on market activity — past and expected.

At smaller regional firms, the entire equity group usually meets: the salesforce, traders, and research analysts. The bigger firms, because of their sheer size, wire speakers to an overhead speaking system, which is

Hungry for more inside scoop? Join Vault.com's popular online
community for finance and banking — www.vault.com

VAULT.com **103**

broadcast to the entire equity trading floor. Institutional salespeople and brokers outside the home office also call in to listen in on the meeting.

In fixed income, meetings are broken down by groups. For example, the government desk, the mortgage desk, the emerging markets desk, and the high yield desk will each have their own morning meetings with the relevant traders, salespeople and research analysts present.

Let's take a look at the participants in morning meetings and their roles:

- In equity, the research analysts review updates to their stocks, present new research and generally discuss the scoop on their universe of stocks. Rating changes and initiation of coverage reports command the most attention to both traders and salespeople on the equity side. In fixed income, meetings will often have analysts who cover economic issues discuss interest rates, Fed activity or market issues, as these often dominate activity in the debt markets.

- Traders cover their inventory, mainly for the benefit of salespeople and brokers in the field. Sometimes a trader eager to move some stock or bonds he or she has carried on the books too long will give quick selling points and indicate where he or she is willing to sell the securities.

- Salespeople, including both brokers and institutional sales, primarily listen and ask relevant questions to the research analyst or to traders, sometimes chipping in with additional information about news or market data.

Morning meetings include rapid-fire discussions on market movements, positions, and trade ideas relevant to them. Time is short, however, so a babbling research analyst will quickly lose the attentions spans of impatient salespeople.

Corporate finance professionals rarely attend morning meetings, choosing instead to show up for work around 9 or 10 a.m.

After the morning meeting, between 8:00 and 8:15, the traders begin to gear up for the market opening. At 8:30 a.m., the fun begins in many fixed income markets — calls begin pouring in and trades start flying. At 9:30 Eastern Time, the stock markets open and a flurry of activity immediately ensues.

The day continues with a barrage of market news from the outside, rating changes from research analysts and phone calls from clients. The first breather does not come until lunchtime, when traders take five to grab a sandwich and relax for a few brief minutes. However, the market does not close at lunch, and if a trade is in progress, the traders go without their meals or with meals swallowed amidst the frenzy.

The action heats up again after lunchtime and continues as before. At 4 p.m., the stock markets officially close and wrap-up begins. Most traders tend to leave around 5 p.m. after closing the books for the day and tying up loose ends. On Fridays, most trading floors are completely empty by 5. For salespeople and traders, golf games, trips to the bar and other social activities are not usually hampered by Friday evenings and nights spent at work.

Day in the Life of a Sales-trader (Lehman Brothers)

Here's a look at a day in the life of a sales-trader, given to us by an associate in the Equities division at Lehman Brothers.

6:30   Get into work. Check voice mail and e-mail. Chat with some people at your desk about the headlines in the *Journal*.

7:15   Equities morning call. You find out what's up to sell. ("I'm sort of a liaison between the accounts [clients] and the block traders. What I do is help traders execute their trading strategies, give them market color. If they want something I try to find the other side of the trade. Or if I have stuff available, I get info out, without exposing what we have.")

9:30   Markets open. You hit the phones. ("You want to make outgoing calls, you don't really want people to call you. I'm calling my clients, telling them what research is relevant to them, and what merchandise I have, if there's any news on any of their positions.")

10:00   More calls. ("I usually have about 35 different clients. It's always listed equities, but it's a huge range of equities. The client can be a buyer or seller — there's one sales-trader representing a buyer, another representing the seller.")

10:30   On the phone with another Lehman trader, trying to satisfy a client. ("If they have questions in another product, I'll try to help them out.")

Hungry for more inside scoop? Join Vault.com's popular online community for finance and banking — www.vault.com

VAULT.com **105**

11:00 Calling another client. ("It's a trader at the other end, receiving discussions from portfolio manager; their discretion varies from client to client.")

12:00 You hear a call for the sale for a stock that several of your clients are keen on acquiring. ("It's usually a block trader, although sometimes it's another sales-trader. The announcement comes 'over the top,' — over the speaker. It also comes on my computer.")

12:30 Food from the deli comes in. (You can't go to the bathroom sometimes, say you're working 10 orders, you want to see every stock. We don't leave to get our lunch, we order lunch in.")

1:00 Watching your terminal ("There's a lot of action. If there's 200,000 shares trade in your name [a stock that a client has a position in or wants] and it's not you, you want to go back to your client and say who it was.)

2:00 Taking a call from a client. ("You can't miss a beat, you are literally in your seat all day.")

2:05 You tell the client that you have some stock he had indicated interest in previously, but you don't let him know how much you can unload. ("It's a lot of how to get a trade done without disclosing anything that's going to hurt the account. If a lot on one stock is up you don't want the whole Street to know, or it'll drive down the price.")

4:30 Head home to rest a bit before going out. ("I leave at 4:30 or sometimes 5:00. It depends.")

7:00 Meet a buy-side trader, one of your clients, at a bar. ("We entertain a lot of buy-side traders — dinner, we go to baseball games, we go to bars. Maybe this happens once or twice a week.")

Success factors in trading

There are many keys to success in trading. On the fixed in side, numbers and quantitative skills are especially important, but truly are a prerequisite to survival more than a factor to success. In equities, traders must not only juggle the numbers, but also understand what drives stock prices. These factors include earnings, management assessments, how news affects stocks, etc.

To be one of the best traders, an instinct about the market is key. Some traders look at technical indicators and numbers until they are blue in the face, but without a gut feel on how the market moves, they will never rank among the best. A trader must make rapid decisions at times with little information to go on, and so must be able to quickly assess investor sentiment, market dynamics and the ins and outs of the securities they are trading.

Hungry for more inside scoop? Join Vault.com's popular online
community for finance and banking — www.vault.com

VAULT.com **107**

Section Five: Institutional Sales — The Basics

Sales is a core area of any investment bank, comprising the vast majority of people and the relationships that account for a substantial portion of any investment banks revenues. This section illustrates the divisions seen in sales today at most investment banks. Note, however, that many firms, such as Goldman Sachs, identify themselves as institutionally focused I-banks, and do not even have a retail sales distribution network. Goldman, does, however maintain a solid presence in providing brokerage services to the vastly rich in a division called Private Client Services (PCS for short).

Retail Brokers

Some firms call them account executives and some call them financial advisors or financial consultants. Regardless of this official designator, they are still referring to your classic retail broker. The broker's job involves managing the account portfolios for individual investors — usually called retail investors. Brokers charge a commission on any stock trade and also give advice to their clients regarding stocks to buy or sell, and when to buy or sell them. To get into the business, retail brokers must have an undergraduate degree and demonstrated sales skills. The Series 7 and Series 63 examinations are also required before selling commences. Being networked to people with money offers a tremendous advantage for a starting broker.

Institutional Sales

Basically a retail broker with an MBA and more market savvy, the institutional salesperson manages the bank's relationships with institutional money managers such as mutual funds or pension funds. Institutional sales is often called research sales, as salespeople focus on selling the firm's research to institutions. As in other areas in banking, the typical hire hails from a top business school and carries a tiptop résumé (that usually involves prior sales experience).

Private Client Services (PCS)

A cross between institutional sales and retail brokerage, PCS focuses on providing money management services to extremely wealthy individuals. A client with more than $2 to $3 million in assets usually upgrades from having a classic retail broker deal with him or her to a

PCS representative. Similar to institutional sales, PCS generally hires only MBAs with solid selling experience and top credentials. Because PCS representatives become high-end relationship managers, as well as money managers and advisors, the job requires greater expertise than the classic retail broker. Also, because PCS clients trade in larger volumes, the fees and commissions are larger and the number of candidates lining up to become PCS reps is longer.

Hungry for more inside scoop? Join Vault.com's popular online
community for finance and banking — www.vault.com

VAULT.com **109**

Section Six: Institutional Sales — The Players

The players in sales

For many, institutional sales offers the best of all worlds: great pay, fewer hours than in corporate finance or research, less stress than in trading, and a nice blend of travel and office work. Like traders, the hours typically follow the market, with a few tacked on at the end of the day after the market closes. Another plus for talented salespeople is that they develop relationships with key money managers. On the downside, many institutional salespeople complain that many buy-siders disregard their calls, that compensation can exhibit volatile mood swings, and that constantly entertaining clients can prove exhausting.

Sales Assistant

This position is most often a dead-end job. It is extremely difficult to move into institutional sales without an MBA, so sales assistants take on a primarily clerical role on the desk. Handling the phones, administrative duties, message taking, letter writing — there's nothing glamorous for the assistants.

Associates

The newly hired MBA is called an associate, or sales associate. Like analogous associates in other investment banking departments, a sales associate spends a year or so in the role learning the ropes and establishing himself. Associates typically spend one to two months rotating through various desks and ensuring a solid fit between the desk and the new associate. Once the rotations end, the associate is placed on a desk and the business of building client relationships begins.

Most sales associates out of business school pull in the standard package on Wall Street: $80,000 base plus bonuses of $25,000 in the first six months. Pay escalation in the first year depends on the bonus, which often ranges from 50 percent of salary to 90 percent of salary. Beyond that, compensation packages depend on the firm — most firms pay based on commissions generated for the firm.

Salesperson

The associate moves into a full-fledged salesperson role extremely quickly. Within a few months on a desk, the associate begins to handle "B" accounts and gradually manages them exclusively. A salesperson's ultimate goal is the account at a huge money manager, such as Fidelity or Putnam, that trades in huge volumes on a daily basis. Therefore, a salesperson slowly moves up the account chain, yielding B accounts to younger salespeople and taking on bigger and better "A" accounts. Good salespeople make anywhere from $250,000 to beyond $1 million per year in total compensation.

Salespeople usually focus by region. For example, an institutional equity salesperson will cover all of the buy-side firms in one small region of the country like New England, San Francisco or Chicago. Many salespeople cover New York, as the sheer number of money managers in the City makes for a tremendous volume of work. Salespeople work on specific desks on the trading floor next to traders. Because so much of their work overlaps, sales and trading truly go hand-in-hand. Here's a look at how a trade works from the sales perspective.

The Flow of the Trade: The Sales Perspective

The salesperson has a relationship with a money manager, or an account, as they say. Suppose a research analyst initiates coverage of a new stock with a Buy-1 rating. The salesperson calls the portfolio manager (PM) at the account and gives an overview of the stock and why it is a good buy. The PM will have his own internal research analysts compile a financial model, just as the sell-side research analyst has done, but likely with slightly different expectations and numbers. If the portfolio manager likes the stock, she will contact her trader to work with the trader at the investment bank.

Sell-side research analyst initiates Buy-1 coverage of stock XYZ.

↓

Institutional salesperson listens to analyst present stock at morning meeting.

↓

Hungry for more inside scoop? Join Vault.com's popular online
community for finance and banking — www.vault.com

VAULT.com · **111**

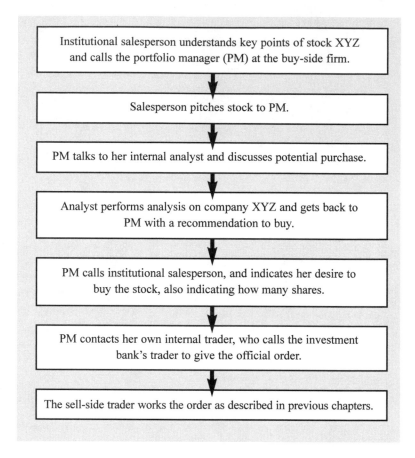

Involvement in an IPO

Corporate finance investment bankers would argue that the salesforce does the least work on an IPO and makes the most money. Salespeople, however, truly help place the offering with various money managers. To give you a breakdown, IPOs typically cost the company going public 7 percent of the gross proceeds raised in the offering. That 7 percent is divided between sales, syndicate and investment banking (i.e. corporate finance) in approximately the following manner:

- 60 percent to Sales

- 20 percent to Corporate Finance

- 20 percent to Syndicate

(If there are any deal expenses, those get charged to the syndicate account and the profits left over from syndicate get split between the syndicate group and the corporate finance group.)

As we can see from this breakdown, the sales department stands the most to gain from an IPO. Their involvement does not begin, however, until a week or two prior to the roadshow. At that point, salespeople begin brushing up on the offering company, making calls to their accounts, and pitching the deal. Ideally, they are setting up meetings (called one-on-ones when the meetings are private) between the portfolio manager and the management team of the company issuing the offering. During the roadshow itself, salespeople from the lead underwriter often fly out to attend the meeting between the company and the buy-side PM. While their role is limited during the actual meeting, salespeople essentially hold the PMs' hands, convincing them to buy into the offering.

The sales routine

The institutional salesperson's day begins early. Most arrive at 7 a.m. having already read the morning papers. Each day a package of research is delivered to the salesperson's chair, so reading and skimming these reports begins immediately. The morning meeting at 7:30 involves research commentaries and new developments from research analysts. The trading meeting usually begins 20 minutes later, with updates on trading positions and possible bargains for salespeople to pitch.

At 8 a.m., the salesperson picks up the phone. Calls initially go to the most important of clients, or the bigger clients wishing to get a market overview before trading begins. As the market approaches the opening bell, the salesperson finishes the morning calls and gets ready for the market opening. Some morning calls involve buy or sell ideas, while others involve market updates and stock expectations. At 9:30, the markets open for business, and salespeople continue to call clients, scrutinize the market, and especially look for trading ideas throughout the day.

Lunchtime is less critical to the salesperson than the trader, although most tend to eat on their desk on the floor. The afternoon often involves more contacting buy-siders regarding trade ideas, as new updates arrive by the minute from research.

Hungry for more inside scoop? Join Vault.com's popular online
community for finance and banking — www.vault.com

VAULT.com **113**

The market closes abruptly after 4:00 p.m. By 4:01, many salespeople have fled the building, although many put in a couple more hours of work. Salespeople often entertain buy-side clients in the evening with ball games, fancy dinners, etc.

Day in the Life of a Sales Associate (Bear Stearns)

Here's a look at a day in the life of a sales associate in the Fixed Income division at Bear Stearns.

6:45 Get to work. ("I try to get in around 6:45. Sometimes it's 7:00.)

6:50 After checking e-mail and voice mail, start looking over *The Wall Street Journal*. ("I get most of my sales ideas from *The Wall Street Journal*. I'd say 70 to 75 percent of my ideas. I also read the *Economist, Business Week*, just for an overview, some *Barron's* and the *Financial Times*. Maybe three issues out of the five for the week for *FT*.")

7:15 Start checking Bloombergs, getting warmed up, going over your ideas and figuring out where things stand.

7:45 Meet with your group in a conference room for a brief meeting to go over stuff. ("We go over the traders' axe [what the traders will focus on that day], go over research, what the market quotes are on a particular issue.")

8:15 Get back to desk, and get ready to start pitching ideas.

9:15 Have a short meeting with your smaller group.

10:00 One of your clients calls to ask about bonds from a particular company. You tell her you'll get right back to her. Walk over to talk to an analyst who covers that company. ("I'm in contact a lot with my analyst. I listen to my analyst.")

10:15 Back on the horn with your client.

12:30 Run out to lunch with another salesperson from your group. ("We often buy each other lunch. Sometimes to celebrate a big deal we'll order in lunch. We go to Little Italy Pizza Place, Cozi's Sandwiches. It's always the same people, and it's always the same six places.")

1:00 Back at your desk, check voice mail. ("If I leave for 30 minutes or so, when I get back, I'll have five messages.)

2:00   One of your clients wants to make a move. ("I trade something every day. Maybe anywhere from one to 10 trades. It's on a rolling basis. You plant seeds, and maybe someday one of them grows into a trade.")

3:15   Another client calls and wants to place an order.

5:30   Still on the phone. ("Although the markets close, that's when you can really take the time to talk about where things are and why you think someone should do something.")

7:30   Head for home, you're meeting a client for a late dinner. ("Often on Thursdays we go out as a group.")

Success factors in institutional sales

Early on, new associates must demonstrate an ability to get along with the clients they are asked to handle. Usually, the first-year sales associate plays second string to the senior salesperson's account. Any perception that the young salesperson does not get along with the PM or buy-side analyst means he or she will be immediately yanked from the account. Personality, ability to learn quickly and fit into the sales group will ensure movement up the ladder. The timing of the career path in sales, more so than in corporate finance, depends on the firm. Some firms trust sales associates quickly with accounts, relying on a sink-or-swim culture. Others, especially the biggest I-banks, wait until they are absolutely sure that the sales associate knows the account and what is going on, before handing over accounts.

Once the level of full-on salesperson is reached (usually after one year to one-and-a-half years on the desk), the goal shifts to growing accounts and successfully managing relationships. Developing and managing the relationships at the various buy-side firms is especially critical. Buy-siders can be thought of as time-constrained, wary investors who follow a regimented investing philosophy. Importantly, salespeople must know how and when to contact the investor. For example, a portfolio manager with a goal of finding growth technology stocks will cringe every time a salesperson calls with anything outside of that focused area. Therefore, the salesperson carefully funnels only the most relevant information to the client.

Hungry for more inside scoop? Join Vault.com's popular online
community for finance and banking — www.vault.com

VAULT.com **115**

Promotions depend on a combination of individual performance and desk performance. The ability to handle relationships, to bring in new clients, and to generate commission sales for the firm are paramount. Those that have managed to join the ranks of institutional sales without an MBA may be at a disadvantage when it comes to promotions into management roles.

Section Seven: Private Client Services (PCS)

The private client services (PCS) job can be exhilarating, exhausting and frustrating — all at once. As a PCS representative, your job is to bring in individual accounts with at least $2 to $3 million in assets. This involves incessantly pounding the pavement and reading the tape (market news) to find clients, followed by advising them on how to manage their wealth. PCS is a highly entrepreneurial environment. Building the book is all that matters, and managers don't care how a PCS representative spends his or her time, whether this be on the road, in the office, or at parties — the goal is to bring in the cash. Culture-wise, therefore, one typically finds a spirited entrepreneurial group of people, working their own hours and talking on the phone for the better part of the day. It is not uncommon for PCS pros to leave the office early on Fridays with a golf bag slung over one shoulder for a game with existing clients or with a few bigshots with money to invest (read: potential clients).

The growth in PCS

Just a few years ago, PCS was considered a small, unimportant aspect of investment banking. PCS guys were essentially brokers, always bothering other departments for leads and not as sophisticated as their counterparts in corporate finance or institutional sales and trading. Times have changed, however. Today, spurred by the tremendous stock market wealth that has been created over the past few years, PCS is a rapidly growing part of virtually every investment bank. While in the past, many banks essentially had no PCS division, or simply hired a few star retail brokers to be PCS representatives, Wall Street is recruiting heavily on MBA campuses today, scouring to find good talent for PCS.

Getting in the door

It takes an MBA these days, or a stellar record as a retail broker to become a private client sales representative. Even firms such as Merrill Lynch, which historically promoted retail brokers to the PCS role, is moving more and more toward hiring only those with business degrees from top schools and proven selling credentials, rather than proven brokers. PCS is also evolving into an entirely different business from traditional retail brokerage.

Whereas retail brokers make money on commissions generated through trades, PCS reps are increasingly charging clients just as money

Hungry for more inside scoop? Join Vault.com's popular online community for finance and banking — www.vault.com

VAULT.com   **117**

managers do — as a percentage of assets under management. A typical fee might be 1 percent per year of total assets under management. This fee obviously increases as the value of the assets increases, thereby motivating the PCS worker to generate solid returns on the portfolio. This move to fee-based management is designed to take away the incentive of a salesperson to churn or trade an account just for the sake of the commissions. One should note, however, that the trend to charge a fee instead of commissions is just that — a trend. Many Wall Street PCS reps still work on a commission basis.

The associate position

Once in the door, as a PCS associate, extensive training begins. The PCS associate must be well versed in all areas of the market and able to understand a wide variety of investing strategies. While a corporate bond salesperson has to know only corporate bonds, a PCS rep must be able to discuss the big picture of the market, equities, bonds, and even a slew of derivative products. Thus, training is said to be intensive in PCS, with many weeks of classroom learning.

Once training is complete, a new PCS associate often works to find his way onto a team, which pairs PCS beginners with one or two experienced PCS reps. (Teams are the latest craze on Wall Street.) The process of matching a new associate onto a team is driven largely by personality and fit. Once paired with an older rep or two, the associate works to understand the process of finding new clients and managing a portfolio of assets.

Generally speaking, PCS hires are given two years to build a book, or establish a reasonable level of business for the firm. While salaries for PCS associates out of business school matches those of other Wall Street hires ($80,000 plus a $25,000 bonus in the first six months), they quickly are shifted to a straight commission basis.

How to Build a Book

PCS associates must establish themselves in the first two years through any means possible. Typically, once the PCS associate has learned how to pitch to clients and how to give money-management advice, he or she begins to look for leads. As PCS is a sales job, leads and clients are developed just like at any other sales job. Phone calls, networking and visiting potential clients are key. To find leads, associates might do any of the following:

- Read the tape (follow market news). Many news articles in the markets discuss companies merging, companies going public, companies selling out, management selling stock in their companies, etc. In these cases, there often are CEOs and others on the management team who will find themselves with gobs of cash that must be invested. These are excellent sources of leads.

- Follow up with leads from other areas within the investment bank. A substantial number of corporate finance bankers represent management teams selling stock in public offerings, or selling stock in mergers. The real bonus is that the bankers already know the CEO or CFO with newfound wealth, and can provide an excellent introduction.

- Network. The power of being a friend of a friend cannot be underestimated. That is why PCS reps spend time at parties, functions, on the golf course, and anywhere else they can find leads. Often an "in" such as an introduction provided by a personal friend is the best lead of all.

Pay beyond the associate level

After a successful client list has been established, the sky is the limit in terms of pay. The best of the best PCS pros can earn well over a $1 million a year. The bottom-of-the-barrel PCS reps, however, may take home a mere $200,000 or so. On average, $500,000 is an annual number for PCS pros working for Wall Street firms. Insiders say it takes an average of five or six years to reach that level, however. Still, there are exceptions. One insider at Goldman Sachs reports that a PCS representative with that firm reached $3.4 million in compensation only five years out of business school.

Hungry for more inside scoop? Join Vault.com's popular online community for finance and banking — www.vault.com

VAULT.com **119**

Managing the portfolio

You may wonder how a PCS representative with a substantial client base and millions of dollars under account manages all these assets. It actually depends on the firm. Some firms break the PCS job into relationship managers and portfolio managers. For example, at J.P. Morgan, some PCS reps solely manage the portfolios of the various accounts, and are even paid a straight salary and bonus, depending on returns, while other reps work on client relations. Other firms, with newly built or bought asset management divisions, are attempting to pair PCS and AM (asset management) in order to utilize the existing money management expertise. Goldman Sachs, for example, has sought to do this, but cultural differences between the divisions and the past ingrained modus operandi may be a hindrance. Regardless of how the portfolio is managed, the movement toward teams will be a key to melding asset management and relationship management expertise on Wall Street.

Key success factors in PCS

One should keep in mind that PCS divisions essentially want to hire good salespeople, not good number crunchers. They don't need or want quant jocks in PCS; they want salespeople and schmoozers to find and land new clients. The key to succeeding in PCS is generating more assets to manage.

Good PCS reps will manage their client relationships extremely well, as these clients become the bread and butter for them over time. Understanding the goals of clients and executing them are extremely important. For example, one finds in PCS that some investors are not out to beat the S&P at all, and would rather earn steady returns without risking their principal. Remember, a wealthy and retired ex-CEO may not care that his $50 million jackpot beats the market. After all, he's got much more than he could spend in a lifetime. Lower risk and decent returns work just fine in some cases, and PCS representatives must be attuned to these individual differences.

Research

If you have a brokerage account, you have likely been given research on stocks that you asked about. The intermediaries between companies and the buy-side, corporate finance and sales and trading, research analysts form the hub of investment banks.

To the outsider, it seems that research analysts spend their time in a quiet room poring over numbers, calling companies, and writing research reports. The truth is an entirely different story, involving quite a bit of selling on the phone and on the road. Analysts produce research ideas, hand them to associates and assistants, and then man the phone talking to buy-side stock/bond pickers, company managers, and internal salespeople. They become the managers of research reports and the experts on their industries to the outside world. Thus, while the lifestyle of the research analyst would initially appear to resemble that of a statistician, it often comes closer to that of a diplomat or salesperson.

Hungry for more inside scoop? Join Vault.com's popular online community for finance and banking — www.vault.com

VAULT.com 121

Section One: The Players and The Product

The players

Research Assistants

The bottom-level number crunchers in research, research assistants generally begin with no industry or market expertise. They come from solid undergraduate schools and performed well in school, but initially perform mundane research tasks, such as digging up information and editing/formatting reports. Research assistants also take over the spreadsheet modeling functions required by the analyst. Travel is limited for the budding research assistant, as it usually does not make sense financially to send more than the research analyst to meetings with company officials or money managers.

Research Associates

Burdened with numbers and deadlines, the research associate often feels like a cross between a statistician and a corporate finance analyst. Long hours, weekends in the office and number-crunching sum up the routine of the associate. However, compared to analyst and associate analogues in corporate finance, the research associate works fewer hours, often makes it home at a reasonable time, and works less on the weekend. Unfortunately, the associate is required to be present and accounted for at 7:30 a.m., when most morning meetings take place.

Mirroring the corporate finance analyst and associate positions, research associates can be bright, motivated kids directly out of top undergraduate universities, or at firms dedicated to hiring MBAs in research, the research associate role is the entry-level position once the MBA has been earned.

A talented research associate can earn much in the way of responsibility. For example, the research associate may field phone calls from smaller "B" accounts (i.e. smaller money managers) and companies less important to the analyst. (The analyst handles the relationships with the biggest buy-siders, best clients and top salespeople.) When it comes to writing reports, some analysts give free reign to associates in writing. Also, research associates focus on one industry and typically work for only one full-fledged research analyst. This structure helps research associates delve deeper into the aspects of one industry group and enable them to work closely with a senior-level research analyst.

To start, research assistants/associates out of undergraduate typically get paid similarly to the corporate finance analyst right out of college. After one or two years, the compensation varies dramatically, depending on performance and the success of the analysts in the industry group as well as the associate's contribution. For the MBA research associate, the compensation is similar to I-banking associates: $80,000 salaries with $30,000 signing bonuses, plus a $30,000 year-end bonus, are typical.

It All Depends on the Analyst

Insiders stress that the research associate's contribution entirely depends on the particular analyst. Good analysts (from the perspective of the associate) encourage responsibility and hand-off a significant amount of work. Others communicate poorly, maintain rigid control and don't trust their assistants and associates to do much more than the most mundane tasks.

Being stuck with a mediocre analyst can make your job miserable. If you are considering an entry-level position in research, you should carefully evaluate the research analyst you will work with, as this person will have a huge impact on your job experience.

Note that in research, the job titles for analyst and associate have switched. In corporate finance, one begins as an analyst, and is promoted to associate post-MBA. In research, one begins as a research associate, and ultimately is promoted to the research analyst title.

Research Analysts

The research analyst, especially in equity, is truly a guru. Analysts follow particular industries, recommend stocks to buy and sell, and convince salespeople and buy-siders why they or their clients should or should not invest in Company XYZ. The road to becoming an analyst is either paved with solid industry experience, or through the research assistant/associate path.

Full-fledged analyst positions are difficult to come by. The skills required to succeed as an analyst include a firm grasp of: 1) the industry and dynamics of stock picking, and 2) the sales skills required to convince investors and insiders alike why a stock is such an excellent buy. An analyst lacking in either area will simply not become the next *II*-rated star (an analyst highly rated by *Institutional Investor* ratings).

Hungry for more inside scoop? Join Vault.com's popular online
community for finance and banking — www.vault.com

VAULT.com   **123**

Research analysts spend considerable time talking on the phone to investors, salespeople and traders, pitching buy and sell ideas or simply discussing industry or company trends. Everyone tries to get the research analyst's ear, to ask for advice or (as we will discuss in-depth later) to pressure him or her to change a rating or initiate coverage of a particular stock. Analysts also travel regularly, visiting buy-siders or big money managers and companies in their field. Indirectly, they are trying to generate trading business with money managers, research ideas from companies or trying to build a reputation in the industry. All in all, analysts must be able to convincingly and quickly pitch an idea, and defend it thoroughly when the time comes.

In this atmosphere, research analysts must scrutinize every company that they maintain under coverage. Any news or company announcements will spur a deluge of phone calls to the analyst, with questions ranging from the big picture to the tiniest of details. They also must maintain a handle on an extremely important aspect of any company — the numbers. Inaccurate earnings estimates, especially when they are far from the mark, reflect poorly on the analyst. Why didn't an analyst know the company stock was going to come out with such low earnings? Or, why didn't the research analyst know that industry growth was slowing down? The analyst is responsible for staying on top of these things.

Compensation packages for research analysts run the gamut. Some *II*-rated star analysts in hot industries command multimillion dollar annual packages, especially during bull markets. Most banks figure their compensation for analysts with formulae that are usually incomprehensible to even the research analysts. The factors that go into analyst compensation typically includes a mix of the following:

- The performance of stocks under coverage (meaning that if their stocks perform like the analyst predicts, they get paid well)

- Trading activity within the firm of stocks under coverage

- Corporate finance business revenues of companies in their industry

- Performance evaluations of the research analyst by superiors

- *Institutional Investor* rankings (Once a research analyst finds himself listed as an *II*-ranked analyst, the first stop is into his boss's office to renegotiate his annual package.)

Note: As they progress in their career, research analysts receive titles similar to investment bankers, namely VP, SVP and ultimately MD. However, the tasks of a research analyst tend to remain somewhat consistent once the analyst level is reached, with perhaps more selling of research and traveling involved at the most senior levels.

The *Institutional Investor* (*II*) Ratings Scorecard

Institutional Investor is a monthly magazine publication that, among other things, rates research analysts. The importance of the *II* ratings to investment banks and even many institutional investors cannot be overstated. Most industry watchers believe and follow the ratings as if they were gospel.

How do the ratings work? Essentially, *II* utilizes a formula to determine the best research analysts on Wall Street, and publishes their rankings annually. Note the bias, however, toward research analysts at bulge bracket firms. *II* 's formula essentially involves surveys of "directors of research, chief investment officers, portfolio managers, and buy-side analysts at the major money management institutions around the world." Major money managers deal primarily with large investment banks for their trading needs and a portion of their research needs.

In 1999, for the second year in a row, Merrill Lynch came in first in the *II* rankings. Merrill had 56 equity analysts receive mention, including 16 analysts on the first team. Salomon Smith Barney came in second with 55 All-Americans, followed by Morgan Stanley Dean Witter (53), Goldman Sachs (43), and Credit Suisse First Boston (40).

The Product

Industry Research Reports

To establish oneself as a knowledgeable analyst, many researchers begin by writing and issuing an industry piece. For example, an industry research report on the oil and gas sector might discuss issues such as commodity prices, the general outlook for the sector and valuations of companies in the industry.

The time required to generate an industry piece depends on the length of the report, the complexity of the industry, and how important it is to show expertise to investors and management teams in the industry. For

Hungry for more inside scoop? Join Vault.com's popular online community for finance and banking — www.vault.com

VAULT.com **125**

completely new industries for new analysts, a full six months or more is given to enable the analyst to fully understand the industry and develop a thorough report. Once it is printed, salespeople will use an industry research report to get up to speed and learn about a particular segment.

Touted as industry gospel, industry research reports take substantial time to produce and earn the firm nothing except awareness that the investment bank follows an industry and has expertise in that industry. However, the brand equity built by an industry piece can be substantial and make corporate finance banker cold-calling a much easier process.

Company-Specific Research Reports

Once an analyst's industry piece has been written and digested by the investment community, the analyst focuses on publishing research reports on specific companies. To create a well-rounded research universe, research analysts will typically write on the top industry players, as well as several smaller players in the industry. Company-specific reports fall into three categories: initiation of coverage, updates and rating changes.

Initiation of Coverage: This is exactly what it sounds like. These reports indicate that an analyst has not previously written research or covered the particular company. Usually an initiation of coverage report includes substantial information about the business, a detailed forecast model and risk factors inherent in the business.

Update: When a stock moves, news/earnings are released, or the analyst meets with management, an update report is put out. Often one-pagers, updates provide quick information important to current movements in the stock.

Change of Rating: Whenever an I-bank alters its rating on a stock (we will discuss these ratings later), a report is issued. These reports vary in length from one to five pages. Reasons for a downgrade include: lower than expected earnings, forecasts for diminished industry or firm growth, management departures, problems integrating a merger, or even overpriced stocks. Reasons for an upgrade include: better than expected earnings, new management, stock repurchases, or beneficial industry trends.

Conflict of Interest

It is crucial to note whether an investment bank has provided corporate finance services to the company under coverage. Usually at the end of a research piece, a footnote will indicate whether this is the case. If so, investors should be careful to understand the inherent conflict of interest and bias that the research report contains. Often covering a company's stock (and covering it with optimistic ratings) will ensure corporate finance business, such as a manager role in equity offerings, M&A advisory services, and so on.

Market Commentary

Analysts usually cover a particular (small) universe of stocks, but some analysts, called market strategists, survey and report on market conditions as a whole. Most large banks publish market commentary reports on a daily basis (sometimes even several within a day), augmented with weekly, monthly and quarterly reviews. Included in such reports is information on the performance of stocks in major market indices in the U.S., major markets worldwide, and in various sectors — such as transportation, technology and energy — in the U.S. Some of these commentaries offer forecasts for the markets or for particular sectors. Naturally, economic data is paramount to stock market performance overall and thus pervades market commentaries.

Economic Commentary

Similar to a market commentary, economic reports are also published periodically and cover economic indicators and trends. These reports are often stuffed with graphs of macroeconomic factors such as GDP, inflation, interest rates, consumer spending, new home sales, import/export data, etc. They provide useful information regarding government fiscal and monetary policy, and often link to fixed income reports. Often the same market strategist writes both the economic commentaries and the market commentaries for a firm.

Fixed Income Commentary

Analysts covering the fixed income markets publish periodic reports on the debt markets. Often tied to the economic commentaries, fixed income market reports comment on the performance of various fixed income instruments including U.S. government securities, mortgages, corporate bonds, commodity prices and other specialized fixed income

Hungry for more inside scoop? Join Vault.com's popular online community for finance and banking — www.vault.com

VAULT.com **127**

securities. The five-point scale for rating stocks is ubiquitous in banking, but the definitions that banks refer to do not accurately measure what the analyst believes. The following scale reflects the general consensus on stock ratings, but keep in mind that these vary by firm.

Rating	Published Definition	Actual Meaning
Buy 1	STRONG BUY. The company's stock is a strong buy, and will outperform the market over the next 18 months.	The stock is a worthy buy. Or, if the investment bank writing the research just completed a transaction for the company, the analyst may simply believe it is a decent company that will perform as well as the market in the next 18 months.
Buy 2	MARKET PERFORM. The stock will perform approximately as well as the market over the next 18 months.	Be wary about buying this stock. It is either richly valued or has potential problems which will inhibit the firm's growth over the next 18 months.
Hold 3	HOLD. The stock will likely perform at or below the market over the next 18 months.	Sell. A hold rating by an analyst usually means that the stock should be sold, but that the analyst does not want to ostracize himself from the company by rating the stock a sell.
Sell 4	SELL. The stock will perform below the market over the next 18 months	Dump this stock as soon as possible. A Sell 4 rating issued by an analyst means the company is going to tank, and soon.
Sell 5	SELL IMMEDIATELY.	Rarely if ever seen. A Sell 4 tells clients to dump the stock, that it is heading into the toilet. A Sell 5 might only be issued after the firm is in bankruptcy.

Section Two: Three Months in Research

The cycle

Many research analysts comment that there's not a typical day, nor even a typical week in research. On the equity side, the workload is highly cyclical. Everything revolves around earnings reports, which come out quarterly during earnings season. The importance of the earnings figures to the stock analyst cannot be stressed enough, and once a quarter, when companies report their earnings data, the job often gets a little crazy.

On the fixed income side, the workflow depends entirely on the product. A high yield or high grade corporate bond research analyst may have some ups and downs in the workload based on the earnings season, but earnings reports are not nearly as critical as they are to equity analysts. We will cover a typical day in debt research in abbreviated form at end of this chapter. First we'll take a look at a three-month period for an equity research analyst.

While we will focus on the analyst himself, keep in mind that the research associate will also perform many of the same tasks, helping the analyst in any way possible.

March

On March 1, four weeks prior to the end of the quarter (March 31), the analyst begins to look at the financial models relating to the companies under coverage. He is worried about his stocks' earnings per share numbers, which will be reported approximately two to four weeks after the quarter's end. If the estimated EPS numbers stray too far from the actual reported EPS when it comes out, the analyst will find himself dealing with many angry investors and salespeople, at the very least.

To finetune his earnings estimates, the analyst begins calling the companies that he covers, testing assumptions, refining certain predictions, and generally trying to grasp exactly where the company and industry stand. Details make the difference, and the analyst discusses with the company CFO gross margin estimates, revenue predictions, and even tax issues, to arrive at an acceptable EPS figure. Conversations such as these can become excruciatingly detailed.

Hungry for more inside scoop? Join Vault.com's popular online community for finance and banking — www.vault.com

VAULT.com **129**

April

The quarter has ended, and in early April the research analyst enters the quiet period. During this time companies are restricted from discussing their upcoming earnings release, as this may constitute sensitive inside information. The calm before the storm, the quiet period (in this case, early April) finds many analysts calling other contacts in the industry to discuss broader trends and recent developments in the field.

Once companies begin reporting earnings (which starts mid-month), the analyst scrambles to quickly digest the information and issue one-page update reports. The deluge of company earnings releases causes long and hectic days for the analyst, who must deal with a barrage of phone calls and the demand for written reports from salespeople and institutional investors. Within two weeks after the earnings release, the analyst will typically publish another three-page report on his companies, often with new ratings, new analysis and revised earnings estimates for the next few quarters.

May

In early May, the analyst finishes writing update reports and is afforded a little breathing room. While earnings season involves putting out fires left and right, the end of the reporting period means the analyst can relax and get back to working on long-term projects. These might include industry pieces, initiation reports or other long-term projects. Banks with large corporate finance businesses may encourage their research analysts and associates to spend time working with investment bankers, developing leads, advising them who to target, and performing a variety of other research tasks.

Writing the report

Where do new research ideas come from? And when and why do analysts change their ratings?

Frankly, many young analysts are told what companies or areas to cover — until one becomes a seasoned analyst, an analyst focuses on ideas based on firm demands. Veteran analysts with more leeway generate ideas either through industry knowledge or new stocks. Typically, investment banks will compel an analyst to follow a particular stock but will not dictate the rating assigned to the stock. The pressure to publish certain ratings, however, is real and cannot be understated, as it can come from all angles.

The writing process is straightforward, and really depends on the type of report needed. For the inch-thick industry report, for example, research analysts utilize research associates and assistants to the utmost. Analysts coordinate the direction, thesis, and basic content of the report, and do much of the writing. For an introductory initiation of coverage report, the work parallels the industry piece. Substantial research, financial analysis and information gathering require much time and effort. Behind the scenes, management interviews and company visits to understand and probe the business render the biggest volume of data.

For less labor-intensive pieces, such as changes in ratings or updates, either the analyst or the associate whips out the report in short time. Keep in mind that the analyst usually produces the idea and reviews the report prior to press time, but the associate may in reality put together the entire piece (and put the analyst's name on top).

For all of these reports, research associates and assistants typically find data, compile other research, edit the written material, build financial models and construct graphs and charts of relevant information. The analyst utilizes his or her contacts within the industry to interview insiders to get a glimpse of the latest trends and current events.

Travel

You'd better like suitcases and hotel rooms if you're aiming for a research analyst position — the position requires a great deal of travel. Usually, the full-fledged analyst (as opposed to the associate) does most of the work requiring travel, including meeting with money managers (the buy-side clients), company management, accompanying corp fin professionals on roadshows. However, associates will fill in for unavailable analysts, attend some due diligence meetings, and attend conferences and trade shows.

These occasional outside meetings aside, research associates spend almost all of their time in the home office. On the plus side, many associates often meet with managers of the companies that come to visit the bank, meaning research associates have the luxury of meeting one-on-one with top management teams and investor relations representatives. This is especially the case in New York, where research analysts with big firms carry a lot of influence.

Hungry for more inside scoop? Join Vault.com's popular online community for finance and banking — www.vault.com

VAULT.com   131

Fixed income research — yawning?

The attitude of many equity bankers, equity sales and traders, and even some equity research analysts is that fixed income research is the most boring area in any investment bank. Why? Unlike stock analysts, many fixed income analysts do not have clients. If a fixed income analyst issues a report on U.S. Treasury bonds, there is no company calling, fewer surprises, and few salespeople/traders to sing the praises of a good research piece. More importantly, there is often less money to make. While equity analysts often can rise to stardom (i.e. *II* ranking), those that do in fixed income play second fiddle to the equity guys. All in all, the fixed income research job is one of the least glamorous on the Street.

A day in the life of a fixed income analyst

How is the debt analyst different than the equity analyst? As previously mentioned, there is no earnings season driving fixed income as much as there is in equity. But corporate bond analysts and high yield analysts do have some seasonal swings. In municipal bond research, emerging markets research, asset-backed research, and government/Treasury research, reports are more evenly spaced and the stress and pressure often lower. But certain monthly events and surprising news (usually macroeconomic in nature) can spark analysts to stay busy. For example, U.S. Treasury research reports often come out around monthly CPI, PPI and quarterly GDP numbers. In general, interest rate news always impacts bonds, and creates work for analysts to interpret.

The day begins early for the debt research analyst just as it does for the equity analyst. Morning meetings take place around 7:30 Eastern Time, no matter where you may happen to work. On the West Coast, an analyst must be ready to go at 4:30 in the morning.

The day includes all of the typical work that an equity research analyst does. The analyst is on the phone with buy-side portfolio managers, doing fundamental research, writing reports, tracking bond prices and yield data, and looking for trade ideas to give to the salesforce. Hours tend to resemble the equity analyst, with 12- to 13-hour days the norm, but with less time on the road.

Key success factors in research

Research Assistants/Associates

To excel initially, research assistants and associates must work hard, learn quickly, and become whizzes at Microsoft Excel and Word. Especially important to research associates are good writing skills, as analysts often hand-off a significant portion of the writing and editing of research reports to the associate. Early on, the biggest mistake a research assistant or associate can make is to mess up the financial models and generally lose sight of the details.

Research is built on a foundation of good models with reasonable assumptions, and research associates must first master that domain. Later on, research assistants and associates must show an ability to handle the phones — answer questions from investors and internal salespeople about the current goings-on at companies they cover, as well as ask smart due diligence questions to company managers in order to generate the next research piece.

Unlike most corporate finance analysts, research assistants/associates can and do rise to the analyst level without an MBA. Some firms promote research assistants to the full-fledged analyst role after one or two years of solid performance, while some hire research associates only for two-year stints, emulating the corporate finance two-year programs. The firms that are less stringent about hiring MBAs full-time for research are more likely to promote internal associates to the analyst position.

Still, the number that makes this jump is a small portion of assistants and associates. Why? Some simply discover that the analyst job is not for them. Many research dropouts move to hedge funds, business school, the buy-side, or institutional sales departments at I-banks. Others simply find that the path to becoming a research analyst nonexistent. Explains one research associate at Morgan Stanley, "A lot of it's demand-driven. If you want to be the head technology analyst, you might have to wait until that person retires or moves to another firm. But sometimes they will add on analysts, maybe they need a retail analyst to bring I-banking business in. And sometimes a new subsector will turn into a new category."

Research Analysts

Newly hired research analysts must start as the associates do — learning, modeling, and working long hours. Beyond the inaugural two

Hungry for more inside scoop? Join Vault.com's popular online community for finance and banking — www.vault.com

VAULT.com **133**

years, analysts begin to branch out and become full-fledged analysts, covering their own set of stocks and their own industry segment or sub-segment. Winning respect internally from corp fin and sales and trading departments may be the first hurdle a new analyst must overcome. This respect comes from detailed research and careful analysis before making assertions about anything. Salespeople can be ruthless when it comes to researchers who make sloppy or unsubstantiated claims. Says one fixed income insider, "There are people who will eat you alive if your analysis is off. They control a huge universe of issues and a huge amount of buyers to make that market liquid, and when you present your analysis you had better be ready. These guys are serious. It's like playing for the San Francisco 49ers; you better be prepared."

Down the road, research analysts — even good ones — are always on somebody's bad side. When the analyst wins respect from the salesperson by turning down a potentially bad IPO, he angers to no end the corporate finance banker who wants to take the company public. When the analyst puts a sell recommendation on a poor stock, the salespeople also cheer, but the company grows angry, sometimes severing all ties with their investment bank. Thus, the best analysts function as diplomats, capable of making clear objective arguments regarding decisions combined with a mix of sweet-talking salespeople and investors.

Do Analysts Need MBAs and CFAs?

Although not required, an MBA undoubtedly opens doors in research. Ten years ago, research departments cared little about educational pedigree and a business school education, but today more and more emphasis is being placed on attaining an MBA. Perhaps even more important than earning an MBA for those in research is becoming a Chartered Financial Analyst, or CFA. The Association of Investment Management and Research (AIMR) confers this designation on those who pass a series of examinations, which are administered in three stages. They are Levels I, II and III and are given at one-year intervals in May. To become a CFA, one must pass all three levels and also have worked for three years (which usually coincides with the testing period). The program and tests are not easy, and according to the AIMR the pass rates have ranged over the past 10 years:

(next page...)

- Level I: 48 percent to 62 percent

- Level II: 46 percent to 65 percent

- Level III: 59 percent to 82 percent

The CFA designation lends the analyst respect and credibility to investors and seems more and more a prerequisite to moving up. As one analyst notes, "All things being equal, promotions will go to the analyst with his CFA examinations complete or with his MBA degree." In addition, a candidate interviewing for a research position will stand out by stating a sincere intention to complete the CFA examinations.

Section Three: Research — The Ties That Bind

Stuck in the middle

Corporate finance bankers press research analysts to be banker-friendly. Salespeople yearn for new stock ideas they can use to solicit trades from clients. Investors demand that research analysts write unbiased research, while companies wish for the best rating possible. Although within the department, research is often less political than corporate finance, those in research face more external pressure than any other area in investment banking. Because the demands placed on an analyst can be severe and multifarious, we will cover in this section the various pressures hurled on the research analyst. We will examine the relationship between research analysts and corporate finance department, outside investors, salespeople and traders, and the companies they cover.

Corporate finance

The reason for disagreement between bankers in corporate finance and research analysts essentially boils down to their incentive systems. Bankers are paid for deals completed and deal size. Nothing in their pay scale takes into account the post-offering performance of the stock. In comparison, a research analyst covering the same stock will generally be paid based on a formula that measures the performance of the stocks he covers, as well as the trading activity in those stocks.

A common analogy used to describe this difference in incentives is that when a company goes public, the banker dates the company, but the research analyst marries the company. Poor stock performance down the road in no way directly impacts the banker, except perhaps in industry reputation. The real scapegoat in the marketplace for a lousy IPO stock is generally the research analyst (if he maintains a buy rating). And the analyst's pay and reputation will be adversely affected when and if the stock tanks.

When does this translate into pressure on the research analyst? Generally when a banker wishes to underwrite an IPO, but the analyst is not convinced that the company and/or management are sound. This pressure from corporate finance cannot be understated, however, as a manager role in a public offerings usually means millions of dollars in revenue for the firm. An analyst's refusal to cover the company or endorse the deal can squelch any transaction in the making.

Sometimes, companies considering a follow-on offering in a few months will hint that favorable research coverage will win the business. Again, the banker will pressure the analyst to publish favorable research before the company begins selecting the managers. Note that once a company begins the process of the follow-on offering (defined by the first working group meeting or the decision by company management to officially pursue a deal), a quiet period ensues, forbidding the managers involved in the secondary offering from publishing any rating changes on the stock.

The Chinese Wall

Between corporate finance and research, firms build what is known as a Chinese Wall separating research analysts from both bankers and S&T. Why? Often, bankers are privy to inside information at a company because of ongoing or potential M&A business, or because they know that a public company is in registration to file a follow-on offering. Either transaction is considered material non-public information and research analysts privy to such information cannot change ratings or mention it, as doing so would effectively enable clients to benefit from inside information at the expense of existing shareholders.

When it comes to certain information, a Chinese Wall also separates salespeople and traders from research analysts. The reason should be obvious. Analyst reports often move stock prices — sometimes dramatically. Thus, a salesperson with access to research information prior to it being published would give clients an unfair advantage over other investors. Research analysts even disguise the name of the company on a report until immediately before it is published. This way, if the report falls into the wrong hands, the information remains somewhat confidential.

Salespeople within the firm

Nothing leads a research analyst quicker to the professional grave than when she touts stocks (to the salesforce) without doing the necessary background checks on the company. Too often, young research analysts fresh out of business school buy into a company's story without really kicking the tires, and publish favorable reports without digging deep enough. Recommending a stock that tanks hurts salespeople, as their clients can become irate at the poor advice given.

Hungry for more inside scoop? Join Vault.com's popular online community for finance and banking — www.vault.com

VAULT.com **137**

Let us further understand why a salesperson can love or hate an analyst. Suppose a research analyst initiated coverage of a company with a strong buy (buy-1) rating. Or that a fixed income analyst put out a new report that was bullish on a certain sector. The research piece immediately ends up on the desks of the relevant salespeople, who proceed to call their clients (investors) pitching a trade. Many clients will actually purchase the security based on the analyst's recommendation, and the salesperson takes home a commission on the trade. However, if the stock drops or the bond declines in value, the relationship between the salesperson and the client can be jeopardized. The salesperson would think twice about extolling the virtues of the next buy-1 research report from that analyst, especially if the cause of the stock falling were something the analyst should have known. To avoid salespeople pitching stocks just to generate trades, many firms pay salespeople based on the performance of the stock or bond, so that a poor stock trade makes less money for the salespeople.

In addition, salespeople lose respect for research analysts who become too banker-friendly. This refers to analysts who compromise research quality to generate corporate finance business, and willingly publish buy-1 ratings simply to help out the bankers gain manager roles. On the flip side, salespeople value analysts willing to sacrifice some income for their reputation.

As noted by one salesperson, a good analyst "reads between the lines of things a company says" and "does industry digging" to ferret out all risk factors and potential landmines. That includes talking to the company's vendors, customers, and even the company's competitors, to understand the stock.

Companies

For obvious reasons, a company wants the best possible rating on its stock. To get such a rating, CFOs and CEOs not versed in the workings of the market may attempt to highlight the positive developments, downplay the risk factors, and influence earnings estimates. Smart companies learn quickly, however, that the backlash from the markets from over-inflated estimates kills credibility with both research analysts and investors alike. Thus, most companies actually understate their expected future earnings. That being said, it is not unheard of for a company to almost threaten to terminate corporate finance relationships without a strong stock rating from the analyst.

Once a research analyst places a sell rating (either a 4 or 5) on a company's stock, the relationship between the company's management and the bankers and research analysts changes forever. In fact, company management may refuse to return calls, give guidance on estimates, or even extend professional courtesy to an I-bank that has issued a sell rating. Thus, it is a rare case indeed when a researcher chooses to issue a sell on a stock.

Outside investors

An investor — whether a large institutional investor or a small retail investor — wants research that accurately reflects a stock's prospects. Investors understand when a research analyst makes a bad call once in awhile, but they must believe that the research analyst's primary goal is to publish unbiased analyses and opinions. After all, analysts are the experts and their primary market is the institutional and retail investor. However, the best institutional investors view Wall Street research with tremendous skepticism, recognizing the inherent conflicts of interests.

Hungry for more inside scoop? Join Vault.com's popular online
community for finance and banking — www.vault.com

VAULT.com **139**

Syndicate:
The Go-betweens

What does the syndicate department at an investment bank do? Syndicate usually sits on the trading floor, but syndicate employees don't trade securities or sell them to clients. Neither do they bring in clients for corporate finance.

What syndicate does is provide a vital role in placing stock or bond offerings with buy-siders, and truly aim to find the right offering price that satisfies both the company, the salespeople, the investors and the corporate finance bankers working the deal.

Syndicate and public offerings

In any public offering, syndicate gets involved once the prospectus is filed with the SEC. At that point, syndicate associates begin to contact other investment banks interested in being underwriters in the deal. Before we continue with our discussion of the syndicate's role, we should first understand the difference between managers and underwriters and how fees earned through security offerings are allocated.

Managers

The managers of an IPO get involved from the beginning. These are the I-banks attending all the meetings and generally slaving away to complete the deal. Managers get paid a substantial portion of the total fee — called underwriting discounts and commissions on the cover of a prospectus, and known as the spread in the industry. In an IPO, the spread is usually 7.0 percent, unless the deal is huge, which often means that the offering company can negotiate a slightly lower fee. For a follow-on offering, typical fees start at 5.0 percent, and again, decrease as the deal-size increases.

As discussed previously in this book, deals typically have between two and five managers. To further confuse the situation, managers are often called managing underwriters, as all managers are underwriters, but not all underwriters are managers. Confused? Keep reading.

Hungry for more inside scoop? Join Vault.com's popular online community for finance and banking — www.vault.com

VAULT.COM **141**

Underwriters

The underwriters on the deal are so called because they are the ones assuming liability, though they usually have no shares of stock to sell in the deal. They are not necessarily the I-banks that work intimately on the deal; most underwriters do nothing other than accept any potential liability for lawsuits against the underwriting group.

Underwriters are selected by the lead manager in conjunction with the company. This role is often called participating in the syndicate. In a prospectus, you can always find a section entitled "Underwriting," which lists the underwriting group. Anywhere from 10 to 30 investment banks typically make up the underwriting group in any securities offering.

In the underwriting section, the list of each participant has next to it listed a number of shares. While underwriting sections list quite a few investment banks and shares next to each bank, it is important to realize that these banks do not sell shares. Neither do they have anything to do with how the shares in the deal are allocated to investors. They merely assume the percentage of liability indicated by the percentage of deal shares listed in the prospectus. To take on such liability, underwriters are paid a small fee, depending on their level of underwriting involvement (i.e. the number of shares next to their name). The managers in the deal will account for the liability of approximately 50 to 70 percent of the shares, while the underwriters account for the rest.

The Economics of a Deal

Suppose there are three managers in an IPO transaction for ABC Corporation. Say the deal is $200 million in size. And let's say that this $200 million is accounted for because the deal is priced at $20 per share and the company is offering 10 million shares to the public. With a 7.0 percent spread (the deal fee percent typical in IPOs), we come up with a whopping $14 million fee.

How is the $14 million divied up? Each department is actually allocated a piece of the deal before the firms divide their shares. First, corporate finance (the bankers working the deal) grabs 20 percent of the fee. So, in our example, $2.8 million (20 percent of $14 million) is split among the three managers' corp fin departments. Then the salespeople from the managing group take their share — a whooping 60 percent of the spread, totaling $8.4 million. Again, this $8.4 million is divided by the few managers in the deal.

This 20/60 split is typical for almost any deal. The last portion of the spread goes to the syndicate group (a.k.a. the underwriters) and is appropriately called the underwriting fee. However, expenses for the deal are taken out of the underwriting fee, so it never amounts to a full 20 percent of the spread. Suppose that this deal had 20 underwriters. The underwriting section in the prospectus might look like:

I-Bank 1 (the lead manager)	7,000,000
I-Bank 2 (a co-manager)	4,000,000
I-Bank 3 (a co-manager)	4,000,000
I-Bank 4	294,118
I-Bank 5	294,118
• • • •	• • • •
I-Bank 20	294,118
TOTAL	20,000,000

The total number of shares accounted for by each underwriter (the number of shares each underwriter assumes liability for) adds up to the total number of shares sold in the transaction. Note that the managers or

(next page...)

Hungry for more inside scoop? Join Vault.com's popular online
community for finance and banking — www.vault.com

VAULT.com **143**

underwriting managers take the biggest chunk of the liability. (In this case, each manager would pay 25 percent of damages from a lawsuit, as 5,000,000 shares represent 25 percent of the 20,000,000-share offering.)

If we return to our example, we see that after the sales and corporate finance managers are paid, the last 20 percent comes out to $2.8 million. This is quite a bit, but remember that the way deals work, expenses are netted against the underwriting fee. Flights to the company, lawyers, roadshow expenses, etc. all add up to a lot of money and are taken out of the underwriting fee. Why? Nobody exactly knows why this is the practice, except that it doesn't seem quite fair to have the syndicate receive as much as the bankers — who put in countless weekends and hours putting together a deal.

Let's pretend that deal expenses totaled $1.8 million, leaving

$2.8 million Underwriting Fees

- $1.8 million Expenses

Underwriting Profit $1.0 million

Therefore, the lead manager gets 35 percent of the underwriting profit (7,000,000 shares divided by the total 20,000,000 = 35 percent). The two co-managers each receive 20 percent of the underwriting profit (4,000,000 divided by 20,000,000) and each underwriter receives approximately 1.47 percent of the underwriting profit (294,118 divided by 20,000,000). Therefore the lead manager gets $350,000 of the underwriting profit, the co-managers each get $200,000, and the other underwriters each get approximately $14,706. Not bad for doing nothing but taking on some risk.

Why the long diversion into the mechanics of what an underwriter is and how much they are paid? Because this is what syndicate spends considerable time doing.

Syndicate professionals:

- Make sure their banks are included in the underwriting of other deals

- Put together the underwriting group in deals the I-bank is managing

- Allocate stock to the various buy-side firms indicating interest in deal

- Determine the final offering price of various offerings

What is involved on a day-to-day basis? Quite a bit of phone time and quite of bit of dealing with the book.

The book

The book is a listing of all investors who have indicated interest in buying stock in an offering. Investors place orders by telling their respective salesperson at the investment bank or by calling the syndicate department of the lead manager. Only the lead manager maintains (or carries) the book in a deal.

Orders can come in one of two forms — either an order for a specified number of shares at any price, or for a specified number of shares up to a specified price. Most buy-siders indicate a price range of some kind. Often, institutions come in with a "10 percent order." That is the goal of the managers, and means that the investor wants to buy 10 percent of the shares in the deal.

In terms of timing, the book comes together during the roadshow, as investors meet the company's management team. Adding to the excitement, many investors wait until the day or two prior to pricing to call in their order. Thus, a manager may not know if they can sell the deal until the very last minute. The day before the securities begin to trade, syndicate looks at the book and calls each potential buyer one last time. It is important to ferret out which money managers are serious about owning the stock/bonds over the long haul. Those that don't are called flippers. Why would a money manager choose this strategy? Because getting shares in the offering is often a sure way to make money, as stocks usually jump up a few percentage points at the opening bell. However, flippers are the bane of successful offerings. Institutional money managers who buy into public deals just to sell their shares on the first day only cause the stock to immediately trade down.

Pricing and allocation

How does syndicate price a stock? Simple — by supply and demand. There are a fixed number of shares or bonds in a public deal available, and buyers indicate exactly how many shares and at what price they are willing to purchase the securities. The problem is that virtually every deal is oversubscribed; i.e., there are more shares demanded than available for sale. Therefore, syndicate must determine how many shares to allocate to each buyer. To add to the headache, because investors know that every successful deal is oversubscribed, they inflate their actual share indications. So, a 10 percent order may in fact mean that the money manager actually wants something like 2 or 3 percent of the deal. The irony, then, is that any money manager that actually got

Hungry for more inside scoop? Join Vault.com's popular online
community for finance and banking — www.vault.com

VAULT.com **145**

as many shares as she asked for would immediately cancel her order, realizing that the deal was a "dog."

In the end, a combination of syndicate's experience with investors and their instincts about buyers tells them how many shares to give to each buy-sider. Syndicate tries to avoid flippers, but can never entirely do so.

After the book is set, syndicate calls the offering company to report the details. This pricing call, as it is called, occurs immediately after the roadshow ends and the day before the stock begins trading in the market. Pricing calls sometimes results in yelling, cursing and swearing from the management teams of companies going public. Remember that in IPOs, the call is telling founders of companies what their firm is worth — reactions sometimes border on the extreme. If a deal is not hot (as most are not), then the given price may be disappointing to the company. "How can my company not be the greatest thing since sliced bread?" CEOs often think.

Also, company managers often mistakenly believe that the pricing call is some sort of negotiation, and fire back with higher prices. However, only on rare occasions can the CEO influence the final price — and even then only a little. Their negotiating strength stems from the fact that they can walk away from a deal. Managers will then be out months of work and a lot of money (deal expenses can be very high). An untold number of deals have been shelved because the company has insisted on another 50 cents on the offered share price, and the syndicate department has told management that it simply is not feasible. It may sound like a pittance, but on a 20 million share deal, 50 cents per share is a whopping $10 million in proceeds to the company.

Politicians

Because of this tension over the offering price, senior syndicate professionals must be able to handle difficult and delicate situations. But it's not just company management that must be handled with care. During a deal, syndicate must also deal with the salesforce, other underwriters, and buy-siders. Similar to the research analyst, the syndicate professional often finds that diplomacy is one of the most critical elements to success. Successful syndicate pros can read between the lines and figure out the real intentions of buy-siders (are they flippers or are they committed to the offering, do they really want 10 percent of the offering, etc.). Also, good syndicate associates are proficient at schmoozing with other investment banks and garnering underwriting business (when the syndicate department is not representing the manager).

It's still a bank, not a cocktail party

Although syndicate professionals must have people skills, a knack for number-crunching and market knowledge are also important. Offerings involve many buy orders at various prices and for various levels of stock. Syndicate must allocate down from the biggest institutional investors to the smallest retail client (if retail clients are allowed to get shares in the deal). And pricing is quite a mix of art and science. Judging market momentum, deal interest and company egos can be trying indeed.

Who works in syndicate?

As for the players in syndicate, some have MBAs, and some don't. Some worked their way up, and some were hired directly into an associate syndicate position. The payoffs in syndicate can be excellent for top dogs, however, as the most advanced syndicate pros often deal directly with clients (management teams doing an offering), handle pricing calls, and talk to the biggest investors. They essentially become salespeople themselves, touting the firm, their expertise in placing stock or bonds, and their track record. Occasionally, syndicate MDs will attend an important deal pitch to potential clients, especially if he or she is a good talker. At the same time, some syndicate professionals move into sales or other areas, often in order to get away from the endless politicking involved with working in the syndicate department.

Beginners in the syndicate department help put together the book, schedule roadshow meetings and work their way up to dealing with investors, other I-banks, and internal sales. Because syndicate requires far fewer people than other areas in the bank, fewer job openings are to be found. Rarely does a firm recruit on college campuses for syndicate jobs — instead, firms generally hire from within the industry or from within the firm.

Hungry for more inside scoop? Join Vault.com's popular online
community for finance and banking — www.vault.com

VAULT.com   **147**

Merge With Us,
And Acquire A Career.

We're smart. Aggressive. Successful. And if that's what you're looking for, we're looking for you. We're one of the fastest growing investment banks on Wall Street. Rather than housing a culture built on old-school tradition and layers of management, we have the personality of a small, progressive boutique. That's why we're an ideal environment for graduates who want to learn investment banking by being an integral part of the team.

www.cibcwm.com

CIBC World Markets is the global marketing name of the investment banking and securities businesses of Canadian Imperial Bank of Commerce and its affiliates worldwide, including CIBC World Markets Corp., member New York Stock Exchange. ©2000 CIBC World Markets

LEADING
EMPLOYERS

Allen & Company

711 Fifth Avenue
9th Floor
New York, NY 10022
(212) 832-8000
Fax: (212) 832-8023

LOCATIONS

New York (HQ)

DEPARTMENTS

Asset Management
Investment Banking
Sales and Trading
Venture Capital

THE STATS

CEO: Herbert A. Allen, Jr.
Employer Type: Private Company
No. of Employees: 200
No. of Offices: 1

UPPERS

• Lucrative profit sharing
• No face time
• Schmooze with the stars

DOWNERS

• Bad deals can savage salaries
• Extraordinarily competitive and
  difficult hiring process
• Must do own research

KEY COMPETITORS

Goldman Sachs
Lazard
Morgan Stanley Dean Witter

EMPLOYMENT CONTACT

Human Resources
Allen & Co.
711 Fifth Avenue
9th Floor
New York, NY 10022

THE SCOOP

A curious firm

Founded in New York in 1922, Allen & Co. is a highly unusual investment bank. Bankers are required to pay their own travel and support expenses, and demands that principals at the company do their own research, anyone in the industry will tell you that bankers from Allen & Co. are among the most highly regarded in the I-banking universe. That's because the firm carries prestige, an impressive array of media clients, and investment opportunities rarely matched by other banks.

Junior's big deal

Brothers Charles and Herbert Allen founded Allen & Co. as a partnership in 1922. The company provided a mix of investment banking (including securities underwriting and mergers and acquisitions), private equity and venture capital, and investment management services. Allen & Co. really took off when Herbert Allen, Jr. took over the reins of the firm in 1966, when he was 26 years old. It took Herb, Jr. seven years to make an impact, but when he did, it was impressive.

In 1973 the younger Allen invested $1 million of his own cash and $500,000 of company capital in Columbia Pictures, buying a controlling interest in the movie studio at $4 per share. The deal had all the makings of a stinker, highlighted by the 1979 revelation that David Begelman, Columbia's CEO, was embezzling from the company. As grim as the situation looked then, Allen managed to turn the company around and sold Columbia to Coca-Cola in 1982 for stock worth $72 per share at the time. The deal that once looked like a youthful mistake for Herb Allen, Jr. skyrocketed in value, and the combined stake owned by Allen personally and by the company is now valued at approximately a half billion dollars. (Coca-Cola later sold Columbia to Sony for $3 billion.)

Media moguls

The Columbia investment made Herb, Jr. and Allen & Co. major players in the media industry. "Deals just don't get done in Hollywood unless [Allen & Co.] are involved," Barry Diller, chairman and CEO at USA Networks, told *Forbes*. Indeed, the firm has been involved in just about every major entertainment deal in the past 20 years. Recent deals of note include the Disney-Capital Cities/ABC merger, the Westinghouse purchase of CBS, and Seagram's purchase of MCA from Matsushita. The company moved seamlessly into the Internet age, representing Priceline.com, Zagat.com, and CDnow, among others.

I-banking, doggy style

Allen, Jr. has some radical ideas when it comes to how I-banks should function, and those ideas have resulted in a somewhat unusual structure for Allen & Co. Allen once told *Forbes*, "Over a long weekend, I could teach my dog to be an investment banker," further noting that he thought the industry was working at "over-capacity." He specifically targeted M&A, saying that corporations should be able to spot a good deal for themselves without help and that most of the bankers working on M&A deals "might as well be hot dog vendors." He also blasted research analysts, saying that most of the opinions are unnecessary and flawed because of the inherent conflict of interest when a bank writes a report while selling shares in a given company.

Allen & Co. is unique in other ways. For example, the firm employs only about 200 people total, as opposed to the thousands of employees common at large banks. The firm's principals are charged with doing their own research, and much of their compensation is non-guaranteed, coming in the form of bonuses that typically start at approximately 100 percent of base salary and proceeds from investments made in deals. "It's a unique culture," Allen, Jr. told *Forbes*. "We have a welfare state for our employees and raw capitalism for the principals." Allen is also proud of not pulling a "bait and switch." As opposed to most investment banks, where senior bankers secure an account, then turn the work over to junior employees, the Allen banker who solicits an account does the bulk of the work on that deal.

From babysitting to media player

One of Allen's superstar principals is Nancy Peretsman, a former banker at Salomon Smith Barney. Peretsman first met Herb Allen while she was at Princeton University, and worked as a babysitter for his children. Eventually, she secured an internship at Allen & Co. She kept in touch with Allen after graduation, and he allowed her to write a fairness opinion on a proposed buyout of Columbia Pictures while she was at Blythe Eastman Dillon. She moved on to Salomon Smith Barney and in 1995 accepted a position at Allen. (According to legend, Salomon shareholder Warren Buffet tried to convince Peretsman to stay until he

Hungry for more inside scoop? Join Vault.com's popular online community for finance and banking — www.vault.com

VAULT.COM   **153**

found out she was going to Allen.) Peretsman, ranked number nine on *Fortune*'s most recent list of the most powerful women in business, has had a hand in numerous big-time deals. She was involved in the sale of MediaOne to AT&T, the sale of King World to CBS, and the IPO of Priceline.com (where she also serves as a director). Additionally, Peretsman has worked with client CDnow, both on a failed merger with Time Warner and Sony and on other merger and fundraising options.

Fun in the Sun (Valley)

Besides its M&A prowess, Allen & Co. is probably best known in the industry for its Sun Valley conference, an annual gathering of entertainment and business elite in Sun Valley, Idaho. It's rumored that the Disney/Capital Cities merger was born out of a 1995 meeting between Disney's Michael Eisner and Capital Cities' Thomas Murphy at Sun Valley. The 1998 conference included Rupert Murdoch, Barry Diller, Intel's Andy Grove, and NBC News's Tom Brokaw. The 1999 gathering, the 17th Sun Valley event, included television stars Oprah Winfrey and Candace Bergen, Dell Computer's Michael Dell, Amazon.com's Jeffery Bezos, Yahoo!'s Jerry Yang, and America Online chief Steve Case.

GETTING HIRED

Allen & Co.'s personnel department does not accept outside calls, does not maintain a job hotline, and does not publicize job openings. The firm does, however, accept résumés mailed to its headquarters. Allen hires only MBAs as bankers and typically requires two to three years of experience. Insiders say getting a job directly out of business school is rare, and getting hired right out of college is "next to impossible."

In an exclusive interview with Vault.com, Allen & Co. Chairman Don Keough had this to say to prospective Allen employees: "My advice to a young person, especially a business school student, interested in Allen & Company is to be sure you become an interesting person. You should develop a full range of interests and not worry about a career. Instead, take courses that interest you — statistics, philosophy, and so on. Secondly, any young person who doesn't put the international world into perspective is a damn fool. Any education in today's world must incorporate some part of it outside the United States." He continues:

"We're interested in people who understand other countries and are fluent in other languages. You have to bring something other than a great MBA background to get in the door [at Allen]. You need experience, which means we rarely take undergrads or someone straight out of business school. You need to come in with some credentials from the business world, and we need to be sure that you want to stay here long term. Because we take so few, we have the luxury of taking our time evaluating new people." Adds another insider, "We do a lot in the entertainment and media field, so an interest in that area is helpful."

OUR SURVEY SAYS

A special, secret society

Bankers say working at Allen & Co. makes them feel like members of "a very special, secret society." Befitting such a group, working conditions are "optimal." Employees describe their offices as "classy," with "lots of dark mahogany on walls and desks" and "original Norman Rockwell paintings." The office "just oozes success." Dress at Allen is "sharp but conservative," even though employees often work with "flashy media clients."

The firm is social, since it is "full of people who schmooze for a living." Senior bankers who have perfected their schmoozing skills take part in Allen & Co.'s "famed annual retreat for media moguls" in Sun Valley, Idaho with "spectacular guests like Bill Gates and Mike Eisner in attendance." This sort of networking means that while Allen "isn't a household name," it "carries almost as much mystique as CAA [Creative Artists Agency]" in the media business. While some insiders mention there are several women in "senior positions," others report that Allen is "still mostly a male firm."

Risk-taking culture

In addition to "above-average" bonuses, our sources adore the opportunity to "invest in Allen & Co. deals and share in profits." One banker says, "The culture here is one of risk-taking, both on a personal and corporate level. You must have a significant portion of your net worth at risk if you want to work here, and you must be a fee generator soon after arriving." Confides another contact: "There's salary plus a

Hungry for more inside scoop? Join Vault.com's popular online
community for finance and banking — www.vault.com

VAULT.com **155**

percentage of the fees from deals that you work on. You get paid when a fee comes in — no waiting for year-end bonus. If you have a bad year, tough luck. On the other hand, there is no theoretical limit on the upside."

Because of this payment structure, the firm is "incredibly entrepreneurial" and suited for "driven and individualistic" employees: "There is no face time or kissing up to get a big bonus." Workload is "very much dependent on what you are working on" but is generally described as "better than your other Wall Street banks," in part because face time is not a priority. "All that counts is your ability to make abnormally high returns for the firm while maintaining an absolutely clean reputation," explains one insider. "The firm's reputation is paramount. Anyone that does anything unethical or illegal will be removed." As one Allen insider summarizes, "While [Allen & Co.] is a great place, it is unlikely that it would be suited for most people."

"The culture here is one of risk-taking, both on a personal and corporate level."

— *Allen & Company Insider*

Banc of America Securities

9 West 57th Street
New York, NY 10019
(212) 583-8000
Fax: (212) 847-6918
www.bofasecurities.com

LOCATIONS

New York (HQ)
Boston
Charlotte
Chicago
Palo Alto
San Francisco
*Numerous other locations in the
U.S. and Canada*

DEPARTMENTS

Corporate and Investment Banking
Credit Products
Debt Capital Raising
Private Client Services
Real Estate Banking
Sales, Trading and Research — Equity
Sales, Trading and Research — Fixed
   Income Products
Sales and Trading — Global Markets
   Group

THE STATS

CEO: Lewis Coleman
Employer Type: Subsidiary of
Bank of America Corp.
No. of Employees: 4,400
No. of Offices: 22

UPPERS

• More responsibility at junior level
• Up-and-coming firm

DOWNERS

• Employee turnover
• Post-merger integration issues

KEY COMPETITORS

Chase H&Q
Donaldson, Lufkin & Jenrette
J.P. Morgan
Lehman Brothers
SG Cowen
Thomas Weisel Partners

EMPLOYMENT CONTACT

Ronni Greenberg
Banc of America Securities Staffing
9 West 57th Street
New York, NY 10019
(212) 583-8000
Fax: (212) 847-6918

THE SCOOP

The heart of San Francisco

Born of complicated merger history, Banc of America Securities is the investment banking arm of Bank of America Corporation, a Charlotte, NC-based commercial bank. Bank of America is the largest bank in the United States with over $614 billion in assets, and provides a solid corporate client base to Banc of America Securities. BofA Securities, as the investment bank is commonly known, has focused on companies in 11 primary industries: technology, consumer, health care, real estate, financial services, insurance, technology, entertainment, media and telecommunications, natural resources, and diversified industries. In addition, the company relies upon its ability to integrate its large research and trading departments, which are the largest outside New York City. The private client services department utilizes the resources of the firm to provide investment services to wealthy individuals and families. The investment banking practice is headquartered in New York, but the firm also maintains an investment banking presence in San Francisco and in Charlotte.

Tricky mergers

In 1997 NationsBank Corp., then the fourth-largest bank in the United States, acquired investment bank Montgomery Securities. NationsBank paid a pretty penny for its new subsidiary — the pact cost NationsBank an estimated $1.2 billion in cash and stock. The investment banking practice was renamed NationsBanc Montgomery Securities. While Montgomery was said to have been searching for a partner to take a minority stake, the overwhelming embrace of NationsBank may have taken the firm by surprise. The changes kept coming. In early 1998, NationsBank announced a merger with BankAmerica in a deal that created the second-largest commercial bank in the U.S. (trailing only Citibank in size). In September 1998, Montgomery Chairman/CEO Thomas Weisel resigned his post after close to a year of power struggles with NationsBank. The bank had been extremely aggressive in its efforts to tame the "highly entrepreneurial" securities firm. Weisel's exit was not a complete surprise — firm insiders report that he had voiced objections to a number of decisions made by NationsBank concerning its new securities division. For example, though it was understood that the investment banking arm would control the firm's combined (and extremely lucrative) high yield business, NationsBank eventually took control of that group, reportedly in preparation for the bank's merger with BankAmerica Corp. The situation was further aggravated when NationsBank announced that the private equity investing business would be turned over to BankAmerica instead of staying with Montgomery. After the merger, BankAmerica renamed itself Bank of America. The new parent also erased the Montgomery name, renaming its I-banking arm Banc of America Securities.

Industry observers expected that bankers loyal to Weisel would follow his lead, and they did. Approximately 100 bankers left BofA within a year of the merger, and many of them joined their former boss at his newly formed firm, Thomas Weisel Partners. BofA's biotech practice was practically decimated, as I-banking insiders whispered that the firm would drop the industry altogether. But Bank of America fought back. Led by Carter McClelland, the former head of Deutsche Bank in the U.S., the firm has been dangling can't-pass-up compensation packages to lure talent from competitors. McClelland told *The Daily Deal* that while the firm lost about 100 bankers, it managed to hire another 125 within the year. Whether the newly made division will be as successful as the former remains to be seen.

Still not free of Weisel

In February 2000, *Securities Week* reported that BofA Securities was suing Thomas Weisel Partners for $500 million in damages. BofA alleged that Weisel had raided BofA for staff at his new firm. The two parties are currently in arbitration.

Though BofA has reportedly re-staffed and moved on after Thomas Weisel's exodus, the small world of investment banks still reunites the two on occasion. In January 2000, BofA advised JDS Uniphase on its $15 billion acquisition of E-Tek Dynamic, serving as a secondary advisor on the deal. The lead advisor was Thomas Weisel Partners. The deal represented the largest M&A mandate (at the time) for both firms and that each firm had to share the success with its old nemesis was not ignored by the press.

Moving on

While 1999 may not have been the year BofA broke into the big leagues, it still proved to be a year of strong improvement for the firm. BofA Securities underwrote 94 common stock transactions worth $23.2 billion, which represents a firm record. BofA also advised on 107

Hungry for more inside scoop? Join Vault.com's popular online
community for finance and banking — www.vault.com

VAULT.com **161**

completed M&A transactions valued in aggregate at $22.6 billion. On the league tables, the firm ranked eighth in investment grade debt (up from number 10 in 1998), 10th in high yield (up from the 12 spot in 1998), 10th among underwriters of all debt and equity (up again from the 12 spot), and ninth among underwriters of asset backed securities (up from the 11th spot previous year). The firm also made major strides in the real estate M&A business, advising on over $10.7 billion in real estate, lodging and gaming M&A transactions in 1999. During 1999 the firm co-lead managed a $790 million common stock offering for EOG Resources, the largest equity offering by an independent oil and gas company. Also in 1999, BofA acted as the sole lead-manager of a $450 million high yield offering for Stater Brothers, a supermarket chain. Finally the company lead-managed IPOs for eCollege.com, Matalink, and Metron Technology. In July 2000, the firm served as co-advisor (along with CIBC World Markets) to JDS Uniphase on its $41 billion acquisition of SDL. JDS, incidentally, was advised by Thomas Weisel Partners. The deal, the largest technology merger to date, represents a major stride by Banc of America Securities towards becoming a major player in the investment banking world.

GETTING HIRED

BofA conducts on-campus recruiting at select universities. Applicants from schools not visited by the I-banking division should submit résumés to jobs@bofasecurities.com. Those who wish to join Banc of America Securities outside San Francisco will be happy to learn the I-banking division has expanded its presence in Charlotte (the headquarters of parent Bank of America) and especially in New York. "The old Montgomery was pretty much all here in San Francisco; now we want to make sure that we have a presence on both [coasts] that's substantial," reports one I-banking analyst. According to BofA recruiting representatives, of approximately 75 analysts hired by the firm in 1999, about 10 were based in San Francisco, 10 in Charlotte, 30 in New York, and about 25 analysts worked in the firm's other offices in cities such as Houston or Chicago. Those interested in M&A should know that the firm's dedicated M&A product group is in New York (although analysts and associates also can work on such transactions through their industry groups). Investment banking co-head Carter McClelland told *The Daily Deal* in early 2000 that the firm will have to double or triple its number of M&A bankers over the next four years.

Finally, in March 2000, the firm moved bankers to a new office in Palo Alto in order to garner more tech deals.

Insiders report that the firm recruits from "Ivy League and larger regional schools." MBAs say candidates can generally expect two rounds of interviews. "The first round is more technical and more 'why do you like us and why do you want to do banking?' The second round is definitely determining whether [the candidate] fits with employees at BofA," says one associate. The firm hires MBAs into I-banking as generalists — they work across product and industry groups before specializing in one of the firm's nine industry groups such as technology or health care, or one of its product groups such as private equity or M&A. Explains one insider about the placement process: "It's almost like a dating deal. You kind of check people out and they check you out until there's a match; this lasts three or four months until Christmas." BofA also hires MBAs as associates into its sales and trading, research, credit products, fixed income, global corporate debt, and private client departments. MBAs are hired into all of BofA offices.

OUR SURVEY SAYS

The turnover

Banc of America Securities insiders do not shy away from admitting that the firm has seen significant changes, most prominently with the turnover that occurred as Thomas Weisel left the firm. "I'm not going to lie to you, there was a period here where there was a lot of turnover and a lot of uncertainty," reports one analyst insider. "Half the class that I came with is not here now. But the people who stayed, they understand what the opportunity is." An associate concurs: "It was a stage of uncertainty that wasn't the most effective time for the firm, but it's a stage that's gone. People had to decide what they want to do, and in a way it was healthy. I mean, you've got to pick your team."

Continues that contact: "As an organization, we have gone through a significant stage of maturity — going from a younger company with a founder to a larger organization. It's not all hoots and hollers — I mean, I liked the old Montgomery, but business demands more capital. We are making the decision that the market's demanding." BofA insiders agree that the atmosphere is now one of optimism, as the firm looks to

Hungry for more inside scoop? Join Vault.com's popular online community for finance and banking — www.vault.com

VAULT.com 163

challenge bulge-bracket firms. "We're constantly getting e-mail memos about moving up in the rankings, that's where the focus is — I think everybody is optimistic," says one research associate. Another associate describes the firm's reputation as "up-and-coming." This associate goes on to explain, "[BofA is] starting to develop great momentum in 2000. We definitely will surprise some people with deal rankings [in 2000]." Insiders worry that the firm has yet to strike a positive cord within the industry. When asked about BofA's perception among the industry, one insider notes, "It's okay but not great. People usually remember the old Montgomery and wonder what happened."

Less uptight

Insiders also report a firm culture that is "a little less uptight than the average investment bank" and "entrepreneurial." Says another source, "I think teamwork is a much more important term than it used to be. Ten years ago at Montgomery, the most important characteristic was individual aggressiveness. It was a very small firm, and individuals had to go out and get an account, and they did it by themselves. Now we are much more about working as a team." "From a corporate finance perspective, we joined with guys who have tons of relationships that we have never cultivated," says another optimistic contact. "There's so many more feet on the street to turn up more ideas too — if we do this right, there should be no shortage of deals." Continues that contact, "There may be a guy on the credit side who has a previous relationship with a company that we've never dealt with, and he'll say, 'This company wants equity research,' and we've never done it before. You have to deal with some of these calls. But sometimes it leads to new business."

"It's not the kind of wild, wild, west banking that there used to be," says one source. "In the past, we were known as the equity shop, doing $20 million IPOs. Well, the fact is, nowadays, our criteria is for bigger and better things. Although we still focus on growth companies, we can now offer them different products, such as credit or high yield." Also, says that insider, "We haven't lost our focus on growth companies or young companies, but we've added the dimension that we can talk to companies that we never talked to before."

Still aggressive

Insiders are quick to point out that the firm is no slow-moving behemoth, but a culture of "deal-driven mentalities." This aggressiveness is a function not only of the firm's size, but also of its clientele, our contacts say. "Both of our institutions [the former Montgomery and former NationsBank] are young, so we don't have century-old accounts which are the firm's accounts," explains one source. "For example, Goldman has been banking Sears for who knows how long, and the way that client is serviced is through a very large, very deep team of people. When I'm working with growth companies, there are thinner teams, and we can give younger people more opportunity." Another associate reports that he has "extensive contact with CEOs and CFOs of all clients." That contact goes on to say, "As with any firm, one needs to prove oneself before getting responsibility. Once you do that, senior bankers give you a lot of latitude. Associates act like VPs." An I-banking analyst agrees: "It's a much more independent kind of analyst experience. I think the staffing here is not as stacked hierarchically. You're going to work one-on-one with your MD and VPs — that's sort of expected." Reports another associate, "We have a flatter organizational structure."

People issues

Insiders at BofA generally speak highly of co-workers. "Everyone is pretty friendly and good to work with," reports one insider. In terms of diversity, most bankers report that the firm is "fairly diverse for the industry," though at least one contact mentions the firm has "very few females" in the senior ranks. Hours are considered "livable" and one M&A associate estimates an average work week as "ranging from 65 to 75 hours." That contact also reports the quality of work as "decent." He explains, "About 65 percent [of my work] is execution of real deals and 35 percent [is] pitching and prospecting."

In describing turnover at BofA compared to that at other investment banks, insider opinions vary from "a little better than other banks" to "turnover seems a little high." One source sees retention as one of the firm's biggest problems. He explains, "[BofA] is so busy trying to move into the bulge bracket that [the firm] overlooks talent that is already here." According to contacts, in order to address lifestyle issues and stem defections, the firm has offered "associate happy hours, business casual dress, and Blackberry wireless devices" among other perks. These changes are generally viewed by insiders as "token gestures," though. One source explains that "[BofA is] not addressing the real issues," one of which is pay. "We believe we are below the Street average and are hearing of other firms raising pay to retain

Hungry for more inside scoop? Join Vault.com's popular online
community for finance and banking — www.vault.com

VAULT.com **165**

employees." Another insider concurs that the current changes are not adequate to retain employees: "If [BofA] gave salary guarantees, that would be different."

San Francisco banking

Insiders at Banc of America Securities' San Francisco office report that there is a definite difference between Bay Area banking and Wall Street. "There are not enough investment bankers in San Francisco to have our own culture," reports one insider. "I think it's more balanced — you don't run around with a bunch of other bankers comparing bonuses. You keep your perspective." "There is a completely different experience out here," contends another BofA analyst. "The people who are out here are out here for a reason. So they are much more conscious of your well-being or your happiness — I think people are more aware of analysts and their happiness than at a normal firm." "If you are banking in San Francisco, you made a decision not to go to Wall Street," says yet another contact, "and that kind of indicates a certain personality, which in my experience means a little more laid-back, a little more approachable, and interested in more than being Gordon Gekko."

"We tend to do the same hours as they do on Wall Street, we just adjust the time zone — at 7 o'clock there are a lot of people, and at 8 at night we tend to thin out," reports one I-banking insider. "It helps to be a morning person." Another source contends that San Fran BofA bankers work slightly fewer hours than bankers on Wall Street, but that the difference is not significant. "In terms of the amount of time, I'm in by 7:30 in the morning, but the fact is most nights I'm not going to leave until 9 or 10," says one analyst. "All in all it's about the same, but I think there's a definite difference in terms of face time as compared to New York."

"As an organization, we have gone through a significant stage of maturity, going from a younger company with a founder to a larger organization."

— *BofA Securities Insider*

Bear Stearns

245 Park Avenue
New York, NY 10167
(212) 272-2000
Fax: (212) 272-4785
www.bearstearns.com

LOCATIONS

New York (HQ)
Atlanta
Boston
Chicago
Dallas
Los Angeles
San Francisco
San Juan

Beijing
Buenos Aires
Dublin
Hong Kong
London
Lugano
São Paulo
Shanghai
Singapore
Tokyo

DEPARTMENTS

Asset Management
Custodial Trust Company
E-commerce
Fixed Income
Foreign Exchange
Futures
Global Clearing Services
Global Derivatives
Institutional Equities
Investment Banking
Merchant Banking
Private Client Services
Real Estate

THE STATS

CEO: James E. Cayne
Co-heads of Investment Banking:
David Glaser and Jeffrey Urwin
Employer Type: Public Company
Ticker Symbol: BSC (NYSE)
1999 Net Revenue: $4.5 billion
1999 Net Income: $673 million
No. of Employees: 9,808
No. of Offices: 17

UPPERS

• Less bureaucratic than most firms
• Responsibility early in your career

DOWNERS

• Not in the big leagues yet
• Rubber bands rare

KEY COMPETITORS

Credit Suisse First Boston
Donaldson, Lufkin & Jenrette
J.P. Morgan
Lehman Brothers
Prudential Securities
UBS Warburg

EMPLOYMENT CONTACT

Investment Banking
Melissa Salerno
245 Park Avenue
New York, NY 10167
Fax: (212) 272-3052

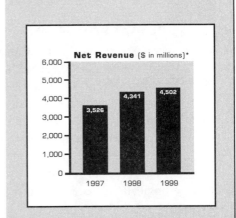

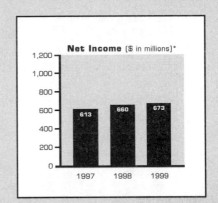

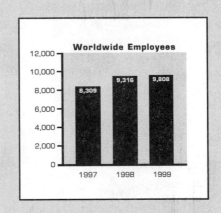

* Fiscal year end June 30

THE SCOOP

Always profitable

Bear Stearns is younger than many of its high-profile rivals, but the firm's reputation stands up to those of its competitors. Known as "Bear" to Wall Street players, the venerable institution is one of the nation's top investment banking, securities trading, and brokerage firms. With about half a million dollars in capital among the three of them, Joseph Bear, Robert Stearns, and Harold Mayer started Bear Stearns in 1923. The firm initially operated with a small staff out of a single office at 100 Broadway. Founded as a partnership, Bear Stearns originally focused on brokerage.

With a gamut of financial services available, Bear Stearns now serves as financial advisor to many of the nation's major corporations, and its clearing operations are a top choice of brokerage and other investment firms around the country, including many of its own rivals. After a few years of profit hibernation during the early 1990s, Bear Stearns has bounced back and is currently outgrowing its office space at a rapid pace. Bear has something of a ferocious reputation for cultivating a sink-or-swim culture and is headed by a colorful chairman so thrifty that he reportedly ties broken rubber bands back together. But Bear employees report being satisfied with the relatively small (by Wall Street standards) organization — and the entrepreneurial possibilities and sense of responsibility that the firm promotes.

Not at the top (but trying)

Despite consistent returns — the firm has topped 18 percent in returns on equity (a common yardstick for a well-performing investment bank) for four straight years — Bear Stearns has not broken into the upper echelon of Wall Street I-banks. Apart from some businesses, such as public finance (underwriting and issuing municipal bonds), in which the firm ranks in the top five consistently, and mortgage backed securities, in which the firm consistently ranks in the top three, Bear Stearns usually hovers at the bottom of the top 10 in the league tables. In 1999 the firm did not make the list of top 10 advisors of completed worldwide M&A transactions or the top 10 underwriters of U.S. IPOs.

Another area where the firm fell behind was European expansion. In 1999 European M&A hit an all-time high, with over $1.2 trillion in transaction volume. However, Bear didn't grab a substantial amount of this expanding pie compared to competitors like Morgan Stanley, Goldman Sachs, or even lower-tiered competition such as Lehman Brothers and J.P. Morgan. According to a March 2000 report in *The Daily Deal*, unnamed sources claim the firm plans to spend about $200 million to grow its investment banking business in Europe. Bear Stearns made great strides in Europe in May 2000, when it poached 11 London-based telecommunication bankers from Dresdner Kleinwort Benson. The team is headed by Michael Phair, who now serves as co-head of telecom banking at Bear. The new hires reportedly more than doubled the staff of the telecommunications group and brought the total number of European bankers at Bear to 65.

Impressive deals

Despite its inability to break into the upper echelon, Bear still manages to participate in some of Wall Street's most notable deals. In late 1999, Warner-Lambert retained Bear for its merger discussions with Pfizer. Bear also advised Honeywell on its merger with Allied Signal during 1999. The Honeywell deal was named "Best Strategic Deal of the Year" by *Mergers & Acquisitions: The Dealmaker's Journal*. The firm also lead-managed the largest municipal bond issue ever — a $3.5 billion issue for the Long Island Power Authority. Bear's reputation as a risk-taking, entrepreneurial-style firm has aided the growth of its technology investment banking area, and the firm has managed several high-profile IPOs for some very successful Internet enterprises. In 1999 the firm took what is now About.com public with an $86.25 million offering, handled the $168 million Prodigy Communications IPO, and lead managed IPOs for Wit Capital and MotherNature.com.

Alan Greenberg: An "Ace" in the Hole

With the odd business guidelines handed down to Bear Stearns employees from the desk of longtime chairman Alan "Ace" Greenberg, people might start thinking that the investment banking powerhouse is scraping for pennies. Greenberg has earned a national reputation for his humorous (and sometimes biting) memos, which were collected into a book entitled *Memos From the Chairman*. Greenberg's memos have espoused the benefits of reusing rubber bands (if they're broken, simply tie the loose ends. Repeat process ad infinitum) and conserving paperclips. Ace even encourages employees to inform upon colleagues who might be breaking one of the chairman's rules (and this goes for all levels of professionals).

Hungry for more inside scoop? Join Vault.com's popular online community for finance and banking — www.vault.com

VAULT.com **171**

Yet Greenberg's own actions outside of the boardroom go a long way toward shattering his kooky-yet-stern image. It is perhaps one of Wall Street's worst kept secrets — though few would risk Greenberg's wrath by dwelling on such non-miserly affairs — that thrifty Ace is also a top-flight philanthropist. For the last 25 years, Greenberg has donated millions of dollars from his own salary to top New York institutions.

Ending the year like the big boys

In late 1999, Bear Stearns announced a change in its fiscal year-end date from June 30 to November 30. Morgan Stanley, Goldman Sachs, Lehman Brothers and many other Wall Street firms have long used November 30 or December 30 as fiscal year-ends. Historically, with Bear's summer year-end, the firm paid bonuses to employees in August. This payment practice made Bear particularly vulnerable to competitors who would try and poach Bear bankers in the early fall. Employees could leave Bear with a full paycheck at the end of August to join a competitor. After Bear paid bonuses in August 1999, the firm lost the co-head of investment banking, two senior managing directors, and six health care bankers to other firms. Eventually, with the new calendar change, bankers will be paid bonuses in January, as they generally are at other firms. Bear is also trying to develop more incentive compensation, handing out some pay in the form of stock options in order to retain more talent.

Like nearly every other major Wall Street bank, Bear's ability to attract and retain bankers has been affected by the increasing number of Internet economy opportunities. In addition to changing the timing and structure of compensation to retain talent, Bear has also headed an aggressive campaign to attract top-notch bankers from other firms. In May 2000, Ilan Kaufthal joined Bear as a senior managing director and vice chairman of its investment banking division. Kaufthal, whom *The Daily Deal* called a "top dealmaker," joined Bear from Schroder & Co., where he was vice chairman and head of mergers and acquisitions.

Clearing the way

Bear Stearns derives more than a third of its profits and 30 percent of its revenue from its clearing business. Clearing firms basically process much of the paperwork that goes along with brokering. The company is hired to execute trades, maintain client records, send out trade confirmations and monthly statements, and settle transactions. Close to

2,900 clients employ Bear for clearing, and even rival firms such as Lehman Brothers have employed the department's services. Primarily smaller brokerages use the firm's services, as the appearance of Bear Stearns' prestigious name on paperwork investors receive is often a selling point.

Unfortunately, Bear Stearns' clearing operations have also generated some unwanted attention. One of the many brokerages for which the firm has cleared transactions, A.R. Baron, collapsed after bilking as many as 8,000 investors out of more than $75 million. The government investigated a possible Bear Stearns role in the Baron case — in particular, the ties between former Baron CEO Andrew Bressman and Richard Harriton, Bear Stearns' chief of clearing. Bear agreed in June 1999 to pay $38.5 million in restitution and penalties to settle the SEC charges. In April 2000, Harriton paid a $1 million fine as a settlement with the SEC. Under the terms of his settlement, Harriton paid the fine and was banned for life from the securities industry but did not admit to or deny the charges.

Bear's clearing troubles were not yet behind it. A few weeks prior to Harriton's settlement, Bear was named in a class action lawsuit by Cromer Finance. Cromer Finance invested in Manhattan Investment Fund, a $400 million hedge fund that lost nearly $300 million. The fund's manager, Michael Berger, is accused by the SEC of covering up these losses. According to the lawsuit against Bear, the company was aware in 1998 that Berger was losing large amounts of investor money but did not act to hinder his activities. The suit also charges that Bear slyly hinted to certain investors, with whom the investment bank had other business relationships, that they should pull out of the fund.

That wasn't the last of the firm's legal problems either. The bank was ordered to pay a Canadian investor $111.5 million by a federal grand jury in May 2000; the trial judge tacked interest onto the verdict, bringing Bear Stearns' payment total up to $164 million. The wealthy investor claimed his Bear Stearns broker failed to disclose the risks involved in currency trades he made in the late mid- to late-1990s. Bear countered that the client, who at one time had currency positions valued at $6.5 billion, was a sophisticated investor well aware of the risks he was facing. The award, one of the largest against a Wall Street firm, led to a significant drag on the bank's second-quarter 2000 earnings, which were $118.4 million — down from $198.1 million for the same period in 1999.

Hungry for more inside scoop? Join Vault.com's popular online community for finance and banking — www.vault.com

VAULT.com   **173**

GETTING HIRED

For investment banking, the firm targets approximately 12 business schools. At these schools, either the co-head of investment banking or another high-ranking official makes a presentation. At about five other business schools, the firm interviews but does not give presentations.

Bear Stearns draws many of its associates through its summer programs. The firm hires about 50 summer I-banking associates (mostly in New York) and about 50 full-time associates worldwide (New York summer associates can move full-time into one of the firm's regional offices). The summer hiring process is condensed into a three-week process. The first round is usually an on-campus, two-on-one interview. While students at some schools will travel to Bear's New York headquarters for second rounds, many will simply interview again that evening on-campus. For example, since the University of Chicago business school does not provide for time off from classes to travel for interviews, Bear conducts both first and second rounds on campus. "Depending on what our competitors' schedules are, sometimes it makes sense to just go ahead and give the offer that night," says one recruiter. According to the firm, anywhere from 55 to 75 percent of I-banking summer associates return for full-time positions.

The firm also generally targets about 40 undergraduate schools each year. It hires about 100 analysts into I-banking worldwide, and about 75 of them work in New York. Although Bear accepts résumés from all undergraduate schools, for summer analyst positions Bear likes to have representation from its core schools — the firm only recruits on campus for summer analysts at Wharton, Dartmouth, Michigan and the University of Virginia.

The firm doesn't recruit undergrads for sales and trading, although those with BAs who complete the firm's operations training program can go into sales and trading. For associates in sales, trading, research, and public finance, the firm recruits on campus at 10 business schools — NYU, Columbia, Harvard, Wharton, Chicago, Kellogg, Stanford, UCLA, Fuqua, and Darden. Says a recruiter, "We do very well with Columbia, NYU, and Chicago; those are our three best." Associates are hired into one of four departments: fixed income, equity, research, or public finance. Candidates in these areas can expect one-on-one interviews, with probably two rounds. "For a full-time hire, you have to have six interviews," according to one insider. Summer hires generally go through an on-campus round and then one callback.

About 50 to 75 percent of the sales, trading, and public finance associate class is hired through the summer program. In these departments, the firm hires about 20 to 25 summer associates and about 20 full-time associates. All fixed income hires complete 12 weeks of rotations, covering six different desks, and are placed after that; the equity division hires students for both specific slots and as generalists. All research positions are hired on an as-needed basis.

OUR SURVEY SAYS

You're not going to a factory

One thing that Bear employees love to point out is that the firm offers "so much responsibility that it automatically becomes a rewarding experience." Explains one I-banking associate, "You're going to a firm that's large and has its fair share of marquee deals, but you're not going to a factory." Says an associate in sales and trading: "The culture's pretty straightforward as far as giving you important work from day one." That contact notes that his B-school friends at other firms were "given projects that the senior managing director already knew the answer to." Another associate reports, "Bear has a little bit of a reputation as an aggressive shop, but I've found the people are very relaxed. There is hierarchy, but it isn't pounded into you. There is a lot of fundamental human respect." Many employees say that they enjoy their "autonomy," which leaves them "free from obnoxious bureaucracy." According to one sales and trading associate: "The SMD [senior managing director] in my group trades. He's not just sitting in an office. It's just like the way Ace [Alan Greenberg] sits on the floor." But surely the firm's chairman doesn't roll up his sleeves to do any serious work? Not so, say insiders. "Alan?" says one. "He trades."

Make your mark

Because "there's very little structure, you have to find your own way" at Bear Stearns. The "flat organization" of the firm enables everyone "to make an impact at any level." Says one source: "Every place *says* they're entrepreneurial — this place *is* entrepreneurial." The firm also allows for "individual stars to shine." Because of Bear Stearns' "thorough commitment to recognizing individual merit, those who perform well can really hold their heads up high." One junior banker

Hungry for more inside scoop? Join Vault.com's popular online community for finance and banking — www.vault.com

V/\ULT.com **175**

explains, "There's an openness here to new ideas. If I do something unique, it's going to get noticed and appreciated."

Concludes one sales associate: "It's not just that they throw you a big ball and tell you to run with it. They maybe give you a little ball, and you can dribble around with it and if you do well then you get a bigger ball."

Sink or swim?

While insiders note the lack of hand-holding that might be present at some other firms, at least one Bear employee says everyone has the "the chance to become a star player for the firm." Some employees say the firm has a "survival of the fittest" mentality which "extends into all ranks." Indeed, Bear has this reputation outside the firm, which other insiders say is overblown. "You hear things, but I quickly found out that it wasn't the case," reports one I-banking associate. "This is not a place where you play 'duck, duck, goose,' but I think there's as much personal contact as at other firms." Bear employees are quick to point out that the firm is not a completely sink-or-swim environment, saying that they are provided support from senior employees. I-banking associates are assigned a junior and a senior mentor (a VP as the junior mentor and an MD as the senior mentor). Says an associate in sales and trading: "The guy who sits behind me is my mentor. The guy who sits in front of me is my mentor. I learn something from them every day." Says another associate: "Bear Stearns is a healthy competitive environment. The bottom line is to make money. If all that they say about back stabbing and sink-or-swim were true, how the hell would we make any money?" While most are very proud of the firm's entrepreneurial, go-getter culture, others express a desire to climb into the big leagues. Says one insider, "We have been considered exciting up-and-comers, but we can't be that forever. At some point, we're actually going to have to make a push for the top tier."

No paper clips for you

The Bear Stearns support staff has been described by employees as "the best available." Unlike at other Wall Street firms, there are plenty of secretaries to go around, though some offices may have a limited number depending upon their needs. Word processing and data entry services are also available and interns are plentiful and available for all research needs. However, several employees confirm that "the firm does emphasize thrift." The firm distributes a bag of paper clips and rubber bands to each new employee, with a memo from Ace Greenberg that reminds them that "the best poker players leave nothing on the table" (i.e., even in booming markets, watching expenses pays off). Says one banker about the dearth of supplies, "No joke, if I see a paper clip on the floor or a pen on somebody's desk — if somebody's stupid enough to leave a pen on their desk — I take it."

In terms of how the firm has changed in order to retain bankers, insiders offer mixed opinions on both the changes and the necessity for them. The firm has initiated a full-time business casual dress policy, and expanded meal and other expense allowances. "Some concessions have been made," says one source, "but Bear tends to attract the kind of person who wants to work on Wall Street. They've always paid well compared to the rest of the Street." Adds another contact, "I have faith in the fundamental fairness of the firm." Not all insiders are so optimistic: "Bear is a very steady organization. While we're very entrepreneurial in culture, we haven't been cutting-edge in changes."

Hungry for more inside scoop? Join Vault.com's popular online
community for finance and banking — www.vault.com

VAULT.com **177**

Broadview International

One Bridge Plaza
Fort Lee, NJ 07024
(201) 346-9000
Fax: (201) 346-9191
www.broadview.com

LOCATIONS

Fort Lee (HQ)
Foster City
Waltham
London
Tokyo

DEPARTMENTS

Investment Banking
Mergers and Acquisitions
Venture Capital

THE STATS

Chairman & CEO: Paul Deninger
Employer Type: Private Company
No. of Employees: 300
No. of Offices: 5

UPPERS

- Extensive contact with clients
- Great responsibility at junior levels

DOWNERS

- Commute to New Jersey
- Not in on the big deals

KEY COMPETITORS

Credit Suisse First Boston
Donaldson, Lufkin & Jenrette
Robertson Stephens
Wasserstein Perella

EMPLOYMENT CONTACT

Justin Kulo
Broadview International
One Bridge Plaza
Fort Lee, NJ 07024

THE SCOOP

Specialists in tech M&A

Founded in 1973, Broadview International has become a major player in the mergers and acquisitions field, especially in middle-market transactions. Broadview has especially become a leader in technology and media deals. The firm executed 125 transactions in 1999, with a cumulative value of $15.4 billion. Broadview ranked 16th overall among advisors of M&A transactions in 1999, but ranked first among advisors of deals valued between $25 million and $500 million. Broadview, once known as Broadview Associates, has 300 employees in five worldwide offices.

100 deals makes you CEO

Broadview is led by Paul Deninger, who has held the chairman and CEO post since 1997. Deninger holds a Harvard MBA and a BS from Boston College and joined the firm in 1987 after three years in the software industry. He has been involved in over 100 transactions, specifically in the tech and Internet fields. In the November 1999 issue of *Fortune*, Deninger advised against the IPO route upon which so many Internet entrepreneurs seem dead set. Instead, he steers them towards a merger or buyout — a little self-serving, given his line of work, but the advice is not without its merits. "If you have the opportunity to be the Cisco of your market, you are crazy not to go public," Deninger told *Forbes*. "But if you will not be the Cisco in your space, you should sell, because your ability to generate long-term shareholder returns is limited. History shows that the cards are stacked against you."

Recent deals

The company's reputation as a heavy hitter in the M&A arena is supported by its recent transactions. In December 1999, Broadview advised Blue Mountain Arts on its $780 million sale to Excite@Home. Later that month, Broadview advised E*Trade when the online stockbroker purchased a 100 percent stake in its British affiliate, E*Trade UK. In February 2000, Broadview advised Aspect Communications on its $55 million purchase of Salem, N.H.-based software maker PakNetX. The company acted as an advisor to RightWorks when the e-procurement software developer sold a 53 percent stake to Internet Capital Group in March 2000. Broadview also served as advisor to BlueGill Technologies when CheckFree purchased BlueGill for approximately $240 million in April 2000. More recent deals include advising PairGain Technologies on its $1.6 billion sale to ADC, announced in February 2000 (still pending), and advising ChiliSoft on its $70 million sale to Cobalt Networks, also pending after a March 2000 announcement.

VC partners

Like an increasing number of investment banks and M&A shops, Broadview has been known to dabble in venture capital. Kennet Capital is a London-based venture capital fund that is the product of a joint venture between Broadview and Electra Fleming Limited, an investment firm with $2 billion of capital under management. AxcessNet is an IT venture fund that focuses on Israeli companies; the company has offices in Israel, London, and Boston. Finally, there's Broadview Capital Partners, a $250 million fund co-managed by Stephen Bachmann, a Broadview managing director and board member, and Steven Brooks, a Broadview managing director and the former head of technology M&A at Donaldson, Lufkin & Jenrette.

GETTING HIRED

Super Saturday

Broadview recruits analysts and associates at leading schools in the U.S. and Europe. Calendars for presentations and on-campus interviews can be found at www.broadview.com. Unlike some other investment banks, Broadview prefers one-on-one interviews to two-on-ones. The process for analysts involves an on-campus interview (or one at the firm's headquarters) and then a "super day," usually a Saturday, with four to six interviews. Insiders say you can expect to see at least two senior bankers, typically managing directors.

Despite the firm's focus on the IT industry, insiders say firm representatives "don't specifically look for a tech background." Explains one contact: "I would say you need to have a passion for tech; there's just as much talk about acronyms like ISDN [Integrated Services Digital Network] as there is about P/E ratios. They'll ask you, 'Tell me

Hungry for more inside scoop? Join Vault.com's popular online
community for finance and banking — www.vault.com

VAULT.com **181**

something about technology that interests you.' If you say the Internet is the coolest thing in the world, they'll ask you to qualify that."

The firm hires undergrads into a two-year analyst program. Analysts begin with a three-week training program in the firm's Foster City, California office, which brings analysts from all of the firm's offices together. "It's all taught by internal people," reports one contact. "It's a lot of finance and some [tech] industry stuff." If an analyst does a third year, which the firm reportedly encourages, he or she can switch offices. The firm will pay business school tuition for outstanding analysts who pledge to return, insiders say. The firm also directly promotes a few analysts to the associate level.

In the past, associate classes at Broadview were comprised of "engineers who went back for MBAs," but as the firm grows, insiders say, it is looking at more business school students with straight finance backgrounds. Reports one insider: "When you come on as an associate at Broadview, [the firm] expects you to become a partner." A company official outlines the career path to partnership: one-and-a-half years until making senior associate, at which time an associate begins to specialize in a sector like software or hardware; then approximately two years to principal; and then two to three years to partnership. All told, the path to managing director takes anywhere from five to six-and-a-half years from one's start date.

OUR SURVEY SAYS

Fortunate niche

Broadview is a rapidly growing firm. Explains one insider: "Basically, Broadview turned a corner from concentrating on a niche that nobody gave a shit about to a niche that everybody gave a shit about. [Broadview] got kind of lucky in that tech went nuts." Still, the firm is far from a machine, and insiders note the firm still provides a lifestyle that is characteristic of working for a smaller firm. Says one contact about the firm's growth in the past several years: "If you take a look at Wall Street — at the typical Wall Street bank — the people are sort of nasty, and the hours are grueling. If that's a 10, Broadview went from being a one to a four or a five." Says that contact: "The hours are maybe 60 to 65 a week — that's a week at Club Med compared to Wall Street."

Another contact pegs the hours a little higher. "You have the occasional all-nighter, but it's all about a deal cycle. It's minimum 60 or 70." Continues that source, "Still, it's not expected that you'll be there on the weekends. Though most people do put some time in the weekends, on Fridays it's not like, 'I'll see you tomorrow.'"

No CEO fear

The firm's small size also influences issues like career path and responsibility, insiders report. "Because you're in a small environment, if you're talented, everyone will know that," explains one insider. "The people who are moving quickly, everyone knows about." One former analyst recounts leading a six-hour meeting with the CEO of a client. "I'm not saying that's typical, but if you know your shit, you'll get to do some cool stuff," says another contact. "One of the great things about working at Broadview is that afterwards, you have no fear. You get on the phone with CEOs, and you have no fear because you're doing this all the time at Broadview." Associates "run the entire M&A process" at Broadview, says one source. Broadview's environment makes it more comparable to an Internet start-up company than a bulge-bracket firm, according to representatives of the firm's HR department. "We focus our recruiting strategy in relation to startups as opposed to bulge-bracket firms," says one rep. Also according to firm HR representatives, in 1999 Broadview offered its MBAs compensation that was approximately 20 percent higher than the bulge bracket.

Fort Lee?

Broadview is headquartered in Fort Lee, New Jersey, just across the George Washington Bridge from Manhattan. "Fort Lee itself sucks, no doubt about it, but I don't think it really matters when you're in the office all day," says one insider. There are other reasons that the location may be less than desirable, contacts note. According to one source, most young bankers "and even some of the marrieds" live in Manhattan and "have to file estimated taxes in New York once a quarter. It's such a pain, the CFO sat us down and told us how to do it." But the actual traveling is not a headache. "It's a nice reverse commute. It's [approximately] 15 minutes to the Upper West Side," reports one contact. And if you live in Manhattan, the firm has recently started providing van or car service to Fort Lee in the mornings. The firm also pays for "a car home after 8 p.m." Says one insider about the cab rides home: "It's a New Jersey taxi cab. The people who don't have cars

Hungry for more inside scoop? Join Vault.com's popular online community for finance and banking — www.vault.com

VAULT.com **183**

know all the drivers and their life stories." For drivers and those not inclined to lending sympathetic ears, Broadview offers "free parking in the building."

I love New York

Although the firm's headquarters may be located in suburban New Jersey, insiders say Broadview bankers maintain social lives more representative of their Manhattan homes. "You meet up with each other in the city on Friday or Saturday night," says one contact, "and there are a lot of firm events. They have a welcome picnic, a Halloween party, and a holiday party." Reports another source: "There's a partner [at Broadview] who shoots hoops with all the analysts. Of course, we suck because we're all investment bankers, but he can practically dunk — and he goes out with you to the bar after." According to insiders, the firm's CEO, Paul Deninger, likes to mix it up too. Says one analyst of Deninger's behavior at firm's functions: "He's the last person to leave the dance floor; he outlasts me. He's just very cool. In some ways, you say, 'Wait a minute, I don't want to see the CEO on the dance floor.' But on the other hand, it's cool."

A broad bill of fare

Aside from firm functions, Broadview bankers enjoy other perks such as dinners when staying late. There's no real "rule" on how late a banker must stay in order to qualify for the dinner. There are also no strict policies on how much a banker can bill for dinner. As one insider points out, "It's New Jersey. It's not like New York, where you could actually bill a very expensive meal. People are reasonable." Another bonus available to employees at the firm's headquarters is catered lunch (on the firm's tab) on Wednesdays and Fridays. "The firm buys lunch for everyone," a contact explains. "It's usually good — it's not Burger King. We've had sandwiches or Italian or sushi. They've gotten very creative."

"Fort Lee itself sucks, no
doubt about it, but I don't
think it really matters
when you're in the
office all day."

— *Broadview Insider*

The Chase Manhattan Corporation

270 Park Avenue
New York, NY 10017
(212) 270-6000
Fax: (212) 270-2613
www.chase.com

LOCATIONS

New York (HQ)
San Francisco
Hong Kong
London

DEPARTMENTS

Advisory Industry Groups
Debt Underwriting
Equity Underwriting
Institutional Brokerage
Mergers and Acquisitions
Private Equity
Syndicated Loans

THE STATS

Chairman & CEO: William Harrison
**Vice Chairman & Head of
Investment Banking:** Geoffrey Boisi
Employer Type: Public Company
Ticker Symbol: CMB (NYSE)
1999 Net Revenue: $13.5 billion
1999 Net Income: $5.4 billion
No. of Employees: 74,801
No. of Offices: 48 principal offices

UPPERS

- Diverse work environment
- Global reach
- Movement within the bank is encouraged

DOWNERS

- Junior bankers get no respect
- Menial work for junior bankers
- Poor support infrastructure

KEY COMPETITORS

Banc of America Securities
Bear Stearns
Deutsche Banc Alex. Brown
Lehman Brothers
Merrill Lynch
Robertson Stephens
Salomon Smith Barney

EMPLOYMENT CONTACT

Global Bank Recruiting
The Chase Manhattan Bank
270 Park Avenue
25th Floor
New York, NY 10017

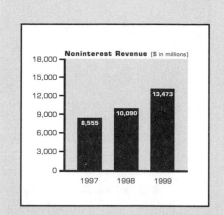

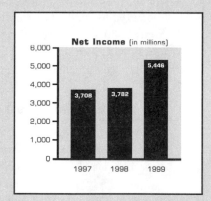

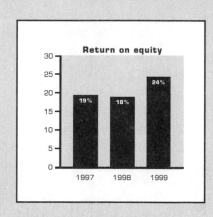

THE SCOOP

Thanks, Gramm, Leach, and Bliley

Chase Manhattan is looking to profit from the work of Senator Phil Gramm (R-Texas) and Congressmen James Leach (R-Iowa) and Tom Bliley (R-Virginia). The three legislators' work, the Financial Services Modernization Act, brought down the barriers separating commercial banking from securities underwriting and brokerage services. Commercial banks like Chase have been all too eager to cash in on the changes. Chase Manhattan has acquired several boutique investment banks (most notably San Francisco-based investment bank Hambrecht & Quist) and has consistently been rumored to be looking to merge with larger firms, including bulge-bracket banks like Merrill Lynch, Goldman Sachs, and Morgan Stanley Dean Witter. While some of those unions are merely wild speculation, Chase has made no secret of its strategy to break into securities underwriting through acquisition. In July 2000, the firm completed its purchase of The Beacon Group, a New York M&A firm, and plans to finalize the purchase of Robert Flemings Holdings, a London-based investment bank, in August 2000.

In the beginning, a historic duel

Chase's beginnings can be traced back to 1799, when The Manhattan Company was chartered to supply water to New York City. Included in the company charter was a provision that capital not needed for the water-supply business could be diverted toward the founding of a bank. Thus, the Bank of The Manhattan Company was formed. Historians are unclear whether Aaron Burr, one of the backers of The Manhattan Company's water business, intentionally inserted the clause so a bank rivaling Alexander Hamilton's could be formed. The two Founding Fathers had a long-running dispute, which came to an abrupt end in 1804 when Burr killed Hamilton in a duel. (The pistols, by the way, have been preserved as part of Chase's historical collection.)

The bank continued to grow, surviving the Great Depression (with a little assistance from the Rockefeller family) and two World Wars. In 1955, the Bank of The Manhattan Company merged with Chase National, a bank founded in 1877 by currency expert John Thompson and named after former Secretary of the Treasury Salmon Chase. The Chase Manhattan Bank, as it became known, went seeking another commercial merger partner in the mid-1990s, settling on Chemical

Bank, the third-largest bank in the U.S. after its 1992 merger with Manufacturers Hanover. The 1996 coupling made Chase Manhattan one of the largest banks in the U.S.

Jimmy Lee, superstar

As the walls separating financial institutions were coming down, Chase was looking to expand into investment banking businesses. For example, the firm became an established leader in syndicated loans, consistently ranking first both in the U.S. and worldwide and often capturing more than a third of market share.

Chase's position in the syndicated loan market can largely be attributed to Jimmy Lee, the firm's former vice chairman and head of the investment banking business. Lee, a respected deal maker, had his status as a superstar firmly cemented when he was featured on the cover of an April 2000 issued of *Forbes*. The *Forbes* piece called him "the next Michael Milken" (Milken, of course, was the junk bond king who rose to power on Wall Street in the 1980s). "He's the greatest relationship banker I've ever seen," Richard Beattie, a partner at law firm Simpson Thacher & Bartlett, told *Forbes*. One industry insider who observed Lee in action told *The Daily Deal*, "He could sell you ice cubes in February and make you feel like you had something special."

The *Forbes* article detailed Lee's career at Chase, which started when his then-girlfriend (now wife) couldn't make a scheduled job interview at Chemical Bank in 1975. She pressured Lee to go in her place, and he, of course, got the job. Lee rose quickly through the ranks, earning accolades by building a merchant bank for Chemical in Australia three years after he was hired. After his return to New York, Lee was befriended by William Harrison, who would go on to become Chase's chairman and CEO three years after the Chase/Chemical merger.

Despite Lee's powerful connections and celebrity status, he received what amounted to a demotion just a month after the *Forbes* piece was published. When Chase acquired The Beacon Group, a New York M&A firm, in July 2000 Geoffrey Boisi, founder and senior partner at Beacon, became vice chairman and head of investment banking at Chase. (Prior to founding Beacon, Boisi was a partner and head of investment banking at Goldman Sachs. Incidentally, Boisi was also the youngest person ever to hold each of those positions at Goldman.) Lee's focus was shifted to "client relationships and significant transactions," according to a Chase press release, which said that Lee

Hungry for more inside scoop? Join Vault.com's popular online community for finance and banking — www.vault.com

VAULT.com **189**

wanted to work more closely on deals and strike a better "work/life balance." While many industry observers accepted that explanation, some felt Lee was pushed aside because he neglected the equity underwriting business Chase has tried so hard to build.

Other I-banking businesses

Chase also ranks high on the league tables for debt underwriting. The firm placed third in investment grade debt in 1999, according to Thomson Financial Securities Data. Chase managed 800 deals totaling $88.7 billion. In March 2000, the bank acted as lead manager on a $5 billion offering for Ford Motor Credit.

Chase placed fourth among underwriters of high yield debt, lead-managing 48 deals worth $10.3 billion. What was missing was equity underwriting, particularly IPOs. Chase apparently plans to address the dearth of equity deals by acquiring other firms.

First, H&Q

Chase's first target was Hambrecht & Quist, a San Francisco-based tech boutique. H&Q was founded in 1968 by William Hambrecht (a finance legend in his own right) and the late George Quist. The firm struggled in the early 1990s, largely due to several bad IPOs. Daniel Case, the older brother of America Online CEO Steve Case, took control of the firm in 1992, as CEO. Case is credited with turning the firm around, and when Hambrecht left to start an eponymous investment bank in 1998, Case became H&Q's chairman.

H&Q was acquired by Chase in December 1999 for $1.35 billion. While the move did give Chase a foothold in an important underwriting niche, not all observers were impressed. *The Wall Street Journal* sniffed, "Even with H&Q, Chase's equity operation will be small compared to its Wall Street rivals." The *Journal* did give Chase some credit for the pickup, saying, "The addition of H&Q could give Chase an earlier entrée into the M&A process and bring with it the accoutrements of equity research and underwriting expertise." The underwriting expertise paid early dividends; Chase H&Q led 14 IPOs in the first five months of 2000 alone, most notably Net.Genesis Corp. In the first quarter of 2000, Chase H&Q announced more transactions than Hambrecht & Quist completed in the entire previous year.

International flavor

Seeking to further its I-banking business overseas, Chase announced the purchase of Robert Flemings Holdings, a London-based investment bank, in April 2000. Analysts speculated that at a purchase price of $7.9 billion for Flemings, Chase had overpaid. "[The price is] stratospheric," Martin Cross, analyst at Teather & Greenwood, told *The Daily Deal*. Whatever the price, Chase scooped up a significant underwriting presence, especially in Asia, as well as Flemings' coveted asset management business. "Flemings brings leadership positions in global asset management and international equities, excellent potential for earnings growth, and a culture of partnership," said Chase chairman and CEO William Harrison in an April release. The Flemings deal looked even better when the company announced record profits of $482.6 million in May 2000 for the previous year. The profits were largely a result of improved business in Asia, a development that bodes well for Chase.

Chase's most recent acquisition was The Beacon Group, a New York M&A firm led by Geoffrey Boisi, a former Goldman Sachs partner. Boisi, the firm also announced, would take over as head of investment banking. The acquisition, announced in May 2000 and completed in July of that year, effectively returns Jimmy Lee to a more deal-focused position at the firm. The purchase price for Beacon was reported to be in the $400 million to $500 million range.

GETTING HIRED

As market gets tougher, so does Chase

Despite the tight labor market and Chase's position outside the bulge bracket, insiders report that the firm is fairly selective in hiring. "I believe we focus on the top-20 MBA schools," says one source. "However, we will add schools if it makes sense and are willing to look outside the top-tier schools for great people." The bank says it recruits at the University of Chicago, Columbia, Cornell, Dartmouth, Harvard, University of Michigan, NYU, and the University of Pennsylvania for both analysts and associates.

Breaking into Chase is "getting harder and harder every day as the firm grows ever more competitive in investment banking." One senior

Hungry for more inside scoop? Join Vault.com's popular online
community for finance and banking — www.vault.com

VAULT.com   **191**

banker who has been involved in the recruiting process for a number of years says, "The selectivity has increased dramatically." That insider goes on to say that Chase now competes with bulge-bracket firms Goldman Sachs and Merrill Lynch for "the same resources," i.e., people. Undergrads must have at least a 3.0 cumulative GPA and, according to the firm, "strong quantitative, analytical, and computer skills and excellent oral and written communication skills." They look for the same basic skills in MBAs but have no minimum GPA requirement.

Interviews: don't expect Regis

Undergrad and MBA recruits can expect a round of on-campus interviews by Chase bankers. If you make the cut, there's a Super Saturday round of interviews with a legion of Chase investment bankers. Those interviews are team-led. MBAs can expect a fairly intense interview experience. "For final rounds [for MBAs] there are five two-on-one interviews and all must agree to hire a particular candidate," reports one source. Expect "many questions dealing with accounting," according to one banker. "[You'd] better know basic accounting and be able to discuss [your] favorite stocks and what you're looking for out of them. Relevant knowledge to the industry in question is important, too. But the questioning is not intense — this is not a quiz show."

Analyst candidates can expect a Super Saturday with four one-on-one interviews. According to one source the level of technical questions depends on a candidate's background: "If you are a finance or accounting major, be prepared. If you are a liberal arts major, then you need to have an aggressive and solid personality. Talking about past experiences, especially sports or life-moving events, is always helpful. Firms like Chase want to know the person they are hiring." Another insider agrees, saying that "questions are not highly technical" but analyst candidates should expect "questions on teamwork, analytical skills, leadership, integrity, and dependability." Another analyst describes the typical interview questions at Chase as "fairly friendly get-to-know you questions — 'Why do you want the job? Why Chase specifically?' Interviewers are trying to gauge knowledge, personality, motivation, and your ability to learn."

In general, Chase bankers note that interviewers are trying to "get a feel for who you are." Says one source, "It is really about your personality and vision, which should be clear." Another banker says, "The ability to sell is important." According to that source, Chase interviewers will be wondering, "Can I put this person in front of a client? Will this person have a positive attitude at 2 a.m.? Will this person run through walls for the firm?"

OUR SURVEY SAYS

Transitional culture

"The culture is still in transition from a corporate bank to an investment bank," says one source. "The culture is therefore mixed depending on the level of evolution reached in individual areas. Syndicated finance, M&A, and many industry groups are totally Wall Street." Others agree that in terms of culture, Chase is in a state of flux. The firm is "very hybrid investment banking/commercial banking," says one banker, who adds that Chase is "more relaxed in general than other firms. People arc not haughty, materialistic, or in-your-face about being bankers." One banker notes that, in general, "the corporate culture is very team-oriented."

Duck!

The complaint shared by most Chase bankers is the lack of respect that senior bankers have for their subordinates. "I have had things thrown at me and been yelled at for no reason," reports one young banker. "Analysts are often excluded from meetings either for some silly reason or sometimes no reason at all. How are we supposed to do models if we aren't invited to the meetings where the company's performance is discussed?" that analyst wonders. Another Chase source concurs with that assessment, saying: "There is often an attitude of condescension by senior people." That source illustrates the point with the following anecdote: "A VP, walking into a meeting — with the client on the line — notices that only associates and an analyst are in the room. [The VP] says 'Well, we can't start. No one who counts is here.'" Ouch.

"There is always the sense that analysts are the grunt workers and disposable to the firm," complains one insider, "as if our presence is just temporary and easily replaceable. Many senior bankers take great advantage of junior people and never take into account that they may actually have a life outside of work as well. Analysts always know their place and there is a great sense of hierarchy." Chase senior bankers

Hungry for more inside scoop? Join Vault.com's popular online community for finance and banking — www.vault.com

VAULT.com **193**

want analysts to prove themselves. "You've got to establish that you're somebody worthy of respect," reports one contact. "After that, they'll listen to your ideas and encourage you to be creative and productive." Some strenuously disagree with that notion. "I know people who quit because they were unable to even meet with human resources personnel to discuss whatever problems they were having," reports one insider. Another complains, "The level of trust has been broken many times. Many associates feel they have been lied to and are not treated with respect."

Considering the apparent animosity between senior and junior bankers, it's not surprising the social atmosphere is underwhelming. "They will not even have cakes for people who leave the group — we have to pay for it ourselves," complains one source. A recent spate of associate departures forced the firm to offer some diversions. "There are many events now, such as bowling outings, drinks, dinners," reports one contact. "However, these are rarely attended by the senior people." More optimistic bankers report Chase "is taking great strides to improve the in-office social environment."

Street work, not Street pay

"Chase underpays versus the Street," fumes one analyst. "Period." One source claims that Chase bankers have "been promised that we 'will be taken care of.' [I'm] not sure what this means. [We're] expected to work Street hours and produce Street product but to date have not been paid Street compensation." While some report that pay "has been revised of late to match industry standards," others point to fundamental problems in Chase's compensation structure. "The fact that there are home-grown employees with contracts serves as disincentive to the rest of us, especially when the compensation numbers are multiples of ours." The firm is reportedly trying to meet these criticisms. Chase recently announced increases in analyst salaries; first-, second- and third-year analysts at Chase will receive starting salaries of $55,000, $65,000, and $75,000, respectively.

On the upside, Chase "allows co-investment with Chase Capital Partners," the firm's venture capital subsidiary. "This is leveraged by Chase." Bankers rave about the plan, saying, "This is a great way to keep us involved in the industry and committed to our careers here. I expect it to increase." Other perks are more typical of the Street. "Chase provides free dinner when you stay late and a car [home]," says an insider. A company gym is available, as are sports tickets. New York bankers have been to the U.S. Open tennis tournament, Yankees, Mets, Knicks, and Rangers games, as well as other events at Madison Square Garden.

Varying opinions on training

Analysts at Chase participate in an 11-week training program that covers topics such as accounting, market dynamics, corporate finance, and financial risk analysis. After training analysts are assigned to product or industry groups. Associate training takes place over eight weeks and includes reviews of topics such as financial analysis and corporate finance. The training also includes Series 7 and 63 prep and presentations from senior bankers and firm executives. After training associates embark on two six-month "rotations" in the financial, advisory, or capital markets area of the firm. After the first year, associates are permanently placed into a group.

Chase bankers disagree on the quality of the firm's training. "[The] rigorous training program is quite challenging to non-business or accounting majors," warns one source. "Be prepared to sweat if this is new to you. If a minimum score is not met on various module examinations during training, you will be given your walking papers and sent on your way." Another contact reports the program consists of a "very good accounting program lasting three weeks. The remainder of the training program covered economics and corporate finance." Finance majors, on the other hand, offer less praise for the training program. "[Chase has a] terrible training program that the company holds up as a wonderful program," rants one insider. "[We're] treated as kindergartners, [and] we often had to point out mistakes by the 'professors.' Absolutely horrendous."

Glorified word processors

Junior bankers report they often have difficulty getting any significant deal exposure. One analyst feels like a "glorified word processor." That analyst goes on to warn, "Any undergrad who thinks they will be a rainmaker should re-examine [his or her] choice. Chase is a great place because you see a lot of deals. But because it is big, you may be left out of the negotiations and logistics and forced to format a pitchbook constantly. If you master MS Office in college, you will be an amazing analyst!"

Hungry for more inside scoop? Join Vault.com's popular online community for finance and banking — www.vault.com

VAULT.com **195**

Things are better on the associate level, but not by much. "Associates are welcomed and encouraged to accept tremendous responsibility and are provided with plenty of room to run," gushes one associate. Overzealous VPs and MDs sometimes encroach on associate territory, though. "Because of MDs often taking on VP or associate roles, all the roles are diminished," reports one insider. "For example, associates are doing work that would typically be done by analysts while analysts are left doing very menial jobs such as formatting or collating." One junior bankers chimes in, "The lack of client contact is simply astounding." Some associates report meeting with clients' senior officers such as CFOs and treasurers, but that seems to be the exception.

"Investment banking hours are long, but you know that going into it," says one analyst. "Typically, expect to work at least 14 hours a day, plus weekends." Indeed, Chase I-bankers work hours on par with the rest of Wall Street. "If you have a hot deal, expect to have no life and to be sending packages to your boss's house," warns one source. Another insider observes, "Suffice it to say that getting out of here before 10 p.m. is a rare occasion. Also, one day or part of a day on the weekend is the norm."

Retention issues

Like most investment banks, Chase is continually fighting to retain talent. "Headhunters are constantly calling to offer me more money," brags one banker. One insider claims that 35 associates left after the first quarter of 2000, compared to 49 for all of 1999. That contact estimates that 40 percent of the defectors went to other banks. Some at Chase feel the firm is making some effort to address turnover. "Overall the bank is very committed to this," says one source. "The dilemma comes [in] balancing the huge growth in investment banking businesses with the personal needs of our limited resources. This is receiving lots of senior management focus." Another banker points out that Jimmy Lee, who recently accepted a demotion presumably to focus on life outside the office, "talks about the importance of a work/life balance."

Commitment to diversity and global scale

"Chase is totally committed to improved diversity and the additional creativity that this brings in the work environment," says one source. Another contact says the firm "[goes] out of its way" to foster a diverse environment. Although some bankers concede there can be few minorities and women in certain groups, they feel that is a by-product of the industry, rather than a failure on Chase's part.

While the size of Chase might scare away some recruits, bankers list that as an advantage of working for the firm. Chase bankers boast of "involvement with nearly all major organizations," and thus the firm has the potential to work with a significant client base. One insider says, "Performers get the opportunity to move around and try different areas of the firm — [Chase is] not a 'siloed' organization." On the downside, the fact that Chase is "still viewed by naïve undergrads as a commercial bank" results in a drag on recruiting. The friction between senior and junior bankers is also a problem at Chase. Junior bankers, sounding like Rodney Dangerfield, report "no respect."

Hungry for more inside scoop? Join Vault.com's popular online
community for finance and banking — www.vault.com

VAULT.com **197**

CIBC World Markets

CIBC World Markets Tower
425 Lexington Avenue
New York, NY 10017
(212) 667-7000
Fax: (212) 667-5310
www.cibcwm.com

LOCATIONS

Investment banking locations:
New York (HQ)
Boston
Houston
Los Angeles
San Francisco

DEPARTMENTS

Asset-backed Securitization
Corporate Finance
Equities
Leveraged Finance
Mergers and Acquisitions
Private Client Services

THE STATS

Chairman & CEO: John Hunkin
Vice Chairman, CIBC World Markets: David Kassie
Chairman of CIBC World Markets U.S: Paul Rogers, CIBC
Employer Type: Subsidiary of CIBC
1999 Revenue: $3.1 billion
1999 Net Income: $345 million
No. of Employees: 4,500

UPPERS

• Contact with senior bankers
• Early responsibility for juniors
• Friendly co-workers

DOWNERS

• Eclectic mix of cultures
• Lack of diversity
• Lack of reputation

KEY COMPETITORS

Banc of America Securities
Deutsche Banc Alex. Brown
Donaldson, Lufkin & Jenrette
Robertson Stephens
SG Cowen
Thomas Weisel Partners
UBS Warburg

EMPLOYMENT CONTACT

CIBC World Markets
Campus Recruiting
One World Financial Center
New York, NY 10281
Fax: (212) 667-5314
E-mail: campus.recruiting@us.cibc.com

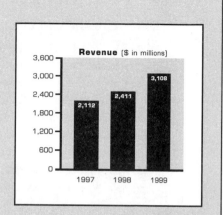

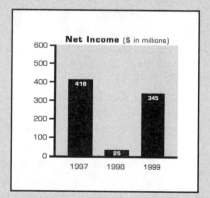

THE SCOOP

One-stop shopping

CIBC World Markets is the investment banking and brokerage arm of the Canadian Imperial Bank of Commerce (CIBC), Canada's second-largest bank. Like most investment banks with a commercial banking parent, CIBC provides a one-stop shopping experience for corporations, allowing clients access to debt and equity markets, asset securitization, leveraged lending, mergers and acquisitions advisory, and everything else a company could possibly need. While many growing investment banking firms seek to become bulge-bracket firms, CIBC has a different approach. Rather than pursuing the big clients that have existing relationships with banking behemoths, CIBC has set its sights on mid-sized corporations. "We believe that there's a big chunk of companies that aren't served well by bulge-bracket firms," Paul Rogers, CEO of CIBC World Market's U.S. operations explained. The firm is looking to develop a significant relationship with these mid-sized companies, to the extent that, in the words of Rogers, "We're their bank. We're their financial institution."

The company decided in 1994 to aggressively develop a U.S. investment banking presence. CIBC executives believed that the investment banking world was not actually "globalizing," but "Americanizing." In 1995 CIBC purchased Argosy, a high-yield boutique run by veterans of Drexal Burnham Lambert. The company added an equity underwriting and research presence in 1997 by acquiring Oppenheimer & Co for $525 million. In 1998, the company suffered a difficult third and fourth quarter due to its operations in derivatives and downturns in world markets. The firm subsequently eliminated its derivatives operations and implemented some global cost cutting measures. In June 1999, CIBC appointed Paul Rogers to replace Michael Rulle as head of investment banking in the U.S. In May 1999, the firm renamed the global investment banking operations CIBC World Markets.

Away from the pack

In addition to its focus on middle-market companies, CIBC is also unique in how the firm has chosen to organize its professionals. The firm was the first Canadian bank to integrate its corporate lending professionals and investment bankers. The firm's 650 person corporate and leveraged finance group allows clients access to all products and services "under one roof." The combination of high yield and leveraged finance into one department also aids the firm's work with financial sponsors, such as Kohlberg Kravis Roberts & Co. Basically, the firm lends money to firms that buy undervalued companies. "Most of what financial sponsors do is complex, involves multiple levels of capital raising, and is done under significant time pressure," Dean Kehler, a CIBC managing director and co-head of the firm's high yield group told *American Banker*. "The more work they [financial sponsors] can do with someone who can streamline the process, the better off they are."

Merchant banking is also a large component of the firm's strategy. This can be an extremely profitable avenue, as CIBC showed with its investment in Global Crossings, a telecommunications firm. According to *Canadian Business*, CIBC realized approximately $176 million on this investment and still holds equity worth over $2 billion in the company. Of course, while investments in young ventures can be extremely profitable they are also very risky. Investing in young companies also offers CIBC the opportunity to gain them as investment banking clients. The firm did precisely this with SpectraSite, a company in which it made a $75 million investment. CIBC has been involved in two public offerings for SpectraSite. As *Canadian Business* noted, some critics question whether investment banks should participate in offerings for companies in which they have significant ownership. CIBC maintains that it generally invests in large companies and is usually only one of many investors. David Kassie, chairman of CIBC World Markets told *Canadian Business*: "Typically other people are putting in real money, which is a lot different than a promotion game where people buy a penny stock and are not putting in very much dough, and [then] promote the next round [of financing.]"

Under Paul Rogers' leadership, the firm's strategy yielded strong results in 1999. That year, the firm's U.S. operations contributed 51 percent of CIBC World Markets revenue. In 1999, CIBC underwrote 114 deals in the U.S. compared to 55 in 1998. According to *The Daily Deal*, the firm ranked first in 1999 among lenders for leveraged buyout loans. The company also advised on 87 M&A transactions during 1999. Because of the bull markets of 1999 and the fact that many of CIBC's clients are technology companies (who experienced a particular boom in 1999), critics worry whether CIBC will be able to continue to prove itself in a bear market. Kassie and CIBC believe the firm's investments in LBOs

Hungry for more inside scoop? Join Vault.com's popular online
community for finance and banking — www.vault.com

VAULT.com **201**

provide another dimension to the company's business if the tech markets evaporate.

Going strong in 2000

In 2000, the firm continued to go strong. In the first quarter of 2000 the firm advised on 10 M&A transactions worth $3 billion. Among CIBC's notable advisory assignments: advising computer hardware manufacturer ATI Technologies on its $400 million purchase of Palo Alto, Calif.-based ArtX. Most impressive was CIBC's role as an advisor (along with Banc of America Securities) to JDS Uniphase in its $41 billion proposed merger with SDL. The proposed deal, unveiled in July 2000, is the largest technology merger announced to date. While the deal is a blockbuster transaction, the deal highlights the success of CIBC's middle-market client strategy. CIBC's relationship with JDS began when JDS was a relatively small company. As JDS grew, CIBC continued to maintain a banking relationship with the company, leading up to CIBC's role as an advisor on this mammoth transaction.

The company also continues to gain equity mandates. CIBC was the lead underwriter for the $100 million offering of Breezecom, a telecommunications firm that went public in March 2000. The company led the $214 million offering of biotechnology firm Tanox in April 2000.

GETTING HIRED

Spreading the word

As CIBC World Markets increases its investment banking presence in the U.S., it is increasing its on-campus profile. "I've seen the transition that we have made in recruiting from an interviewing side," reports one associate who has taken part in talent-finding missions.

Those going through on-campus interviews participate in the "super day" affairs common on Wall Street. "They have a dinner and cocktails with all analysts and some associates the evening before," reports one recent analyst hire. "On the interview day, it's a half-day, with five or six interviews. The interviews are 30 minutes, one-on-ones with senior-level people." As for the questions, says that contact, "Some people go straight for finance and technical, and some people go for 'Do you have any sort of life?'" Says another insider, "We definitely look for smart analytical people who are also the kind of people you want to hang out with."

Insiders agree that because the firm doesn't have the same cachet as the premier bulge-bracket firms, interviewers are impressed by candidates who are targeting CIBC. "I think they're looking for people who have a strong interest in the firm," says one insider. "[CIBC is] a relative unknown, so they're looking for someone who, if they can extend an offer, is going to take it. It matters how strong your interest is."

The firm has recently started a summer associate program for MBAs. In the summer of 2000, the firm hired 18 summer associates. Insiders say the firm's relatively smaller size and large number of high growth clients makes it an interesting place for MBAs interested in nontraditional investment banking opportunities. Says one senior insider, "We offer a lot of the exciting opportunities of a dot-com without as much downside risk."

OUR SURVEY SAYS

Work hard, but not as a slave

"I'm working just as many, if not more, hours as my peers at other banks," reports one CIBC World Markets insider. Contacts at the firm agree that CIBC World Markets employees definitely work normal I-banking hours. However, they express less burnout than their peers at other firms. "[The firm] definitely does not have a face-time culture," says one insider. "The firm is very generous about benefits," reports another contact. "There's good sick time, vacation — basically good HR policies." Says another, "The A-No. 1 reason I chose this place was the emphasis on lifestyle. Don't get me wrong, there have been times when I've killed myself." However, that insider emphasizes that the firm pays attention to its employees' happiness. "It's all about keeping the best people in the firm, so they are really good about making sure you're happy. If that means switching to another group or another location or whatever, that's fine." Another insider agrees, saying: "I think typically people come here and stay for a long time. They try to nurture people and keep the good people here."

Hungry for more inside scoop? Join Vault.com's popular online
community for finance and banking — www.vault.com

VAULT.com **203**

No highfalutin attitude

The firm wins praise not just for management's emphasis on lifestyle and retention, but for an overall laid-back and down-to-earth attitude. "We absolutely have some of the friendliest, most talented people here," says one I-banking associate. Says another insider who has worked at bulge-bracket Wall Street firms: "[At other firms], the attitude is win-win-win, get your deals, where the attitude here is a lot more team-oriented, more 'win on our principles.'" "It's a friendlier place," says one contact. That insider continues: "[CIBC World Markets is] a pretty hardworking place, but they're not up there managing their league table status, whereas at larger banks, I know they're managing their status. They don't pursue the large Fortune 500 companies. They stick with, not the middle market, but middle-sized larger companies." Insiders say this mid-sized role leads to a less snobby atmosphere than at other Wall Street firms. "You're not judged by a piece of paper, and your school means nothing — it's what you do at work," says one insider. "You get people from all types of schools, from Harvard to wherever." Another agrees, saying, "Because we don't chase after the highest-profile clients, we don't have to have this highfalutin attitude that we're better than everyone else." The firm, like most of its investment banking peers, adopted a full-time business casual dress policy in nearly every unit. Of course, for client meetings employees are required to dress as the clients do.

Insiders also report a healthy amount of camaraderie at CIBC World Markets. Reports one associate who joined CIBC from a large Wall Street firm, "I don't think I was ever invited over to a senior guy's house there. Here, the head guy of M&A has an outing every year, and some of the other guys have had us over. It's a better working environment."

Welcome, CIBC

Despite the initial industry reactions to the merger, contacts are also pleased at how the CIBC/Oppenheimer integration has proceeded culturally. "People-wise I think it was OK," reports one associate insider who was originally hired by Oppenheimer. "It's not like a commercial bank without any introduction to investment banking acquired us. They had already done that when they had acquired Argosy Group. So in the U.S., their presence was largely from an I-banking perspective anyway. Their culture was not a 9-to-5 bank culture." Says an analyst, with friends whose mid-sized firms have also undergone recent acquisitions, "My friends complain that it's a pain to work for the commercial banks, and that 'They handcuff us.' I'm grateful that that hasn't been the case here."

All in all, the combination has proved fruitful, insiders say. "There has been more work, more marketing, and things are busier, as we have more products to offer. I think the bar was raised as far as expectations for group heads to generate revenue. At the same time, there is more opportunity to close transactions as we have deeper resources." Says one associate, "It feels very much like one firm now." Some bankers still feel the mergers have led to a mix of cultures that maintain some separation. "The firm doesn't have a 'corporate culture,' as many groups still retain their pre-CIBC cultures," says one insider. "The high yield group, for example, stems from the Drexel culture — an aggressive, arrogant, and exciting environment."

Still separate, sort of

Although CIBC and Oppenheimer have merged, operations in New York are still "split between [CIBC's] 425 Lexington, and the Oppenheimer space in the World Financial Tower." According to insiders, the New York corporate and leveraged finance group is located at 425 Lexington. "Getting everybody under one roof is definitely a priority," says one associate. The firm says it has signed an agreement to build a new building at 42nd Street and Madison Avenue. In the meantime insiders report favorably on the ability to work with colleagues in different offices. "All the infrastructure from the technology standpoint is pretty good, as far as shared files and e-mail," reports one insider about maintaining two main offices.

Early opportunity

Like their peers at other mid-sized firms, CIBC World Markets insiders enjoy early responsibility and client contact, as they work on smaller deal teams and with growth companies. One analyst, talking about his first assignment, says, "I was at the pitch, and I was there all the way to the IPO. I got to know the CEO of the company, and developed even more than an investment banking relationship, a personal relationship. "I went to Hawaii with the CEO's kids, and [the CEO] e-mails me." Another insider tells a similar story. "I have friends that are analysts at other banks, and they don't do the same type of work that we do here. Because we are smaller, you are afforded more responsibility, and I think associates would feel the same. I have some friends at [a bulge-

Hungry for more inside scoop? Join Vault.com's popular online community for finance and banking — www.vault.com

VAULT.com **205**

bracket firm], and they don't have buyer contacts. If we're on the sell-side, we are calling [potential buyers], answering questions." Associates agree with this assessment. One contact, who joined CIBC from one of the bulge-bracket firms, says his previous employer "had way too many people on a deal team, and you didn't get to learn as much. You didn't get to take as much of an active role as at CIBC. Here you actually get to run transactions sometimes." Says one associate, "Because we're focused on middle-market companies, we have the capability to grow with our clients."

Some insiders criticize the firm's lack of diversity, though they note that it is also a function of the industry. "CIBC is still a white male enclave," says one source. "Certain departments are exceptions to the rule, but management so far has not identified the recruitment of minorities as something they need to focus on. The complete lack of any racial, gender, or ethnic diversity is a real problem here although no one seems to notice it or discuss it." That source goes on to say that "more top-level women have been leaving the firm [recently] to go to competitors." One female insider disagrees, saying that the firm is "very flexible and family friendly." That source reports that the firm offers talented female bankers many "options for balancing work and family." The firm reports that 40 percent of the 2000 analyst class is either a minority or female.

"I think typically people come here and stay for a long time. They try to nurture people and keep the good people here."

— *CIBC World Markets Insider*

Credit Suisse First Boston

11 Madison Avenue
New York, NY 10010
(212) 325-2000
www.csfb.com

LOCATIONS

New York (HQ)
Baltimore
Boston
Chicago
Houston
Los Angeles
Palo Alto
San Francisco

London (HQ)
São Paulo
Zurich
57 offices in 38 countries

DEPARTMENTS

Investment Banking
Equity
Fixed Income
Private Equity

THE STATS

CEO: Allen D. Wheat
Co-heads of Equities and Investment Banking:
Brady W. Dougan and Charles G. Ward
Head of Fixed Income:
Stephen A.M. Hester
Employer Type: Subsidiary of Credit Suisse Group
1999 Revenues: $9.8 billion
1999 Net Income: $1.3 billion
No. of Employees: 15,185
No. of Offices: 57

UPPERS

• Diverse, friendly environment
• Deal exposure
• State-of-the-art gym

DOWNERS

• Lack of strong firm culture
• Lots of bureaucracy
• Poor support

KEY COMPETITORS

Deutsche Banc Alex.Brown
Donaldson, Lufkin & Jenrette
Goldman Sachs
Lehman Brothers
Merrill Lynch
Morgan Stanley Dean Witter
Salomon Smith Barney
UBS Warburg

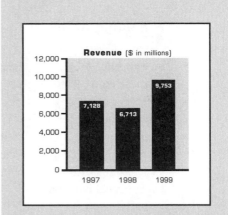

EMPLOYMENT CONTACT

North America

Investment Banking
Jennifer Bruch, *MBA Recruiting*
Pauline Ma, *BA Recruiting*

Fixed income
Catherine Curley, M*BA Recruiting*
Cynthia Marrone, *BA Recruiting*

Equity
Dolores Daly, *MBA Recruiting*
Robyn Bogash, *BA Recruiting*

11 Madison Avenue
New York, NY 10010

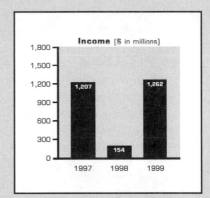

Europe

Investment Banking
Sophie Walker, *MBA Recruiting*
Omar Iqbal, *Undergraduate Recruiting*

Equity/Fixed Income
Michelle DeSena

One Cabot Square
London E14 40J
United Kingdom

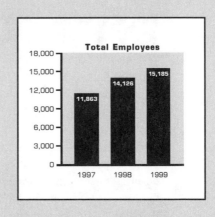

THE SCOOP

A bulging bracket

Credit Suisse First Boston is one of New York's most renowned investment banks and a member of Wall Street's prestigious bulge bracket of top securities firms. Credit Suisse First Boston is the wholly owned investment banking unit of the Credit Suisse Group of Switzerland. Credit Suisse Group (formerly known as CS Holdings) initially invested in First Boston in 1988, renaming the investment bank CS First Boston. Since that infusion of Swiss cash, the firm itself has changed significantly. Credit Suisse First Boston now has a much larger capital base than First Boston ever had.

From New York to Zurich

Credit Suisse First Boston has a history that spans nearly 70 years. The firm began as the investment banking arm of First National Bank of Boston. When the Glass-Steagall Act and other legal reforms set up barriers between commercial banks, investment banks, and insurance companies, the investment banking arm became the independent First Boston. In 1988 Credit Suisse, the Zurich-based bank, renamed itself CS Holding and became a parent company/shareholder of a newly renamed CS First Boston. The alliance became more formalized in 1997, when CS Holdings swallowed the whole investment banking unit and both parent and child emerged with new names: Credit Suisse Group (a global bank headquartered in Zurich) and investment banking arm Credit Suisse First Boston (headquartered in New York).

Boldly growing the business

Since its absorption by the Credit Suisse Group, Credit Suisse First Boston has aggressively built its I-banking business, making several high-profile moves. In a deal announced in December 1997, the firm acquired several divisions of Barclays Bank's investment bank, BZW. First, CSFB bought the British and European mergers and acquisitions, corporate finance advisory, and equity capital markets businesses. A couple of months later, the firm acquired BZW's British and European equity sales, trading, and research groups, as well as BZW's Asian businesses. And in September 1998, it bought Garantia S.A., Brazil's top investment bank, for $675 million in cash and stock. (This price didn't seem like such a bargain when Brazil's market began collapsing shortly after the deal was made.) The firm also made substantial waves with its acquisition of individual talent. In October 1998, CSFB snagged John Nelson, the former deputy chairman of famed investment bank Lazard, to head its European investment banking business. Most notably, the firm hired about 150 technology bankers and analysts, led by superstar investment banker Frank Quattrone, from rival Deutsche Bank in the summer of 1998.

In 1999 CSFB was recognized as an unquestioned leader in tech transactions. That year CSFB lead-managed IPOs for 54 technology companies including Phone.com, QXL.com, Wavecom, and Informatica. On the M&A front in 1999, CSFB advised Whittman-Hart on its $7.9 billion acquisition of USWeb, Cerent on its $7.5 billion sale to Cisco, and Ascend Communications on its $24 billion sale to Lucent. In 2000 CSFB co-lead-managed (alongside Goldman Sachs) a $2.7 billion offering for ASM Lithography and lead-managed IPOs for such companies as Interactive Investor, Trader.com, Telecocity, and Handspring.

Too much tech?

Quattrone's advent made headlines and most industry insiders attribute CSFB's subsequent success in technology-related businesses largely to Quattrone's presence. Of course, the unprecedented boom in tech and Internet-related banking coincided nicely with Quattrone's arrival in 1998. Over the last two years, the firm has quickly become a major player in equity underwriting. In 1999 the firm ranked fourth among lead managers of common stock issues (right behind the big three: Goldman Sachs, Morgan Stanley, and Merrill Lynch), climbing up from the eighth spot on the list in 1998 according to Thomson Financial Securities Data. As mentioned previously, much of this equity success at CSFB is due to the firm's strong technology banking group. In 1999 48 percent of the dollar volume of CSFB's underwriting represented transactions for technology companies (for the first half of 2000, that number climbed to 54 percent).

The high percentage of tech deals, according to many industry experts, shows a dependence on tech that could prove dangerous if the robust market for tech stocks turns sour. Quattrone himself isn't cheap, and industry experts question how much business he brings versus how much compensation he receives. Reportedly, his compensation structure includes a generous profit-sharing plan which drains much of

Hungry for more inside scoop? Join Vault.com's popular online community for finance and banking — www.vault.com

VAULT.com 211

the profit from CSFB's bottom line. According to CSFB's 1999 annual review, the company experienced a 44 percent increase in "staff costs…primarily as a result of increased incentive bonus awards and related payroll taxes." The annual review also makes mention of the "significant investment" made in mid-1998 to acquire "a group specializing in technology banking and equity research." In addition to the cost of keeping him happy, Quattrone also has a history of jumping ship and taking large numbers of staff with him. Quattrone left Morgan Stanley for a lucrative offer from Deutsche Bank, and then walked away from Deutsche just two years later to join CSFB. During the early months of 2000, industry insiders circulated rumors that Quattrone was planning to jump again (according to *The Wall Street Journal*, Merrill Lynch and Lehman Brothers were rumored destinations). However, in June 2000 Quattrone extended his contract with CSFB. His previous contract expired in 2002 and the new agreement provides a rolling, three-year extension of the original contract, according to the report in the *Journal*.

Not just tech

While CSFB has a strong presence in tech, the firm is certainly trying to gain similar momentum in other industries. In the summer of 1999, CSFB poached a group of health care bankers from Deutsche Banc Alex. Brown. In March 2000, the firm expanded operations in Japan by acquiring the Japanese division of the securities group of Schroders. The next month, the firm led a nearly $3 billion IPO for Met Life. The deal was the largest IPO in CSFB's history and served as an indicator that the firm could excel in other industries. The firm also topped the list of underwriters of asset-backed securities in 1999 and has a strong presence in global mergers and acquisitions. According to TFSD, the firm ranked fourth (ranked by total deal value) among worldwide advisors of announced M&A transactions in 1999 with 333 deals valued at a combined $529 billion. Some major mandates of the year included representing AT&T on its $64 billion acquisition of MediaOne Group, advising Totalfina on its $54 billion acquisition of Elf Acquitaine, advising Union Carbide on its $11.6 billion merger with Dow Chemicals, and advising AMP Incorporated on its $12 billion acquisition by Tyco.

Attracting more talent

In May 2000, CSFB celebrated victory in the telecom banking space. The firm announced that it had hired Christopher Lawrence, a Salomon Smith Barney vice chairman, as the head of global telecommunications investment banking. Lawrence, a staple at SSB since the old Salomon Brothers days, was one of Solly's top bankers, managing relationships with many phone service providers such as AT&T, WorldCom, and Qwest Communications. Lawrence's presence is especially crucial since CSFB lost telecom banker Laurence Grafstein in March 1999 and telecom research analyst Frank Governali in November 1999.

Lawrence was the not the first Solly employee that CSFB poached. Shortly after SSB announced its acquisition of Schroders, CSFB stole Justin Funnel and Darren Ward, telecom equity research analysts. Continuing to fill out its telecom banking business will be a challenge for CSFB as well as other banks, as many top bankers have moved on to other pursuits.

Nerves of steel

One word rarely used to describe CSFB and its management is gutless. The firm and its parent take risks and continue aggressively where others might shy away. In 1998 the firm experienced some serious setbacks. First, the firm caught some unwanted publicity for stonewalling the descendants of Holocaust survivors who demanded access to dormant Swiss accounts. Credit Suisse Group, along with Swiss banking competitor UBS, eventually agreed in August 1998 to pay Holocaust survivors $1.25 billion over 30 years. In May 1998, CSFB settled with Orange County in its well-publicized bankruptcy lawsuit. The $52.5 million settlement served as partial restitution for the California county's losses, but the bank denied undertaking unsubstantiated risks. (Other Wall Street biggies like Merrill Lynch and Morgan Stanley Dean Witter also made multi-million dollar payments.) Also in 1998, the firm ran into severe problems in Russia, where the firm was caught with suddenly devalued positions resulting from the collapse of the country's economy. CSFB announced major trading losses in the fall of 1998, and began slashing its staff in Russia. For the year, the firm had to swallow a $1.3 billion write-off in Russia, dragging down the rest of the firm. Overall, Credit Suisse First Boston reported a net loss of $154 million in 1998. However, CSFB's woes did not prevent the firm from continuing to pursue its I-banking business. Rather than panicking, the firm took a philosophical approach to the

Hungry for more inside scoop? Join Vault.com's popular online community for finance and banking — www.vault.com

VAULT.com **213**

losses. As CFO Richard Thornburgh told *The New York Times* shortly after the Russian market collapsed: "The criticism that everyone can make is that our concentration on Russia was too high. But there was nothing wrong about the activity in itself. This is what banks do." CSFB's solid performance in 1999 validated the company's aggressive strategy.

Another problem area for CSFB was Japan, where the firm was accused in the spring of 1999 of helping Japanese clients cover up losses and also of hindering the investigation by Japanese regulators. Later that year, Japanese police arrested and jailed Shinji Yamada, the former head of CSFB's Japanese derivatives group. CSFB admitted that some of its staff had hindered the investigation and issued an apology, but it continued to receive the cold shoulder in Japan. According to a March 2000 report in *Financial News*, "Despite millions of dollars spent on legal fees and personal representations from the most senior executives of Credit Suisse, the firm is losing business in Japan and is being excluded from some prized business mandates." However, the firm continues to work to expand and strengthen its franchise in Japan, especially through the recent purchase of the Japanese securities division of Schroders.

Whether or not CSFB can expand into other banking businesses and surpass Goldman Sachs or Morgan Stanley in the all-important league tables is impossible to predict, of course. However, the firm's top execs are clearly optimistic. Charles Stonehill, CSFB's deputy head of I-banking in the Americas told *Investment Dealers' Digest*, "We spend a lot of time thinking about what we need to get ahead. But I like the cards we've got right now. We're not in the game to play; we're in it to win."

GETTING HIRED

Credit Suisse First Boston posts a list of entry-level job openings on its web site, located at www.csfb.com. The firm's on-campus recruiting program is managed on a firm-wide basis and organized by each of the bank's target schools. Each school is assigned an "ambassador" (a member of the firm's operating committee), a "team captain" (a director or managing director), and a "team leader."

At all of the bank's target schools, there is a campus presentation, which provides an overview of the firm and a Q&A session, and in some cases a dinner. The firm also participates in other get-to-know-you events such as golf tournaments and various student-organized functions. Applicants with bachelor's degrees are hired as analysts. MBAs are hired as associates. At the associate level, the firm also hires JDs into its Investment Banking division and PhDs into its Fixed Income division (because of the math-heavy derivatives and risk management products).

CSFB conducts a summer analyst program for college students. Students are placed in the investment banking, fixed income, or equity divisions. CSFB also offers a summer associate program that gives students finishing their first year of business school a chance to learn about the investment banking industry; the program runs for a minimum of 10 weeks. Summer associates participate in new business presentations, financial advisory assignments, and the completion of transactions. The firm has a sales and trading summer associate program, which allows summer associates to be exposed to as many functional areas as possible within the Fixed Income and Equity divisions. In their final week, summer associates in the sales and trading rotational program can remain in the product area of their choice. CSFB also has an equity research summer associate program, where summer associates are assigned to work with a research analyst for the summer. According to the firm, all summer associates are assigned mentors and reviewed periodically.

OUR SURVEY SAYS

Friendly folks

Credit Suisse First Boston fosters a "collegial" environment in which new employees enjoy a large degree of "interaction with senior management." One former associate reports: "We would go out at least once a week. Anytime there was someone new in our group visiting from one of the other CSFB offices, it was basically their duty to take you to a bar." One former analyst notes that the best aspect of working for the firm was "definitely the people. I've made some great friends at the firm, both in my analyst class and in my group. I still keep in touch with many of them…I was also struck by how genuinely nice people were compared with what I had expected when I went into investment banking." Insiders also rate the firm favorably in terms of diversity. Says one source, "CSFB is one of the most diverse banks on Wall

Hungry for more inside scoop? Join Vault.com's popular online community for finance and banking — www.vault.com

VAULT.COM **215**

Street." That source mentions a downside to diversity, though: "I think the diversity does hurt [CSFB] in one respect because the firm lacks a strong sense of firm culture. I don't think [the people] here take as much pride in the firm as counterparts at other firms." CSFB emphasizes "teamwork" and says its employees must possess "quantitative and modeling skills."

CSFB employees "regularly" receive free tickets to sporting and cultural events, as well as opportunities "to go out for nice dinners in restaurants like Lutece, Dawat, River Cafe, Remi, and Four Seasons." The only problem is that CSFB people spend so much time in the office; "Who really has time for anything else?"

Nice work and you get it

Insiders note the deal flow as "incredible" and "excellent, particularly in the technology group." One analyst says simply, "You work on lots of live deals here." Junior insiders also praise the opportunity to interact with a "wide range of bankers." One source notes, "I have worked with guys who are absolutely technically brilliant and others who are great relationship guys." Support services, such as word processing and graphic design, receive low marks and are described by one insider as "one of the weakest points at the firm." Administrative assistants are rated in similarly poor fashion. Says one contact, "Secretaries are terrible." That grumbler goes on to complain, "My phone never got answered…[my secretary] was technically supposed to be able to do word processing as well, but I wouldn't for a second trust him to do any of it."

While insiders note that the work flow hasn't slowed down, they do say the firm has made lifestyle improvements in order to retain talent. To help with the long hours, CSFB has improved the meal policy. "We used to have one of the stingiest meal allowances on the Street," reports one insider, "and they have relaxed that considerably." Along with a business casual dress policy, salary increases are being implemented and employees are also offered honeymoon and paternity leave in addition to standard vacation packages. For associates, the firm is offering a "wealth creation" plan in which associates can take advantage of private equity opportunities. CSFB has also introduced "fast-track promotion" where exceptional analysts are promoted to associate after two years. Analysts who are promoted to associate are given a one-month paid leave and the firm has introduced sabbaticals for employees who have been with the organization for a minimum of five years.

Where nobody knows your name

Insiders at CSFB say that one major issue in working for CSFB is that the firm's name doesn't wield the same "prestige" as other bigger name banks. According to some insiders, this is the firm's own fault. "Our perception in the industry, I believe, is very strong," notes one insider. "But to the uneducated outsider, we're not as readily recognized." One analyst agrees, noting that, "[CSFB] does a terrible job at marketing our firm and our brand name. You go down to recruit and you say CSFB and [college students] have no idea who the hell we are; people recognize firms that are tiers below us."

However, not all insiders are anxious to embrace the bulge-bracket style. Since CSFB lacks the marquee name and underwriting franchise that some of its competitors enjoy, contacts say the bank maintains an entrepreneurial culture in which employees are "encouraged to go out and win business for the firm."

Healthy options

Working at CSFB offers other, more basic benefits. "[The firm offers] lots of health care options, including one in which you can save money for health care expenses tax-free," says one insider. "So say you know that later in the year you'll have $2,000 in medical expenses that won't be covered by insurance. You can save for that in a pre-tax account. So if you didn't have that account, you might have to earn $2,800 to pay for the $2,000 in expenses." For those looking to re-energize, there's the firm's health club. The monthly fee for the club depends on one's position — "for people below VP it's $30 a month." Perhaps the biggest perk, say New York employees, is that "you get to live in Manhattan — and earn enough money to enjoy it."

Don't see anyone over 30

Like most on Wall Street, CSFB's employees contend with "long," "intense" workdays and "excruciatingly tight deadlines." According to one analyst, "The hours vary. I pulled almost no all-nighters, but I worked a lot of days until four or five in the morning." Another analyst says, "You burn out by the time you're 30. Most people only last until

Hungry for more inside scoop? Join Vault.com's popular online community for finance and banking — www.vault.com

VAULT.com **217**

they're about 35, then go off and do something else." Many employees comment that their jobs "require a high level of energy and dedication."

"Our perception in the industry, I believe, is very strong. But to the uneducated outsider, we're not as readily recognized."

— *CSFB Insider*

Deutsche Banc Alex. Brown

31 West 52nd Street
New York, NY 10019
(212) 469-5000
Fax: (212) 469-3660
www.db.com

LOCATIONS

New York (HQ)
Atlanta
Baltimore
Boston
Chicago
Los Angeles
San Francisco
Washington

Frankfurt (HQ)
Geneva
London
Tokyo

DEPARTMENTS

Asset Management
Global Corporates and Institutions
 (Global Equities, Global Markets,
 Global Investment Banking, Global
 Banking)
Private Banking

*(Note: a fund affiliated with DB Alex. Brown
holds an investment in Vault.com)*

THE STATS

Chairman: Rolf E. Breuer
CEO of the Americas: John Ross
**Head of Global Corporates and
Institutions:** Josef Ackermann
**Co-heads of Global Investment
Banking:** Yves de Balmann and
Mayo Shattuck
**Head of Global Equities and Global
Markets:** Edson Mitchell
Head of Asset Management:
Michael Philipp
Employer Type: Public company
1999 Revenue: $21.2 billion
No. of Offices: 200

UPPERS

• Global presence
• Growing in the U.S.

DOWNERS

• Bureaucracy
• Slow on perks for juniors

KEY COMPETITORS

Credit Suisse First Boston
Donaldson, Lufkin & Jenrette
J.P. Morgan
Lehman Brothers
Merrill Lynch
UBS Warburg

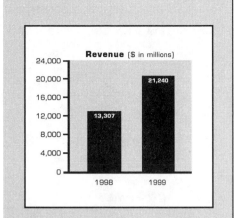

EMPLOYMENT CONTACT

United States

Investment Banking
Nebal Fahed
1251 Avenue of the Americas
25th floor
New York, NY 10020
Fax: 212-469-3660

Sales, Trading & Research
Caryn Blumenfeld
1251 Avenue of the Americas
25th floor
New York, NY 10020
Fax: 212-469-3660

Asia

Sallyann Birchall
Graduate Recruitment, Asia
Deutsche Bank AG, Hong Kong
Branch
51/F Cheung Kong Center
2 Queen's Road Central
Hong Kong
Fax: 852 2203 7374

London

Nadia Capy
email: nadia.capy@db.com

THE SCOOP

Ties to the Rhineland

Deutsche Banc Alex. Brown is the marketing name for the U.S. investment banking operations of Deutsche Bank AG, the world's largest financial institution. The firm has a history that includes one of the oldest names in corporate America. Deutsche Bank, which reported $21.2 billion in revenue for 1999, is based in Frankfurt, Germany. The company was founded in Berlin in 1870 and has had a presence in the Americas since the 19th century.

Old-timers

Alexander Brown & Sons (the predecessor to today's Deutsche Banc Alex. Brown) was founded in 1800 by Alexander Brown, an Irish immigrant living in Baltimore. (Investment banking prowess apparently ran in the family; Brown's sons founded the firm now known as Brown Brothers Harriman in 1818.) The company funded railroads in the early 1800s; after the Civil War, Alexander Brown & Co. helped finance the reconstruction of the Southern United States. Alex. Brown moved into a brick-and-Tiffany glass building in 1900, a structure that would survive a 1904 fire that destroyed much of downtown Baltimore. (Alex. Brown financed the rebuilding of its neighborhood after the fire.) The firm went public in 1986, ending 186 years of private partnership. In 1997 the company moved out of its 97-year-old offices and into a skyscraper in downtown Baltimore.

The first and second marriages

After 197 years as an independent company, Alex. Brown was acquired by Bankers Trust for $1.6 billion in 1997. The merger was expected to combine Bankers Trust's corporate lending business, which included a well-known high yield practice, with Alex. Brown's niche investment banking business, creating a full-service investment bank. The combined company, BT Alex. Brown, failed to live up to expectations. Bankers Trust reported a $73 million loss in 1998, including losses of $500 million from investments in junk bonds and Russian securities in the third quarter alone. The company also suffered problems integrating corporate cultures.

In June 1999, Bankers Trust was purchased by Deutsche Bank for approximately $9 billion. The German giant was seeking to add BT's corporate lending practice as well as Alex. Brown's underwriting and private client business to its mammoth commercial banking and debt underwriting operations. The merger was met with less than enthusiastic response from industry insiders. "I'm not bullish on this deal," Evangelous Kavouriadas, an analyst at Sanford C. Bernstein, told *The Baltimore Sun* when the deal was announced in November 1998. Others doubted the corporate cultures of the two companies could be successfully melded. "I think they're very different in their philosophies," James Nesbit, assistant manager of syndications in the London office of Dai Ichi Kangyo Bank, told *Investment Dealer's Digest* in December 1998.

The merger created the expected skittishness at BT Alex. Brown. "There [were] definitely a lot of people doing some soul searching whether they wanted to stay on this boat or whether they wanted to move on," a former Alex. Brown employee told *The Baltimore Sun*. In June 1999, the company lost four managing directors in the health care investment banking group to rival Credit Suisse First Boston, including Russell Ray, who became head of CSFB's global health care group. The managing directors took over 30 additional employees to CSFB's new Baltimore office. The losses were especially frustrating to Deutsche Bank, which had lost tech banking superstar Frank Quattrone and his entire 132-person team to CSFB in June 1998.

What's in a name?

As bad as Alex. Brown's personnel losses were, they could have been worse had Mayo Shattuck, now co-head of investment banking, not won a major battle shortly after the close of the merger. *The Baltimore Sun* reported that Shattuck (formerly president and COO of Alex. Brown) convinced Deutsche Bank executives to keep the Alex. Brown name. Some within the firm felt the Alex. Brown name, despite its place in the history of Baltimore and the investment banking community, was no longer necessary after the transfer of ownership. Shattuck's point of view won out and Deutsche Bank agreed to keep Alex. Brown with the DB name tacked on the front. The year 2000 marks the 200th anniversary of the founding of Alex. Brown in Baltimore, and the firm continues to be a major corporate fixture in the city.

Hungry for more inside scoop? Join Vault.com's popular online community for finance and banking — www.vault.com

VAULT.com **223**

Looking good

A year after the close of the DB/BT merger, the once-derided deal has received praise from analysts. Though the deal "was marked by the usual clash of cultures that occurs when a commercial and investment bank come together, Deutsche Bank has done a terrific job now in getting over the hurdles and moving forward with the acquisition," Robert Bostrom, head of the financial institutions practice at New York law firm Winston & Strawn, told *The Wall Street Journal* in November 1999. The best praise, however, came from a competitor: J.P. Morgan research analyst Stuart Graham said in a research report, "We consider there is now no doubt that Deutsche has created a bulge-bracket investment bank." Graham's glowing analysis includes the firm's international I-banking business as well as Deutsche Banc Alex. Brown. According to the *Financial Times*, in 1999 Deutsche was "Europe's most profitable investment bank."

According to Thomson Financial Securities Data, Deutsche Bank ranked ninth among all lead-underwriters of common stock in 1999. In the U.S., the company lead-managed the August 1999 $24 million IPO of HotJobs.com. One month later, Deutsche Banc Alex. Brown led the $73.1 million offering of Web marketing company Luminant Worldwide. The firm also led OnDisplay's $98 million IPO in December 1999. In March 2000, the firm lead-managed IntraBiotics Pharmaceuticals' $112.5 million IPO and Eprise's $60 million offering. The sweetest of all IPOs lead-managed by Deutsche Banc Alex. Brown, however, was the April 2000 offering of Krispy Kreme Doughnut Corp, which raised $63 million.

Not this time

While the company has certainly received praise for pushing itself into the bulge bracket, Deutsche Bank recently failed in an attempt to become even more formidable. In March 2000, Deutsche Bank announced plans to merge with Dresdner Bank AG, the third-largest German bank. The deal, estimated at $31.6 billion dollars, was the second union the banks had planned; the firms had previously discussed combining retail operations in 1999, but the talks went nowhere. The full merger rapidly fell apart amid a dispute over the future of Dresdner's investment banking division, Dresdner Kleinwort Benson (DKB). According to published reports, Deutsche wanted DKB closed or sold, a move opposed by Dresdner chairman Bernhard Walker, who was slated to become co-CEO at the combined firm. In April 2000, with the dispute over DKB's future raging on, Dresdner called off the deal. Deutsche's Breuer told *The Wall Street Journal* that "no solution acceptable to both sides could be found," and that Deutsche had no other mergers in the pipeline. As a result of the failed merger, Dresdner CEO Bernhard Walter resigned. While industry observers, including *The Daily Deal*, wondered whether Breuer would be the next to go, Deutsche's chairman remains in power.

GETTING HIRED

Show some initiative

Deutsche Banc Alex. Brown's recruiting process for investment banking usually begins with an on-campus interview. A pared-down group of candidates is then invited to visit the firm's offices in New York or Baltimore, where candidates typically interview in a "Super Saturday" format with several of the firm's bankers. The firm says that it looks for candidates who demonstrate "initiative" and "excellence" and who will work well in a team environment. MBA candidates who are interested in international opportunities generally interview on campus before being invited to offices in Europe or Asia. Current bankers suggest applicants "talk to people with experience in the industry" before interviewing at the firm. Consult either the firm's job hotline or its web site, www.db.com, for a list of current job openings.

Both analysts and associates are recruited by, and hired directly into, specific departments. One financial analyst reports that the firm "looks for smart people and thinks that grades are very important in determining mental horsepower. Also, the company looks for a strong work ethic, and an outgoing and engaging personality, because you have to get along with clients when away from the office and with peers when working 100 hours a week." Those who join the firm as full-time investment banking analysts participate in eight to 12 weeks of training in London. Those who sign on as investment banking associates attend a four-week training program in New York.

The firm also offers summer analyst and associate positions. Summer positions for investment banking are available in New York, Singapore, and Hong Kong, and last anywhere from six to 10 weeks between June and September.

Hungry for more inside scoop? Join Vault.com's popular online
community for finance and banking — www.vault.com

V∧ULT.COM   **225**

OUR SURVEY SAYS

Less intense

Insiders describe the firm as being both "less intense" and "less structured" than its Wall Street peers. One insider speaks favorably of the firm's merger: "Things have moved very smoothly with Deutsche Bank — it wasn't 100 percent seamless, but it was a fluid transition. The firm had a great 1999 and there is a lot of positive sentiment here." Another insider adds, "[The merger] played out well." That source, however, also notes that the firm has become "more bureuacratic since the merger, which was expected, but not necessarily welcome."

Employees in the firm's Baltimore office give the location mixed reviews. One insider says that unlike New York, Baltimore rents are "really cheap." Another insider is less optimistic: "Baltimore is really limited in the number of places where you can live." Insiders in the New York office describe "a typical Wall Street feel" at the firm's offices. Says one associate, "There is a lot of energy here." That source goes on to note, "They have also paid more attention to bankers on the junior level. We weren't on track with the market before, but I think we are now."

Employees at various locations offer praise for the perks. "All the facilities are top-notch," says one analyst, "especially in the San Francisco branch, where the offices are on the top floor of a building that overlooks the city and the bay." Other perks include: overtime meals, taxis, and bonuses. "When you travel you stay in the top hotels," notes another source. Bankers in all American locations enjoy a full-time business casual dress policy.

"Things have moved very smoothly with Deutsche Bank — it wasn't 100 percent seamless, but it was a fluid transition."

— *Deutsche Banc Alex. Brown Insider*

Donaldson, Lufkin & Jenrette

277 Park Avenue
New York, NY 10172
(212) 892-3000
Fax: (212) 892-7272
www.dlj.com

LOCATIONS

New York (HQ)
Atlanta
Baltimore
Boston
Chicago
Dallas
Houston
Los Angeles
Menlo Park
Miami
San Francisco

Buenos Aires
Frankfurt
Hong Kong
London
Mexico City
Paris
São Paulo
Seoul
Taipei

DEPARTMENTS

Equities
Financial Services Group
Fixed Income
Investment Banking

THE STATS

CEO: Joe Roby
Type of Employer: Public Company
Ticker Symbol: DLJ (NYSE)
1999 Net Revenue: $5.6 billion
1999 Net Income: $600.7 million
No. of Employees: 10,200
No. of Offices: 29

UPPERS

• Entrepreneurial culture
• Responsibility for junior professionals

DOWNERS

• Long hours
• Terrible clerical and creative
  support staff

KEY COMPETITORS

Bear Stearns
Credit Suisse First Boston
Goldman Sachs
Lehman Brothers
Merrill Lynch
Morgan Stanley Dean Witter
Salomon Smith Barney

EMPLOYMENT CONTACT

Investment Banking
Rachel Graves
277 Park Avenue
New York, NY 10172

Investment Services Group,
Equities and Fixed Income
Gladys Chen
280 Park Avenue
New York, NY 10017

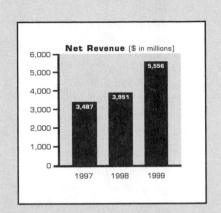

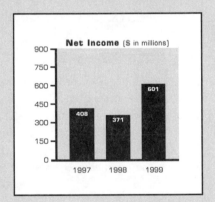

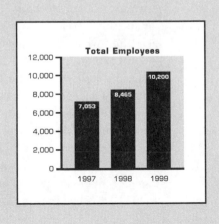

THE SCOOP

A splashy beginning

Founded in 1959 by three Harvard MBAs, Donaldson, Lufkin & Jenrette (DLJ) has grown into one of Wall Street's most influential investment banks. DLJ was first known on Wall Street as a research firm. Its reputation soon expanded — in 1970 DLJ created a media sensation by becoming the first member firm of the New York Stock Exchange to go public. DLJ leapt wholeheartedly into the hostile takeover market of the 1980s, advising legendary corporate raider T. Boone Pickens on some of his more audacious forays. In 1985 DLJ was purchased by Equitable, which was subsequently acquired by AXA Financial. In October 1995, AXA took DLJ public yet again. As of December 1999, AXA owned approximately 70 percent of DLJ's outstanding stock. The firm has over 10,200 employees, 1,000 of whom are classified as investment bankers.

DLJ divisions

DLJ's operations are organized around four major groups: investment banking, equity, fixed income, and the financial services group. Investment banking includes DLJ's M&A advisory business, the firm's successful merchant banking operation, venture capital (the Sprout Group), and the new security issues management and underwriting. The equities and fixed income divisions provide research, securities trading, and sales services to institutional clients.

The financial services group rivals the other groups in revenue and far exceeds them in number of employees. Aside from asset management, the financial services group's main businesses are subsidiaries that do not offer what are generally considered core I-banking services. Several of these, such as DLJdirect (one of the country's leading online brokerage systems) and the Pershing Division, have been pioneers in the use of technology in the financial services industry. Pershing provides a range of trade execution, clearing, and information management services to securities services and investment advisors and was an early entry in electronic distribution. Due in large part to the success of DLJdirect and Internet IPO fever, as well as the anticipation of a spin-off of the online trading subsidiary, the firm saw its stock rise in 1999. DLJ issued tracking stock for DLJdirect in May 1999.

King of a smaller kingdom

DLJ had a solid year in 1999. For the full year, the firm reported record profits of $600.7 million, a 62 percent increase over 1998's results. Still, DLJ probably won't be offended if you call it junky — the firm has profited enormously from underwriting junk bonds (high yield debt) at a time when other banks thought the category was dead for good. In fact, when the fiefdom of junk bond czar Michael Milken and Drexel Burnham Lambert imploded in 1991, DLJ zoomed in and scooped up Drexel's best and brightest, unlike other firms that shied away from the scandal. Today, DLJ is the perennial leader in junk bond underwriting. According to Thomson Financial Securities Data, in 1999 the firm was first among all underwriters of high yield debt, lead-underwriting $17.5 billion in junk bonds. While DLJ is the undisputed heavyweight of junk, the high yield market has shrunk significantly in recent years, leaving DLJ with a larger piece of a smaller pie. In 1999 DLJ lead-managed $17.5 billion of junk bonds, which represented a 18.3 percent market share. The previous year, the firm underwrote $21.5 billion of junk bonds, which represented a 15.4 percent market share. Essentially, the high yield market is slowing down significantly. As this trend continues, it becomes increasingly important for DLJ to become more dominant in other I-banking businesses.

Not all junk

While capitalizing on its strong junk bond practice, DLJ is also looking to grow other businesses. In more high-profile business areas, such as stock underwriting and M&A advisory, DLJ is making a push towards Wall Street's leaders. The firm ranked sixth among lead managers of common stock offerings in 1999 (according to TFSD), lead managing IPOs for Goto.com, Jupiter Communications, SciQuest.com, and Xpedior. In mergers and acquisitions, DLJ is playing some impressive catch-up. The firm ranked 12th in completed global M&A in 1998 and climbed up to the seventh slot in 1999. DLJ gained notice for advisory roles in deals such as AT&T's $70 billion acquisition of Telecommunications Inc. (working for TCI) and Olivetti's much-publicized hostile takeover of former Italian monopoly Telecom Italia in 1999. In 1999, as in previous years, DLJ ranked 10th among the lead managers of investment grade bond issues, according to TFSD. DLJ has also been targeting growth in convertible securities. The firm recently hired several senior investment bankers to build this business.

Hungry for more inside scoop? Join Vault.com's popular online
community for finance and banking — www.vault.com

VAULT.com **231**

DLJ's merchant banking group is one of the most well-regarded areas of the firm. Through this group, the company invests in venture capital deals, leveraged buyouts, real estate, and a variety of other opportunities. At the end of 1999, the group managed funds with $10 billion in committed capital. Increased strength in technology banking should also complement DLJ's successful venture capital affiliate, the Sprout Group. In January 2000, the Sprout Group co-led a $21 million second round of investment in Silicon Access Technology.

London calling

DLJ's current focus is on expanding overseas, particularly in Europe where advisory and equity underwriting represent the largest growth sectors in banking. The firm has especially emphasized growing its presence in London. In early 1997, DLJ agreed to buy a London-based firm, Phoenix Group, as part of its efforts to penetrate the European market. That year, DLJ established a junk bond group in the London office and boosted other investment banking capabilities. The firm also set up a private banking operation in London, specializing in "off the screen" entrepreneurial investments. The private banking group was the first such overseas group for the bank. When longtime CEO John Chalsty stepped down and handed the reins to Joe Roby in February 1998, the expansion in Europe, and particularly in London, was Roby's main stated concern. (Incidentally, Chalsty stepped down as CEO but remains chairman of the firm.) In the past two years, DLJ has created 1,000 jobs in London alone. At the end of 1999, 1,700 individuals worked for DLJ outside of the U.S.

The company's early efforts in international expansion have seen some results. In 1999 the firm co-advised AXA on its acquisition of Guardian Royal Exchange in addition to working on the Olivetti-Telecom Italia takeover. In November 1999, DLJ announced plans to hire up to 75 more investment bankers in Europe. Jim Alexandre, president of DLJ International, told the *Financial News* that DLJ International is "absolutely, positively in aggressive growth mode right now." However, according to many industry experts, DLJ will have to pick up the pace on European expansion if the firm wishes to remain competitive with the bulge bracket.

In the spring of 2000, a stumbling stock market resulted in a dip in the share prices of the publicly traded brokerage companies, including DLJ. The firm initiated a plan to buy back 10 million of its shares in May

2000. In reporting on the share buyback, the *Financial Times* noted, "DLJ has had a rough ride. It is a smaller participant in the largest growth areas of its sector's business — such as European M&A and equity underwriting. And its strengths, such as emerging markets and junk bonds, have not lately been as lucrative." In June 2000, DLJ announced that Joel Cohen, head of global M&A for the firm, would be moving to London to head up DLJ's European investment banking operation. By sending the highly successful Cohen and several other top managers abroad, DLJ clearly signaled that it did not want to fall behind in the race to gain European market share.

Making promises

In late 1999 and early 2000, DLJ, like much of Wall Street, felt the impact of new economy opportunities as an increasing number of bankers left the firm for dot-coms and venture capital companies. In an attempt to make lifestyles more agreeable, Wall Street firms switched to a full-time business casual dress policy and offered more generous expense plans; DLJ met the Street perk for perk. Then, in April 2000, DLJ shocked Wall Street by offering salary guarantees to junior bankers. The industry was accustomed to guaranteed pay packages for high-level deal makers, but DLJ was the first firm to offer compensation promises to associates. According to a report in *The Daily Deal*, "The deals will be based on an individual's historic rankings within his or her class and the guaranteed figure will serve as the floor." Insiders say first-year associates can expect a minimum of $300,000 total compensation for the first year and $400,000 for the second year. The firm also raised salaries for investment banking analysts, and insiders say they expect analyst bonuses to rise beyond Street averages. No promises, however, were made to analysts, who remain the lowest rung on the ladder of the investment banking deal team.

GETTING HIRED

DLJ manages its recruiting process from its New York headquarters in coordination with its regional offices. The firm hires undergraduates and graduates for investment banking into multiple domestic and international offices. The firm says it is very interested in candidates seeking positions outside of New York. For a comprehensive list of the dates and locations of DLJ's on-campus recruiting, visit the firm's

Hungry for more inside scoop? Join Vault.com's popular online
community for finance and banking — www.vault.com

VAULT.COM **233**

Career Opportunities web page, located at the firm's web site, www.dlj.com. At key schools the firm makes presentations, sending bigwigs such as the CEO or head of investment banking.

Get psyched

The firm conducts three rounds of interviews for undergraduates interested in analyst positions in investment banking. The first and second rounds are conducted on campus. The third and final round is a "super day." This super day involves a trip to the office where the candidate is being considered, usually on a Saturday, but sometimes a Friday or another day. On these days, the firm brings in many candidates, maybe 20 to 30, on the same day. For analyst positions, the super day is actually a half-day; the candidates arrive in the morning and have five to six half-hour interviews. Most interviews involve one candidate and two interviewers. Insiders report that the level of technical questions depends on the interviewee's background. One source reports, "What they're primarily looking for are people who are really psyched about going to DLJ. You probably wouldn't get asked any technical questions unless they have any questions about your technical abilities."

Final decisions are made shortly after the candidates leave. "At the end of the day, all of the interviewers get together in a room and debate for several hours until they reach consensus on all candidates," explains one recruiter. "They also have all written feedback from earlier rounds in front of them." According to one analyst, "The core school on the undergrad level is Penn, specifically Wharton." However, this source notes that in recent years the firm has had to widen its net.

MBA recruiting

DLJ holds three rounds of interviews for MBAs in hiring for investment banking associate positions. The first round is held on campus, the second at a hotel near the school, and the third, "super day" round takes place at the office for which the candidate is being considered. Both of the first two rounds involve two-on-one interviews. The MBA super day process (the final round) is similar to the final round for analysts — expect four to five hours. Insiders tell us that DLJ will call candidates for a fourth round of interviews if a candidate is being considered for a specialty group position and has not had a chance to meet enough bankers in that group.

The firm recruits at over 20 schools for its Investment Services Group (the division that covers high net worth and small institutions). For investment services, the first round is on campus, the second round at the local office the candidate is being considered for, and a third round in New York. For the equities division, the firm holds a first-round interview on campus and a second round in New York. For each of these, the first round is a two-on-one interview.

DLJ holds two to three rounds of interviews for MBAs interested in fixed income. The first round is held on campus and subsequent rounds are held in New York. Interviews are generally one-on-one meetings with managers from sales, trading and research.

OUR SURVEY SAYS

Fierce entrepreneurs

DLJ has a "fiercely entrepreneurial" culture that is "individualistic and exciting," employees say. One Los Angeles-based analyst suggests that "to understand DLJ's culture, think of DLJ and Goldman as being the two opposite poles of the world of investment banking. Goldman is solidly conservative and extremely team-oriented. DLJ is daring and individualistic." DLJ's Los Angeles office has a particularly "freewheeling and risk-friendly" attitude because of all "the people who came over from Drexel and brought the Drexel attitude over." An associate in the New York office comments that because of DLJ's aggressive attitude, "people are better rewarded here for their performance than in other banks." In general, insiders give DLJ high marks for pay, saying that the firm "consistently exceeds industry standards for compensation." Another insider notes, "DLJ is more of a meritocracy than other firms. If you work hard, you move through the whole spectrum of jobs really rapidly. Everything that goes on is really based on performance. So there's nothing in the way of people getting moved up more quickly or getting higher compensation if they're doing something good. DLJ keeps the politics away." An insider in sales and trading agrees: "It is really a meritocracy here — if you get in, you get an opportunity to really excel. If you're making the firm money, then the sky's the limit. The title is less important than your bonus." Says yet another insider at the firm's headquarters: "It's managed very well, and it's not as political as other places."

Hungry for more inside scoop? Join Vault.com's popular online
community for finance and banking — www.vault.com

VAULT.com **235**

High pressure

This freedom comes at a price. Insiders say DLJ "puts a lot of pressure on you to perform. DLJ works you harder than some of the other investment firms." The amount of pressure varies from group to group. On the sell side, for example, "high grade is a lot more laid-back than high yield." Says one research associate about high yield salespeople and traders: "There are people who will eat you alive if your analysis is off. They control a huge universe of issues and a huge amount of buyers to make that market liquid, and when you present your analysis you had better be ready. These guys are serious. It's like playing for the San Francisco 49ers — you better be prepared." One of DLJ's vice presidents in the Los Angeles office notes, "I think there's a risk that anytime there's a freewheeling culture it can be a tougher place to be for an individual than in places that have sort of a team attitude and group-think culture." Insiders are quick to add, however, that DLJ has a "friendly, social corporate environment. There's a lot of firm activities going on around here." An I-banking analyst adds: "I think DLJ has a reputation of being a sweatshop, but it is much more laid-back. People here are goal-oriented."

Pay with an edge

At the entry level, DLJ pays "better" than other investment banks, especially when it comes to bonuses, according to recent hires. But even better than the above-average salary is DLJ's merchant banking program. The firm allows bankers to invest in the merchant banking (similar to private equity or venture capital) investments that the firm chooses. Although not all DLJ professionals are eligible to make the investments, junior insiders report that the firm is organizing investment opportunities for junior bankers as well. "People make a lot of money that way," reports one contact. "There are lot of people who won't leave because of these merchant banking deals, because they aren't completely vested, and also because the gravy keeps coming." Another source explains the merchant banking program: "If it goes bust, you don't owe them anything. It's all upside, no downside."

Dressing down and taking taxis home

Dress at DLJ's corporate headquarters in New York is business casual every day, with exceptions for certain client meetings. Investment banking insiders report dinner allowances of $25 and car service that is available starting at 10:00 p.m. "You can expense a cab anytime after 8:00 p.m.," one insider notes. "But you hardly ever get out that early."

Hungry for more inside scoop? Join Vault.com's popular online
community for finance and banking — www.vault.com

VAULT.COM **237**

Goldman Sachs

85 Broad Street
New York, NY 10004
(212) 902-1000
Fax: (212) 902-3000
www.gs.com

LOCATIONS

U.S.

New York (HQ)
Atlanta • Boston • Chicago • Dallas •
Houston • Los Angeles • Memphis •
Menlo Park • Miami • Philadelphia •
Princeton • San Francisco • Tampa •
Washington, DC

Outside the U.S.

Australia • Bangkok • Canada • China •
France • Germany • Grand Cayman •
Hong Kong • India • Italy • Japan •
Korea • Mexico • Russian • Sweden •
Singapore • South Africa • Spain •
Switzerland • United Kingdom

DEPARTMENTS

Equities
Fixed Income, Currency, Commodities
Global Investment Research
Information Technology
Investment Banking
Investment Management
Merchant Banking

THE STATS

CEO: Henry M. Paulson, Jr.
Head of Investment Banking:
Steven Heller
Employer Type: Public Company
Ticker Symbol: GS (NYSE)
1999 Net Revenue: $13.3 billion
1999 Net Earnings: $2.7 billion
No. of Employees: 15,361
No. of Offices: 41

UPPERS

• Excellent support staff
• Talented co-workers
• Top-quality name brand

DOWNERS

• Grueling hours
• More bureaucracy since IPO
• Overbearing culture

KEY COMPETITORS

Credit Suisse First Boston
Merrill Lynch
Morgan Stanley Dean Witter
Salomon Smith Barney

EMPLOYMENT CONTACT

Bob Gottlieb
Goldman Sachs
85 Broad Street
New York, NY 10004

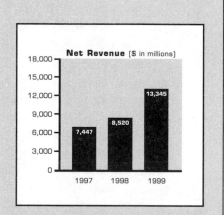

Net Revenue [$ in millions]

1997	1998	1999
7,447	8,520	13,345

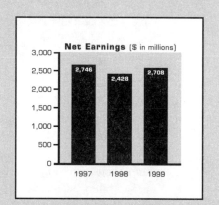

Net Earnings [$ in millions]

1997	1998	1999
2,746	2,428	2,708

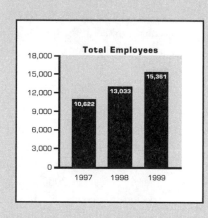

Total Employees

1997	1998	1999
10,622	13,033	15,361

THE SCOOP

CULT-ure of success

Founded in 1869 by Marcus Goldman, a European immigrant, Goldman Sachs is one of the nation's oldest and most prestigious investment banking firms. Goldman has not only distinguished itself from its competitors with its conservative attitude but has also created a reputation among both employees and outsiders that the firm is the pinnacle of investment banking success. By insisting that the firm come first and individual egos a distant second, Goldman Sachs has achieved unparalleled success among American I-banks in prompting high-flying corporate whiz kids to bow to the overall interests of the firm. Goldman is also legendary for its secrecy. The firm rarely lets the media see what's going on behind the scenes. Even former employees tend not to speak to the press — perhaps as a result of the legal clauses that Goldman reportedly inserts in every employee's contract, which ensure that he or she will never speak out in public about even the smallest detail of office life.

Top of the heap

In 1999 Goldman Sachs soared to the top of nearly every major league table, according to Thomson Financial Securities Data. The firm ranked first among advisors of completed (and announced) worldwide M&A transactions, advising on 369 deals with a combined transaction value of $915 billion. Goldman also topped the list of IPO underwriters, lead-managing 54 deals and raising $14.5 billion in proceeds. Finally, Goldman was the top underwriter of all equity transactions, lead-managing 123 issues and raising proceeds of $33.7 billion. The firm is also ranked in the top 10 among lead underwriters of high yield issues, asset-backed securities, and investment grade debt.

The trouble with research

While Goldman topped the league tables for underwriting, it took a slight hit in sell-side equity research. The firm fell two spots in a Greenwich Associates poll of buy-side analysts. In recent years, Goldman had consistently captured the first or second slot but fell to number four in 2000. According to *Wall Street Letter*, the analysts polled in the survey said Goldman's Investment Research Division has recently been affected by especially high turnover and low morale.

The firm's research division picked up some more negative press in June 2000 when *The Wall Street Journal* issued a story about a recently released Goldman e-commerce report. In the report, one of the firm's research analysts grouped 32 e-commerce companies into three categories depending on survival prospects. The analyst listed eight companies as having the best chances of surviving, seven of which were Goldman clients. The second tier, with poorer survival chances, included only one Goldman client, and the last tier of companies included no Goldman clients. The analyst, Anthony Noto, defended his report, insisting, "My research is independent from our corporate relationships." Some Wall Street insiders agreed and lauded Noto for his report. Noto also noted that it was reasonable to think that his evaluative criteria and that of Goldman's underwriting professionals might overlap. Others, including the *Journal* article's author, said that the report "raises anew questions about how high Wall Street has erected the 'Chinese Wall' between its research and investment-banking activities."

The IPO trail (and trials)

Contributing to Goldman's mystique for years was its status as a major Wall Street private partnership. In 1998, however, the firm's partners voted to change this status and offer stock to the public. Analysts believe that two major factors drove the decision. One issue was that without stock "currency" Goldman could not acquire other banking businesses and would eventually not be able to keep pace with competitors like Merrill Lynch and Morgan Stanley Dean Witter. Additionally, observers felt that Goldman's partners sensed that the market was at its peak and wanted to cash in their chips.

However, with world financial markets in turmoil in the late summer and fall of 1998, Goldman execs shelved the IPO. The firm's longtime head, Jon Corzine, resigned from his post as co-CEO in January 1999. The firm had absorbed an estimated $500 million to $1 billion in trading losses because of the troubled markets, and industry observers believe that Corzine, who had advocated a public offering, was pushed out of the firm's top spot by other senior execs, including Henry Paulson (who had shared the CEO position with Corzine and now is the firm's sole CEO) and co-COOs John Thornton and John Thain. Firm spokespeople asserted that relieving Corzine of CEO duties would give him the time to concentrate on IPO-related matters.

Hungry for more inside scoop? Join Vault.com's popular online
community for finance and banking — www.vault.com

VAULT.com **241**

Skeletons in the IPO closet?

In filings for its planned IPO, Goldman revealed details of its finances that had until that time been kept secret. While Goldman's M&A and underwriting businesses were always recognized as impressive, the firm was more dependent on its trading operations (both for clients, when it takes a commission, and on its own account) — far more so than its closest competitors. For example, in 1999, the firm earned 43 percent of its revenue from trading. In comparison, Morgan Stanley earned just 20 percent of its revenue from trading. In every year from 1995 to 1999, Goldman's trading revenues outpaced investment banking revenues. Trading, especially proprietary trading (when a firm trades its own capital rather than that of clients), is a volatile business, heavily dependant on market conditions. Analysts have warned that Goldman's dependence on proprietary trading makes it vulnerable to market downturns. Industry observers interpret the changeover from Corzine to Paulson to be a reflection of the firm's concern over its dependence on trading. Corzine rose through the ranks as a bond trader and is thought to have pushed the firm in that direction; Paulson climbed the corporate ladder as a banker. The firm, of course, denied any internal struggles. As of July 2000, Corzine was running for the U.S. Senate as the Democratic candidate for New Jersey and Paulson still held Goldman's reins.

The moment the Street was waiting for

In the spring of 1999, Goldman announced that IPO plans were back on track. In response, investors rushed to secure shares. A week before the company went public, the offering was eight times oversubscribed. Goldman faced so much demand that it was able to choose its investors. On May 4, 1999, Goldman went public. In the second-largest U.S. IPO at that time (behind Conoco's $4 billion offering in 1998), the firm raised $3.66 billion and issued 69 million shares. The offering valued Goldman at a hefty $33 billion. The IPO ended 130 years of private partnership and converted the 222 partners into the largest shareholders.

Can't get too comfortable at the top

While Goldman Sachs may have achieved penthouse status in the Wall Street world, it is not resting on its laurels. The firm is clearly interested in growing its asset management business. Asset management, a fee-based business, is less volatile than trading or banking. Currently, the firm lags behind Morgan Stanley and Merrill in this department.

However, Goldman has been pouring personnel and money into building asset management accounts.

Sensing more potential change in the investment banking industry, in March 1999 Goldman purchased a 22 percent ownership stake in Wit SoundView, an online investment bank, for approximately $20 million. The investment, according to Goldman, will expand the firm's distribution channels by allowing Wit customers the chance to get in on deals underwritten by Goldman. The investment also marks Goldman's interest in the online sector and its belief that the Internet will affect the future of investment banking.

Goldman also experienced its share of wins and losses in the war for talent. Notable gains included Roberto Mendoza, former vice chairman of J.P. Morgan, who joined Goldman's London office as a managing director in June 2000. In 1999 Goldman captured the lion's share of advisory business in Europe (46.6 percent of all European M&A deals, according to Thomson Financial Securities Data), and Goldman hopes Mendoza's presence will expand the firm's presence on the continent. In March 2000, Goldman made headlines when the firm poached Jack Levy, head of mergers and acquisitions at Merrill Lynch. Levy joined Goldman as co-chairman and co-head of global M&A. While acquiring Levy may have been a major coup for the firm's investment banking group, Goldman soon received some payback from Merrill Lynch. By the end of March, five of Goldman's top-producing brokers jumped ship to Merrill. The five brokers managed a collective $6 billion in assets.

Smudges on the white shoe

Goldman, much to the shock of the financial world, received some unusually negative press in the first half of 2000. In May 2000, after some serious dips in the stock market sobered tech-hungry investors, Goldman's name emerged in the aftermath. A report in *Wired* revealed that of 32 companies for which Goldman had lead-managed IPOs in 1999, nearly half were trading below the initial offering price by April 2000. The list included high-profile disappointments such as iVillage, eToys, 1-800-Flowers.com, and TheStreet.com. The *Wired* article noted that observers were criticizing Goldman, usually a bastion of quality inspection in its underwriting practices, for "push[ing] through so many companies with dubious prospects in over-hyped markets." Goldman representatives said the press was being unfair in its evaluation. Kathleen Baum, a Goldman spokesperson, explained, "A snapshot of

Hungry for more inside scoop? Join Vault.com's popular online
community for finance and banking — www.vault.com

V/\ULT.com **243**

time really isn't representative." Industry insiders speculated that the poor performance of Goldman-managed 1999 IPOs might hurt the company's efforts to win more IPO mandates.

Goldman received more criticism for its underwriting — this time overseas — after the IPO of World Online (a Dutch Internet provider) in Amsterdam in March 2000. After the offering, it was revealed that World Online's chairperson and founder, Nina Brink, had sold shares before the offering. Goldman and fellow lead underwriter ABN Amro were criticized for not disclosing the situation to investors before the offering. A World Online shareholders group filed a suit against Goldman (as well as against World Online and ABN Amro).

GETTING HIRED

Getting the third degree

Goldman's interviewing process is notorious for its grueling intensity. Candidates undergo at least three rounds of interviews and often many more. The first and second rounds usually consist of two half-hour sessions, during which the applicant interviews with two Goldman professionals, typically one associate and a vice president. The third round is the most rigorous; it consists of five or six two-on-one interviews, each of which is 45 minutes long and involves one or more of the firm's directors. There is no clear delineation of personal and professional questions during the three rounds; candidates must be prepared to answer any question at any time. And the interview process may go beyond the ordinary five-to-six person format. Says one insider: "Goldman is a very, very consensus-driven place. I think in the full-time hiring process, you could literally meet 25 people during that process, which is unheard of at other banks."

One of us

Goldman cares a lot about fit — a lot. This is the unanimous emphasis of firm insiders, who believe that more than any other Wall Street firm, Goldman weeds out those who will not fit with the firm's culture. All candidates are questioned on their willingness and ability to work hard as team players in an intense and demanding work environment. Interviewers say that they look for "people with smart personalities who aren't afraid to work hard. We especially don't want big egos around the place, so we try and find out how you will be able to work with someone you don't like too much personally." "They stress over and over again that anybody graduating from a top MBA program can do what they want them to do," says one source. "But they can't change his personality or make him pleasant to work with. They really put a lot of effort into the personality part." In fact, one recent hire reports that he received "rapid-fire personal questions: 'Why did you go to that school?' 'How were your grades?' 'How were you perceived by your peers?' 'Your professors?'"

When screening potential summer associates, Goldman generally conducts two on-campus rounds and a third round at the firm's headquarters, which is described as "sort of a super day, but a miniature version," with about four 30-minute interviews. For summer associates "trying out" for full-time positions, contacts say, "there's very strong attention paid to how well people work together." Play nice!

OUR SURVEY SAYS

Putting big egos in their place

Goldman Sachs' workplace is legendary for an "intense, goal-driven" ethic, where "success is taken for granted." While the rest of the world may exalt Goldman employees as the "Masters of the Universe," insiders themselves note that the firm "cuts their egos down to size." Goldman Sachs makes it clear from the beginning that "individual personalities are insignificant" and that "the firm comes first, second, and last." Says one recent hire: "I've seen some people from top schools who came across as a bit arrogant, and they were very unwelcome [at Goldman]."

New hires take some time to get used to the careful scrutiny to which they are subjected, and employees sometimes feel that they "are under constant surveillance." At the same time, analysts and associates praise their fellow employees for being "intelligent and perceptive," yet also "prepared to make the sacrifices that have to be made for the team to succeed." Reports one associate: "Teamwork is a word that's clichéd and overused, and I sort of cringe when I hear it elsewhere, but in some sense that's really what the firm prides itself on." How does teamwork

Hungry for more inside scoop? Join Vault.com's popular online community for finance and banking — www.vault.com

VAULT.com **245**

play out in everyday office life? "If you need to talk to someone, they're not going to stop everything they're doing to talk to you, but they'll say come back at the end of the day. Even senior people are very accessible," reports one contact.

However, working as part of a team of Goldman Sachs employees "can also be challenging because you have to hold up your end, and there's always pressure to measure up to your co-workers' high standards." Some insiders also feel that Goldman's emphasis on teamwork comes at a cost — "Individuality and creativity usually are considered much less important than being a good team player," says one contact. Even the most enthusiastic confess that "occasionally the stress of work can get to be too much, and you come close to cracking." Another contact says that the culture can not only cramp individual style but might be limiting the firm as a whole. Explains that source, "Because of the corporate culture and the goody two-shoes image, [the firm is] less inclined to take risks."

Hand your life to Goldman

Goldman Sachs employees work "extremely long hours," but that comes as no surprise. At one of the top investment banks, employees are guaranteed a hefty workload. After all, one of the most commonly asked questions in a Goldman interview is, "How will you cope with working 90-hour weeks, or longer, for three years?" One associate complains that the hours are "long" and "unnecessary." He goes on to say, "While it is somewhat due to the nature of the business, my biggest complaint is they don't hire enough junior people." This paucity of junior people can increase the workload, depending on how far down the chain you happen to be. "For the first few years, analysts usually work between 80 and 110 hours a week" and generally come in to the office "at least six days a week, though you're usually there every day of the week." Working until 10 at night is virtually a daily affair, and "all-nighters are pretty frequent" as project deadlines draw near. Even those employees who say that they love working for Goldman concede that the hours "just get a bit too much at times." New hires, however, should take heart from the fact that "the hours loosen up as you get promoted." Vice presidents rarely work all day on weekends; they reportedly usually "just drop in for a couple of hours on Saturday mornings, tell the analysts and associates what to do, and then leave."

Insiders say the firm is recognizing the effects of the grueling lifestyle. Defections to dot-coms have affected even almighty Goldman. One source says the firm has paid "much more attention to [lifestyle issues] since people have been leaving to dot-coms. They have not created solutions to ease the workload, but rather to make your life easier while you keep working." These changes include Goldman's switch to a business casual dress code policy. Goldman announced the move in February 2000, and became the second major player to make the change (the first was J.P. Morgan). The firm also offers a concierge service that will pick up dry cleaning and perform other daytime errands for employees trapped in the office.

Full support

Goldman's support staff wins high marks from employees for being "thoroughly efficient and professional." According to insiders, Goldman bankers enjoy support services that are as good as they get on the Street. Analysts have secretaries to answer their calls, although they have to share — usually one secretary is assigned to four or five analysts or associates. Goldman's support staff infrastructure ensures that backup secretaries are always available to fill in any gaps caused by illness or absence among the regular support staff. The highly paid support staff (like other Goldman employees, support staff receive year-end bonuses) not only perform standard administrative and clerical duties such as faxing and filing but also help associates and analysts with making graphs, setting up databases, and creating charts and tables. Every floor at Goldman's New York headquarters has a word processing room staffed with "friendly, knowledgeable" people. Goldman's data resources and library staff members are also "superb" but tend to "grumble about last-minute requests." Overall, Goldman employees remark that the top-notch support staff plays an "integral" role in ensuring the smooth execution of pitchbooks and presentations.

Posh offices

Goldman Sachs' New York headquarters is split into two main locations; 85 Broad Street, Goldman's headquarters, houses the investment banking business and Goldman's administrative functions, while the sales and trading business is located across the street at One New York Plaza. (The firm also has a few smaller offices in New York.) Goldman's offices are "modern" and "beautiful," and the lobbies and hallways are bedecked with "expensive artwork by renowned artists

Hungry for more inside scoop? Join Vault.com's popular online
community for finance and banking — www.vault.com

VAULT.com **247**

such as Jasper Johns." All analysts and associates are assigned their own cubicles. Our sources complain that working in cubicles eventually "gets tiresome," because they afford very little privacy; one analyst notes that "everyone can listen in on all of your personal phone calls." Junior employees are particularly irked that "senior people can tell whether you are working or slacking off." One associate complains that "it's obvious whether you've gone home early" and said he took to leaving his suit jacket on his chair if he left the office before 9 p.m. Another former associate recalls, "You can't even read the paper at your desk without the whole floor knowing, so a lot of people take papers to the bathroom and read them in the stalls." However, as employees ascend the corporate hierarchy, the amount of privacy increases considerably. Vice presidents get their own "nice but small" offices, and managing directors have the luxury of large corner offices.

Dot-coms woes overpower IPO

Many industry observers wondered if Goldman's IPO would disturb the mystique and hush-hush culture of the private partnership. Insiders say that post-IPO, the mystique is safe and sound. Explains one associate, "The people who were partners [now managing directors] still control the majority of the firm. The power structure remains the same." That contact goes on to say, "The culture [at Goldman] has changed more because of the dot-coms." One source says the IPO has changed compensation: "Before people would be paid in all cash — now a good portion of your comp will be in stock." That source also notes that the firm has "become more bureaucratic since going public."

One favorable consequence of the IPO was a one-time stock grant by Goldman to junior bankers. In what industry analysts consider a move to stave off defections to dot-coms, the company issued two million shares to 8,000 analysts and associates. The amount of each bonus was calculated as a percentage of prior year's pay. According to an insider, the stock bonus was the equivalent of "20 percent of last year's compensation" and will be paid out "over the next three years."

"I've seen people from the top schools who came across as a bit arrogant and they were very unwelcome [at Goldman]."

— *Goldman Sachs Insider*

Jefferies & Company

11100 Santa Monica Blvd.
11th Floor
Los Angeles, CA 90025
(310) 445-1199
Fax: (310) 914-1014
www.jefco.com

LOCATIONS

Los Angeles (HQ)
Atlanta
Boston
Chicago
Dallas
Houston
New Orleans
Stamford
New York
San Francisco

Hong Kong
London
Tokyo
Zurich

DEPARTMENTS

Convertibles - Sales, Trading and
    Research
Corporate Finance
Equity - Sales, Trading and Research
High Yield - Sales, Trading and
    Research
International
Prime Brokerage Services
Trading Technology

THE STATS

CEO: Frank Baxter
Head of Global Investment Banking:
Chris M. Kanoff
Employer Type: Public Company
Ticker Symbol: JEF (NYSE)
1999 Net Revenues: $640.1 million
1999 Net Earnings: $61.7 million
No. of Employees: 875
No. of Offices: 19

UPPERS

- Early responsibility
- Easy movement between groups
- Leader in third-market trading

DOWNERS

- Lack of structure can lead to chaos
- Little training
- Niche-market player

KEY COMPETITORS

CIBC World Markets
Donaldson, Lufkin & Jenrette

EMPLOYMENT CONTACT

Corporate Finance
Dee Dee Bird-Jhawar
(310) 575-5252
11100 Santa Monica Blvd.
11th Floor
Los Angeles, CA 90025
E-mail: dbird@jefco.com

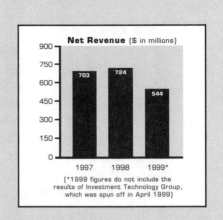

Net Revenue [$ in millions]

[*1999 figures do not include the results of Investment Technology Group, which was spun off in April 1999]

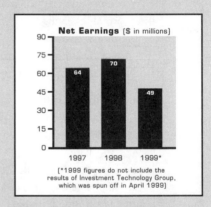

Net Earnings [$ in millions]

[*1999 figures do not include the results of Investment Technology Group, which was spun off in April 1999]

Total Employees

[*1999 figures do not include the results of Investment Technology Group, which was spun off in April 1999]

THE SCOOP

The cowboy way

Founded in 1962 by Boyd Jefferies, Los Angeles-based Jefferies & Company, Inc. has developed a reputation as a maverick firm. Jefferies, a UCLA graduate, spent three years as a cowboy on his uncle's ranch, ropin' steer. In 1956 Jefferies joined Noble Tulk, a Pasadena, California securities firm, as a clerk on the Pacific Coast Stock Exchange (PCSE). Boyd rose quickly through the ranks and became a partner in 1962. His aggressiveness and secretiveness, however, rubbed his partners the wrong way; Jefferies often declined to disclose for whom he was placing an order, an unusual practice at the time. In December 1962, he left the company to found Jefferies & Co. with $30,000 in borrowed capital. The new firm made its mark in the 1960s and 1970s as a broker of over-the-counter ("third-market") trades — trades made outside of the normal exchanges (like the NYSE). Boyd developed a solid reputation as an aggressive go-getter who would go to great lengths for his clients, qualities that would eventually contribute to his removal from the securities industry.

While the firm is still known as an equity trading house, it has in recent years focused on expanding its corporate finance and research divisions. In the 1990s the firm grew its high yield business tremendously. In 1990 CEO Frank Baxter hired approximately half of the high yield bankers, traders, and salespeople from Mike Milken's collapsed junk bond shop, Drexel Burnham Lambert. The firm, still led by Baxter, continues to provide investment banking services to mainly small and mid-size companies. "There is a tremendous value in mid-cap companies that the market has overlooked," Baxter told *Investment Dealers' Digest* in 1999. At the end of 1999, the firm employed approximately 70 bankers in 12 offices.

History: back to Boyd

When Jefferies opened its doors for business in 1962, the firm had only two employees. From these humble beginnings, Jefferies continued to grow and began trading on other regional exchanges (including Detroit, Boston, and Philadelphia) before gaining a seat on the New York Stock Exchange in 1967. In 1969 Jefferies was purchased by Investors Diversified Services, or IDS (now known as American Express). At the time, exchange rules required that broker-dealers and their parent companies derive at least 50 percent of their revenues from broker-dealer operations. IDS did not meet that requirement, and Jefferies was forced to give up its seat on the NYSE, as well as the regional exchanges. The firm became a full-time third-market brokerage.

In the early 1970s, because of many factors including market downturns, IDS became less interested in the brokerage business. In 1973 Boyd Jefferies agreed to buy the compay back from IDS. Back in Boyd's hands, the company continued to grow and dominate other third-market firms. In October 1983, the firm sold 1.75 million shares of Jefferies Group, Inc. to the public for $13 per share.

Et tu, Ivan?

In 1987, 35 years after founding his firm, Boyd Jefferies was forced out of the securities business. Jefferies' legendary love of secrecy eventually may have caused his downfall. Many big investors preferred dealing with Jefferies because the firm's brokers only identified investors by number and letter, thus providing them with anonymity. One of Jefferies' preferred clients was the legendary Ivan Boesky, a speculator in stocks of takeover targets. When the Securities and Exchange Commission came knocking at Boesky's door with charges of insider trading, Boesky named names in order to reduce his own sentence. One of the names he delivered was that of Boyd Jefferies. Jefferies pled guilty to two charges, including that of "parking" securities on Boesky's behalf. Basically, in parking transactions for Boesky, Jefferies purchased securities on behalf of the firm with the intent to sell them to Boesky at a later date. This practice allowed Boesky to acquire large chunks of a company without having to immediately disclose the purchases to the SEC. Boyd Jefferies was fined, suspended from securities activities for five years, and forced to resign. The firm received only censure. Though the firm claimed ignorance in the Boesky matter, the company's credibility suffered after Boyd Jefferies' resignation. The onus fell upon Frank Baxter, the new CEO, to restore order. Baxter, a marathon runner and strong proponent of meditation, proved up to the challenge, and the company has recovered from one of Wall Street's darkest periods.

Restoring order

Until 1999 Jefferies Group, Inc. was a holding company that controlled both Jefferies & Co. and a computer-automated stock trading company

Hungry for more inside scoop? Join Vault.com's popular online community for finance and banking — www.vault.com

VAULT.com 253

for institutional investors, Investment Technology Group. In the spring of 1998, as its profits soared, Jefferies Group announced that it would spin off both Jefferies & Co. and Investment Technology Group (in separate offerings) in a complex transaction designed to allow Jefferies & Co. to remain an institutional brokerage but also to concentrate more on investment banking. In April 1999, the firm completed its spin-offs. All subsidiaries of the former Jefferies Group were spun off to create "New JEF" (trading on the New York Stock Exchange under the familiar JEF symbol). ITG was spun off as well and immediately merged with the old Jefferies Group. The combined new entity was renamed Investment Technology Group.

The firm's investment banking businesses, which aside from underwriting also includes M&A and other advisory work, targets small to mid-size companies in specific industries. While the company doesn't appear on the league tables with bulge-bracket firms, it has tried to carve out niches in several industries, including business, information and Internet services, e-finance, energy, gaming, media, and telecommunications.

In 1999 the firm reported record revenues. However, the firm's corporate finance area has not contributed greatly to the success. In 1997 the firm reported a record $228.6 million in corporate finance revenues; the following year it reported $126.7 million and just $80.8 million in 1999. Among Jefferies' offerings in 1999: the January 1999 IPO of Packaged Ice and the May 1999 Ziplink IPO.

In recent years, the firm's highly successful high yield business has suffered some setbacks. In 1999 the high yield markets experienced serious declines, resulting in high default rates for many firms. Jefferies' focus in the energy sector caused the firm to have a default-to-issuance rate of 23.6 percent (the highest of any major firm) from 1997 to 2000 for bonds issued between 1995 and 1999, according to *Investment Dealers' Digest*. The *IDD* report noted that many of Jefferies' problems related to one specific issuer, TransAmerican Energy Corp., whose bonds comprised more than half of the $2.6 billion in defaults. "The default rate is what you'd expect for a company that dominated the energy sector in 1997 and 1998," Chris Kanoff, executive VP and director of corporate finance at Jefferies, told *IDD*. He also asserted that despite the problems in the energy sector, "We have a very active high yield business."

New hires

In April 1999, the firm announced plans to expand its investment banking business. "We think there's plenty of opportunity to poach from competitors that are now part of larger commercial banking organizations, where several bankers may be disenchanted by the new expectations being placed on them and would be attracted to Jefferies' more entrepreneurial environment," CEO Baxter told *Investment Dealers' Digest*.

The firm embarked on a hiring spree during 1999 and 2000. In March 1999, Jefferies hired Steve Black, formerly of Deutsche Bank Securities, as director of equity research. In July 1999, the firm hired David Wachter as a managing director in the firm's business, information, and Internet services group. In December 1999, the company hired Frank Bracken from Prudential Securities as a senior equity research analyst in the energy exploration and production industry. In May 2000, the firm stole another Prudential Securities research analyst when it hired Michael Legg to join the firm's Internet equity research team. Also in May, the firm announced it had added four sales professionals from Schroders to its high yield group. Later that month, Jefferies hired Robert Kramer as managing director of e-finance investment banking and Craig Peckham as an equity research analyst in the banking technology sector. Both Kramer and Peckham joined the company from Bear Stearns.

GETTING HIRED

Typical banking

Jefferies recruits at select college and business school campuses. Says one insider about the firm's interviews: "I would classify it as typical I-banking. You get some technical questions — it depends on the interviewer. Some are real lax, others are real intense." Unlike some firms which employ two-on-two interviews, however, "all we do pretty much is one-on-ones," reports an insider. Although in the past Jefferies has recruited primarily for full-time rather than summer positions, the firm is developing a more structured summer associate hiring process. "They're definitely moving that way, because they've grown so much," reports one insider. In 1999 the firm hired eight summer analysts and

Hungry for more inside scoop? Join Vault.com's popular online community for finance and banking — www.vault.com

VAULT.com **255**

associates. For full-time positions, the firm hired 12 analysts and four associates that year.

Those who have a banking or finance background have perhaps more of an edge over other applicants than they would at other firms, insiders say. "By and large, Jefferies likes to hire people who've been in banking before, because they don't have a large training program that the bulge-bracket firms have," reports one contact. That source describes the firm's analyst training program as "helpful, but it's only a week. It's modeling, Excel, just kind of walking you through the basics."

OUR SURVEY SAYS

Those Drexel guys are everywhere

One insider at Jefferies explains the firm's recent history: "It's traditionally a high yield firm. When Drexel [Burnham Lambert] blew up, basically half of the bankers went to DLJ, half went to start Jefferies Corporate Finance. Over the last four years, we've moved into basically every product group." That contact says the notorious aggressiveness of Mike Milken's bankers at Drexel has been preserved at Jefferies. "I would say it's very aggressive, very hardworking. There's some competition amongst bankers."

What does this "aggressive" atmosphere mean for bankers looking at Jefferies? "It's one of the few places where you can have a completely general experience. You're not pushed into a product group right away. Although they have those groups, you're free to move on your own," reports one source. "Maybe there's a lack of controls, but that's just the trade-off. You've got to be aggressive. If you're looking for structure, you're not going to be happy."

Because Jefferies is a small firm, insiders report that "analysts and associates are going to meetings, not just doing spreadsheets." Another Jefferies employee is impressed by the responsibility afforded at a smaller firm: "You definitely have much more responsibility. As a second-year analyst, you're pretty much playing an associate role. It's not as structured. There are a lot of deal teams without an associate or VP, just an analyst going to work with a managing director."

More personality

"I think they pay above market," says one banker. "Definitely in the bonus; the base is on par with Wall Street. When you're a smaller firm, sometimes that's the only way you can differentiate yourself." Also, the firm reportedly has an outstanding 401(k) program. "The matching is pretty attractive," reports one insider. "It's based on Jefferies' profitability, so it can be over 100 percent." How hard do the bankers work for the money? "It's right on par with most Wall Street firms. Analysts are at about 80 to 85 [hours] per week, associates maybe 70." Work may be less painful, though, our contacts say. "It's a more casual atmosphere, more of a West Coast feel, without a doubt," says one insider. "There's more personality."

Hungry for more inside scoop? Join Vault.com's popular online
community for finance and banking — www.vault.com

VAULT.com **257**

J.P. Morgan

60 Wall Street
New York, NY 10260
(212) 483-2323
www.jpmorgan.com

LOCATIONS

New York (HQ)
Atlanta
Boston
Chicago
Los Angeles
San Francisco
Washington, DC

Brussels
London
Rome
Singapore
Tokyo
Locations in 54 other cities worldwide

DEPARTMENTS

Asset Management Services
Global Markets
Investment Banking
Internal Consulting Service

THE STATS

Chairman & CEO: Douglas Warner III
Employer Type: Public Company
Ticker Symbol: JPM (NYSE)
1999 Net Revenue: $7.1 billion
1999 Net Income: $2.1 billion
No. of Employees: 15,512
No. of Offices: 66

UPPERS

• Great diversity
• Huge focus on employees' quality of life
• Prestige

DOWNERS

• Emphasis on teamwork not for everyone
• Pay below Wall Street average
• Somewhat stuffy

KEY COMPETITORS

Chase Manhattan
Credit Suisse First Boston
Deutsche Bank
Donaldson, Lufkin & Jenrette
Lehman Brothers
Salomon Smith Barney

EMPLOYMENT CONTACT

Human Resources
60 Wall Street
New York, NY 10260
www.jpmorgan.com/careers

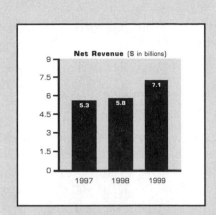

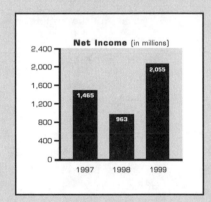

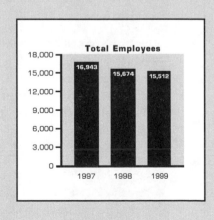

THE SCOOP

Becoming less commercial

With a history that spans over 160 years, J.P. Morgan is one of the most respected names in the annals of American business. The firm survived the Great Depression and two World Wars, but one of its greatest obstacles may have been the Glass-Steagall Act of 1933. J.P. Morgan was forced to abandon its investment banking operations after the passage of the law, which separated investment and commercial banking. The company became a commercial bank, and only within the past 15 to 20 years has it returned to I-banking. Unlike other large commercial banks, such as Bank of America and Deutsche Bank, which have built their I-banking practices by acquiring firms, Morgan has decided to grow its business from within. In addition to its historically stellar reputation in the U.S., the firm has a solid international presence. Over half of the firm's revenues are derived from outside of the U.S.

Rich in history

J.P. Morgan traces its roots back to 1838, when American George Peabody opened a London merchant bank. Junius S. Morgan became Peabody's partner in 1854, and eventually the firm became known as J.S. Morgan & Company. Seven years later, Junius' son, J. Pierpont, established J.P. Morgan & Company, a New York sales office for securities that were underwritten by his father. Working on both sides of the Atlantic, the Morgans were responsible for bringing capital from Europe that was crucial to U.S. growth. In 1895, five years after Junius' death, J. Pierpont consolidated the family businesses under the J.P. Morgan name.

The firm's growth continued unimpeded until the enactment of the Glass-Steagall Act in 1933. Because of the newly formed barriers between commercial and investment banking, the firm experienced many changes. Several partners, including Harry Morgan (grandson of J. Pierpont) left the firm to form an investment banking firm, Morgan Stanley. J.P. Morgan, after a merger with Guaranty Trust Company, moved into the commercial and personal loan business.

In the 1960s, J.P. Morgan began underwriting securities in Europe, where there were fewer banking regulations. The company craved such business in the United States, especially once corporations looked to bonds as a cheaper alternative to bank loans. In 1989 J.P. Morgan received permission from the Federal Reserve to enter debt underwriting; one year later, the door to equity underwriting was opened.

The times they are a changin'

Wall Street analysts have been impressed by J.P. Morgan's ability to grow its investment banking practice so quickly. Morgan reported net income of $2.1 billion for 1999, compared to $963 million the previous year. It also reported return on equity (ROE) of 18.4 percent for 1999. While the firm's expansion efforts — combined with an outstanding economic boom — produced solid results in 1999, the firm still hovers in the lower half of most important league tables of top-10 underwriters and financial advisors. According to Thomson Financial Securities Data, the firm ranked seventh among underwriters of common stock offerings, lead-managing 27 deals worth $9.6 billion. The company also ranked seventh among lead underwriters of domestic IPOs, underwriting offerings with combined proceeds of $2.8 billion. J.P. Morgan continues to succeed in debt underwriting — the firm ranked sixth among underwriters of asset-backed deals, with 51 deals worth $16.9 billion. The company captured ninth place among underwriters of investment grade debt, underwriting 238 deals worth $31.8 billion. Finally, the firm placed fifth among advisors of completed worldwide M&A transactions, offering opinions on 235 deals worth $364.2 billion.

The firm has also continued to emphasize the importance of attracting talented bankers in order to grow its investment banking business. J.P. Morgan hired nearly 100 investment banking professionals in 1999 with the intent of boosting services to technology companies. Specifically, the company hopes to gain more mandates for IPO underwriting and M&A advisory assignments to telecommunications, high tech, and Internet companies. Like other investment banks, J.P. Morgan has experienced its share of losses in the scramble for talent. In February 2000, Roberto Mendoza, the firm's vice chairman, resigned after 32 years with the organization. (While Mendoza originally announced the departure as his retirement, he was quickly lured away from his life of leisure by Goldman Sachs. In June 2000, Mendoza joined Goldman as a managing director in the firm's London office.)

In addition to focusing on growing its banking business, J.P. Morgan has made other efforts to change with the times. One of the firm's latest initiatives is LabMorgan, an in-house incubator that develops e-finance businesses and ideas generated both inside and outside the firm.

Hungry for more inside scoop? Join Vault.com's popular online
community for finance and banking — www.vault.com

V/\ULT.com **261**

LabMorgan functions similarly to other incubators, providing office space, advice, and technological help to accelerate the development of potential businesses that originate from Morgan employees or contacts — the firm calls them "intrapreneurs." "We do all the things a typical incubator does during the time-to-market phase and we probably do them at least as well as any incubator," Thorkild Juncker, the managing director who heads LabMorgan, told *Euromoney*. "Where we are unique is in the time-to-value phase, that is, in taking the new venture from launch to critical mass, to making it a real player. We excel here because of our client reach and knowledge of the underlying financial markets." Despite these enormous strides to keep up with technology, the firm received some derisive press in June 2000, when the J.P. Morgan web site was deactivated because the firm (through a clerical error) missed a $35 payment — a renewal fee for the domain name jpmorgan.com.

Getting casual

Known as the consummate white-shoe firm, J.P. Morgan made headlines with a change in its dress code policy. In February 2000, the firm initiated a full-time business casual dress policy. While other I-banks were already allowing casual Fridays or summers, J.P. Morgan was the first to issue a full-time policy of khaki pants and button-down shirts. A former J.P. Morgan employee expressed his astonishment regarding the change to *The New York Observer*: "What are the firms you would absolutely expect not to change? I would say that J.P. Morgan's at the top of the list."

Courtroom drama

J.P. Morgan has faced its share of adversity while building its business. In August 1999, a federal judge unsealed a $735 million lawsuit leveled at Morgan. The suit, filed by Japanese trading company Sumitomo, alleges that Morgan lent money to a rogue trader in Sumitomo's employ and then demanded restitution at usurious rates. Sumitomo contends that neither the loans themselves nor the payments back to Morgan were on the up-and-up. Officials at J.P. Morgan have sworn to fight the charges, claiming that Sumitomo is merely attempting to pass the buck.

GETTING HIRED

Changing with the times

Like the bank itself, Morgan's recruiting process has changed dramatically in the past decade or so. The firm's different divisions recruit separately (rather than relying on a cumbersome and less-focused unified recruiting effort). Also, although the firm doesn't generally shell out huge signing bonuses to attract name-brand Wall Street talent, the firm no longer limits its hiring to recent graduates. Clayton Rose, who heads Morgan's investment banking business group, told *The Wall Street Journal* recently: "We have become comfortable with the notion that loyalty doesn't only come from being born and bred here."

J.P. Morgan has extensive recruiting literature on its web site, www.jpmorgan.com. The firm recruits at 40 undergraduate schools and 15 business schools. At business schools, the firm does one company-wide presentation, after which individual groups make more focused presentations. These presentations are generally club-sponsored. Sometimes the firm holds brown bag lunches or cocktail presentations. For lucky schools, such as UCLA, Morgan holds beer busts.

Getting to know you

Morgan also hosts dinners at the major business schools. "The goal is to get to know you," explains one recruiter. These dinners are usually held one to two months before interviewing begins. There is also an "after-offer" dinner for recruits.

Candidates applying to Morgan through the firm's on-campus recruiting efforts weather a lengthy on-campus interview and then a full day of callbacks at the firm's New York headquarters. (For summer hires, the second round is held locally.) The firm's investment banking department holds a "Super Saturday," when many candidates are brought to the headquarters to run the interviewing gauntlet. A candidate usually interviews with five to eight people during the second round.

MBAs who receive offers are asked back for sell days, when the candidate meets members of the group who schmooze and try to get the prospective employee to sign up. Most new MBA hires are brought aboard in New York, London, Brussels, Singapore, and Tokyo.

Hungry for more inside scoop? Join Vault.com's popular online community for finance and banking — www.vault.com

VAULT.com **263**

OUR SURVEY SAYS

First-class

J.P. Morgan's mantra, bankers say, is "first-class business in a first-class way." Translation: an emphasis on civility and teamwork, with a touch of old-school elitism and bureaucracy. Despite the shift in dress code policy, one analyst in the firm's equity research department describes the culture as "very corporate" and "white collar." Another insider comments on the firm's "notably high ethical standards." Says a different source in the fixed income department: "It's somewhat conservative, extremely politically correct, and very elite." However, one associate says this reputation is overstated: "It's professional, but not as haughty as is sometimes thought." Underlying this conservative culture is a commitment to employees not often matched on Wall Street. J.P Morgan has long had a reputation as an employee-friendly firm, offering quality-of-life perks well before the labor market forced other banks to follow suit.

Insiders agree that J.P. Morgan is "on the friendly end of the Wall Street spectrum," with "very little petty office politics," according to at least one insider. An associate in investment banking explains, "It's generally very inclusive and team-oriented. There's not much back-stabbing. Managing directors and vice presidents are concerned about developing junior people."

But in this imperfect world, even Morgan's emphasis on teamwork is considered an outmoded drawback by some. Says another analyst: "The team environment sometimes leads to failure to recognize those working harder or on more advanced assignments." An associate in investment management agrees: "The consensus-driven approach makes accountability and contrarian thinking difficult to achieve." Says another I-banking analyst: "[J.P. Morgan] is friendly and cooperative, but it can become too entrenched in its own history at times and not aggressive enough." According to one associate in sales: "The only thing that really bugs me is that we tend to keep weak people circulating in-house rather than aggressively firing those not up to par."

Diverse by Wall Street standards

The opportunities for both women and other minorities at Morgan are "surprisingly good for this business," employees say, emphasizing J.P. Morgan's "excellent gender diversity." Reports one I-banking analyst:

"I work in a very diverse group — several different races and good representation of women." One insider comments that "there certainly are more women here than at any other Wall Street firm — Morgan puts a big effort forward in this area, and it's definitely paying off." An associate in investment banking comments, "The head of my group is a woman and almost half of all junior personnel are women." But Morgan is still on Wall Street, and some women believe their opportunities could be improved. "The firm appears to try and reach out to women in hiring for junior positions, but there are very few women in leadership positions or in positions to mentor or support young women," according to one female analyst. One woman associate says that while receptivity to women is "very good," "it becomes increasingly difficult to rise to the 'next level' with each promotion. While this is true for men, too, I think it is more pronounced for women."

As for minorities, "J.P. Morgan's diversity efforts are known by all employees," says one vice president. In 1999 and again in 2000, Morgan was the only Wall Street firm named one of the "50 Best Companies for Minorities" by *Fortune*. The firm maintains a Diversity Steering Committee (DSC), which is composed of managing directors from each business group who oversee the diversity issues affecting the firm on a global basis. One insider reports: "If you're a minority and you want to leave the job, they'll sit you down for an interview to try to find out what it was that made you want to leave this place."

Morgan is a leader when it comes to gays and lesbians, too. In 1997 Morgan announced same-sex domestic partner benefits, the first Wall Street firm to do so. The firm has brought in speakers like Allen Gilmour, a retired vice chairman of Ford Motor, to speak to employees about being openly gay in the workplace. One analyst puts it simply: "Morgan has a huge diversity initiative."

On the low-end for the Street, but c'mon?

Insiders say Morgan is known for being on the low end of pay on the Street; contacts suggest that the firm's prestige and job satisfaction allow it to get away with paying salaries below those of competitors. One employee gossips: "There's a rumor going around that so far has proven to be pretty true — if you take a job at, say, Salomon Smith Barney, you'll get paid more than at J.P. Morgan because Morgan has a better reputation." Says one associate in investment management: "Morgan is on the low end, and buy-side is lower than sell-side, but

Hungry for more inside scoop? Join Vault.com's popular online community for finance and banking — www.vault.com

VAULT.COM **265**

there's a fair amount of predictability and stability." Concludes one young VP: "I was worried that at J.P. Morgan I would not be paid as much, and I believe I am underpaid compared to my peers at other firms, but I love my job and don't want to work anywhere else." The firm reports that its starting salaries are competitive, and that starting salaries are reviewed continuously for benchmarking purposes.

It's not as if bankers at Morgan are going hungry. Although first-year salaries are sometimes called "a bit low," insiders say they are on par with "industry averages, if you consider your signing bonus." Says one second-year analyst in investment banking: "I'm not sure how this compares to other Wall Street firms, but straight out of college, I couldn't expect much more." Afterwards, analysts suggest that "increases depend on whether or not you make associate." If you do, "expect to be pushed way up the pay scale." One associate in sales and trading describes his compensation as the "standard top-tier Wall Street package." The firm also offers an incentive compensation program for which employees are eligible from day one of employment.

"[J.P. Morgan] is friendly and cooperative, but it can become too entrenched in its own history at times and not aggressive enough."

— J.P. Morgan Insider

Lazard

30 Rockefeller Plaza
New York, NY 10020
(212) 632-6000
Fax: (212) 632-6060
www.lazard.com

LOCATIONS

New York (U.S. HQ)
Chicago
San Francisco
Washington, DC

London
Paris
Beijing
Cairo
Frankfurt
Hamburg
Hong Kong
Jersey Channel Islands
Madrid
Milan
Montreal
Mumbai
New Delhi
Seoul
Singapore
Stockholm
Sydney
Tokyo
Warsaw

DEPARTMENTS

Asset Management
Capital Markets
Corporate Advisory Services
Principal Investing

THE STATS

Chairman & CEO: Michel David-Weill
Employer Type: Private Company
No. of Offices: 23

UPPERS

• Above-average pay
• Great deal flow
• International prestige

DOWNERS

• Insane hours
• Poor infrastructure
• Senior-level turnover after merger

KEY COMPETITORS

Allen & Company
Goldman Sachs
Morgan Stanley Dean Witter
Merrill Lynch
Salomon Smith Barney
Wasserstein Perella & Co.

EMPLOYMENT CONTACT

Corporate Advisory Services
Basil Bliss
Lazard
30 Rockefeller Plaza
New York, NY 10020

Capital Markets
L. Gregory Rice
Managing Director — Equities

F. Harlan Batrus
Managing Director — Bonds

John Rohs
Managing Director— Research

Michael Weistock
Managing Director— High Yield

Lazard
30 Rockefeller Plaza
New York, NY 10020

Asset Management
Amy DeAngelo
Lazard Asset Management
30 Rockefeller Plaza
New York, NY 10020

THE SCOOP

A classic

Lazard might be called the classic advisory boutique, specializing primarily in providing mergers and acquisitions advice. The firm also has a small underwriting and trading practice and a respectable asset management arm with approximately $80 billion under management. Despite the firm's specialization, Lazard's profits and influence are hardly limited. Lazard is known for a superstar culture: its elite, connected bankers are known as the trusted advisers of the princes of business. The firm touts itself as "the only private partnership in global investment banking." In 2000 the firm finalized a merger of its London, Paris, and New York practices and changed its name from Lazard Frères to Lazard.

French bred

The Lazard family's U.S. business ventures can be traced back to 1848, when the clan immigrated to the United States from France and opened a dry goods enterprise in New Orleans. In 1849 the family moved to San Francisco after a fire destroyed the New Orleans operation. The Lazards arrived just in time for the gold rush and the resulting economic boom caused by arriving prospectors. The company began banking operations in Paris in 1852, adding offices in London in 1877 and New York in 1880.

Much of the firm's growth is attributed to Alexandre Weill, a cousin of the Lazards who opened the New York office. The company has remained in the hands of the Weill family for over 120 years. Michel David-Weill (the family hyphenated the family name to David-Weill in the 1920s to add aristocratic luster) took the helm of the company in 1977.

M&A powerhouse

Lazard's most notable strength is in mergers and acquisitions advisory, and the firm's prominence is evident in the league tables. In 1999 the bank ranked ninth among advisors of completed worldwide M&A, according to Thomson Financial Securities Data, advising on 158 transactions worth $168.2 billion. The firm has been involved in some of the most high-profile mergers including Pfizer/Warner-Lambert, SBC/Bell South, Terra/Lycos, Viacom/Paramount, and IBM/Lotus.

While M&A advisory is the firm's primary expertise, it isn't Lazard's only business. The company's asset management business is well-respected and has approximately $80 billion in capital under management, both from institutions and wealthy individuals. The firm's equity underwriting is less impressive, as Lazard does not have equity distribution channels like those of competitors such as Morgan Stanley Dean Witter or Goldman Sachs. The firm co-managed a handful of deals in 1999, including two offerings for Equant in January and December that raised a total of $7.8 billion. Lazard is currently co-managing the $115 million Rosetta Inpharmatics IPO and co-lead managing IPOs for Granada Media (estimated at $2 billion) and Orient Express Hotels (estimated at $215 million).

Coming together

The firm, traditionally known for its avoidance of publicity, has been in the news in recent years. In the late 1990s, Lazard garnered negative press that eventually resulted in changes at the firm. Michel David-Weill's son-in-law and expected successor, Edouard Stern, left the firm in mid-1997 after the two clashed repeatedly over issues such as Stern's role in the company and the company's direction. Felix Rohatyn, who gained fame by orchestrating New York City's recovery from bankruptcy in the 1970s, also left Lazard in 1997 to become the U.S. ambassador to France. As a result, David-Weill was forced to reevaluate Lazard's management structure.

David-Weill's solution was to consolidate the firm's London, Paris and New York offices. Post-merger, the firm changed its name from Lazard Fréres to Lazard. The firm is now managed by a seven-person committee headed by David-Weill. The merger, announced in June 1999 and finalized in March 2000, met with some resistance from partners before its completion. *Investment Dealers' Digest* reported that two partners in the Paris office, Antoine Bernheim and David-Weill's son-in-law Stern (who retained an ownership stake despite leaving the firm in 1997), balked at the reorganization. Their specific objections were never publicized, but the concerns were a significant issue because under French law a partnership cannot be reorganized without unanimous partner approval. David-Weill acknowledged the need for cooperation, telling *Business Week*, "[The reorganization] has to be done in a spirit of partnership and avoiding the feeling that any part of the firm would dominate any other part." He added, "What is clear is that in some respects the businesses have to be unified." David-Weill

Hungry for more inside scoop? Join Vault.com's popular online community for finance and banking — www.vault.com

VAULT.com **271**

quashed speculation that the company would go public after the consolidation, saying a public Lazard would "tend to serve two masters: your [outside] owners and your clients."

Going places

The merger led some Lazard executives to seek greener pastures. Steven Rattner, David Tanner, Peter Ezersky, and Joshua Steiner left to form Quadrangle Group, a private equity firm, in March 2000. Rattner's departure was expected. A well-respected M&A player, whom David-Weill called "a wonderful business getter and a deal guy" in *Business Week*, Rattner stepped down as deputy CEO after the announcement of the combination and took the title of deputy chairman. The other departing bankers, while not as high-profile, still represented significant losses for the firm. *The Daily Deal* reported that Ezersky's client roster included Polygram and America Online and called Steiner, 34, a "young rising star." Thomas Dunn and Ira Handler, the heads of the asset management group's fixed income department, departed the firm in January 2000 after a poor performance by the fixed income group.

One of the president's men

The firm did manage to add some muscle to its business — Lazard added 12 partners after the June 1999 merger announcement. Pehr Gyllenhammar, chairman of U.K. insurer CGU and former CEO of Volvo, joined Lazard in December 1999. Gyllenhammar was the second-most important addition to Lazard that month; the firm also added Vernon Jordan, formerly a partner at Washington, DC law firm Akin, Gump, Strauss, Hauer & Feld. (Jordan stayed on at the law firm as "of counsel," a title usually reserved for senior, non-equity lawyers.) Jordan, a close friend of President Bill Clinton, was previously scrutinized for his role in finding intern Monica Lewinsky a job after her time in the White House. "Life is about new occasions and new duties, and this is another hill to climb," Jordan told *Black Enterprise* regarding his new position. Jordan's hiring led to speculation that the big man himself, President Clinton, would join Lazard after leaving office. Media reports said the President would receive an annual salary of $10 million. Lazard immediately dismissed the reports. The White House, for its part, said the president did not have any relations with that firm.

GETTING HIRED

Looking for talent

Lazard's investment banking division recruits at undergraduate colleges and business schools, but other departments, such as asset management, fill their open slots primarily through word of mouth, sources say. A recruiting schedule for investment banking and contact information for other departments are available at the firm's web site, www.lazard.com. Like other Wall Street firms, Lazard aims to hire full-time associates through its summer associate program. However, the firm also tries to find candidates through on-campus recruiting efforts. Lazard also maintains a summer analyst program for college juniors.

B-school insiders report mostly two-on-one interviews. At some schools, after the initial screening round, "they call you later on that night and have you come back and do some more interviews, and they will give you the offer then." Other contacts report, "They fly people to New York." "They don't interview many people," says one insider. While it is not an explicit requirement, insiders say, "you need to have M&A experience to work at Lazard [as an associate]." The firm instituted a two-week training program for associates in 1999.

Hey good lookin'

Lazard insiders advise showing up for your interview at the firm with a "nice expensive suit." "The people they hire — there's no way to say this, really — but they tend to be attractive people," says one Lazard insider. "They're not looking for the nerdy number-cruncher that you get at some of the banks like Goldman. They want it so when there's a meeting, you can tell Lazard walked in the door."

Reports one recent interviewee: "One question they like to ask is, 'What was the hardest thing you did — what was the most complicated deal?' If you brought up an M&A deal, then from talking to you about that deal, they can tell where you are." Says that contact: "I strongly stress to anyone who wants to work there as an associate — you've got to be a banker. They expect you to walk in the first day and be ready. My first day, my phone rang, and they said you're late. I said, 'I'm late? I just walked in the door.' It was a secretary of one of the senior people, and she tells me, 'There's a meeting up on 62 and you've got to get up there.' I get up there and there's the CEO and he's talking about what

Hungry for more inside scoop? Join Vault.com's popular online community for finance and banking — www.vault.com

VAULT.com **273**

type of company he wants to acquire. I start taking notes. That evening and the rest of the night I cranked out merger models."

OUR SURVEY SAYS

You have no life

To say Lazard "demands total commitment" is an understatement. "Working hours are just crazy," says one insider, who sometimes wishes for "more time for family, friends, and non-professional areas of interest." Says another: "You will definitely work over one hundred hours during an average workweek." Another insider puts the figure at "110 to 130" hours weekly. One employee criticizes the "superhuman expectations" at the firm. "You can't work any harder than they work," a former Lazard banker attests. "There were people carried out by ambulance — they had collapsed from exhaustion." The firm says these reports are exaggerated.

How bad it is for Lazard bankers depends almost entirely on where one is on the totem pole, according to sources. Contacts concur that "analysts have no life." Explains one insider: "The attitude is that the analysts are not bankers. It's 'I want to work you for two years and then spit you out, and you're lucky to be here.'" That source continues: "The analysts do not exercise, they do not leave, they are there all the time." "The analysts for the most part are extremely bitter," says one associate. "I think they're going to do better in the future, because they're starting to realize that it's not good," says that contact. Despite Lazard's hard-work reputation, the firm reports that in 2000, 10 out of 24 second- and third-year analysts stayed on at the firm after the completion of the analyst program.

Associates don't have it much better, insiders say, but "they know what they're getting into" and morale is pretty high. "The first three years as an associate — you're throwing those years away," says one banker. "You're just trying to survive." Why do associates put up with the intense work? For the promotion to VP that happens in three or four years. "If you can survive the four years, you're looking at a pretty good lifestyle," explains one insider. "A VP at Lazard is very different from a VP at other places. At other places, the VP gets dragged down to do associate work and still gets dragged into the office on weekends.

A VP at Lazard — they really know their shit, and if they want to, which pretty much everyone wants to, they refuse to do associate-level work. They want to be working on getting clients and things like that." During the week, insiders report, VPs are there "until 9:00 — even MDs put in long hours at Lazard"; on the weekends "they'll be at the Hamptons with a fax machine."

I've never seen so much decadence

"Lazard is like Wall Street was in the early 1980s," says one former insider. "Cigar smoke is thick on the floor by 10 in the morning — they're all smoking. They play polo. They've got their polo gear in the office. I've never seen so much decadence in a firm. They all had huge houses in the Hamptons, and they didn't mind talking about it — 'Oh, the roof in my Hamptons house is leaking, and now I can only sell it for $3 million.'"

The amazing luxury that the Lazard lifestyle affords is the reason the firm's bankers endure the almost unconscionable hours. "Bankers at Lazard are usually paid 25 to 50 percent more than the market salary [for] comparable positions at other banks," says an analyst. "They basically tell you that their goal is to be the highest-paying firm, and they're looking to start private equity stuff up in order to expand what they can do as far as compensation," reports another banker. "This is serious stuff."

Insiders also agree that Lazard is at the top of the list when it comes to prestige. "It's an amazing place," says one source. "They really do have great relationships with the CEOs of major companies." Says another: "We're the cutting edge of management and finance theory. The culture is very focused on production, merit, and profits." Says a former banker: "They're not spinning their wheels, working their hours. They really put some time and thought into the work they're doing."

Not great diversity

One employee maintains that the firm is "relatively progressive, with active recruitment of women and minorities," but notes that "there are very few women investment bankers at Lazard, not because we do not hire them, but because many of them leave due to the inhumane working environment." Another I-banker is more caustic: "There's one female managing director, and then there are some among the associates, but basically it's men. And it's not very diverse at all, it's a

Hungry for more inside scoop? Join Vault.com's popular online
community for finance and banking — www.vault.com

VAULT.com **275**

bunch of white guys." Says that contact: "It's a lot more of the old-boy WASPy network rather than the Jewish network at other banks." One employee criticizes Lazard's "limited resources," noting that the firm's lack of consolidated databases forces employees to "fish for information using highly unorthodox methods, sometimes making life miserable. If you were working at a bulge-bracket firm, most of the information would be a telephone call or a click of the mouse away."

"The attitude is that the analysts are not bankers. It's 'I want to work you for two years and then spit you out, and you're lucky to be here.'"

— *Lazard Insider*

Legg Mason

100 Light Street
Baltimore, MD 21202
(410) 539-0000
Fax: (410) 454-4923
www.leggmason.com

LOCATIONS

Baltimore (HQ)
Philadelphia
Reston
Washington, DC
140 locations in the U.S.

DEPARTMENTS

Capital Markets
Investment Advisory
Private Client Group

THE STATS

Chairman & CEO:
Raymond A. Mason
Employer Type: Public Company
Ticker Symbol: LM (NYSE)
2000 Net Revenue*: $1.2 billion
2000 Net income*: $142.5 million
No. of Employees: 4,350
No. of Offices: 140

UPPERS

• Rich history
• Supportive culture

DOWNERS

• Decline in I-banking deals
• Lacking in prestige

* Fiscal year-end March 31

KEY COMPETITORS

First Union Securities
Merrill Lynch
Raymond James Financial

EMPLOYMENT CONTACTS

Investment Banking
Lucille Hughes
Capital Markets Recruiting and
Training Manager
(410) 454-5892

Other Opportunities
Joseph Timmons
(410) 454-3301

Human Resources
100 Light Street
Baltimore, MD 21202

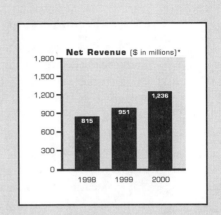

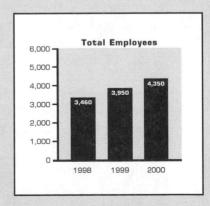

Fiscal year-end March 31

THE SCOOP

100 years and counting

Legg Mason recently celebrated its centennial, but the firm insists it is still a growing enterprise. In March 2000, the firm reported a record fiscal year for revenues and net income. Through a number of subsidiaries, the firm offers investment advisory, securities brokerage, investment banking, and commercial mortgage services to individuals and institutions. The firm provides investment banking services through two subsidiaries, Legg Mason Wood Walker and Howard, Weill, Labouisse, Friedrichs (a smaller subsidiary which handles only energy-related investment banking and brokerage from a New Orleans office). Legg Mason Wood Walker lists the following as core industries: e-business and consumer services, education, electronic commerce, financial services, health care, industrial, professional sports, real estate, technology, and telecommunications. The company also employs a team of analysts in both equity and fixed income research.

Name changes

Legg Mason traces its roots back to 1899, when George Mackubin founded George Mackubin & Co., a brokerage house in Baltimore. Mackubin was only 25 but had prior experience with two brokerages. Mackubin eventually hired John Legg, Jr., a 19-year-old board boy. (In the early days of the stock market, board boys would write changes in stock prices on a chalk board in the firm's office for the benefit of clients who sat on benches, eagerly awaiting news of their fortunes.) Legg made partner in 1904 and gained control of the company 45 years later, after he and Mackubin had a falling out. (Mackubin went on to join a competitor, Robert Barrett and Sons.) After Mackubin's departure, Legg renamed the firm John C. Legg & Co. The firm became Legg & Co. after Legg's death in 1963. Legg & Co., stung by the economic decline of the 1960s, sought a merger partner in the latter part of the decade. In August 1970, the firm joined with Mason & Co., a brokerage firm founded in 1962 by Raymond "Chip" Mason, an ambitious young trader like Legg's former friend, George Mackubin.

Help us, Chip

Legg Mason acquired Wood Walker & Co. in October 1973, a deal that turned out to be a disaster. Though the Wood Walker name survives —

the bulk of the company's investment banking business operates under the Legg Mason Wood Walker name — Legg Mason struggled to integrate WW, a New York-based brokerage and money manager. Investors, angered by ongoing integration issues, showed up at Legg Mason's door with the business equivalent of pitchforks and torches and demanded that Chip Mason assume control of the firm, which he did. Chip led the firm out of the morass, and the company went public in 1983, raising $14 million. When the firm celebrated its centennial in 1999, Chip rang the opening bell at the New York Stock Exchange. At age 62, Chip is still going strong but is rumored to be seeking a successor.

Recent news

Legg Mason hasn't rested on its 100-year-old laurels. In December 1999, the bank announced a merger with Johnson Fry Holdings, a London investment firm. In May 2000, the firm finalized an agreement to pair with Perigree, Inc., a Canadian investment management firm. Earlier in the year, Legg Mason had announced a partnership with Bingham Dana, a Boston law firm, to create Bingham Legg Advisors. The autonomous partnership provides legal and financial advice and takes advantage of a recent American Bar Association ruling allowing law firms to partner with firms outside the legal industry. The company has also recently implemented online brokerage and has announced plans to offer online banking.

The online moves apparently weren't enough for one senior executive at Legg Mason. William McVay, director of investment consulting at Legg Mason Capital Management, left the bank in June 2000 to become executive vice president and chief business development officer at Financeware.com, a company that offers a variety of web-based financial tools. In another career switch, Glenn Mueller, head of equity real estate research, left Legg Mason to become a professor at Johns Hopkins University.

Other peoples' money

Legg Mason is perhaps best known for the asset management business it has worked so hard to grow recently. Legg Mason's Value Trust fund, a $13 billion fund managed by Bill Miller, was the only equity mutual fund tracked by research firm Lipper, Inc. to beat the S&P 500 index for the nine consecutive years ending 1999. For the fiscal-year ending in March 2000, the company reported record earnings and revenues,

Hungry for more inside scoop? Join Vault.com's popular online
community for finance and banking — www.vault.com

VAULT.com   **281**

mostly attributable to growth in Legg's asset management businesses. For the year, the firm reported a 60 percent increase in net earnings over 1999 and a 30 percent increase in net revenue. The firm's asset management subsidiaries experienced a 24 percent increase in revenues over the previous year and the brokerage business reported a 19 percent increase in revenues.

Less stellar in banking

The firm's investment banking operations experienced less success for the year. In the company's 2000 annual report, the chairman's letter noted a 9 percent decline in investment banking revenues from 1999 figures. The decline was mostly blamed on a decrease in equity issues. This was not the first year the firm experienced a decline in investment banking. In fiscal 1999, the company reported a 20 percent decline in I-banking revenues compared to 1998. Overall for fiscal 2000, the firm's capital markets division reported a 18.9 percent increase in revenue and a 35 percent decrease in pre-tax earnings.

GETTING HIRED

Legg Mason recruits are first interviewed on campus. Promising candidates are flown to headquarters in Baltimore for a second round of interviews. For financial advisors and trainees, Legg Mason says a Series 6 or 7 registration is preferred; financial analysts are hired at the college graduate level without previous experience for a two-year generalist program which involves exposure to mergers and acquisitions, public offerings, and private placements of debt and equity. The firm's web site, www.leggmason.com, has an employment section that lists job openings and has an online application form.

OUR SURVEY SAYS

Fast-paced but supportive

Legg Mason is described as "a great place to work." One employee at the firm's Baltimore headquarters describes the culture as "very warm and friendly" and "much more of a pleasant and helpful atmosphere than in New York." The environment is described as fast-paced and supportive. The pay and hours vary but are described as competitive for a firm of Legg Mason's size and stature. All full-time employees are eligible for benefits from the day of hire.

Well-protected prestige

Employees call the company "prestigious" and say it has "a good name." Says one insider, "Chip Mason [the CEO] and the other powers-that-be at Legg Mason protect that reputation carefully." In the words of another employee, "Legg Mason is a great company with a bright future." One analyst says, "Anyone interested in investment banking should look at Legg Mason. While money management and brokerage are huge, and research is getting better, investment banking is relatively small — but Legg Mason wants to grow that business."

Hungry for more inside scoop? Join Vault.com's popular online
community for finance and banking — www.vault.com

VAULT.com 283

Lehman Brothers

3 World Financial Center
New York, NY 10285
(212) 526-7000
Fax: (212) 526-3738
www.lehman.com

LOCATIONS:

New York (HQ)
Atlanta
Boston
Chicago
Los Angeles
San Francisco
Washington, DC

Beijing
Hong Kong
London
Paris
Tokyo

DEPARTMENTS:

Equities
Fixed Income
Investment Banking
Private Client Services
Private Equity

THE STATS:

Chairman & CEO:
Richard S. Fuld, Jr.
Head of Investment Banking:
Bradley H. Jack
Employer Type: Public Company
Ticker Symbol: LEH (NYSE)
1999 Net Revenue: $5.3 billion
1999 Net Income: $1.1 billion
No. of Employees: 8,340
No. of Offices: 39

UPPERS

- Meritocratic culture
- Private equity opportunities on the way
- Relaxed atmosphere

DOWNERS

- Can be a pressure cooker
- Constant merger rumors
- Sometimes fratty atmosphere

KEY COMPETITORS

Bear Stearns
Donaldson, Lufkin & Jenrette
J.P. Morgan
Merrill Lynch
Salomon Smith Barney

EMPLOYMENT CONTACT:

Kim Cockrell
Associate Recruiting

Leslie Pellettieri
Analyst Recruiting

3 World Financial Center
15th Floor
New York, NY 10285

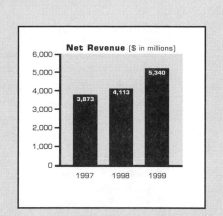

Net Revenue [$ in millions]

1997	1998	1999
3,873	4,113	5,340

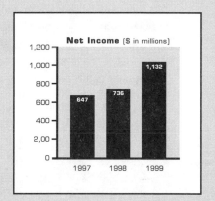

Net Income [$ in millions]

1997	1998	1999
647	736	1,132

Total Employees

1997	1998	1999
8,340	8,873	8,340

THE SCOOP

Southern roots

Lehman Brothers was founded in 1850 in Montgomery, Alabama by brothers Henry, Emmanuel and Mayer Lehman. The enterprise began as a commodities brokerage and trading firm and opened a New York office in 1858. In 1887 Lehman acquired a seat on the New York Stock Exchange and underwrote its first stock offering two years later. Expanding over the last 150 years, the company is currently a full-service global investment bank providing a wide range of services including fixed income and equities sales, trading and research, M&A advisory, public finance, and private client services.

An auspicious start

American Express purchased Lehman in 1984 as part of its strategy to become a full-service institution covering all consumer and business financial needs. Amex changed its tune 10 years later, deciding to refocus on core businesses. Amex's new strategy resulted in a spin-off that once again created an independent Lehman Brothers.

The newly independent Lehman Brothers stumbled out of the starting gate, implementing considerable layoffs and cost cuts to survive. The firm managed to rebound and made significant strides in high-margin businesses such as equity and high yield underwriting and M&A advisory. Rumors of a potential Lehman merger with commercial banks Chase Manhattan or Deutsche Bank circled the industry in 1998. The rumors were just that, and the vanishing of prospective merger partners, along with a market-wide slump, caused Lehman's stock price, which had reached the mid-$80 range in July 1998, to plummet. The company's stock sank to the mid-$20 range before recovering in late 1998. Between February 1999 and February 2000 the stock traded as low as $46 1/8 and as high as $85 9/16.

Despite the share-price roller coaster, Lehman Brothers has been one of the most profitable investment banks in recent years. While competitors such as Merrill Lynch were announcing staff cuts in mid-1998, Lehman, which has a reputation for lean staffing, reported no layoffs. The bank announced record profits of $736 million in 1998, then more than doubled that number with $1.1 billion of profits in 1999, with a return on equity of 21.8 percent.

In Fidelity?

In June 1999, Lehman Brothers announced an alliance with Fidelity Investments, the Boston-based asset management and mutual fund firm, to provide Fidelity customers access to Lehman-led debt and equity offerings as well as Lehman's research products. As a result of the partnership, Lehman could access a larger distribution network for public offerings and presumably attract more deals from companies eager to issue securities.

At the time of its announcement, the partnership yielded speculation that the two firms would merge. The rumors disappeared shortly after the announcement, only to resurface a year later. *The Wall Street Journal*, which first resurrected the rumors in June 2000, conceded that a merger was "a long shot" and said formalization of the Lehman/Fidelity distribution alliance was more likely. A Fidelity spokesman quashed the gossip, telling *The New York Times*, "We have no such plan[s] and there is nothing under discussion."

In July 2000, Lehman boosted its private client business, acquiring SG Cowen's high net worth business. According to *The Wall Street Journal*, the deal was worth $50 million, much of which was money set aside for retention bonuses for the 140 SG Cowen brokers joining the Lehman team.

Top 10 lists

If Fidelity did purchase Lehman, it would be getting a firm securely entrenched on several league tables. In 1999 Lehman ranked sixth among lead-managers of all debt and equity transactions, according to Thomson Financial Securities Data, underwriting 951 deals in 1999 worth $164.3 billion. The firm ranked eighth among lead underwriters of common stock ($6.6 billion, 54 deals), eighth among underwriters of high yield debt ($4.3 billion, 27 deals), seventh among underwriters of investment grade debt ($45.0 billion, 304 deals), sixth among lead managers of IPOs ($2.9 billion, 32 offerings), seventh among advisors of announced U.S. M&A transactions ($197.3 billion, 125 deals) and eighth among advisors of worldwide M&A transactions ($182.0 billion, 84 deals).

In March 1999, Lehman lead managed a $201 million IPO for Wesco International. In May of that year, Lehman co-managed the $290 million Time Warner Telecom IPO. One month later, the company led a $194 million IPO for High Speed Access. Lehman has also

Hungry for more inside scoop? Join Vault.com's popular online
community for finance and banking — www.vault.com

VAULT.com   **287**

participated in sizable follow-on offerings for Qualcomm ($1.08 billion) and Hanvit Bank ($1 billion).

Lead-managed debt offerings included a $5.75 billion, multi-tranche offering for Wal-Mart, named "U.S. Dollar Bond Deal of the Year" and "U.S. Investment-Grade Corporate Bond Deal of the Year" by *International Financing Review*. The firm also managed a $2.8 billion offering for Ford Motor, a $2.3 billion offering for Pepsi Bottling Group and a $1.25 billion offering for Liberty Media Group. M&A transactions of note include the MediaOne/AT&T merger. (Lehman is representing MediaOne in the $63.1 billion merger, announced in May 1999.) The bank also advised US West on its $48.5 billion pairing with Qwest Communications. In addition to investment banking divisions which focus on underwriting and M&A advisory assignments, Lehman has substantial groups devoted to sales and trading, research, private client services, and private equity.

GETTING HIRED

Make a good impression

First impressions are key at Lehman. After meeting students at colleges and business schools, the firm's recruiters will focus on a number of top candidates. Says one recent MBA hire: "I was targeted and was pursued hard." In fact, the firm prefers to have identified its targets by the time campus interviewing starts.

Lehman focuses on 10 graduate business schools (Chicago, Columbia, Wharton, Tuck, Fuqua, Stern, UCLA, Kellogg, Harvard, and MIT's Sloan) for recruiting MBAs. For analysts, Lehman conducts on-campus interviews at top-20 schools but will interview write-in candidates from other schools. One Lehman analyst from a top-20 school reports, "We do hire a lot of write-ins."

Playing the game

How does Lehman pick its targets? In part, through on-campus get-to-know-you functions. For example, the firm's sales and trading recruiters host a "Trading Game" on campus, where they simulate three to four "pits" similar to those on the Chicago Futures exchanges. The "game" (read: tryout) lasts four to five hours. The trading game allows

Lehman to observe students in action so it can identify strong candidates. Lehman also hosts cocktail parties to identify targets. Despite the ulterior motives, the firm tries to keep the events as informal and social as possible, insiders say: "The focus is on personalities."

Like the summer programs at most bulge-bracket firms, Lehman's summer associate programs act as a feeder system for full-time hires. Summer associates receive their offers within two weeks of the end of the program. Most associates report an excellent recruitment process. Says one: "There was no bullshit in the recruiting process. They were honest with us." Interested candidates should visit the firm's web site, www.lehman.com, which is chock full of detailed recruiting information, including a list of contacts for several departments.

OUR SURVEY SAYS

Effort rewarded

Perhaps the most attractive aspect of working for Lehman, employees say, is that "the firm rewards effort. This place is as close to a meritocracy as it gets." An associate calls the company's culture "fluid" commenting that "managers tend to move around the firm." "I've been given more responsibility than I'd ever imagined," says one associate in trading. Another associate in Lehman's fixed income group calls the firm "an aggressive firm that will let you take risk, if you can justify it." According to one capital markets associate, "[Lehman gives] lots of responsibility early. They push employees to progress quickly." Another associate in that area boasts, "The opportunity is fantastic. The firm has focused on a number of growth opportunities and is aggressive about getting people involved." That doesn't mean analysts are free of cumbersome tasks. One I-banking analyst warns, "It's easy to get pigeonholed into doing a lot of pitches."

Insiders generally report a "young culture" that is "very entrepreneurial." Reports one insider, "The firm is very open to people moving around departments where it makes sense; they don't really mess around — if something makes sense, they just do it." One Lehman analyst complains the firm is a little behind the bulge bracket in terms of pay, though the bank did come through with raises in response to competitor increases. First-year analysts received 40

Hungry for more inside scoop? Join Vault.com's popular online
community for finance and banking — www.vault.com

VAULT.COM **289**

percent raises, second-years 45 percent, and third-years 54 percent. Lehman also offers a leveraged investment account for all employees.

Scrappy, friendly survivors

Lehman's culture is one of "survivors and fighters — people have been through a lot together, and they are very loyal to each other," according to one recent hire. Employees speak enthusiastically about Lehman's "social" corporate offices, where "most employees are extremely nice and friendly and very down-to-earth, unlike at some other places on the Street." As one new hire says, "[Lehman's] culture is open," largely because of the "affable" upper management who "make an effort to be readily approachable." "Culture very much depends on which business and which desk, but overall, it is not at all stuffy," says one associate in trading. "There are fairly honest professional people."

"Lehman has more of a laid-back collegial environment than other firms that I've worked at. I've seen all the other firms, and also over the summer I visited a bunch of firms," says one associate who summered at Lehman. "It's not laid-back in that people are easygoing, it just doesn't have the pretension that you might have at other places," continues that associate. "People work hard, but people also are welcoming, no one's putting on airs, that's the feeling that I got. I've been all around the firm, and I never had a situation where someone blew me off or wasn't interested in talking." Says one analyst in the firm's research department: "It's warm and less intense than your typical Wall Street firm." Some insiders believe the firm's culture and growth story are selling points to employees at competitor firms. Explains one I-banking analyst, "We're getting more people from top-tier firms like Morgan Stanley and Goldman interested in us."

Frat brothers

Although Lehman may be laid-back in the sense of not being stuffy or aristocratic, that doesn't mean the temperature doesn't rise at the firm. One ex-employee in New York notes, "There's a lot more yelling at Lehman Brothers than at my current firm." Insiders say that Lehman, like most major investment banks, has a "macho culture" and "many arrogant attitudes." According to one: "Antics are somewhat unprofessional. Many employees have something of a locker-room, fraternity culture." Reports another: "It's meritocratic but can be easily abused by overly aggressive people." Another associate says, "This is definitely a culture of a work ethic…they put in the hours." Still, insiders generally note the firm has been receptive to recent changes in the industry. In addition to salary and expense improvements, one insider notes that "management is showing more of an interest in people having well-rounded lives."

Hungry for more inside scoop? Join Vault.com's popular online
community for finance and banking — www.vault.com

VAULT.COM   **291**

Merrill Lynch

World Financial Center, North Tower
250 Vesey St.
New York, NY 10281-1332
(212) 449-1000
Fax: (212) 236-4384
www.ml.com

LOCATIONS

New York (HQ)
Atlanta
Boston
Chicago
Dallas
Houston
Los Angeles
San Francisco
Puerto Rico
*Offices in 43 countries on six
continents.*

DEPARTMENTS

Asset Management
Corporate and Institutional Client
International Private Client
U.S. Private Client

KEY COMPETITORS

Donaldson, Lufkin & Jenrette
Goldman Sachs
J.P. Morgan
Morgan Stanley Dean Witter
Salomon Smith Barney

EMPLOYMENT CONTACT

Investment Banking

Carrie Higginbotham
Assistant Vice President, BA Recruiting

Denise Patton
Vice President, MBA Recruiting

Sales and Trading

Claudine Rippa
Vice President

Merrill Lynch
World Financial Center
250 Vesey St., 2nd Fl.
New York, NY 10281-1302
Fax: (212) 449-3130

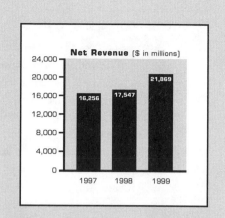

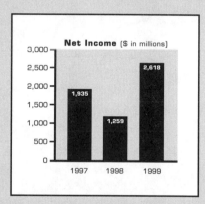

THE SCOOP

Strong as a bull

In 1914 Charles Merrill formed an underwriting firm, Charles E. Merrill & Co. Merrill took on Edmund Lynch as his partner, and the firm was renamed Merrill, Lynch & Co in 1915. Following the market crash in 1929, Merrill decided to focus on investment banking and sold off its retail operations to E.A. Pierce, a brokerage firm. A decade later, Merrill recaptured the retail business when Merrill, Lynch & Co. merged with E.A. Pierce. Charles Merrill (who ran Merrill Lynch until his death in 1956) was a true renaissance man. In addition to his activities in the financial world, he founded *Family Circle* magazine (you've likely seen it at the grocery store checkout line) and even played semi-pro baseball as a young man. He quickly decided his fortune lay not in the hit-and-run but in sales and trading. In 1971 Merrill Lynch became the second Big Board member to have its shares listed on the New York Stock Exchange (the first was Donaldson, Lufkin & Jenrette). Later in 1971, the company unleashed its "Merrill Lynch is bullish on America" ad campaign. For better or worse, the firm has been linked to its bull mascot since then.

Ranking high

Part of the investment banking "big three" (which also includes more white-shoe firms Goldman Sachs and Morgan Stanley), Merrill Lynch is a global powerhouse. The firm has a top-notch research staff and private equity group, and employs 1,600 investment banking professionals in 22 countries. Almost all of Merrill's departments are at the top of their respective league tables or, at the very least, hover somewhere in the top five. According to Thomson Financial Securities Data, the bank ranked first among lead-underwriters of all equity and debt in 1999, raising $333.6 billion for clients in 2,049 deals. Merrill's market share for domestic issues (debt and equity) was a whopping 16.8 percent; its closest competitor, Salomon Smith Barney, boasted a market share of only 12.8 percent. In the all-important IPO table, ML ranked third among lead-managers, raising $7.7 billion in 41 offerings. Also in 1999, the firm was the leader in global debt and equity underwriting for the 11th straight year.

In the advisory business, Merrill slipped a bit in 1999, ranking third among advisors of worldwide M&A transactions. The firm lost its number two spot to Morgan Stanley Dean Witter (number one was Goldman Sachs). In 1999 the firm advised Phillips Petroleum on its merger with Duke Energy. Beginning that year, Merrill served as one of three advisors to Mannesman on its highly publicized merger with Vodafone. The $190 billion deal, the largest merger to date, began with a hostile offer from Vodafone, but was eventually approved by Mannesman's management.

The new millennium has been good to Merrill so far. The firm lead-managed John Hancock Financial Services' mammoth $1.9 billion IPO in January 2000. Merrill was one of three lead managers for the $10.6 billion IPO for AT&T Wireless in April 2000. In the Internet sector, Merrill led the February 2000 Buy.com IPO, which raised $209.3 million; a few days later, Merrill lead managed a $94.9 million IPO for Pets.com.

Merrill's underwriting prowess would mean little if not for its distribution capabilities. The firm employs over 19,000 financial consultants and account executives. Brokers' commissions consistently contribute the largest chunk to Merrill's annual net revenues (in 1999, for example, commissions represented 29 percent of total net revenues).

Departures from the top

Many industry insiders were stunned in July 1999 when Herb Allison, Merrill Lynch's president and chief operating officer, resigned from the firm after 28 years. Allison had held a variety of senior positions during his tenure, including treasurer, CFO, and vice president of human resources. Though Merrill tried to put the typical spin on his departure — the bank said he was retiring and that he planned to pursue the ubiquitous "other interests" — speculation held that Allison left because he had been told he would not be considered for the chairman spot (which would be vacated within the next several years with the retirement of David Komansky). Also a factor, according to observers, was the addition of an online brokerage. Reportedly, a cadre of powerful Merrill executives, including Allison, felt online trading was a fad that would never be profitable; additionally, the opponents of online brokerage also wanted to protect Merrill's brokers from losing commissions to the online service. The firm began offering Web-based trades in June 1999 for $29.95 per trade. While Allison and his alleged anti-Web cohorts might not have been pleased by the decision, Merrill's online platform has won several awards.

Hungry for more inside scoop? Join Vault.com's popular online community for finance and banking — www.vault.com

VAULT.com   295

Several months later, in March 2000, news of another departure at Merrill made headlines. Jack Levy, head of mergers and acquisitions, resigned from Merrill to join M&A rival Goldman Sachs as co-chairman and co-head of global M&A. The move occurred after a year in which Merrill dropped from second to third in the M&A league tables. According to Thomson Financial Securities Data, Merrill advised on 342 completed deals worth $521.5 billion worldwide and 178 transactions valued at $483.2 billion in the U.S. While many firms would celebrate such numbers, Merrill's drop in the league tables (Merrill lost the number two slot to Morgan Stanley) rendered 1999 a subpar year in M&A by Merrill's standards. Steven Baronoff and Daniel Dickson were picked to fill Levy's big shoes in M&A.

Levy was not the only loss in investment banking for Merrill. Mark Shafir, head of the technology investment banking group at Merrill, left to join Thomas Weisel Partners in February 2000. Shafir was replaced by Joseph Schell, who left Banc of America Securities in January 1999. Schell had spent 14 years with BofA predecessor Montgomery Securities.

Shaken by the Levy departure (and, to a lesser extent, by that of Shafir), Merrill unleashed an unusual initiative to retain employees. *The Daily Deal* reported in March 2000 that the firm offered written compensation guarantees to senior bankers in the M&A department. The exact terms of the agreements were not disclosed (Merrill has declined comment on the issue), but the packages have been substantial enough to prevent other firms from stealing Merrill's banking stars.

Getting commercial

Merrill caused a stir in February 2000 by announcing plans to compete with commercial banks for customer deposits. For years, Merrill had provided customers with Cash Management Accounts (CMA), a combination of brokerage accounts and interest-bearing checking accounts. Under the company's proposed plans, any customer funds in a brokerage account that are not invested in securities will be swept into accounts insured by the Federal Deposit Insurance Corporation (FDIC). Previously, these funds were swept into a money-market fund that was not FDIC-insured. Merrill owns two banks that will hold the accounts and lend the money out (as is the standard practice with deposits at commercial banks). Merrill also plans to offer higher rates on deposits than other commercial banks. This move, made possible by the Financial Services Modernization Act, took some of the risk out of investing but was met with skepticism by the FDIC. The government agency was worried that if other banks followed suit, it would overtax the system by creating too much insured money. In the worst-case scenario (a complete market collapse similar to the one in 1929), the FDIC would have insufficient funds to pay off all insured accounts.

The firm further embraced commercial banking activities in April 2000, when it announced a billion-dollar partnership with London-based HSBC Holdings to form an online financial services company for individuals outside the U.S. The alliance will offer investors integrated banking and brokerage services.

Hot water for brokers

While Merrill likes to publicize the fact that it employs over 69,000 individuals worldwide, the company is also subject to a larger pool of potentially errant employees. Merrill has been hit with a handful of small client lawsuits alleging misrepresentation and misappropriation of funds on the part of Merrill brokers. In addition to small-scale suits, the company was involved in a brouhaha in the Middle East in January 2000. An employee in Merrill's Egypt office was accused of helping himself to almost $40 million of a client's money. The Merrill employee was an ex-employee of the client, Arab International Bank (AIB), which helped him in landing the account. He was accused of transferring the cash to a private account. Merrill reimbursed AIB immediately upon learning of the malfeasance, then tried to reclaim the money after turning the newly fired, alleged perpetrator over to Egyptian authorities. According to a report in *The New York Times*, industry analysts believe "the incident highlights one of the risks financial services firms such as Merrill, based in New York, face in managing far-flung networks of brokers and offices worldwide." Merrill faced another problem a little closer to home when two Merrill brokers caught the attention of Massachusetts authorities. One broker, accused of fraud, reportedly invested clients' money in risky stocks and options after promising them investments in funds. The other broker was accused of concentrating too much investor money into too few stocks. The firm paid a $750,000 fine (the largest ever imposed by the Massachusetts Security Division) for failing to supervise the brokers adequately.

Hungry for more inside scoop? Join Vault.com's popular online
community for finance and banking — www.vault.com

VAULT.com   **297**

GETTING HIRED

Merrill Lynch accepts résumés by regular mail, fax, and e-mail. Applicants can consult Merrill Lynch's employment web site, www.ml.com, in order to find out about job openings and contact information for the various groups within the company.

Résumés submitted to Merrill through both college career resource centers and direct mail are sorted by Merrill's recruiting personnel; all qualified applicants are invited for interviews. The first round of interviews is held on the applicant's campus, and those candidates who make the cut are invited to further rounds at the New York office. Merrill Lynch often gives preference to applicants who have worked as summer associates or analysts at the firm. However, one Merrill employee confesses that "in recent years, Merrill has over-hired for its summer programs, with the result being that only 50 percent of the summer class has received offers to work at the company." Insiders also report that Merrill's interviews — even the initial on-campus screening interviews — "can last a lot longer than the typical half-hour interviews that other firms conduct." Summer hires who receive offers of employment are generally required to respond within 30 days.

OUR SURVEY SAYS

No more elephants

Gigantic Merrill is known for having many subcultures, as insiders say that Merrill's culture varies "from department to department." According to one analyst, the investment banking division "is more laid-back than at most bulge-bracket investment banks, primarily because investment banking at Merrill is relatively new." Says that contact, "Historically, you must remember, Merrill was a 'huge lumbering elephant' because that was the culture in the dominant retail side of business. However, things are changing as Merrill becomes one of the top three investment banks, and we're becoming more like Goldman or Morgan Stanley day by day." One contact adds, "We're different from other places. The people are nicer than at other banks." Another source says Merrill has a "midwestern corporate culture — bland, collegial, inoffensive; nobody swears in public." One insider notes, "As with any big company, there will be people who are nasty for no particular reason. But there are fewer at Merrill."

Merrill Lynch is "probably the leading firm on Wall Street that is attempting to improve its diversity," according to Tony Chappelle, publisher of *Securities Pro*, a New York newsletter for African-Americans in the financial industry. Most recent hires say that they "are truly impressed by Merrill's efforts to diversify." However, one analyst says, "Although the company may be making a real effort to get non-whites, you don't see too many of them around — yet."

Do you read Kafka?

The major drawback of working for Merrill, most agree, is the "horrendous" bureaucracy, which "can sometimes combine with office politics to make life miserable and incomprehensible." An insider repines, "Sometimes, for no apparent reason, you get blamed for things you didn't do and get assignments you're not supposed to have, and there's no one to complain to — life becomes like a page from a Kafka novel." Another source agrees, "While I'm in the world outside, I'm proud to be working for Merrill. But on the inside, I know that bureaucracy and politics can make life pretty miserable."

Merrill Lynch's headquarter offices are "impressive and large." While "they're not furnished in a particularly lavish fashion, they're always tastefully decorated." Employees at the New York office state that "the most impressive feature of Merrill's offices is that they're located in the World Financial Center — Merrill has an entire building to itself." A source remarks, "The views from that office are spectacular! The analysts are actually housed in a bullpen and you have a corner view of the Statue of Liberty." A different contact describes the office's surroundings: "The World Financial Center neighborhood has great bars and shops, though everything is priced exorbitantly." While the view might be nice, insiders say the firm spends most of its decorating cash on impressing clients. One source notes, "The conference rooms and other areas visited by clients are very nice, but some of the analyst bullpens are kind of dumpy."

How low can they go?

One area where Merrill lags is pay. While the firm is around the industry average, insiders complain ML is slow to match competitors' increases. Gripes one banker, "[The firm] doesn't ask, 'How much do

Hungry for more inside scoop? Join Vault.com's popular online community for finance and banking — www.vault.com

VAULT.COM **299**

we have to pay to get people to stay?' but 'How little do we have to pay people to get them to stay?' They look at Morgan Stanley Dean Witter and Goldman Sachs and then price at the lowest."

Perks at Merrill, according to employees, are "the same as those you get at other banks. If you stay past a certain hour, you get dinner and transportation home." Officially, you have to stay past 8 p.m. to get a car, and past 7 p.m. to get dinner. The firm's dinner plan utilizes restaurants with which Merrill has negotiated discounts. Some insiders say they get sick of the food, "but a lot of the associates love it." Those who work on Saturday or Sundays get three meals covered.

Other perks include "free travel and accommodations when you travel with clients." "When you travel," one analyst notes, "you have it pretty good because you use airlines and hotels that must be up to the standard of your clients." The dress code, as at most bulge-bracket firms, is now all business casual.

Living large

The lifestyle at Merrill certainly doesn't help employees stay in shape. One New York analyst complains: "I worked so many hours at the office that I gained a substantial amount of weight. I got fat, to avoid euphemisms. The problem is, you spend so much time sitting at your desk, with no time to exercise, and you're always eating a lot at meetings at night or ordering food from different restaurants. There's no company gym for easy, during-the-day access to weights or jogging." There is an "executive gym" in the building for those high up on the ladder; as for the hardworking junior employees, "some associates go to the nearby Marriott, some go to another club."

"[The firm] doesn't ask, 'How much do we have to pay to get people to stay?' but, 'How little do we have to pay people to stay?'"

— *Merrill Lynch Insider*

Morgan Keegan

Morgan Keegan Tower
50 Front Street
17th Floor
Memphis, TN 38103
(901) 524-4100
Fax: (901) 579-4406
www.morgankeegan.com

LOCATIONS:

Memphis (HQ)
Atlanta
Austin
Baton Rouge
Boston
Charlotte
Durham
Ft. Lauderdale
Gainesville
Houston
Jackson
Louisville
Montgomery
New York
Raleigh
Richmond
46 total offices in 13 states

DEPARTMENTS

Asset Management
Corporate Finance
Private Client Services
Research
Sales and Trading

THE STATS

CEO: Allen B. Morgan, Jr.
Employer Type: Public Company
Ticker Symbol: MOR (NYSE)
1999 Revenue: $438.6 million
1999 Net Income: $45.8 million
No. of Employees: 1,900
No. of Offices: 46

UPPERS

• Great perks, including tuition reimbursement
• Team-oriented culture

DOWNERS

• Lack of diversity
• Small-market player

KEY COMPETITORS

First Union Securities
Legg Mason
Raymond James
Robinson Humphrey

EMPLOYMENT CONTACT

Investment banking analysts:
Alper Cetingok
Morgan Keegan Tower
50 Front Street
19th Floor
Memphis, TN 38103

Investment banking associates:
Wilbur Ellis
Morgan Keegan Tower
50 Front Street
19th Floor
Memphis, TN 38103

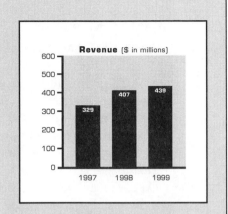

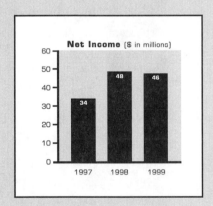

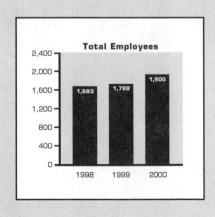

THE SCOOP

Southern comfort

Memphis-based Morgan Keegan & Co. was founded in 1969 by Allen Morgan, Jr., Jim Keegan, and two associates with a total of $500,000 in capital. One year after its founding, the company nabbed a seat on the New York Stock Exchange. Six years later, Morgan Keegan entered the underwriting business. The firm first went public in 1983 and was listed on the NYSE two years later. Morgan Keegan began offering asset management services a year later and in the late 1980s started an acquisition binge. The firm, originally a broker-dealer, has expanded into equity and debt underwriting, asset management and investment advisory and, strangely, a sports agency, through a series of purchases.

Y'all from around here?

The company stuck by its Southern roots throughout its acquisition phase, acquiring Geary & Patterson of Mississippi in 1988, and T.J. Raney & Sons of Arkansas, Alabama's George M. Wood & Co., and Louisiana-based Scharff & Jones in 1989. Alabama-based Porter White & Yardley and Texas-based Capitol Securities Group were acquired in 1993. J. Lee Peeler & Co. of North Carolina and Kentucky's Commonwealth Securities Group were added in 1994.

Athletic Resource Management (ARM), a Memphis-based sports agency, was acquired in 1995. ARM counts among its clients Southern sports stars such as Reggie White and Scottie Pippen; in addition to representing athletes in contract negotiations and endorsements, the firm provides asset management. (Incidentally, ARM isn't the firm's only link to the sports world; Olympic gold medalist Mary Lou Retton is married to a broker in Morgan Keegan's Houston office.)

Morgan didn't stop with ARM. The firm bought Atlanta underwriter Knox, Wall & Co. in 1997; soon after, the company acquired Weibel, Huffman & Keegan, a Memphis investment management firm run in part by Morgan Keegan co-founder Jim Keegan, who in 1985 had left Morgan Keegan. (At the time, Keegan said he was seeking a smaller, more intimate environment; Morgan Keegan was a growing firm while his new employer consisted only of two founders). Despite all the purchases, the firm has a reputation for allowing the companies it acquires a great deal of autonomy. Usually, the firm keeps the original names of its Southern partners intact after an acquisition.

Dain, Dain, go away

Morgan Keegan, faced with a rash of employee defections to a competitor in 1998, fought back. The firm filed a lawsuit against Dain Rauscher, claiming that the Minnesota-based bank unfairly lured away Morgan Keegan traders after Dain opened a Memphis office. The suit was quickly settled with neither side disclosing terms.

The company has experienced additional courtroom drama, though not always with the enthusiasm it brought in its suit against Dain. Brokers at Morgan Keegan have had several run-ins with the law recently. In December 1999, two brokers from the Nashville office were suspended amid allegations that they benefited from inside information. After receiving inside information on a merger involving two Bermuda-based insurers, the two brokers allegedly made trades on their own behalf and tipped off two dozen clients. In March 2000, two Bowling Green, Kentucky brokers were charged in an insider trading scheme that netted $8 million in profits, according to the Securities and Exchange Commission. The two brokers, like the ones in Nashville, were suspended pending the outcome of the case. Morgan Keegan has not been implicated in either instance.

Small deals

Like other Southeastern investment banks, Morgan Keegan has experienced downturns in the number of lead-managed investment banking mandates. According to *The Wall Street Journal*, in 1998 seven Southeastern I-banks lead-managed 17 IPOs, while in 1999 those same firms lead-managed only seven IPOs. According to the *Journal*, there are a few reasons for this decline. For starters, the number of offerings by industrial businesses (the traditional clients of Southern banks) has decreased as technology companies have come into market favor. Also, the bulge-bracket firms have increased their presence in the South — both Morgan Stanley and Goldman Sachs have recently opened offices in Atlanta. In 1999 Morgan Keegan did not lead manage any IPOs and co-managed just six initial public offerings. Minor Perkins, director of investment banking for Morgan Keegan, told the *Journal*, "It is frustrating. We are, on the one hand, delighted and appreciative of the opportunity to be involved as a co-manager. On the other hand, we would certainly have liked to be lead manager on all of these transactions."

While its underwriting operations will never be confused with those of a bulge-bracket firm, Morgan Keegan has carved a niche for itself in the

Hungry for more inside scoop? Join Vault.com's popular online
community for finance and banking — www.vault.com

VAULT.com **305**

South. The firm reports it has raised $12.7 billion in proceeds through equity underwriting since 1991, including $2.7 billion in 1999. Morgan Keegan has been the leading IPO underwriter in the Southeast since January 1994. Recently, Morgan Keegan co-managed the $67.5 million, October 1999 offering of Crossroads Systems. In November 1999, Morgan Keegan co-managed Finisar Corp.'s $155.8 million IPO. Altogether, the firm participated in 23 equity offerings in 1999. Corporate debt deals include a $15 million offering for Schlotzky's, Inc. in March 1999.

GETTING HIRED

Year-round hirin'

The firm's web site, www.morgankeegan.com, has a careers section that posts corporate finance, private equity, and brokerage openings. The site allows interested candidates the chance to apply for positions online. The firm accepts résumés and evaluates applicants on a continual basis, rather than focusing on a recruiting season as many bulge-bracket firms do.

OUR SURVEY SAYS

Not all Southern hospitality

Morgan Keegan prides itself on being "a Southern company with Southern manners." Employees say co-workers are "warm and friendly," and everyone is "eager to help." Sources also report that "if you don't like someone hovering over you while you work, this is the place." They say Morgan Keegan is a "great place to learn the ropes," and "opportunities for advancement are great." Still, life at the firm is not all mint juleps and Southern hospitality. Insiders in the firm's I-banking department say, "this is still a man's business," so "if you have difficulty taking criticism, or standing up for yourself, this is not the place." "Signs of discrimination," are not evident, however, and women are reportedly "treated fairly." Insiders do concede "there is not an overabundance of minorities" employed by firm.

Tough hours, but love that stock plan

Workers have different experiences with the hours. While some remark happily that "face time is not encouraged," others bemoan "tough" hours for investment bankers. But benefits are universally praised — they're "really good," with "several different options" for health plans, a tuition reimbursement program, and a "terrific" 401(k) program that allows employees to decide how their money is invested. The company also sponsors an outstanding stock purchase plan — 54 percent of the firm's stock is owned by its employees and directors.

Hungry for more inside scoop? Join Vault.com's popular online
community for finance and banking — www.vault.com

VAULT.com **307**

Morgan Stanley Dean Witter

1585 Broadway
New York, NY 10036
(212) 761-4000
Fax: (212) 761-0086
www.msdw.com

LOCATIONS

New York (HQ)
Atlanta
Boston
Chicago
Houston
Los Angeles
Menlo Park
Philadelphia
San Francisco

Beijing
Hong Kong
London
Paris
Tokyo
Other offices in 25 countries

DEPARTMENTS

Asset Management (Institutional,
    Individual)
Credit Services
Institutional Securities (Investment
    Banking, Institutional Sales and
    Trading, Research)
Private Client Group

THE STATS

Chairman, CEO & Director:
Philip J. Purcell
President & COO: John Mack
Employer Type: Public Company
Ticker Symbol: MWD (NYSE)
1999 Net Revenue: $22 billion
1999 Net Income: $4.8 billion
No. of Employees: 56,058
No. of Offices: 560

UPPERS

• Bulge-bracket prestige
• Associate rotation system lets you
  get a taste of everything
• Work with talented bankers

DOWNERS

• Bad press from recent scandals
• Brutal hours
• Rigid organization

KEY COMPETITORS

Donaldson, Lufkin & Jenrette
Goldman Sachs
Merrill Lynch
Salomon Smith Barney

EMPLOYMENT CONTACT

Firmwide Recruiting
Erika Rosek, Manager
1221 Avenue of the Americas
44th Floor
New York, NY 10020
Attn: Division of Interest

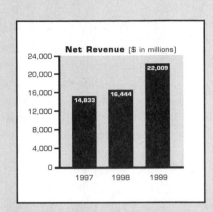

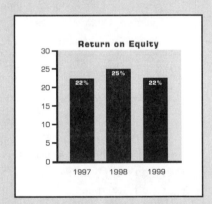

THE SCOOP

Silver only to Goldman?

Morgan Stanley Dean Witter (MSDW) is unquestionably one of the premier bulge-bracket investment banking firms. The firm reported over $4.5 billion in I-banking revenues in 1999 and is ranked in the top 10 of every significant league table. The firm's retail operations are even more lucrative. Morgan Stanley took in almost $6 billion from its brokerage in 1999. In addition to its securities businesses, MSDW also has departments devoted to asset management and research. Additionally, the bank owns Discover Card, the third-largest credit card company. While the firm's reputation within the I-banking world is fairly spectacular, it might suffer from a second-fiddle complex in its recent competition with fellow bulge-bracket firm Goldman Sachs. According to Thomson Financial Securities Data, in 1999 Morgan Stanley Dean Witter ranked number two behind Goldman on three key investment banking league tables: lead underwriters of common stock, lead underwriters of IPOs, and advisors of worldwide M&A transactions.

Dodging Glass-Steagall

Morgan Stanley Dean Witter was created in 1997 through the merger of Morgan Stanley and Dean Witter, Discover & Co. Dean Witter was founded in 1924 in San Francisco. Dean Witter milestones include the firm's IPO in 1972, its 1978 merger with New York-based securities firm Reynolds & Co. (at the time, the largest securities industry merger), its purchase by Sears Roebuck in 1981, the 1986 launch of Discover Card, and the 1992 spinoff of the Dean Witter, Discover Group.

Morgan Stanley traces its roots to the former securities operations of J.P. Morgan. In 1933, after the passage of the Glass-Steagall Act, which prohibited firms from operating both commercial and investment banking business, two J.P. Morgan partners (Howard Stanley and Harry Morgan, son of J.P. Morgan) and several other employees split from the bank and formed Morgan Stanley. The new firm was created in order to concentrate on the securities business while J.P. Morgan remained a commercial bank. Great moments in Morgan Stanley history include its admission to the New York Stock Exchange in 1941 and its 1986 IPO.

Accolades

While many feared the merger with retail-oriented Dean Witter would damage the powerful, white-shoe operations of Morgan Stanley, the combined firm's results have hushed the critics. MSDW posted a bevy of achievements during 1999. The firm was named "Best Investment Bank" by *Euromoney* and received four out of a possible 16 "Deal of the Year Awards" by *Investment Dealers' Digest*. Morgan Stanley finished second in U.S. IPO and common stock underwriting, lead managing 49 IPOs worth approximately $14.0 billion and 99 common stock offerings worth $32.7 billion, according to Thomson Financial Securities Data. MSDW ranked second in completed worldwide M&A advisory, advising on 377 deals worth $630.3 billion. The bank didn't rank as highly (by Morgan Stanley standards) in debt underwriting, but it is nonetheless considered a major player. MSDW was fifth among both investment grade and high yield debt underwriters, lead managing $66.6 billion of issues in the investment grade market and $8.7 billion in high yield offerings. The firm also rounded out the top five list of underwriters of asset-backed securities, underwriting 133 offerings worth $20.6 billion. The year 2000 began with a bang for MSDW. During the first quarter of 2000 the firm advised on 88 completed worldwide M&A deals with a total transaction value of over $207 billion.

While continuing to break I-banking records, the firm has also been expanding its retail business. In November 1999, Morgan Stanley jumped headfirst into online trading. Previously, the firm's online clients traded on Discover Brokerage Direct. The bank opened Morgan Stanley Dean Witter Online, its new online trading option, in November after months of asserting that its clients weren't interested in online alternatives. MSDW charged $29.95 for trades, gradually moving all Discover Brokerage clients who had been paying $14.95 per trade up to the new scale. While many price-sensitive Discover clients moved their accounts to other online banks, analysts felt the firm made the right move, stating that existing Morgan Stanley clients were clamoring for a high-quality alternative. The company is also reportedly investigating "cross-selling" opportunities with Discover Card. The firm hopes to develop brokerage relationships with vendors that currently accept the Discover Card, according to a June 2000 report in *Financial NetNews*.

Blessed is Meeker

MSDW also employs a large research team, which includes superstar Internet analyst Mary Meeker. Cited as "the Net analyst with the most

Hungry for more inside scoop? Join Vault.com's popular online
community for finance and banking — www.vault.com

VAULT.com **311**

influence on stock prices and thinking on the Street" by *The Industry Standard*, Meeker is probably the most well-known analyst on Wall Street. From 1995 to 1997, Meeker and her team members wrote groundbreaking trend reports regarding the Internet. According to *Business Week*, these reports became "virtual bibles for investors and CEOs alike." John Chambers, CEO of Cisco, told *Business Week*, "[Meeker] gets it, got it earlier than most, and was able to articulate it to the business community in a way they could understand." Meeker's reputation and knack for picking winners have made a buy recommendation from her one of the most coveted calls on Wall Street. Her presence is often cited as a factor in Morgan Stanley's success with technology companies. "Undoubtedly, the lure of a recommendation from Meeker has many Net startups eager to have Morgan Stanley take them public," *The Standard* hypothesized in 1999. Though the firm and Meeker herself try to modestly downplay the analyst's influence, Meeker was reportedly paid $15 million in 1999 for her efforts.

Dealing, MSDW style

Morgan Stanley Dean Witter likes to boast quality along with quantity in terms of investment banking mandates. Notable IPOs include Martha Stewart Living Omnimedia (a $129.6 million offering completed in October 1999), United Parcel Service's enormous $5.47 billion offering in November 1999, and John Hancock Financial Services' nearly $2.0 billion deal completed in January 2000. More recent deals include Palm's $874 million IPO and Sun Life Financial's $1.2 billion offering, both completed in March 2000. In April 2000, the company lead-managed the $497.7 million IPO of Germany's QS Communications AG.

In the tech sector, M&A clients include Healtheon, which Morgan Stanley advised on its $7.9 billion purchase by WebMD. MSDW advised @Home on its $6.7 billion purchase by Excite and Broadcast.com on its $5.7 billion sale to Yahoo!. Outside of the tech area, MSDW advised Monsanto on its $27 billion merger with Pharmacia Upjohn and, in the European sector, Morgan Stanley represented Germany's Hoechst on its $50 billion merger with Rhone-Poulenc of France.

Some embarrassing moments

While every bank has skeletons in its closet, Morgan Stanley's metaphorical wardrobe has some bones which the firm probably wishes would stay buried. In April 2000, *The San Francisco Examiner* revealed that San Francisco Mayor Willie Brown had been granted access to several hot IPOs underwritten by Morgan Stanley, making tens of thousands of dollars in profits. It's not unusual for banks to give influential individuals access to high-profile IPOs — in fact, it's almost a standard practice. However, the situation yielded some embarrassment when the *Examiner* reported that a Morgan Stanley spokesperson initially said the firm did not have any bond business with the city; in fact the firm had underwritten numerous bond offerings for San Francisco. The Morgan Stanley spokesman later explained that he did not mention the bonds because "all those bonds were competitive, meaning they were done on a sealed-bid basis where the [bank offering] the low true interest cost to the city wins. There is no opportunity for influence." According to the report, an unidentified "young broker" sold the shares to the mayor, independent of the investment banking relationship with the city, in order to develop a relationship with him.

In January 2000, MSDW was fined $495,000 by the National Association of Securities Dealers (NASD). The NASD alleged that in 1995, six Morgan Stanley traders manipulated the stock prices on nine Nasdaq stocks. According to the allegations, the six quoted artificially high prices for the stock before the market opened, raising the share prices to artificially high levels. The traders were fined $2,500 each.

The firm encountered trouble with another regulatory agency in June 2000 when the Equal Opportunity Employment Commission (EEOC) ruled the bank had discriminated against a high-level female broker. Allison Schieffelin, an employee in the firm's institutional equity division, alleged in 1998 that she had been subject to discrimination and harassment at Morgan Stanley and that less-qualified male traders were promoted to managing director while she remained a principal. The bank denied the allegations; if it fails to reach a settlement with the EEOC, the federal agency could file a lawsuit against MSDW.

Where do we go from here?

Like many I-banks, Morgan Stanley Dean Witter is the constant subject of merger rumors. With the 1999 repeal of the Glass-Steagall Act (the act that led to the founding of Morgan Stanley in 1933), some industry analysts believe an increasing number of bulge-bracket firms will merge with commercial banks to form full-service financial "supermarkets." *The Banker* published just such a rumor in May 2000,

Hungry for more inside scoop? Join Vault.com's popular online
community for finance and banking — www.vault.com

VAULT.com   **313**

saying Morgan Stanley's directors were in constant debate on the merits of merging with Chase Manhattan. Other innuendo has the firm acquiring boutiques to grow specific niche businesses or pairing with another bulge-bracket firm to create an I-banking über-giant.

GETTING HIRED

Wide variety of interviews

Morgan Stanley Dean Witter's interviews are, according to some current employees, "quite formal, even for the investment banking industry." Technical questions are reportedly common; one business school student interviewing for a trading job reports that for his final round he was asked to sit in a chair while a senior director peppered him with macroeconomic questions. "All he did was pace around and throw questions at me — if I was wrong he'd correct me, and then just go to the next one. I remember thinking, 'God, I'm glad I know some of this stuff.' It was a lot of macroeconomics: inflation, interest rates, currencies." Says that contact: "They had me interview with pretty senior people, the head of all treasury trading, and the second in charge of all fixed income." Some recent associate-level hires report undergoing more than one callback round during the business school recruiting process. "I had three more rounds, all in New York [after the on-campus round]," reports one contact.

MBA recruits for investment banking tell a different story. One associate reports a far less grueling interview process. "It's all in who you meet here," that source explains. "Since it's such a large place, you are going to meet people with very different interviewing styles...I also think that if they have confidence in your technical skills and coursework, then you won't hit many technical questions at all." Another investment banking contact reports that at his business school, MSDW holds only two rounds (one on-campus and one at an office) for both summer and full-time associate hires. "They make very quick decisions," reports that contact. "That's the difference between Goldman and Morgan Stanley." That insider reports that there was one two-on-one interview ("good cop, bad cop"), though "other people had one-on-ones." The second round was all one-on-ones for this contact.

OUR SURVEY SAYS

Talk the talk and walk the walk

As one of Wall Street's preeminent "white-shoe" firms, Morgan Stanley Dean Witter cultivates an "extremely professional environment" geared toward the "bright, motivated individuals who fill the halls." Insiders say that "everyone seems to have an MBA from a top business school" and state that "no other firm matches Morgan Stanley in terms of education and attitude." One former banker says the firm was "a great place to learn how to work in an intense environment with smart people." Not everyone appreciates this atmosphere, however. One former analyst calls "the people at Morgan Stanley" his "biggest disappointment." He explains: "They are boorish, aggressive, and elitist — even more so than the rest of Wall Street."

Sources say the firm cultivates a conformist culture. "If you don't fit in, you stand out a lot," observes one banker. "You kind of have to walk the walk and talk the talk." Another insider complains of Morgan Stanley's "extremely rigid organization" and "heavy-handed culture." That insider says the firm takes pride in "the Morgan Stanley way. The firm has this attitude of 'this is how we've always done things and this is how we'll continue to do things.'" However, that insider does concede that the bank puts "a lot of time and effort into developing people."

Contacts report that though the merger has been a rousing success, some prestige-oriented investment bankers are reluctant to embrace the Dean Witter name. Says one source, "The bankers still call the place Morgan Stanley. On voice mail or in conversations, you never hear bankers using the Dean Witter name. Recently the firm announced we would have to start using the Discover Card more instead of the corporate Amex and everyone kind of groaned silently."

Investment banking associates at MSDW are offered a generalist program with three rotations through industry or product groups. These rotations last four months each. Comparing Morgan Stanley Dean Witter to its chief competitor, Goldman Sachs, one insider comments, "There's an incredible amount of mobility when compared to Goldman. You spend your first year as a total generalist and then after two years, if you want, you can switch groups."

Hungry for more inside scoop? Join Vault.com's popular online
community for finance and banking — www.vault.com

VAULT.com **315**

Free fruit and shop at J. Crew

The firm, like its Wall Street counterparts, recently embraced a full-time business casual dress policy. The firm also issued a brochure highlighting the major do's and don'ts for dressing appropriately at work. Some don'ts: shirts without collars or open-toed shoes. Some do's: khakis and polo shirts in the summer. Like other firms on Wall Street, MSDW also negotiated discounts at local retailers including J. Crew and Banana Republic so employees could pick up some new casual threads. The firm provides tuition reimbursement, subsidized health club memberships, laptops, car service, meal allowances on nights and weekends, and other standard investment banking perks. In addition, insiders say the firm sponsors "lavish" company outings and parties: "I feel like this firm really cares about making people feel like they are working for a top-notch organization." For the health-conscious, the firm reportedly offers free fruit on every investment banking floor.

Beep!

One of the famed aspects of Morgan Stanley Dean Witter's culture is that bankers are required to wear beepers, which some other banks enjoy pointing out as a MSDW shortcoming during MBA recruiting season. "Depending on how you think about that, [omnipresent beepers are] a good thing or a bad thing," reveals one associate. "The bad thing is, everyone's got access to your number. But the good side is that if you ever want to take a two-hour lunch, you can, because they can page you. If anyone ever complains that you weren't in the office, you can just say 'Why didn't you page me?'"

360-degree evaluations

Morgan Stanley Dean Witter is also famed for its innovative evaluation system. The 360-degree review evaluation process takes place once a year, but most analysts are reviewed mid-year as well. "So everyone you work with, you put on your list, and that list goes to the HR department," explains one insider. "The HR department sends an evaluation form to everyone you work with. [Morgan Stanley] takes this very seriously. Everyone you work with will give you a formal evaluation. All the evaluations are collected, and a VP or managing director who's in your group is assigned to collate all the information and pull together what the overall evaluation should be."

"You not only get feedback from people above you, but you give them evaluations. The downward evaluations are named, upward are anonymous," says one former analyst. "So if your associate is being a total pain in the ass, you slam [him or her] in the reviews. They take very seriously the opinions of the junior people when evaluating for bonuses, so associates go out of the way to be helpful." "I'd say that is a very unique thing about Morgan," says one banker, who points out that the Morgan Stanley evaluation model was actually a case study at his business school.

Everything's coming up bulge bracket

Since Morgan Stanley is an unquestioned industry leader, all of the positives and negatives of working in I-banking are exaggerated. The hours required can be brutal — analysts can expect nightmare 100-hour workweeks. Of course, the firm pays well to compensate for the hours at the office, though not well enough for everyone: "The most frustrating aspect of being [at Morgan Stanley] is that it is such a well-respected name and they know it. They can get away with cutting corners in compensation." MSDW has recently made an effort to stop cutting corners, but insiders report that "the initiatives the firm has put in place are nice but not enough."

Hungry for more inside scoop? Join Vault.com's popular online
community for finance and banking — www.vault.com

VAULT.COM   317

PaineWebber Group

1285 Avenue of the Americas
New York, NY 10019
(212) 713-2000
Fax: (212) 713-4889
www.painewebber.com

LOCATIONS

New York (HQ)
Boston
Chicago
Houston
Los Angeles
Orlando
Philadelphia
San Francisco
Washington, DC
More than 380 offices worldwide

DEPARTMENTS

- Capital Markets (Equity, Fixed
  Income, Investment Banking,
  Municipal Securities Group,
  Research)
- Retail (Private Client Group, Asset
  Management, Insurance)
- Transaction Services
  (Correspondent Services, Prime
  Brokerage and Stock Loan)

THE STATS

Chairman & CEO:
Donald B. Marron
Head of Investment Banking:
Brian Barefoot
Employer Type: Public Company
Ticker Symbol: PWJ (NYSE)
1999 Net Revenue: $5.29 billion
1999 Net Income: $629 million
No. of Employees: 20,008
No. of Offices: 380 +

UPPERS

- Company fitness centers
- Laid-back culture

DOWNERS

- Fragmented culture
- Low prestige for I-banking

KEY COMPETITORS

Merrill Lynch
Prudential Securities
Salomon Smith Barney

EMPLOYMENT CONTACT

Investment Banking Recruiter
PaineWebber
1285 Avenue of the Americas
13th Floor
New York, NY 10019
E-mail:
ibdanalyst_recruiter@painewebber.com
ibdassociate_recruiter@painewebber.com

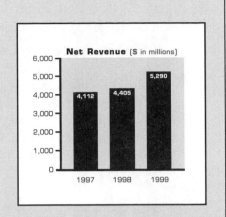

Net Revenue [$ in millions]

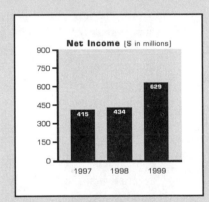

Net Income [$ in millions]

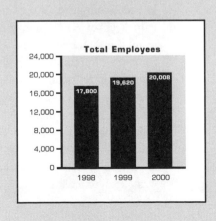

Total Employees

THE SCOOP

The financial services spectrum

While PaineWebber's greatest strength is in its retail brokerage business (the firm employs more than 8,400 brokers who serve over 2.7 million individual clients), the company is a diversified financial services firm, offering investment banking, asset management, and insurance services. The firm's capital markets division includes three investment banking groups: a general investment banking group, a real estate investment banking and principal transactions group, and a municipal securities group.

The urge to merge

In July 2000, the firm announced it would be acquired by UBS, the Swiss banking group. Initial reports said that UBS would pay approximately $10.8 billion in cash and stock. Donald Marron, CEO of PaineWebber, issued a statement in which he said, "This is the right merger, with the right partner, at the right time." According to early reports, if the merger is completed, UBS officials said PaineWebber would continue to operate under its existing brand name.

Most reports noted that UBS had long been interested in reaching more wealthy investors in the U.S. Industry insiders have said that PaineWebber's focus on retail brokerage would hinder the company in an era when most retail brokerages were expanding into investment banking and other financial services. The acquisition ended years of adamant statements by PaineWebber officials that the company intended to remain independent. According to *The Wall Street Journal*, PaineWebber CEO Marron had "been viewed on Wall Street as a stumbling block to a deal." In 1995 the *Journal* reported that Marron responded to rumors of a PaineWebber sale by telling employees: "We continue to be staunchly independent and are proud of our heritage as one of the very few such firms left in our industry." Despite Marron's assertion, merger rumors persisted. In 1998 the firm was reported to be negotiating a merger with Prudential Securities. Shortly thereafter, PaineWebber was approached by Dresdner for a merger that also did not materialize. In April 2000, Marron noted in an interview that PaineWebber was "open to anything that would enhance our growth rate."

Beantown roots

The firm traces its roots back to 1879, when William Paine and Wallace Webber opened a brokerage house in Boston. Before the turn of the century, PaineWebber obtained a seat on the New York Stock Exchange. PaineWebber moved into the financial big leagues in the 1960s, when it moved its headquarters to New York; the firm continued its expansion by opening international offices. After the stock market crash of 1987, PaineWebber decided to scale back operations, shedding some of its non-core businesses (including a venture capital arm and its commercial paper operations). In 1994 PaineWebber purchased Kidder Peabody, the defunct financial services subsidiary of General Electric. Prior to the acquisition by UBS, GE held a 23 percent stake in PaineWebber.

Serving the rich

PaineWebber's mutual fund business, which had $73 million in assets under management after the first quarter of 2000, is handled by the firm's subsidiary, Mitchell Hudson Asset Management. The firm's entire private client group (or retail brokerage) focuses on wealthy individuals, defined as those with annual income greater than $100,000 and/or net worth exceeding $500,000. According to the company, the firm's private client division is striving to "gather assets from affluent and emerging affluent individuals." Donald Marron told *Barron's* in November 1999, "Our strategy has been to be in the center of the flow of household financial assets from the more affluent segment of the population." Some have questioned that strategy, noting that Internet trading has led to a sizable increase in investment by less-affluent individuals. However, the firm's research predicts that the amount of assets controlled by affluent individuals is increasing by nine percent per year. For PaineWebber clients, it is more like 20 percent, according to *Barron's*. "How many industries are there in this country where the underlying demand for the product is growing that fast?" Marron asked rhetorically.

Tennessee studs

In June 2000, PaineWebber completed its acquisition of J.C. Bradford & Co., a Nashville, TN-based firm. The acquisition, valued at $620 million, gives PaineWebber a retail presence in the Southeast, an area where PaineWebber had sparse representation at best. The Bradford name was eliminated after the merger and approximately 20 percent of Bradford's 2,700 employees, including approximately 72 of 100

Hungry for more inside scoop? Join Vault.com's popular online
community for finance and banking — www.vault.com

VAULT.com   **321**

employees in the municipal bond sector, were terminated. In 1999 PaineWebber's municipal securities group ranked second in negotiated senior underwriting while Bradford came in ninth, according to Thomson Financial Securities Data. Therefore, PaineWebber wanted to replace the Bradford muni employees with its own staff. "It's a very good acquisition for PaineWebber," an anonymous analyst told *The Bond Buyer*. "It's a good fit for them and will generally help their strategy. I don't think they will have to alter their strategy at all."

See you in court

PaineWebber's lawyers were called into action shortly after the Bradford deal. PaineWebber filed a lawsuit against Morgan Stanley Dean Witter in May 2000, alleging unfair hiring practices. PaineWebber claimed Morgan Stanley's recruiting efforts targeted Bradford brokers after the deal was announced, which amounted to an attempt to "injure PaineWebber's business." The suit against Morgan Stanley was not the first legal action launched by the firm against its competition. In March 2000, the firm filed a similar suit against Prudential Securities, accusing the competitor of illegally recruiting three star brokers from PaineWebber's Oklahoma City office.

Co-manager's special

While PaineWebber competes with Merrill Lynch and Morgan Stanley in the fierce battle for retail clients, the firm's corporate finance practices are not in the same league with the top-tier investment banks. Beyond municipal underwriting, PaineWebber most often acts as a co-manager in deals and is not a presence on top 10 rankings of domestic or international equity underwriters. That's not to say the firm hasn't been in on any significant deals. The firm co-managed IPOs for Goldman Sachs and Juno Online Services in May 1999. The firm also co-managed the August 1999 Blockbuster IPO and the April 2000 offering by AT&T Wireless. PaineWebber acted as lead manager for the April 1999 CompuCredit IPO, worth $69 million.

GETTING HIRED

PaineWebber's web site has a detailed career section with job openings all over the world and contacts for those positions. For I-banking, the firm conducts campus recruiting for both analysts and associates. Schools range from the normal top 20 entries (Harvard, Columbia and Stanford) to regional private and public colleges. The firm generally recruits for investment banking from November to March. On-campus interviews conducted by bankers follow a presentation by the firm. If selected for the next round, candidates are invited to New York for final interviews. According to the firm, all associates train in New York but work in New York, San Francisco, Houston, Los Angeles, Washington, DC, Philadelphia, Orlando, Boston, or Chicago, depending on individual preference and the firm's staffing requirements. During training, associates have the opportunity to meet bankers from various industry and product groups.

OUR SURVEY SAYS

Everything to everyone

While PaineWebber would like to be all things to all people, potential employees are cautioned that "PaineWebber is a brokerage firm first and an investment bank second." Still, insiders say that the firm is committed to the goal of "growing and establishing a presence as a premier bank on Wall Street." According to one veteran banker, "PaineWebber definitely offers a better lifestyle than other firms. The atmosphere is collegial and the hours, while long at times, are much better than at other firms." While life at PaineWebber is as "challenging, demanding, and rewarding" as at any firm in the industry, the corporate culture is said to be much less "stuffy" and "overbearing" than that at many of its competitors. Employees in real estate praise the firm's top executives for "being so approachable," and insiders generally say that "PaineWebber, despite its size, has a small-business feel." Says one source who served a stint as a summer associate with PaineWebber in New York while in business school: "It was a very good experience. I had exposure to VPs constantly. Exposure to [managing directors] was limited to special meetings — three to five during the summer."

Hungry for more inside scoop? Join Vault.com's popular online community for finance and banking — www.vault.com

VAULT.com 323

Employees in New York and New Jersey say, "There are fitness centers here, and if you live in New York City, you can take the ferry free to PaineWebber at Lincoln Harbor [in Weehawken, NJ] if you work there." Otherwise, in car-clogged New Jersey, "the commute is a nightmare." At PaineWebber, "women and minorities are treated very well, and women constitute a good portion of management. Complaints regarding harassment and discrimination are handled very seriously." While employees think the firm is "relatively liberal" — one contact reports seeing "some long-haired and multi-earringed employees" — and "sensitive, for a place on the Street," some say "the culture is fragmented and people tend to keep to their own divisions."

"PaineWebber definitely offers a better lifestyle than other firms."

— PaineWebber Insider

Peter J. Solomon Company

767 Fifth Avenue
New York, NY 10153
(212) 508-1600
Fax: (212) 508-1633
www.pjsolomon.com

LOCATIONS

New York (HQ)

DEPARTMENTS

Bankruptcy and Restructuring Advisory
Financing Advisory
Mergers and Acquisitions Advisory

KEY COMPETITORS

Lazard
Wasserstein Perella

EMPLOYMENT CONTACT

Diane M. Coffey
Managing Director
Peter J. Solomon Company
767 5th Avenue
New York, NY 10153
Email: careers@pjsolomon.com

THE SCOOP

Hip eponymous

Peter J. Solomon Company (PJSC) is a boutique investment bank specializing in mergers and acquisitions, restructuring, and financing advisory. The firm was founded in 1989 by Peter J. Solomon and has completed over 175 advisory assignments. The company employs 45 individuals, approximately half of whom are investment banking professionals.

Solomon himself is quite the accomplished banker. He started his career in the corporate finance department at Lehman Brothers in 1963 and became a partner in 1971. Four years later, he was appointed a member of the board of directors. In 1978 Solomon was named New York's Deputy Mayor of Economic Policy and Development under Ed Koch. Two years later, he was appointed Counselor to the United States Treasury by President Jimmy Carter. He returned to investment banking and Lehman Brothers in 1981 as a senior managing director; after the firm's purchase by American Express, he became chairman of the M&A department. In addition to leading his self-named firm, Solomon is also currently on the board of directors of several companies, including Office Depot, Baker, Fentress & Company, and General Cigar Holdings.

Merger boutique

While PJ Solomon can't claim to compete with the big boys, the firm has established an interesting niche in the M&A marketplace. In January 1999, the firm advised McKesson Corp. on its $14.5 billion merger with HBO & Co., a deal that created the world's largest health care services company. That same month, PJ Solomon advised Centennial Cellular on its $1.6 billion sale to an investor group. Other companies seeking PJ Solomon's advisory skills include Bedford Fair Industries (regarding a sale to Fingerhut), Hedstrom Corp. (sold to buyout firm Hicks, Muse, Tate & Furst), Office Depot (purchased Viking Office Products and The Office Club) and Perry Drug Stores (merged with Rite Aid). PJ Solomon has advised on several bankruptcies and restructurings. Clients include Barney's, Bradlees, Discovery Zone, R.H. Macy & Co., Today's Man, and Zenith Electronics. The firm also has a private placement group that specializes in both debt and equity financings.

GETTING HIRED

Know your discounted cash flows

Insiders report that Peter J. Solomon Company is stepping up its recruiting. "[PJSC] recruits at Harvard, Wharton, Stanford, Berkeley, maybe Yale. But I don't think they've had too much luck," says one contact. "They've just started hiring associates in the past year or two — on-campus — at Harvard and Wharton." The firm also recruits from Brown, Columbia, Dartmouth, the University of Chicago, the University of Michigan, and the University of Virginia.

"I think it's better there to have a quantitative or finance background. You do go through training — it's about a month — and they do bring in accountants, but they really want you on the job quickly," explains one insider. "If you have some experience, you're going to be happier. That's not to say that you can't get there without it." Says that contact: "The Wharton candidate is almost the ideal candidate for [PJSC]. They come in understanding discounted cash flows." As for those discounted cash flows and other yummy quantitative finance questions, sources say, "if you have it on your résumé, you better be sure you can talk about it. If you have zero experience, you better be focused on the fact that you're smart. Bring up examples where you've been quantitative."

Applicants can expect to travel to PJSC's headquarters twice and "definitely meet all the senior people at the firm." What about the big man himself? "Peter — if he's around — he'll pop his head in and say why Peter Solomon is great, but he won't ask you questions."

OUR SURVEY SAYS

Deep M&A know-how

"If you really want to learn how an M&A deal works," comments a firm insider, "you'll get depth at Peter J. Solomon. You'll get depth, though you won't get the breadth." That contact explains: "They don't underwrite, so you don't get financing experiencing. You're not going to do an IPO... You'll get to see it, but you won't actually work on it." On the upside insiders say they "definitely work on smaller teams. At Peter Solomon, the working group [list] is one page of people. If you

Hungry for more inside scoop? Join Vault.com's popular online
community for finance and banking — www.vault.com

V/\ULT.com **329**

look at DLJ or Goldman, the working group list is 100 people." "You see a much smaller piece of a bigger deal at a bigger bank," says one insider. "At Peter Solomon, you're much more likely to see something from start to finish. You won't necessarily get to see as many things, but you'll know a lot more about what you've seen."

Think like an owner

Getting to see more of deals also means working more closely with senior bankers, according to contacts at the company. "The senior banker contact is great. You just walk into the partners' offices — there's no appointment-making," says one insider. "Even if there's a conference call, you can just walk into the office and listen to it if you want to, even if it's not something you're working on." Working at a small firm also provides for an extra type of learning experience for the business-minded. "At a lot of banks, you think of yourself as an investment banker and not part of a business," explains one source. "At Peter Solomon, you get both. It's small enough so you understand what it's like to run a business — which computer to buy, how best to market the firm. And if you're entrepreneurial and interested in what its like to run a professional services firm, that's really interesting."

The astounding Peter Solomon

Working with senior bankers, of course, can mean working with Peter Solomon. One banker notes: "You would hear the secretary say who was on the phone. It's incredible. If you think about the mid- to late-1980s or early '90s, and who were the hitters — it's those names, all the time." As far as working with Solomon is concerned: "He's extremely demanding, so he just expects you to know everything," says one source. "He'll cut you some slack because you're a junior person, but if he wants something done, if you happen to be in his line of sight, you'll be the person to do it, whether it's VP work or not."

Peter J. Solomon bankers work in "offices with a beautiful view overlooking Central Park in Manhattan." An employee reports that "there are lots of places to go shop nearby, though you have no time to do that. You will be there for dinner all the time, it's just a better place than downtown." The firm pays for its bankers' dinners, and "you get taxis home, and they reimburse you for those." Peter Solomon bankers take taxis "because to take a car from Midtown to Downtown it's $15, for a cab it's $8. Those little things count. They'll take care of you, but you have to recognize that they're a small firm and they have to take into account those things."

Although small benefits like cabs versus car service may differ between PJSC and larger firms, "your hours won't be any different than at a big firm. [Workweeks are] definitely sometimes over 100 [hours], sometimes less than 70." Those late-night hours might look a bit different at a smaller firm, though. "At a big firm if you're there at 10:00 or 11:00 at night, it looks like 4:00 in the afternoon. At a smaller firm, late at night, it gets a little lonely, but it's not that bad, you're getting work done." The firm helps make up for solitary nights with pretty decent social contact. "In the summer there are outings. We went on a fishing trip one time in the Hamptons. There was some other boat cruise thing that they did. We go bowling, do things at Chelsea Piers," says one former Peter J. Solomon banker. "There are times when, because you have that senior banker contact, the senior guy will say, 'OK, who wants to leave and can go to dinner?' Before you know it, you and two other analysts will be out at a nice place and talking to a managing director about whatever."

Hungry for more inside scoop? Join Vault.com's popular online
community for finance and banking — www.vault.com

VAULT.com   **331**

Prudential Securities

One New York Plaza
New York, NY 10292
(212) 778-1000
Fax: (212) 778-6880
www.prusec.com

LOCATIONS

New York (HQ)
Atlanta
Boston
Chicago
Houston
Los Angeles
San Francisco
Palo Alto

DEPARTMENTS

Asset-Backed Securities
Business Origination/Development
Convertible Securities
Corporate Finance
Equity Products
International
Mergers and Acquisitions
Private Debt
Private Equity
Proprietary Capital

THE STATS

President & CEO:
Hardwick Simmons
Employer Type: Subsidiary of
Prudential Insurance
1999 Net Income: $813 million
No. of Employees: 18,000

UPPERS

• Friendly and laid-back culture
• Good exposure to interesting deals
• Lots of responsibility

DOWNERS

• Compensation
• Less prestigious than bulge-
  bracket firms
• Turnover

KEY COMPETITORS

Bear Stearns
PaineWebber
SG Cowen

EMPLOYMENT CONTACTS

Investment Banking
PSI
Jane Meyer
One New York Plaza
18th Floor
New York, New York 10292
Fax: (212) 778-6880

THE SCOOP

Big backer

Prudential Securities is the financial services division of Prudential Insurance, the insurance behemoth that reported $26.6 billion of revenue in 1999. The investment banking unit provides the usual services — debt and equity underwriting and mergers and acquisitions advice — in seven industries: consumer products and services, energy, financial services, health care, real estate, technology, and media. Additionally, Pru Securities handles private equity placements and provides private client services.

Pru Sec's roots

The company traces its history back to 1879, when Leopold Cahn founded Leopold Cahn & Co. Brokers and Investment Bankers. The next year, Cahn's nephew, Jules Bache, joined the firm at the tender age of 19. Within a short time Bache became treasurer and, by 1873, a partner. In 1892 the firm was reorganized under the name J.S. Bache & Co. In 1944, when Jules Bache died, he was succeeded by his nephew, Harold Bache, and the firm was renamed Bache & Co. Bache & Co. went public in 1971; 10 years later, it was purchased by Prudential Insurance for $385 million. Eventually, it was named Prudential Securities. In more recent news, the firm entered the online trading foray in May 1999, setting up an online brokerage shop that charges $24.95 per trade.

Merger binge

Prudential Securities went down the merger path in 1999, first acquiring Vector Securities International, a boutique investment bank specializing in health care and life sciences. The plum pickup, however, was Volpe Brown Whelan & Co., a San Francisco-based firm specializing in technology and health care, which Pru acquired in December 1999. Volpe was a leader in the Internet IPO craze; co-managed deals included About.com and Stamps.com in March and June 1999, respectively. At the time of the merger, Prudential Securities CEO Hardwick Simmons said, "The Volpe Brown Whelan acquisition establishes us as a key player in the vital technology business."

The key player status Simmons hoped for has yet to materialize. Prudential had been lead-managing fewer transactions at the same time

Volpe's star was on the rise; Prudential hoped to capture that momentum by snagging the services of Volpe's bankers. That strategy evaporated when approximately 10 percent of Volpe's 200-member staff quit in January 2000, a month after the merger closed. The hemorrhaging didn't stop there; in a May 2000 article in the *San Jose Mercury News*, Ken Sawyer, former head of mergers and acquisitions at Volpe, estimated that between 80 to 90 percent of Volpe's staff had departed, including 25 of 30 managing directors. A Prudential spokesman disputed the numbers but did concede that "we lost a number of people we wish we had not lost."

Who wants to marry a tech boutique?

Among the departures was James Feuille, who had taken over day-to-day operations at Prudential Volpe Technology Group (as the unit is now known) from former Volpe CEO Thomas Volpe and partner Robert Whelan. Feuille left in March 2000, claiming Prudential wouldn't allow its new technology branch enough autonomy. *The San Jose Mercury News* trashed Prudential's handling of the deal, saying it made the Fox special *Who Wants to Marry a Millionaire?* "look like a model long-term relationship." Specifically, the paper charged that Pru Securities made little effort to preserve the Volpe culture. According to the report, in the first month after the merger, Volpe employees had expense account reimbursements returned because they didn't fit Prudential's requirements. Additionally, Volpe employees were forced to switch personal trading accounts to Prudential, which charged higher commissions. Small complaints, true, but indicative of the differences between the Volpe way and the Prudential way. A former Prudential insider told Vault.com, "The firm acquired this small boutique (Volpe) that had a certain culture and tried to integrate — really dictate — that boutique into Pru's culture." While analysts feel that Prudential will wind up making its money back from the Volpe acquisition, it's clear the departures will cause the Volpe group to lose some stature in the tech underwriting field.

Spanked by the NASD

The firm suffered a blow its credibility in March 2000 when the National Association of Securities Dealers (NASD) slapped Prudential Securities with a $100,000 fine and a stern scolding for the company's actions in trying to win a 1996 IPO. According to the NASD, Prudential was seeking the lead underwriter slot on a $59 million IPO in February

Hungry for more inside scoop? Join Vault.com's popular online
community for finance and banking — www.vault.com

V/\ULT.com   **335**

1996. Prudential wanted to charge the issuer a 7 percent fee, the standard IPO underwriting fee for a large investment bank; the issuing company didn't want to pay more than 6 percent and had found a boutique firm willing to accept those terms. The NASD didn't name the issuer or the competitor bank, but *Red Herring*, via process of elimination, identified the issuer as First Alliance and the investment bank daring enough to charge 6 percent as Friedman, Billings, Ramsey Group. Prudential, according to the NASD, tried to pressure Friedman, Billings, Ramsey into ceding the lead underwriter position, saying the smaller bank couldn't handle the deal. Pru, of course, hoped to get the lead-underwriter's share of the 7 percent fee, rather than a paltry co-manager's cut. The NASD decision came at an inopportune time for investment banking giants; the regulatory commission is investigating I-banks for unfairly fixing underwriting fees at 7 percent, a price some feel is too high.

The NASD punishment hasn't shut Prudential Securities out of the IPO market. For example, the Volpe unit co-managed the AT&T Wireless IPO in April 2000. The $10.6 billion offering was the largest initial public offering in history.

GETTING HIRED

Top 20 or bust

Considering Prudential Securities' position outside the bulge bracket, it's surprising how selective the firm is. The company hires from "Ivy League and top-20 schools almost exclusively," according to one contact. The firm's web site, www.prudentialsecurities.com, lists recruiting contacts and the recruiting schedule for analysts and associates.

For those lucky enough to make Pru's cut, expect one or two on-campus interviews and follow-up interviews at the New York office with five or six bankers. "Interviews will vary," says one insider, "but corporate finance knowledge must be demonstrated and communications skills must be superior for a candidate to do well." Bankers say "questions vary [and include] case studies, technical, and general interest [questions]."

OUR SURVEY SAYS

(Almost) everybody's happy

Prudential insiders describe the company as "friendly, fun and entrepreneurial." One source raves, "The people here are very smart and work very hard. Unlike at some other banks, the people here are fun to work with and really care about quality of life issues." One former Pru associate reports that many bankers socialize outside the office by "going out for happy hour" and "meeting for poker games." Insiders also give the firm good marks for diversity, and report minority and female representation is "good by Wall Street standards." One source says there is "an open-door policy with senior bankers very willing to teach and to let you take on greater responsibility." Unfortunately, not everybody's having fun. "Right now, the morale is very low," reports one banker. "People feel as though they are not valued by the firm." Insiders also complain that "feedback is rare, unless you seek it out," and there is a "lack of mentors." One young banker complains that he's "treated as a resource as opposed to an educated analyst."

Pay is an issue

One contact complains that compensation "is slightly lower than average among our competitors for associates." To some, the pay issue is somewhat offset by the fact that "on average, [Pru bankers] probably work less hours than [bankers at] some of the bulge-bracket firms." Another source explains the lack of face time by noting, "If you are not busy, you don't have to stay in the office just to put in face time." Insiders report that since early 2000, the firm has implemented some changes in compensation and other perks offered to bankers. The firm went to a business casual dress policy, issued laptops, and offered "speedier promotions" and "increased pay," according to one insider. While some sources report that the initiatives are aiding retention, another hints that "the culture needs to improve more than the money does." Yet another contact notes that Prudential faces a different situation from that of the bulge-bracket I-banks that lost significant talent to Internet companies. This insider, a member of the highly publicized and problematic technology group, explains, "People weren't leaving to go to dot-coms. They were leaving to go to other banks."

Hungry for more inside scoop? Join Vault.com's popular online
community for finance and banking — www.vault.com

VAULT.COM **337**

Refresher course

The company offers a four-week training program that insiders rate as average. "The training program was just a refresher on some of the basics covered in business school," says one banker. Another repines, "One huge mistake was [an] entire week of fixed income." On-the-job training varies. "It is important to find an aggressive and smart banker and use [him or her] as a mentor," advises one contact. Pick carefully, though. "Senior bankers [are] not seasoned in corporate finance," according to one insider. "The technology group [is] really a hodge-podge of people from private placements and equity capital markets — they tried to build from within [with] individuals who didn't have experience in the industry." On the plus side, "a lot of responsibility is given to capable junior people," and deal teams usually consist of "a senior banker, one associate, and one analyst."

"Unlike at some other banks, the people here are fun to work with and really care about quality of life issues."

— *Pru Securities Insider*

Raymond James Financial

880 Carillon Parkway
St. Petersburg, FL 33716
(727) 573-3800
Fax: (727) 573-8244
www.raymondjames.com

LOCATIONS

St. Petersburg (HQ)
Atlanta • Chicago • Dallas • Detroit •
Los Angeles • New York • Princeton •
West Palm Beach • Buenos Aires •
Brussels • Brugte • Calgary •
Dusseldorf • Geneva • Istanbul •
Lausanne • London • Luxembourg •
Milan • Mumbai • Paris • Stuttgart •
Toronto
Over 1,700 financial advisor offices

DEPARTMENTS

Asset Management
Equity Capital Markets
    -Investment Banking
    -Equity Research
    -Private Client Group
    -Institutional Sales
    -Institutional Trading
Fixed Income
Merchant Banking
Office of the Chairman

THE STATS

Chairman & CEO:
Thomas A. James
Co-heads of Investment Banking:
Jim McDaniel and Dav Mosby
Employer Type: Public Company
Ticker Symbol: RJF (NYSE)
1999 Revenues: $1.2 billion
1999 Net Income: $85 million
No. of Employees: 4,480*
No. of Offices: 1,700

UPPERS

• Shorter hours than most banks
• Warm and fuzzy culture

DOWNERS

• Recent troubles in I-banking
• Stringent hiring process

** Does not include approximately 3,200
independent financial advisors*

KEY COMPETITORS

Legg Mason
Morgan Keegan
Robinson Humphrey

EMPLOYMENT CONTACT:

Human Resources
Raymond James Financial
880 Carillon Parkway
St. Petersburg, FL 33716

MBA Recruiting
E-mail: mbarecruiting@exec.rjf.com

Undergraduate Recruiting
E-mail: employment@hr.rjf.com

Employment applications available online

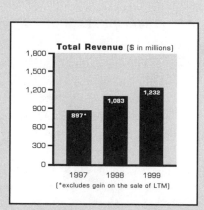

Total Revenue [$ in millions]

1997: 897*
1998: 1,083
1999: 1,232

(*excludes gain on the sale of LTM)

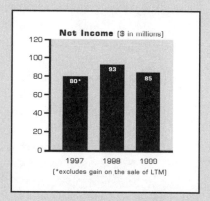

Net Income [$ in millions]

1997: 80*
1998: 93
1999: 85

(*excludes gain on the sale of LTM)

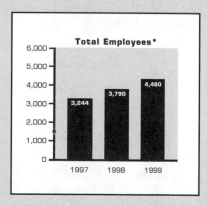

Total Employees*

1997: 3,244
1998: 3,790
1999: 4,480

* Does not include independant financial advisors

THE SCOOP

Everybody loves Raymond

Raymond James Financial is a full-service financial firm based in St. Petersburg, Florida. The company traces its roots back to 1962 when Robert James, whose son Thomas is now company CEO, founded Robert A. James Investments. Two years later, Robert merged his firm with Raymond & Associates. Raymond James & Associates, which began as a brokerage, eventually moved into underwriting (the company's first deal was completed in 1969), research (1972) and asset management (1975). The firm gained admission to the New York Stock Exchange in 1973 and went public in 1983. Football fans may recognize the company name; Raymond James bought the naming rights to the Tampa Bay Buccaneers' stadium in 1998.

Looking to add strength to its retail operations, Raymond James spent $80 million in April 1999 to purchase Roney & Co., a Detroit brokerage, from Bank One. Though the deal added 320 brokers to the Raymond James team, it was not a problem-free transaction. Roney executives were reportedly miffed at having less responsibility in the new firm. CEO Thomas James went to Detroit in June 2000 to speak at a series of management meetings and smooth things out. According to *Investment News*, James pointed out that though many mid-level Roney managers had been given different titles, due to increased hiring these managers would have more people serving under them. Despite early gripes, most observers praised the Roney acquisition. One industry analyst told *Investment News* the pickup was "an especially astute move," as it quickly added to Raymond James a bevy of experienced brokers. The transaction also increased the number of products available to Roney brokers.

I-banking slump

While the brokerage business is growing briskly, Raymond James' investment banking has been suffering recently. The firm's investment-banking revenues slipped to $75 million in fiscal 1999, down from a record $110 million the previous year. The falloff was attributed to the firm's lack of technology coverage as well as a slump in obtaining M&A work. M&A fees were down from $20 million in 1998 (another Raymond James record) to $16 million in 1999. However, Raymond James did manage to get in on a handful of deals in 1999. The firm led

Insurance Management Solutions Group's $36.9 million IPO in February 1999 and co-managed offerings for Pinnacle Holdings ($308.4 million in February 1999) and Paradyne ($117.3 million in July 1999), for example. More recently, Raymond James co-managed T/R Systems $34.5 million IPO in January 2000 and Fargo Electronics' $86.3 IPO in February 2000. While the company experienced weak results in 1999, it started the new millennium on the upswing. For the first half of 2000, the company reported 49 percent and 65 percent increases in revenues and net income, respectively, over the prior year.

Raymond James also employs a substantial research staff. The firm's equity research team is composed of 40 analysts and 80 research associates and other support staff. In August 1999, the firm hired Bob Anastasi to head up its equity research department. In 1995, Anastasi was named one of the 20 executives to watch in the computer industry by *Computer Reseller News*. He has ranked in the top five of *The Wall Street Journal*'s "All-Star Analyst Survey" four times since 1993.

Trouble with the law

Federal juries and regulatory agencies have affected Raymond James in recent months. A jury in Cincinnati returned a $40 million verdict against the firm in March 2000. The jury ruled that one of the company's discontinued subsidiaries, RJ Mortgage Acceptance, failed to dispense $18 million in interim financing to Corporex, a Cincinnati-based real estate management company, as required by a conditional letter of intent. The jury awarded Corporex $10 million in damages and a $30 million punitive award. Raymond James has said it plans to appeal the verdict. In April 2000, the Securities and Exchange Commission fined the firm $165,000 for improper record keeping. Raymond James accepted the fine without admitting or denying the charges. Finally, the bank lost $4.45 million in a decision by a NYSE arbitration panel in May 2000. The panel was adjudicating a dispute between Raymond James and Principal Financial Securities and Everen Securities. Raymond James had been in talks to acquire Everen in late 1997; Everen was purchased by Principal in December 1997. Everen and Principal claimed Raymond James used confidential information obtained during merger talks to lure over 80 employees from Everen, including 16 branch managers, 63 brokers and the firm's general counsel. Again, Raymond James said it intends to appeal the decision.

Hungry for more inside scoop? Join Vault.com's popular online
community for finance and banking — www.vault.com

VAULT.com   **343**

Single and loving it

Though the firm has received overtures from several large banks (including, reportedly, a handful of foreign banks), insurance companies, and a few broker-dealers in recent years, don't expect Raymond James to be next on the list of small firms bought out. The company is said to value its independence too much. Thomas James told *Investment News*, "Right now, there is a great benefit to being perceived by advisors and clients as an independent financial firm committed to clients and not having a change in management and all that stuff going on every day."

GETTING HIRED

Be the teacher's pet

Raymond James' web site, www.raymondjamesfinancial.com, provides information on applying for jobs at the St. Petersburg headquarters, at other U.S. offices, and at overseas offices. The site includes job descriptions, contact information, and recruiting schedules at both undergraduate schools and graduate business schools. The firm hires one recent business school graduate each year to serve as an assistant to Thomas James for a two-year period. One insider describes that position as largely focused on special projects like geographic expansion or new business. That contact describes the position as ideal "if you wanted to see how investment banking works from 30,000 feet — how the whole thing works." One insider who has held the position notes, "It offers unprecedented access to senior management of the firm."

Raymond James' recruiting effort for MBAs for positions as investment bankers and research analysts (for both summer and full-time positions), is rather unique. To start with, "the recruiting is done by a fairly high-level individual, the number two guy with the firm," reports one insider. "He does the interviewing for equity capital markets on campus. He usually brings in another banker, typically a junior banker, but he asks most of the questions." The questions asked in the screening interview are somewhat atypical as well; candidates are reportedly often asked about high school and other areas of life not normally covered in on campus interviews. "Not many people ask you questions like that," says one insider. "They'll ask you about things on your résumé or throw out some finance questions. Raymond James asks about high school: 'What were you doing in high school?' Were you doing well in class? Were you playing any sports?' [The interviewer] may ask you, 'Did you just bum through high school?' What he wants to know is: 'Did you take on all you can handle and still do more?'"

Dinnerview questions

The same day as the screening interview, several candidates at the school are called and invited for a "dinnerview." Explains one contact: "They'll go to dinner and see how you act in a dinner environment. It's usually at one of the best restaurants around — and you'll just talk about whatever." The firm waits until it completes its on-campus interviews before deciding on callbacks to the firm's headquarters. While thorough, "the interview process is also a little nerve-wracking. If you're at one of the first schools they visit, it could be a while before you get the call, and you get a little acid indigestion."

The visit to Raymond James' headquarters isn't much stress relief, though the firm makes sure to provide amusement. Candidates are usually flown to Florida on a Thursday evening and go through a "full slate of interviews in the morning." These interviews are usually two-on-one or three-on-one. "They're all just peppering you with questions, just to get a sense of who you are," recounts one recent candidate. After lunch, candidates take a set of five 10-minute tests. "All of it's just fundamental math. It's not one of those 'Here's this shape and do something funky with it.' It's: 'You've got 10 minutes to solve these fraction multiplication problems.' You've got to do a bunch of these and do them in a hurry." After these tests, the firm administers a standardized personality test on a Scantron form. "It's like one of those where you have two choices: 'I'm standing in a line, and someone cuts in front of me. I would fly into a rage, or approach them calmly.' It's something like 300 questions." All of the candidates take the test in the same room: "Everybody's just sitting around and plugging away." (All employees at Raymond James take these tests.)

After the interviews and tests, the firm finally lets the candidates relax. On the Saturday after interviews, Raymond James' hopefuls have been treated to deep-sea fishing and golf in recent years. Some lucky candidates have been treated to Tampa Bay Buccaneers football games.

Hungry for more inside scoop? Join Vault.com's popular online community for finance and banking — www.vault.com

VAULT.com **345**

OUR SURVEY SAYS

A very intense family

Raymond James bankers enjoy a working environment that is "not as stuffy as some of the workplaces in New York City." Reports one source: "RJ's culture is still like that of a small firm — almost like family." Although some describe the firm as laid-back, one I-banking insider disagrees. "I personally find that the laid-back term is not an accurate term — everybody there is extremely competitive. I was actually kind of surprised. They're all extremely intense." Continues that banker: "What they want to do is fit work into their life. They get to work in the morning and they work real hard until 8:00 and then they quit. There's not a whole lot of sitting around staring at the ceiling — you're pretty much on task from the moment you get there. [There's] not a whole lot of gabbing in the hallway."

Movin' on up

Insiders say RJ is "very well run," and "a great company to work for." "There is a strong sense of teamwork and respect," according to bankers. Says one insider: "Associates are often the point person for clients." Insiders are especially pleased with the company's policy of promoting from within. One longtime employee describes ascending from a back-office position to an I-banking VP spot. Says one trader: "I have gained more experience at RJ than I could have with a larger firm. There's an excellent training program, and it's easier to get on the trading floor than at a bigger firm." One I-banker agrees about the opportunities the firm affords. "You get exposure there pretty quickly to just about everybody," says that associate. "I could go knock on virtually everybody's door." That contact reports that this emphasis creates a selective hiring process. "They like to look at it as if they're hiring a partner, someone who will be with them for a long time."

Fun in Florida

Salaries for incoming MBA's at Raymond James are on par or slightly below bulge-bracket firm averages. However, the salaries are extremely attractive given Tampa's low cost of living and the fact that Florida does not have a state income tax. Another insider says he came to Raymond James "not for the money, but rather the working environment." Benefits include insurance ("good if you are single, a bit expensive for families"), a 401(k) with employer matching, profit sharing, and a "good" employee stock purchase plan. Employees also observe with pride that "RJ supports a lot of local arts programs." Sources say "the company does lots of neat things," including "Breakfast with the Boss" each quarter, and "yearly employee days at Busch Gardens or Sea World." The firm also sponsors an annual cultural awareness week, complete with "exhibits, food, and information from different countries." RJ employees also enjoy "going all out with the decorations" at Halloween and fundraising for each department's favorite charity during the winter holidays. These firm-sponsored social events notwithstanding, don't expect to be partying hard with colleagues at Raymond James, insiders say. "A lot of the bankers are married," says one. "They make really no bones about spending time with family."

Raymond James' offices are located in a campus setting in St. Petersburg, about 20 minutes from downtown Tampa. "St. Pete is a little more of a retirement area, but it's right across from the water from Tampa. Most of the bankers live in Tampa, and they seem to really like it — there's a nice trendy area in South Tampa," reports one insider. In one of the two towers, the firm houses most of its institutional finance groups (investment banking, research, and trading, but not asset management). "There are two cafeterias, they have a barber shop, and a guy who shines your shoes. You can drop your laundry off there." The company even boasts a "superb" art collection at its headquarters — the hundreds of pieces at the headquarters come from the personal collection of Tom James, who is one of the biggest benefactors of the arts in the Southeast.

"As with most male-dominated industries," relates one female insider, "the climb for women is much harder, but it is possible." She goes on to add, "there are minorities here, but not many." Most insiders report that opportunities for women and minorities, however, are wide open. Says one woman: "I think that everyone is treated equally by most of the company." Comments another insider: "There are many cultures at all levels. Your success is based on your merit and determination."

Hungry for more inside scoop? Join Vault.com's popular online community for finance and banking — www.vault.com

VAULT.com **347**

Robertson Stephens

555 California Street
Suite 2600
San Francisco, CA 94104
(415) 781-9700
Fax: (415) 248-4110
www.rsco.com

LOCATIONS

San Francisco (HQ)
Atlanta
Boston
Chicago
Menlo Park
New York

London
Munich
Tel Aviv

DEPARTMENTS

Capital Markets
Convertibles
Corporate Finance
Mergers and Acquisitions
Private Client Services
Private Capital
Research
Sales and Trading
Venture Capital

THE STATS

President & CEO: Robert Emery
Employer Type: Subsidiary of
Fleet Boston Financial
1999 Revenue: $1 billion
No. of Employees: 1,374
No. of Offices: 9

UPPERS

- Excellent investment opportunities
- Great corporate culture
- Significant deal and client exposure

DOWNERS

- Can't always compete with bulge-bracket firms for big deals
- Lack of hierarchy can lead to disorganization
- Lack of infrastructure

KEY COMPETITORS

Chase H&Q
Credit Suisse First Boston
Deutsche Banc Alex. Brown
Morgan Stanley Dean Witter
Thomas Weisel Partners

EMPLOYMENT CONTACT

Investment Banking
Leah Lovelace
IB_Recruiter@rsco.com

Financial Services Department
Robin Nakao
Robin_Nakao@rsco.com

Research
Catherine Myers Paul
Catherine_Myers_Paul@rsco.com

Sales and Trading
Rosan Lam
Rosan_Lam@rsco.com

THE SCOOP

Leading the charge

Founded in 1969, Robertson Stephens (affectionately known as Robbie Stephens) is one of the leading underwriters in the red-hot technology, Internet, and e-commerce sectors. The firm was the top underwriter of so-called growth IPOs from 1995 to 1998. In 1999, the firm advised on 10 of the 15 largest internet M&A transactions. It also boasts a large sales and trading staff, and a well-respected equity research division.

Merger history

Like many other San Francisco area boutique banks (Hambrecht & Quist and Montgomery Securities being the two most notable examples), the firm became a merger target in the late 1990s. In 1997 Robbie Stephens chose BankAmerica, then the third-largest bank in the U.S., as its partner. BankAmerica, seeking to take advantage of Robbie's underwriting and M&A capabilities, paid $540 million for Robbie Stephens. BankAmerica's deep pockets enabled Robbie Stephens to expand its staff and to venture outside its high tech industry base. The ink was barely dry on the BankAmerica/Robbie Stephens merger agreement when the parent decided to merge again. In April 1998, BankAmerica merged with NationsBank, which had previously snapped up an investment bank — Robbie Stephens' cross-town rival Montgomery Securities. Neither Montgomery nor Robbie Stephens was happy about the prospect of being paired. The two firms had, in the words of a Robertson Stephens spokesman, a "notoriously different approach" to doing business.

In order to avoid an I-banking death match, BankAmerica agreed to sell off Robbie Stephens' investment banking operations (at the time, Montgomery seemed the far better catch) to BankBoston for $800 million in the summer of 1998. BankAmerica went on to relaunch itself as Bank of America, and renamed its investment banking arm Banc of America Securities.

Shortly after the acquisition by BankBoston, Sandy Robertson, Robbie Stephens' founder and former chairman, left the firm, along with Misha Petkevich, the head of investment banking. Though such high-level departures usually open up the floodgates, few senior bankers left the firm. The $400 million employee-retention pool was a big factor, but observers say that Robbie Stephens and BankBoston handled the transition well in general, in stark contrast to the BankAmerica/ Montgomery combination.

Yet another merger

Try as it might, Robbie Stephens couldn't go a year without being involved in another merger. BankBoston coupled with Fleet Financial Group in October 1999, Robbie Stephens' third dance partner in less than three years. Robertson Stephens' independence, which had survived more or less intact throughout the turmoil, was secure even after the Fleet acquisition. Fleet, which has a reputation for allowing its subsidiary units to function autonomously, restored the Robertson Stephens name. (The firm had previously been saddled with the clumsy moniker BancBoston Robertson Stephens.) In May 1999, Bob Emery, previously COO and head of investment banking, was named president of Robertson Stephens. Todd Carter, who joined the firm in 1993, was named head of investment banking.

Banking prowess

Robbie Stephens rebounded nicely from a sub-par 1998, reappearing on the 1999 league tables in its core industries. The company ranked fifth among advisors of technology M&A transactions and ranked third in the all-important Internet sector. All told, the firm completed over $60 billion worth of M&A transactions in 1999. Notable clients include WebMD in its $7.5 billion sale to Healtheon, Excite in its $7.2 billion purchase by @Home Network, and CMGI in that company's $2.3 billion purchase of AltaVista. In 2000 Robbie Stephens advised Ask Jeeves on its $507 million purchase of Direct Hit Technologies, E*Trade Group on its $1.8 billion acquisition of Telebanc Financial, and Healtheon/WebMD in a $1 billion investment by News Corp.

In a red-hot tech IPO market, equity underwriting was another booming business for Robbie Stephens. In 1999 the firm lead managed numerous IPOs, including the $98 million December offering by OnDisplay, the $108.8 million offering by IBasis in November, and the $145.5 IPO for Value America in April. Co-managed deals included MP3.com's $344 million July 1999 offering and Autoweb's $70 million March 1999 deal. In 2000 the firm lead managed OrphaPharma's $72 million March IPO, as well as the $77 million IPO for Opus360 and the $168 million IPO for DDI, both completed in April 2000. The company

Hungry for more inside scoop? Join Vault.com's popular online
community for finance and banking — www.vault.com

VAULT.com **351**

was also involved as a co-manager on Palm, Inc.'s $874 million offering in March 2000 and the $180 million IPO of EMachines in June 2000.

GETTING HIRED

400 résumés for 12 positions

Like many niche investment banks, Robertson Stephens is fairly selective in hiring. "Robertson Stephens is still 'who you know' and in Boston, Ivy League is almost a must," says one contact. The Ivy League is preferred for all locations, as are other top schools. College and MBA recruiting is especially selective. "It's not uncommon for us to receive 400 résumés from a school for 12 interview spots," says one banker. "I think students recognize that this is a great place to work." Getting in may be getting easier, especially for lateral hires, because of the shrinking pool of experienced investment bankers. "[Robbie Stephens] has lowered its standards, given the firm's rapid growth within banking and the need for people," according to one source. Another insider observes that when it comes to lateral hires, "we hire less qualified people."

Thinking on your feet

Insiders report "one round of two-on-one on-campus interviews and then a Super Saturday consisting of an entire day of interviewing — six or so interviews back-to-back." "Be prepared to present your real self," advises one source. "We'll be interested in your ability to think practically and on your feet, and in your people skills. We don't merely want a smart kid, we want someone who can communicate with others and work well with normal people." There are "hardly any technical questions" from most interviewers and the firm is looking for "personality fit." One warning: "Don't be thrown off by a lack of structure." Hit the gym, too — "We like athletes, historically."

OUR SURVEY SAYS

Culture of innovation

Bankers say the culture is "the best part of Robertson Stephens." It's "a go-get-'em culture" that's "entrepreneurial to the extreme." One insider says, "[The] firm promotes a culture of innovation, maximizing individual responsibility and paying for performance." "We take our culture seriously," says another contact. "All the analysts in San Francisco work in one area — the bullpen. We pride ourselves on working with each other, helping one another out so that everyone has an easier time with the demands that are placed on us." Analysts in New York and Boston also enjoy the bullpen life. For those in the bullpen, "the firm provides fruit, sodas, and snacks."

New Yorkers at Robbie Stephens report a satellite feel. "The New York office is only now rising to the level of the Boston office," says one banker. "As a satellite office, there are unique challenges in staying in the loop. We will never be on par with San Francisco, but our experience here is possibly more humane, and we are in the center of the universe for all things civilized here in the Big Apple. There are trade-offs, of course, but I have been generally happy with my decision to stay in New York rather than relocating to San Francisco." Another New York-based employee adds, "The firm is very laid-back and very much concerned about employees' happiness."

No hierarchy

Relationships between senior and junior bankers are smooth. "We're too busy for people to have big egos," says one source. "I've been very pleased with the senior bankers," says one young contact. "I view them not just as bosses and co-workers, but rather as generally good people. I think there's a pretty good understanding about the pressures on a young banker's life, so they are sympathetic and empathetic." Observes another insider: "The senior bankers at Robertson Stephens treat the younger [bankers] with much more respect than at other banks."

In keeping with the congenial culture, the firm promotes a healthy social environment. "The majority of bankers here have very athletic backgrounds and this carries over into the overall feel of the bank," reports one contact. "Firm-sponsored events are common, with Friday afternoon beer bashes every month, group dinners and lunches, off-sites

Hungry for more inside scoop? Join Vault.com's popular online community for finance and banking — www.vault.com

VAULT.com **353**

every quarter, and the occasional firm trip to Colorado for skiing." Insiders feel "the firm is committed to creating a positive social environment that makes the day-to-day enjoyable."

A manageable life with varying pay

"Robertson pays as well or better than any other bank in San Francisco," according to one banker in that city. Another banker adds, "[The firm] will pay up for its superstars. The phone rings all day long with headhunters, and management knows they need to remain competitive." In other cities, Robbie Stephens bankers express more concern. "The pay is all over the board," says one Boston banker. "You have to pressure the firm to step up." In New York, the pay is "not the highest, but certainly good compensation. The firm is considering ways to crank up the compensation for junior bankers who currently can't participate in our private investments." Reportedly, the firm recently raised analyst compensation to match Street increases.

Speaking of investment opportunities, insiders agree that the firm is trying to extend their programs to more junior people. "[A] new program began this year for associates," says one source. Robbie Stephens offers the usual meal allowances and cab rides when working late. Insiders at the San Francisco office have access to a gym in the lobby. Additionally, the firm offers a dry cleaning service, the aforementioned bullpen snacks, and discounts to local art exhibits.

Hours at Robbie Stephens are on par with or better than industry average according to most insiders. One source says M&A analysts can expect 100-hour workweeks, with 80 hours for corporate finance. "Our travel schedule can be a little more demanding than at other firms because of the level of client contact and small deal teams," says another banker. Of course, in the words of one contact, "We do work hard, but it's a trade-off, too. Anything worth doing will require a commitment." Another source concurs: "If you want a nine-to-five job, don't get into investment banking. The hours are long but rewarding." The hours also vary by group. Says one San Francisco banker: "The hours in my group are very manageable, with little work on the weekends."

CFO? Who cares?

"Deal teams are relatively thinly staffed," says one source, "which translates into more responsibility for younger members of the team."

Analysts and associates at Robbie Stephens don't have to settle for just doing comps or, worse, photocopying. Says one senior banker: "There are always those days you wish you stayed in bed, but at RS junior bankers get a significant amount of responsibility." Another source claims, "Robertson tends to let analysts do things they would not be allowed to do at other banks."

Client contact is the norm at Robertson Stephens. "I have traveled on multiple road shows with senior management and have direct contact with them," brags one banker. "Everyone from MD to analyst has a personal relationship with the executives of all our clients," according to another contact. "I had a two-on-two meeting with Michael Eisner, the CEO of Disney, my first year here," says one lucky source. "I'm not even impressed by the title CFO anymore," says another insider.

Great strides in training

If you're going to be meeting with CEOs and CFOs, you'd better be prepared. One contact reports "Robertson Stephens has only recently begun having formal training for associates. We have made great strides in this area but still have more work to do." For analysts, there's a "four-week training program followed by a period of time when you work directly under second-year banking analysts." The training program includes "very general accounting [and] finance training," according to one analyst who gushes that the "instructor was awesome."

Informal training is also one of Robbie Stephens' strong points. "The bankers in my group have made a concerted effort to be sure that I am learning a lot and participating in higher-level discussions," says one source. Another chimes in, "The bankers at [the firm] are very good at spending time to walk you through concepts and strategy."

Trouble with diversity

While all investment banks have trouble maintaining a diverse work environment, Robbie Stephens seems to be a little worse off than most. "[The firm's] efforts are good," says one source, "but the firm is not extremely diverse." It's not much better for women. "The firm makes a good effort with women, [but] there are few senior women in banking at any firm," says an insider.

Hungry for more inside scoop? Join Vault.com's popular online community for finance and banking — www.vault.com

VAULT.com **355**

Salomon Smith Barney

388 Greenwich Street
New York, NY 10013
(212) 816-6000
Fax: (212) 793-9086
www.salomonsmithbarney.com

LOCATIONS

Institutional Locations:

New York (HQ)
Atlanta
Boston
Chicago
San Francisco
Los Angeles

London
Hong Kong
Tokyo
Sidney
Over 500 additional retail offices

DEPARTMENTS

Asset Management
Equity
Fixed Income
Investment Banking
Public Finance
Research
Sales and Trading

THE STATS

Chairman & CEO:
Michael A. Carpenter
Head of Investment Banking:
Eduardo Mestre
Co-heads of Investment Banking:
Michael Klein and Bob Morse
Employer Type: Subsidiary of
Citigroup
1999 Net Revenue: $13.8 billion
1999 Net Income: $2.8 billion
No. of Employees: 36,250
No. of Offices: 500+

UPPERS

• Celebrated training program
• Growing in the bulge bracket
• Improving atmosphere for analysts

DOWNERS

• Increased bureaucracy after
  Citigroup merger
• Onerous workload
• Support staff

KEY COMPETITORS

Credit Suisse First Boston
Donaldson, Lufkin & Jenrette
Goldman Sachs
Morgan Stanley
Merrill Lynch

EMPLOYMENT CONTACT

Investment Banking Recruiting

Caitlin McLaughlin
Vice President, MBA Recruiting

Sales and Trading Recruiting

Susan Glendon

Equity Research Recruiting

Debbie Bertan

388 Greenwich Street
New York, NY 10013

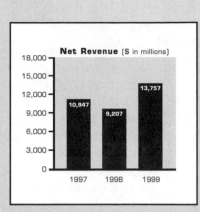

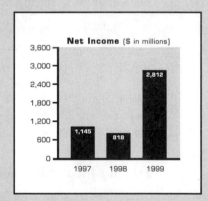

THE SCOOP

Merger mania

Salomon Smith Barney, now the investment banking arm of Citigroup, has a long history of mergers. The firm traces its roots back to 1873, when trader Charles Barney founded a securities firm in Philadelphia. In 1892 Edward Smith started his brokerage business in the City of Brotherly Love. The two firms eventually combined to form Smith Barney. Smith Barney was acquired by Primerica, a financial services firm run by Sanford "Sandy" Weill, in 1987. Primerica was sold to Hartford-based insurance giant Travelers Group in 1993. In December 1997, Travelers bought Salomon Brothers for more than $9 billion, and merged Salomon Brothers with Smith Barney to create Salomon Smith Barney. Travelers then merged with Citicorp, the New York-based commercial bank, creating the merged entity Citigroup in October 1998.

As a full-service investment bank, SSB offers sales, research and trading for individuals and institutions, underwriting, advisory and specialty financing for corporations and government entities, mutual fund services, and futures and asset management. SSB is also the second-largest retail brokerage firm in the U.S. The firm employs an army of nearly 11,000 brokers who manage more than 6.2 million client accounts, representing over $816 billion in client assets.

Getting into the big leagues

Though the coupling with Travelers went smoothly, it took the 1998 merger with Citicorp to thrust Salomon Smith Barney into the big leagues of investment banking. According to *Crain's New York Business*, Weill (by then CEO at Travelers) initiated contact with Citibank CEO John Reed in 1998 with the intention of forming a financial service powerhouse. The two CEOs began discussions in February 1998 and by April had secured board approval for the merger, valued at $70 billion.

The merger faced another hurdle after board approval. The Glass-Steagall Act, the Depression-era law prohibiting a mix of financial services business, threatened to cancel the deal. The companies were able to buy some time under the Bank Holding Company Act of 1956, a rule that allowed financial service partnerships for five years, but Weill and Reed knew that if the merger was to survive, they had to act to facilitate repeal of the Glass-Steagall Act. (Such a move had been discussed in both political and business circles, but no significant progress had been made.) Weill and Reed took the initiative in affecting change, phoning President Bill Clinton the night before the merger announcement to enlist his help in repealing Glass-Steagall. Eventually, their efforts proved successful and the Financial Services Modernization Act of 1999 has removed the obstacles to full-service financial institutions. (According to *Crain's New York Business*, Weill has the pen used by President Clinton to sign the Financial Services Modernization Act into law displayed in his office.)

Initial results from the Citicorp/Travelers merger were excellent and analysts raved about the company's future. *Euromoney* named Salomon Smith Barney "Most Improved Investment Bank" in July 1999. In October 1999, SSB was able to lure former Treasury Secretary Robert Rubin to the firm, making him chair of the executive committee and part of the chairman's office. After his appointment, rumors surfaced that Rubin was under consideration for the CEO post at Citigroup and the position of chairman of the Federal Reserve. Those rumors have been extinguished as Rubin has denied interest in becoming the company's CEO and Alan Greenspan was reappointed Fed chairman.

Transitions were reportedly not as smooth at Citigroup's headquarters, however, as Weill and Reed (who were co-chairmen and co-CEO) struggled for control of the company. Reed retired in February 2000, saying he sought the tranquility of life outside of corporate America. In April 2000, *The Wall Street Journal* published a far different account, saying that Reed and Weill had clashed over a number of issues, including the bank's Internet strategy, and that some senior managers found the presence of two CEOs disruptive. Citigroup's board of directors debated the issue for several hours in February 2000. At one point, Reed rejected a compromise that would have made him non-executive chairman and left Weill as CEO. After that, the board voted to ask Reed to retire.

Inroads in Europe

After SSB secured its place in the U.S. bulge bracket, the firm turned its attention towards expanding in Europe. In February 2000, SSB announced it would acquire the investment banking operations of Schroders plc, a London-based firm that was 50 percent family-owned. Weill told *The New York Times* that the acquisition, valued at $2.2 billion, would put his firm "two or three years ahead of where we would

Hungry for more inside scoop? Join Vault.com's popular online community for finance and banking — www.vault.com

VAULT.COM **359**

have been" in investment banking in Europe. In Europe, the firm will be known as Schroders Salomon Smith Barney. Schroder's U.S. operation, known as Schroder & Co., was folded into Salomon Smith Barney and the firm laid off Schroders employees who overlapped with existing I-banking personnel. The Schroders family retained the asset management and private banking units.

Mergers for others

In addition to its own merger activity, Salomon Smith Barney has also been busy in advising its clients on mergers and acquisitions. The firm was ranked fourth among advisors of announced U.S. M&A transactions in 1999, according to Thomson Financial Securities Data. The company advised on 212 domestic announced deals worth $363.4 billion. Among advisors of completed worldwide M&A, Salomon Smith Barney ranked sixth, advising on 400 deals worth $355.1 billion.

Despite the firm's status, some industry observers were surprised when Salomon Smith Barney was chosen as lead adviser to America Online in its blockbuster merger with Time Warner, announced in January 2000. The bank was a surprise choice because others in the industry perceived SSB's technology and Internet teams as weak. "I don't even know the names of anyone over there," one competitor admitted to *The Standard* after the deal was announced. That competitor should take note of the name Eduardo Mestre. Mestre not only led the AOL deal team, he led the team that advised WorldCom on its acquisition of MCI in 1998. The transaction helped him capture the Banker of the Year award from *Investment Dealers' Digest* that year.

Debt expertise

Salomon Smith Barney is a perennial leader in underwriting fixed income offerings and providing liquidity in those markets. According to TFSD, SSB ranked second among lead underwriters of both investment grade and high yield debt in 1999, underwriting 773 investment grade issues worth a total of $111.8 billion and 62 high yield deals worth a total $13.4 billion. The firm took third place in asset-backed securities, completing 177 deals worth $35.4 billion. One client of note is Rite Aid; along with J.P. Morgan, Salomon Smith Barney helped Rite Aid restructure $550 million in notes so the drug chain could avoid bankruptcy.

Though Salomon Smith Barney's equity underwriting practice doesn't match its debt figures, the company is still a top-ten underwriter. SSB ranked fifth among underwriters of all common stock in 1999, lead managing 73 issues with total proceeds of $13.2 billion. In the lucrative IPO underwriting business, SSB ranked ninth among domestic lead managers. The firm underwrote 22 deals in 1999 worth $2.5 billion. Recent deals of note include Blockbuster's $465 million August 1999 IPO, John Hancock Financial Services' $2.0 billion January 2000 offering and the massive, $10.6 billion April 2000 AT&T Wireless deal.

A little trouble

No big company is exempt from public relations disasters, and Salomon Smith Barney is certainly no exception. In December 1999, the treasurer's office of San Bernardino County, California accused the firm of yield burning. (Yield burning is the practice of overcharging for U.S. Treasury securities.) Dick Larsen, the current San Bernardino County treasurer, claimed Salomon Smith Barney bilked his predecessor, Tom O'Donnell, out of $308,000 in the county's 1997-1998 fiscal year.

A few months after the San Bernardino accusations became public, Salomon Smith Barney was wrapped up in a conflict-of-interest brouhaha. In March 2000, Dime, a New York-based savings and loan, sued Salomon Smith Barney to prevent the investment bank from representing North Folk, another New York savings and loan, in an attempted hostile takeover of Dime. According to the suit, Salomon Smith Barney had signed a confidentiality agreement with Dime when it represented the commercial bank in a 1997 transaction. A federal judge agreed with Dime in April 2000, barring Salomon from further participation in the deal. Salomon Smith Barney said it would appeal the decision, which will cost the firm $8.4 million in fees.

GETTING HIRED

Looking for bankers in all the right places

Like most bulge-bracket firms, Salomon Smith Barney focuses its recruiting on top-20 schools. However, like many banks, SSB has been forced by recent market pressures to look elsewhere for talent. Top regional schools (contacts give examples like Berkeley, Vanderbilt,

Hungry for more inside scoop? Join Vault.com's popular online
community for finance and banking — www.vault.com

VAULT.COM **361**

Washington University and Emory) are becoming increasingly important in the bank's recruiting strategy. This expanded recruiting strategy receives mixed reviews. "Salomon always was selective in choosing candidates that fit the culture of intelligent and hard-working people," says one source. "Yet I feel the current batch of both analysts and associates has definitely moved downstream in terms of quality — mainly of intelligence and work ethic," that source gripes. Another insider disagrees, saying: "Some of our best recruits come from the lesser-known schools."

Recruits — no matter what school they're from — can expect two or three rounds of interviews with up to 10 Salomon Smith Barney bankers. In most cases, expect one or two preliminary rounds followed by a Super Saturday, "with an average of four one-on-one interviews." According to one source, "Interviewers are mostly interested in gauging a candidate's understanding of the job responsibilities and the candidate's eagerness to embrace these responsibilities." The specific questions will vary. "Questions are usually not ridiculously difficult or abstract and will definitely be appropriate for your background," offers one New York banker. A recruit with a finance background had better be prepared. For example, one insider warns, "If you are a CPA, you had better know your accounting." Don't sweat too much, though. "[The] company usually stays away from trick questions," reports another source.

OUR SURVEY SAYS

A culture in flux

Salomon Smith Barney employees call the firm "hard-working," "entrepreneurial" and "scrappy." With all of the recent merger activity, though, it's no surprise that the bank's culture is in a state of transition. One contact says the company is "somewhat a conglomerate and mix-match of the mergers." The firm is "a mix of the old Salomon cowboy culture with Smith Barney's better management and oversight." Another banker complains that "senior management is dominated by the old Solly side, [which is] as anal-retentive as they come." That insider says the anal-retentive management has a complex when it comes to competitors. "Senior management uses every presentation to compare Salomon to Goldman, Morgan and Merrill. [They need] to get the chip off the shoulder and realize Citi is a fantastic bank for a whole host of reasons the other guys can't compete with."

Insiders also describe the firm as a meritocracy where "individuality is encouraged." "The firm's culture is best characterized by aggressive entrepreneurialism," says one source. "The firm adheres to its commitment to meritocracy and looks after the best interests of its star employees." Additionally, "Salomon's social environment is über-friendly." One source claims there is "lots of fun and talking and laughing" at the office, though the company is somewhat lacking in firm-sponsored events.

Generalist MBA associate program

Salomon Smith Barney is praised by insiders for the amount of flexibility it affords its MBA graduate hires. Over 10 months, newly hired MBA-level associates rotate through five groups — either industry or product groups — and can also be sent overseas to Europe or Asia or to offices in Chicago, Los Angeles, San Francisco or Toronto. As of 1999, insiders say, the firm offered rotations in Australia. "The first benefit of the program is to get around and get to know a lot of people," explains one associate. "Also, you get a broad base of experience."

A bit of a sweatshop

As at most firms, bankers at Salomon Smith Barney put in a lot of time at the office. "This just sucks," says one insider. "[I'm] not sure when, if ever, they will successfully address the workload issue." While the workload is in part a function of the profession, the company culture is also a factor. "People say Salomon is a bit of a sweatshop," reports one insider. "This is somewhat true, because I think the Salomon legacy, in part, mandates the use of complicated analysis whenever simple analysis will do the job."

Of course, the more senior you are, the fewer hours you work. "You will work longer hours when you are a first-year analyst and less as a third-year analyst," states one source. A third-year analysts concurs: "I have been working on only live projects for the past six months and my weekends have typically included at least one full day off." In contrast, this source says, "The summer between my first and second year was awful — I had to come into the office every day for three months."

Hungry for more inside scoop? Join Vault.com's popular online community for finance and banking — www.vault.com

VAULT.com **363**

Making improvements

Problems with the firm's culture were thrust into the spotlight in April 2000. Troubled by analyst defections, senior bankers and members of the recruiting committee asked a second-year analyst to collect employee complaints and submit a memo with suggestions on how the firm could retain its junior bankers. Among the complaints, which ranged from deadly serious to mundane, were a general lack of respect shown to analysts by associates and senior bankers, an onerous system for reimbursement of expenses and an absence of laptops for analysts. The firm apparently took the complaints to heart. Though one source complains that "to an extent, analysts are viewed as resources," another insider says, "Overall, I feel that Solomon values its analysts more than most firms." A junior banker agrees, saying improvements "[were], a year ago, just lip service. Now there seems to be a genuine focus."

Bulge-bracket pay

Compensation at Solly is hardly an issue as the firm "has always been tops in compensation for analysts." Insiders say the firm has "also recently pledged to widen the compensation bands, allowing exceptional analysts to be paid at associate levels, if deserved." Recent market pressures have forced the firm to bump up pay at all levels. The one common complaint is that Salomon Smith Barney "tends to be reactionary" and reluctant to set the standard for pay.

The firm offers the typical perks, including meals, car service and access to a company gym. Additionally, the firm offers "free cell phones, calling cards and your very own HP calculator." Rumored to be in the works: a concierge service that will attend to errands (e.g., dry-cleaning and shopping) for bankers stuck in the office. A leveraged investment plan, which includes a four- to five-year vesting period, is available for associates and first-year vice presidents.

Boot camp for I-bankers

Insiders say Salomon Smith Barney has "probably the most thorough training program on the Street." For associates, "Salomon has a 10-week training course which is basically a review of your two-year MBA program. Helpful if you forgot it over the summer or never studied it in the first place." One insider also notes, "The accounting program was excellent. However, the finance segment was less comprehensive and not as well taught." For analysts, the training program is famous for, in the words of one analyst, "turning liberal arts graduates into accounting and finance gurus in a mere six weeks."

In terms of mentoring and further professional training, insiders say the situation will be determined more by your individual co-workers than any firm-sponsored initiatives. "I've had an MD and a VP take an immense interest in my personal and professional development here at Salomon," explains one contact. On the other side of the coin, one analyst reports that "there is a lack of attention or interest in an analyst's learning experience and it is really up to the analyst to be very proactive and ask questions in order to learn."

Biggest cubes on the Street

New Yorkers seem generally satisfied with SSB's office space. Some complain about the location; the firm's main office is located in Tribeca, an area of Manhattan with little in the way of public transportation. Insiders do note, though, that the area "makes for great dinner options, with a plethora of bars and restaurants unmatched on Wall Street or in Midtown." The physical space once won rave reviews, but a recent remodeling has put a damper on that. "Our cubes were rumored to be the biggest on the Street but have recently been 'densified' to accommodate everyone under one roof." Bankers in London "just moved to Canary Wharf," which insiders say is "much more civilized, though it is a trek to get here."

Good diversity — for Wall Street

SSB has faced many of the same challenges as other Wall Street firms in recruiting and retaining women and minorities. Contacts at the company report that junior levels are often staffed with a significant number of women and minorities, but at the higher levels, representation by those groups seems slimmer. SSB bankers also report a positive atmosphere for homosexuals. The firm recently instituted domestic partner benefits. "I have a friend who requested help networking with other gay individuals at the firm," reports one banker. "He was immediately directed towards the appropriate people here."

Hungry for more inside scoop? Join Vault.com's popular online
community for finance and banking — www.vault.com

VAULT.com **365**

SG Cowen

1221 Avenue of the Americas
New York, NY 10020
(212) 278-6000
Fax: (212) 278-4284
www.sgcowen.com

LOCATIONS

New York (HQ)
Boston
Chicago
San Francisco
Washington, DC
London

DEPARTMENTS

Corporate Bond Brokerage
Fixed Income
Institutional Sales and Trading
Investment Banking
Private Client Services
Research

KEY COMPETITORS

Banc of America Securities
Deutsche Banc Alex. Brown
Robertson Stephens

EMPLOYMENT CONTACT

**Investment Banking
(Boston, Chicago, New York,
Washington, DC, London)**

Analyst Recruiting
Debbie Shalam

Associate Recruiting
Chip Rae

SG Cowen
1221 Avenue of the Americas
New York, NY 10020

**Investment Banking (San
Francisco)**

Analyst and Associate Recruiting
Wendy Ruggiero
SG Cowen
4 Embarcadero Center
Suite 1200
San Francisco, CA 94111

Research (Boston)

Analyst and Associate Recruiting
Kathleen Finn-Dean
SG Cowen
Two International Place
Boston, MA 02110

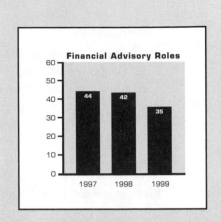

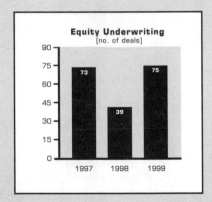

THE SCOOP

French kiss

SG Cowen was formed in 1998 when French bank Société Générale acquired Cowen & Co., a New York boutique investment bank specializing in the health care, technology and communications industries. Société Générale paid $540 million for Cowen, which was founded in 1919. The French parent had immediate plans for its new toy. While Cowen had traditionally focused its investment banking operations on three core industries, Société Générale made plans to expand to other areas. Additionally, as a result of the buyout, Cowen's once-robust asset management and mutual fund business were scaled down.

The changes kept on coming, even well after the merger was completed. BNY Clearing, a subsidiary of the Bank of New York, acquired SG Cowen's clearing operations in February 2000. (Clearing refers to the paperwork necessary to complete a trade; small firms often outsource this function to larger institutions.) Neither the terms of the deal nor the size of SG Cowen's clearing business were disclosed. However, industry observers speculated that Cowen's operations were relatively small (the clearing business is dominated by Bear Stearns), though profitable.

The firm has accelerated its growth through recent hires. In April 2000, SG Cowen lured a five-banker M&A team from competitor Deutsche Banc Alex. Brown to open a Washington, D.C. area office. The team, which specializes in technology, is led by managing director Paul Mellin, a four-year veteran of Alex. Brown who had previously worked for Smith Barney. Mellin was joined by a vice president, an associate and two analysts. In June 2000, SG Cowen hired seven professionals into its Global Leveraged Finance group. The Cowen newbies included two directors from Robertson Stephens, Robert Whiteman and Jeff Schachter. In July 2000, the company jettisoned its private client services unit, selling the business to Lehman Brothers. According to the *Wall Street Journal*, Lehman paid approximately $50 million in cash for the purchase.

Let's make some deals

SG Cowen has seen a fairly steady stream of deals. The company underwrote 75 equity deals worth $20.3 billion in 1999. In Europe, for example, SG Cowen lead-managed Air France's $557.6 million offering in February 1999 and Aerospatiale Matra's $1.4 billion IPO four months later. Stateside, the firm led Crossroad Systems' $77.6 million IPO in October 1999 and was a co-manager for Agilent Technologies' $2.2 billion IPO in November 1999. More recently, the firm was the lead manager for ActivCard's $306 million follow-on offering in March 2000 and co-managed the Charles River Laboratories $224 million IPO in June 2000.

SG Cowen also focuses on mergers and acquisitions advisory work. In January 1999, the bank advised Arterial Vascular Engineering on its sale to Medtronic for $3.9 billion. One month later, SG Cowen advised Cogen Technologies regarding its purchase by Enron for $1.4 billion. In July 1999, the firm advised Sierra Pacific Resources on that company's $1.1 billion merger with Nevada Power Company. The merger momentum carried over into 2000 as SG Cowen was tapped to advise on 31 transactions in the first six months of the new year. The bank advised Yankee Energy System on its $478 million merger with Northeast Utilities in March 2000. The following month, the firm advised Software.com on that company's $374.5 million sale to @mobile.com.

SG Cowen has also handled its share of private equity transactions, managing $30 million in private placements for Morton Grove Pharmaceuticals, Ciphergen Biosystems, and HighGround Systems, and a $34 million offering for Wireless Online, for example.

We're not gonna take it

The firm also boasts a respected research group, with four analysts making the prestigious *Institutional Investor* "All-America Research Team." Insiders report that SG Cowen has a firm commitment to research. "The research people don't take any shit from the bankers," explains one insider. "Those guys have built enough power, since they were there first. They never felt any pressure from the bankers to do anything more than they wanted to do."

GETTING HIRED

Thirsty for learning

SG Cowen says it looks for accomplished and motivated individuals with strong academic backgrounds, and analytical, computer, and communication skills. Visit the investment banking section of SG

Hungry for more inside scoop? Join Vault.com's popular online
community for finance and banking — www.vault.com

VAULT.com **369**

Cowen's web site, www.sginvestmentbanking.com, for job descriptions and contact information. For analyst positions, the firm recruits at 12 schools in October, November, and January. For associate positions (MBA-level positions), the firm recruits at 10 schools in October and November. One recent associate hire explains her interview process: "I did a two-on-one for the first round. The second round was a round robin of one-on-ones. I interviewed with four people, and each interview was 30 to 45 minutes."

The firm offers five weeks of training for associates beginning in early August. The training program includes such topics as accounting, financial modeling, and corporate finance. Associates also prepare for and take the Series 7 examination during training. In addition, various corporate finance groups make presentations to the training class. Analysts at SG Cowen report to a four-week training program in July. The analyst training includes instruction in areas such as financial analysis, modeling and pitchbook presentation. Analysts and associates are assigned to a product or industry group shortly after they are hired.

While a deep knowledge of an industry isn't necessary, insiders say "what's important to [the firm] is that you have a thirst to learn. In underwriting you have to write documents describing the company, and its products and strategy, so you have to exhibit that interest." While in the past the firm has promoted analysts to associate without requiring an MBA, it is selective in such promotions. The firm promoted five third-year analysts to associate in 1998, and five more in 1999.

OUR SURVEY SAYS

Friendly culture

With a small- to medium-size company atmosphere, insiders note that each department and office at SG Cowen has its own distinct culture. The firm's technology group, for example, has reportedly been more fractious than its health care group in the past. However, insiders agree that bankers are in general closer to each other at SG Cowen than at bulge-bracket firms. One source praises relationships with the company brass, saying upper management is interested in developing the abilities of its staff and are "even willing to make themselves available to anyone who needs them." Others "manage to get together outside the office, which is nice." Says one associate in the firm's San Francisco office: "It's a friendly, family-like environment. I think the lines between professional and personal relationships get crossed. People know when someone's been on a date, and people celebrate birthdays a lot." "The culture here is very team-oriented," says one insider. "Most of the people who have been brought in have many years of previous bulge-bracket experience." Reports a former analyst in New York: "The MDs take people out once a month to have a big event, whether it's bowling, or out for drinks, or whatever, just to keep morale high. Another insider says, "People here are very responsive. [If] you leave a voice mail you get a response in a couple of hours from even the most senior people."

Lots of responsibility

According to insiders, the "the majority of the firm's clients are emerging growth companies." Says one contact, "We don't cover 15 sectors like Merrill or another bulge-bracket firm. We want to be very, very focused. Everyone here wants to work with emerging growth companies." Sources say that because of the nature of the firm's clients and the firm's size, entry-level bankers are given high levels of responsibility from the start. "In your first year here," says one analyst, "you will get to work with CEO clients, something that would not happen in a larger firm." Another banker concurs: "Junior people get tremendous deal experience, greater-than-usual client contact and greater-than-usual opportunity to travel and attend meetings."

But even though employees are proud that "SG Cowen is a company with a history of success," they acknowledge that "there are drawbacks. You will also perform the mundane tasks that would not be required of you in a larger company. You will do copying, filing — whatever needs to be done."

The SG acquisition

Reports one insider about the acquisition of Cowen & Company by Société Générale: "There were some cosmetic changes — new business cards, new stationary, new logos, templates for producing pitchbooks changed." That contact continues: "The policies changed a bit; there were more people added to committees. One of the things that SG did well was actually reduce the number of steps that had to be taken before deciding to take on a deal." One source gives the merger a great review:

Hungry for more inside scoop? Join Vault.com's popular online community for finance and banking — www.vault.com

VAULT.com **371**

"The merger has worked out exceptionally well. [Société Générale] has taken a very hands-off approach."

More important than cosmetic or policy changes, however, is a change in name recognition and identity. "From a marketing standpoint, it changes somewhat," explains one insider. "You now have a parent company that's a French bank, you try to offer more products for clients, and you're able to do debt and equity. But some people don't understand what SG means, whereas NationsBank or Bank of America is more recognizable."

The merger also resulted in some cultural changes and the inevitable turnover, most notably at the firm's New York headquarters. Reports one associate: "Some of the SG people are coming in and taking over more; the head of I-banking is an SG person, where it used to be all Cowen." Another insider reports: "Basically the tech group got decimated, a lot of them didn't stick around to see how it would work out. Also, a lot of the dead wood got fired." Despite the initial departures, insiders emphasize that the firm is expanding itself skillfully. Says one source, "The firm is selectively choosing people who fit the mold and have the industry expertise."

"I think the lines
between professional
and personal relationships
get crossed. People know
when someone's been
on a date, and people
celebrate birthdays a lot."

— SG Cowen Insider

TD Securities

31 West 52nd Street
New York, NY 10019
(212) 827-7000
Fax: (212) 827-7232
www.tdsecurities.com

LOCATIONS

New York (HQ)
Chicago
Houston

London
Montreal
Toronto
Tokyo
Vancouver
*12 other offices in Canada, Europe,
Asia, and Australia*

DEPARTMENTS

Investment Banking
Sales and Trading

KEY COMPETITORS

Chase Manhattan
CIBC World Markets
J.P. Morgan
Lehman Brothers

EMPLOYMENT CONTACT

Recruiting Manager
31 West 52nd Street
New York, NY 10019
(212) 827-7000
Fax: (212) 827-7248

Human Resources — Recruitment
55 King Street West
19th Floor
PO Box 1
Toronto-Dominion Bank Tower
Toronto, Ontario Canada M5K 1A2
Fax: (416) 982-2766

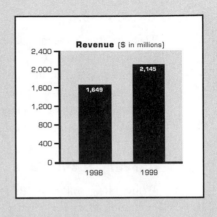

Revenue [$ in millions]

	1998	1999
	1,649	2,145

THE SCOOP

Oh, Canada

TD Securities is the investment banking unit of Toronto Dominion Bank Financial Group, Canada's largest bank (in terms of market capitalization). TD Bank, which reported revenues of $10.66 billion in 1999, also consists of retail bank TD Canada Trust, TD Commercial Banking, TD Asset Management and TD Waterhouse, the world's second-largest online securities broker.

Carving out a niche

While fairly unknown in the U.S., TD Securities has an excellent reputation in its Canadian homeland. The company was named "Best Securities Firm in Canada" by *Euromoney* in 1998 and 1999. Financial research firm Brendan Wood International rated TD the number one "Reputational Franchise" in 1999 and number one in quality of equity research in 1998 and 1999. Most of the company's underwriting activities focus on certain industries in which the firm excels, including media and communications (TD's strongest group), forest products, and energy. Recent years have witnessed major geographic expansion for TD Securities. The firm opened a New York office in 1996. In April 1998, TD received approval from Japan's Ministry of Finance to open an office in Tokyo.

History lesson

TD Bank was formed in 1955 by the union of the Bank of Toronto and the Dominion Bank. Over the next 40-plus years, the firm added the units that have made it one of Canada's best, including asset management and securities brokerage. (Trivia buffs, take note: TD claims to have set up the first automated teller machine in 1976.) A proposed merger with the Canadian Imperial Bank of Commerce was blocked by the Canadian government in December 1998. TD's deal was not the sole victim of zealous government regulation — at the same time, the Canadian government also rejected a planned merger between the Royal Bank of Canada and the Bank of Montreal.

TD deals

ATM trailblazer or not, TD Securities is active in all areas of corporate finance, including debt and equity underwriting. The firm was rated number one in Canadian corporate debt underwriting in 1999 by the *Financial Post*; it had previously been named the "Loan House of the Year" for 1998 in the U.S. media and telecommunications sector by *International Financing Review*. On the equity side, the firm was involved in numerous IPOs in 2000. In March 2000, TD assisted on Sun Life Financial Service of Canada's $1.2 billion IPO. The following month, 360networks (the bandwith company headed by former Microsoft CFO Greg Maffei) retained TD Securities as a co-manager for its $654 million IPO. Two months later, TD was in on the $57.9 million Certicom IPO. The most important offering, however, was the June 1999 offering of TD Waterhouse, TD Securities' brokerage affiliate. The offering raised $1 billion.

Junk on the rise

In 1999 TD securities made an impressive showing in the league tables for managing high yield debt. The firm ranked 15th, up from 25th in 1998, raising $911.4 million in total proceeds. While that number may be paltry compared to heavy hitters like DLJ and Salomon Smith Barney, it is a significant jump in the tables and the result of some savvy hiring by TD. The firm poached some of the industry's top junk professionals, including Fernando Guerrero, former head of DLJ's junk department. TD also lured John Chester, a former Morgan Stanley Dean Witter research analyst, to become head of high yield research at TD. Derrick Herndon, head of high yield trading, sales, and research at TD, told *High Yield Report*, "We've never tried to be all things to all people. We've leveraged our strengths to certain industry groups." While TD is trying to grow its underwriting business, it still has some room for improvement. In 1999 underwriting represented a little over five percent of total revenue.

GETTING HIRED

Interviews: light on technical questions

TD Securities' web site, www.tdsecurities.com, advertises for analyst and associate positions in the firm's Toronto, New York, and Calgary

Hungry for more inside scoop? Join Vault.com's popular online
community for finance and banking — www.vault.com

VAULT.com **377**

offices. The site lists additional positions in research, sales and trading, and operations. Applicants should send résumés to the office of interest and keep an eye out for TD Securities' on-campus representatives.

The interviews themselves are described as "not very intense." One contact recalls, "My interviews [were] pretty laid-back. Not much technical stuff, mostly questions relating to the right fit." Other sources report the same experience, saying interviewers asked a "lot of feel questions." For those who meet with a campus representative, there are usually three to four second-round interviews, with an additional round if necessary. All told, prospective TD Securities employees can expect to meet with three to six people. The company is described as "less competitive than bulge-bracket firms, although [some] groups, including M&A and high yield, have high standards and are very selective."

OUR SURVEY SAYS

Making clients happy

Insiders at TD Securities say the company "promotes open communication and has a lean organizational structure." The firm is "fairly relaxed" and "there is some attention paid to quality-of-life issues." That contact concedes that TD "can be quite aggressive when going after deals," but the bank is "team-oriented" and exudes a desire to "make the clients happy and get the job done well." The firm has had a full-time business casual dress policy since April 2000.

A banker at TD Securities reports "close interaction between the managing directors, department heads, and associates. Associates are respected for their abilities and are given a substantial amount of responsibility at an early stage." Another source says, "Respect is critical here. Everyone is really nice." "The review process is informal, with constant feedback given to employees throughout the year," reports one insider. How informal? Too informal, in the opinion of some, including the contact who claims, "I have not seen a single review since I've been here."

Good hours/pay ratio

While insiders say pay at TD Securities is a notch below that of bulge-bracket firms, the hours required are reportedly also much lower. A

New York banker says the firm requires "great hours for the pay." Another source adds that "hours can be heavy in certain groups such as high yield and M&A. However, there is some flexibility and face time is not very important. In general, hours range from 65 to 100 per week." Additionally, the firm offers investment opportunities, "typically at the vice president level and above, although junior team members are often allocated shares if available." Firm representatives add that the firm offers incoming analysts and associates starting salaries that are on par with the Street.

On the plus side, those working the 100-hour weeks get significant deal exposure. "It is not unusual for an associate to be working on a lead transaction and several co-managed transactions in addition to marketing for new business," says one contact. People skills are also a necessity at TD, according to insiders. One contact explains: "Associates are often invited to accompany the MD to pitches, dinners, meetings, etc. During a live deal, the associate often has responsibility for day-to-day dealings with the clients, which is often at the CEO, CFO, COO and treasurer levels."

One-size-fits-all training

TD Securities offers newly hired associates and analysts a "thorough seven-week formal training program plus extensive on-the-job training." Specifically, you can expect "a week of presentations from all groups of the firm." Subjects covered during training include accounting, credit, Series 7 exam preparation, business valuation, and capital markets. One source calls the training program "helpful, but not very useful in my position." Another contact says, "Mixing analysts and associates was a mistake," because "experience levels varied greatly."

Not a major player

While some TD employees enjoy the lighter hours and laid-back atmosphere, others emphasize the downside of being at a firm that is "not even close to a major bank." In describing the quality of support services, one analyst explains that analysts are "the word processors of the firm." One insider also adds, "The bank could step up the budget for non-work activities."

Hungry for more inside scoop? Join Vault.com's popular online
community for finance and banking — www.vault.com

VAULT.COM **379**

Thomas Weisel Partners

One Montgomery Street
San Francisco, CA 94104
(415) 364-2500
Fax: (415) 364-2695
www.tweisel.com

LOCATIONS

San Francisco (HQ)
Boston
New York
London

DEPARTMENTS

Private Client
Private Equity and Asset Management
Research
Sales and Trading
Strategic Advisory and Investments
Banking

THE STATS

Chairman & CEO: Thomas Weisel
Co-directors of investment banking: Steven Bottum, Michael Ogborne, Mark G. Shafir
1999 Revenue: $186 million
Employer Type: Private Company
No. of Employees: 630
No. of Offices: 4

UPPERS

- Classy offices
- Contact with clients
- Entrepreneurial environment

DOWNERS

- Competing with established banks
- Lack of support staffers
- Poor marks for diversity

KEY COMPETITORS

Chase H&Q
Credit Suisse First Boston
Donaldson, Lufkin & Jenrette
Robertson Stephens
Wit SoundView

EMPLOYMENT CONTACT:

Human Resources
Thomas Weisel Partners
One Montgomery Street
San Francisco, CA 94104
(415) 364-2500
Fax: (415) 364-2695
Submit résumés to jobs@tweisel.com

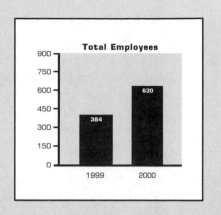

Total Employees

Year	Employees
1999	384
2000	630

THE SCOOP

A San Francisco "merchant bank"

Thomas Weisel Partners was founded in January 1999 by Thomas Weisel, Frank Dunlevy, J. Sanford Miller, Derek Lemke-Von Ammon and Alan Menkes. The firm bills itself as a merchant bank rather than an investment bank — an allusion to the fact that the firm seeks to invest in private companies through an equity fund that has now reached $1.29 billion in assets under management and is integrated within the firm. Weisel Partners' growth has been phenomenal; the company advised on 106 investment banking transactions in 1999 worth $23 billion, including 54 IPOs (six of which were lead-managed by Weisel Partners). The firm had 630 employees in June 2000 after a little more than a year and a half in business. Additionally, according to *Investment Dealers' Digest*, the bank — under Weisel's capable leadership — turned a profit after only four months in business.

Weisel himself has a long history of founding firms. He was a founding partner of Robertson Coleman Siebel and Weisel. However, after a now-famous falling out with his partner Sandy Robertson, Weisel left to form Montgomery. Robertson, on the other hand, went on to form Montgomery's San Francisco rival, Robertson Stephens.

I am outta here

Thomas Weisel founded Montgomery Securities in 1978. He sold Montgomery to Nationsbank in 1997 for $1.2 billion. (Weisel himself reportedly netted between $100-$120 million in the deal.) Weisel originally intended to retain control over Montgomery after the sale. His plan, however, fell by the wayside when NationsBank merged with BankAmerica (now Bank of America). Weisel clashed repeatedly with NationsBank CEO Hugh McColl after the union with BankAmerica. "At NationsBank, in effect, they were taking the entrepreneurial spirit away," Weisel would later tell *Forbes*. Specifically, after the NationsBank/BankAmerica merger, Weisel felt the bank was trying to fold Montgomery into the combined firm, an action which Weisel told *Red Herring* constituted "a violation of the merger agreement and of my employment contract." He finally quit in summer 1998. Weisel told *Red Herring*: "It was very easy for me to say, 'Fine, see you later.' I had no interest in being around people who don't keep their promises."

You worked at Banc of America Securities? Me too!

Shortly after splitting from Montgomery, Weisel started assembling a team with the intention of forming an investment bank of his own. Many observers felt Weisel, who was already well-off financially and possessed numerous outside interests, took on the burden of forming an investment bank mainly out of a desire to stick it to his former colleagues at the new Banc of America Securities, a charge Weisel denies. "I wish them well," he told *The San Francisco Chronicle* of his former firm. "There's no animosity. I'd like to work with them."

Whatever his motives were, Weisel's actions certainly annoyed the new management of BofA. His new venture took approximately 150 former Montgomery employees, including 36 of 68 partners. Weisel took so many employees, in fact, that BofA struck back. In December 1998, a handful of analysts resigned from the old Montgomery, shortly after receiving $60,000 bonuses. Not so fast, said NationsBank officials, withdrawing the bonuses. After some reconsideration, some of the money was restored, minus what NationsBank said were incremental bonuses paid upon promotion to associate — a promotion the analysts obviously refused when they jumped ship for Weisel Partners.

In February 1999, BofA went a step further, filing a lawsuit against Thomas Weisel Partners alleging unfair hiring practices and theft of proprietary information. BofA pointed to the large number of former Montgomery bankers at Weisel and alleged that these employees had not left BofA's offices empty-handed, but had helped themselves to pitchbooks and other sensitive information. According to reports in *Securities Week*, BofA was seeking $500 million in damages in the suit, which is currently in arbitration. (Employment law experts say that in order to win the suit, BofA will likely have to prove that Weisel recruiters knowingly convinced bankers to break employment contracts with BofA.)

Renaissance man

Weisel himself is described by those around him as intense and driven. He holds an AB from Stanford and a Harvard MBA and is an accomplished athlete. In fact, he is a five-time speed skating champion who won his first title at the age of 14. (Rumor has it that Weisel just missed making the 1960 Olympic team.) Weisel has also served as chairman of the U.S. Ski Team. More recently, he sponsored Lance Armstrong and the U.S. Postal Service biking team in the 1999 Tour de

Hungry for more inside scoop? Join Vault.com's popular online community for finance and banking — www.vault.com

VAULT.com **383**

France. Weisel is also a frequent financial contributor to the San Francisco Museum of Modern Art and a wing at the museum is named after him. His business prowess has also been recognized. He was named "Executive of the Year" in December 1999 by the *San Francisco Business Times* and won a 1999 "Banker of the Year" award from *Investment Dealers' Digest*.

New partners

While 1999 was a solid year for the company, 2000 got off to a great start as well. The California Public Employee Retirement System (CalPERS) invested $100 million for a 10 percent stake in the company in January 2000. The investment valued the firm at approximately $1 billion after just a year in business. According to reports in *Investment Dealers' Digest*, CalPERS also agreed to invest $500 million in Thomas Weisel Partners' private equity funds and an additional $500 million "to support new business activity by the firm."

The bank added some new blood in February 2000 when Mark Shafir and Jamie Streator came aboard as partners. Shafir arrived from Merrill Lynch, where he was head of global technology investment banking. He joined Weisel as co-director of investment banking and co-director of the bank's M&A advisory practice. Streator had been a health care banker at Hambrecht & Quist (now Chase H&Q) and serves as head of the health care investment banking practice at Weisel.

Quick splash

The firm has quickly made an impact in I-banking circles. One of its first transactions was advising Yahoo! on the Internet portal's $4.7 billion acquisition of Geocities in May 1999. The bank also advised REZsolutions on the company's $250 million purchase by Pegasus Systems in January 2000 and SDL on its proposed mammoth $41 billion merger with JDS Uniphase. The JDS mandate was a major win for the firm over larger I-bank competitors. In speaking about the deal, Mark Shafir, co-head of investment banking told Dow Jones, "The big firms do not have a monopoly on M&A talent."

Thomas Weisel Partners has also been active in the equity markets, though it has not lead-managed many transactions. In August 1999, the bank co-managed the $96.6 million Red Hat IPO. The firm handled an October 1999 IPO and a March 2000 follow-on for Cysive. Thomas

Weisel Partners was also one of several co-managers for the enormous $10.6 billion AT&T Wireless IPO in April 2000.

GETTING HIRED

Growth industry

As at many start-up organizations, insiders report that the hiring process at Thomas Weisel Partners is still being refined. The majority of investment banking professionals are lateral hires (many of them from the former Montgomery Securities), but the firm is now also recruiting on campus for junior positions. Insiders report a "very quick response [from the firm] if an individual is seen to have strong potential. People take recruiting very seriously. At times, the firm gets carried away with candidate pedigree, but this is changing." The firm's target schools are the "same as most of Wall Street, typically top-20 schools, but we will consider candidates from other [schools]."

Candidates can expect one or two preliminary rounds, either on campus or at one of the satellite offices. After the preliminary rounds, candidates are "flown out to San Francisco for a series of final interviews." Interviewees meet between seven and 10 people who ask "very technical banking skill questions as well as personality questions."

OUR SURVEY SAYS

New economy feel

Insiders at Thomas Weisel Partners say the firm is "very interested in doing it differently from the old guard." People at Weisel Partners are "entrepreneurial, passionate about investment banking and private equity, energetic, [and] enthusiastic." According to insiders the firm is "interested in multi-talented people with top skills and desires to accomplish more in life than just being defined by their jobs." Weisel bankers dress business casual, a trend one insider (who apparently forgot about huge bonuses and outlandish perks) calls the "best thing that ever happened to Wall Street."

Hungry for more inside scoop? Join Vault.com's popular online
community for finance and banking — www.vault.com

VAULT.com **385**

Junior bankers at Weisel Partners report an excellent relationship with superiors. "Everyone is extremely friendly and approachable," says one source. "Although you probably wouldn't ask a partner how to build a dilution model, if you are having any problems that need senior attention, they almost always drop what they're doing to listen to you." Don't worry about screamers, either. Insiders are happy to report that there are "no real senior leaders with attitude problems at the firm." One contact gushes, "As a smaller firm, each individual really makes a difference, and that fact is not lost on the senior bankers."

On the downside, the firm is "pretty male-dominated, [though] very receptive to people's performance, irrespective of race, background, gender, and such." Diversity seems to be an issue throughout the firm. Most say that Weisel makes an effort to recruit and retain women and minorities, but the end result is still a less diverse workforce than at most Wall Street shops. One banker says the firm is "average at best" in terms of minority recruiting efforts, though that source notes that "people of a variety of different ethnicities [work at Weisel]." Firm representatives say the company is actively trying to address this issue.

Pay, if not location, near the Street

As far as pay goes, insiders say Weisel Partners "aims to be competitive with all the bulge brackets, especially Donaldson, Lufkin & Jenrette." In its short history, the firm has tried to set the bar for other banks, a strategy which has sometimes backfired. "As one of the first to pay bonuses, the firm needs to be more careful in not being surprised by where the market comes in," says one source. For senior bankers, pay is augmented by the firm's private equity investment opportunities, which are available only to qualified investors. The perks offered by Weisel are on par with most of the industry, including cars and meals after 8 p.m., gym discounts, free cell phone calls, and a "generous business travel policy" which includes upgrades on flights over four hours long and business class travel on red-eyes. The firm recently began offering bankers free concierge service as well.

The place for morning people

Unfortunately, employment at Thomas Weisel Partners requires working brutal hours similar to those at other investment banks. "[I] work from 7:30 a.m. — typical for most — to 8:30 p.m., with some Sunday work that is usually avoidable with some advance planning," reports one West Coast banker. "As a morning person, this fits my schedule much better than the typical Wall Street model of in at 9 to 9:30 and out at midnight." When you're done, go home. That source continues, "Face time is extremely discouraged and individuals who require [face time from junior team members] find themselves at a disadvantage in how they are perceived to be managing their resources."

While you're working all those hours, though, you can expect a lot of client contact: "This organization is pretty flat, so you have a lot of contact with the senior bankers and clients." Insiders rave about the quality of work available to all bankers at Weisel. "We have been fortunate to have mostly live deals," says one source. Another contact says there is ample responsibility and "plenty of business to go around." That source continues, "Unlike [at] Wall Street firms, vice presidents [at Weisel] are expected to lead a transaction and be a major point of contact with the client, leveraging the partner's time." One optimistic junior banker says, "As my ability as an analyst increases, I am sure that the level of work that I do will also increase."

Since most Weisel bankers have significant experience, training hasn't been a large priority for the firm. As the bank expands, more formal training will likely be instituted, but for now junior bankers rely on the wisdom of their superiors. "The senior bankers are very experienced and they really know their spaces," says one source. "The problem," complains another banker, "comes from their availability to share this knowledge, as we are all extremely busy."

Thom's taste

Due to Thom Weisel's reportedly excellent taste and willingness to spend money, the firm's office space is top notch. "Thom buys the best space with the best view, regardless of the price, and outfits it with $3,000 desks, $1,000 chairs, and priceless works of art on the walls. Each office is created with Thom's careful input and reflects his taste." Bankers are also complimentary of the support staff, the quantity of which is being increased. "[We] recently added a dedicated word processing and presentation group which does all the PowerPoint presentations for the firm," says one Boston banker. In San Francisco, a space crunch has meant the bank has less support staff than needed, though insiders say "that should change next year when [the firm] acquires more space."

Hungry for more inside scoop? Join Vault.com's popular online
community for finance and banking — www.vault.com

VAULT.COM **387**

UBS Warburg

299 Park Avenue
New York, NY 10171-0026
(212) 821-3000
Fax: (212) 486-8077
www.ubswarburg.com

LOCATIONS

London (HQ)
New York
Chicago
San Francisco
Stamford
Zurich
Offices in 39 countries

DEPARTMENTS

Investment Banking
Private Client
Private Equity
Sales and Trading

THE STATS

Group CEO: Marcel Ospel
CEO of UBS Warburg:
Markus Granziol
Employer Type: Subsidiary of UBS AG
No. of Employees: 12,700

UPPERS

- Growing in the U.S.
- Laid-back culture
- M&A specialists

DOWNERS

- Commute to Connecticut for some
- Problem with mergers
- Second-tier image in the U.S.

KEY COMPETITORS

Credit Suisse First Boston
Deutsche Banc Alex. Brown
Donaldson, Lufkin & Jenrette
J.P. Morgan
Lehman Brothers

EMPLOYMENT CONTACT

Human Resources
677 Washington Boulevard
Stamford, CT 06901

You can also also submit your
résumé and apply online at
www.ubswarburg.com

THE SCOOP

Neutral parent

UBS Warburg represents the investment banking operations of UBS, the Swiss-based financial services behemoth with nearly 50,000 employees. Besides investment banking, UBS offers private and corporate banking services through UBS Switzerland and asset management and mutual funds through aptly named UBS Asset Management. After a tumultuous history of mergers and acquisitions, the firm hopes to become a major player in the U.S. markets. In May 2000, the firm listed its shares on the New York Stock Exchange. At the time of the listing, firm representatives made it clear that UBS Warburg had expansion and acquisitions on its agenda. That projection came true in July 2000: UBS acquired Painewebber for $10.8 billion.

Multi-mergers

The company's story begins in 1872 with the founding of the Swiss Bank Corporation (SBC). SBC grew internationally (the London office, the bank's first outside Switzerland, opened in 1898) and by the 1990s had established alliances or subsidiaries in the world's financial centers. In the mid-1990s, the firm became a major player in the investment banking world by purchasing the securities business of S.G. Warburg Group, a firm started in London in the 1930s by German Siegmund Warburg, who was fleeing Nazi persecution. The new firm was dubbed SBC Warburg. SBC Warburg expanded into the U.S. with its September 1997 acquisition of Dillon, Read & Co., a New York I-bank founded in 1832. The firm was then named Warburg Dillon Read. In June 1998, SBC merged with UBS, taking the name UBS AG. UBS had been formed in 1912 by the merger of two regional Swiss banks, the Bank of Winterthur and Toggenbirger Bank.

Early reports of the UBS/SBC/Warburg combination were not favorable. The newly combined firm reported a profit of $4.2 billion for 1999, which was nearly double the 1998 profits. However, in 1998 the firm was hit with one-time write-offs (including an investment in hedge fund Long-Term Capital Management) that dragged profits down and made 1999's performance look artificially good in comparison. *The Economist* called UBS "a directionless and unhappy institution" and said the bank's problems resulted from the merger with SBC, which it felt was poorly managed. One issue was the departure of talent. For example, according to *The Economist*, 19 out of 20 partners from O'Connor & Associates, a derivatives shop bought by SBC in 1992, had left the bank.

New order for the new millennium

Like its investment banking competitors, the firm has been working actively to expand its base of banking professionals. From December 1999 to January 2000, the firm hired three syndicated loan professionals from Lehman Brothers. According to *American Banker*, the arrival of Steve Rielly, Brendon Dillon and Chris Ryan from Lehman suggests that "Warburg may be poised for a big entrance into U.S. leveraged lending."

In June 2000, UBS Warburg named James Feuille as global head of the firm's technology sector. Feuille had previously worked for the firm (from 1995 to 1998) before leaving for Volpe Brown Whelan, a technology boutique now owned by Prudential Securities. Feuille's hiring is the beginning of a rebuilding project in the technology group. Bob Hotz, UBS Warburg's head of investment banking for the Americas, told *Tech Finance News* in July 2000 that the firm intends to double its technology team, increasing the corporate finance staff from 30 to 75 within six to 12 months.

In addition to ramping up its personnel, the firm has made structural changes. In February 2000, the bank's operations were reordered into its current format and the investment banking arm was renamed UBS Warburg. In May 2000, UBS began trading on the New York Stock Exchange (the first financial services firm based outside the United States to trade on the Big Board). CEO Marcel Ospel told CNBC that the NYSE listing would enable the company to "act in the United States on the acquisition front." Additionally, Ospel emphatically denied the possibility of the firm retreating from the investment banking business. "These rumors have absolutely no substance; to the contrary, investment banking is very important for our group, we are determined to grow it with a focus to here — North America."

Thank you, PaineWebber

The focus of UBS Warburg's expansion plans turned out to be PaineWebber, the 121-year-old investment bank. In July 2000, UBS announced it was acquiring PaineWebber for $10.8 billion in cash and stock. The purchase connects PaineWebber's considerable U.S. retail

Hungry for more inside scoop? Join Vault.com's popular online community for finance and banking — www.vault.com

VAULT.com   **391**

presence (the firm was the nation's fourth-largest broker at the time of the deal) with UBS Warburg's growing banking practice. "The combination of UBS' international reach and product range, with PaineWebber's leading position in the U.S. market for affluent and high net worth individuals, will create a premier global investment services firm," UBS' Ospel said in the release announcing the coupling.

Analysts were optimistic about the deal, though surprised to a degree. "We thought they would enhance their investment banking," Beat Kaeser, head of Swiss equity research at privately held Bank Darier, Hentsch & Cie, told *The Daily Deal*. "It is a very coherent move for UBS," concurred Oliver Prucheut, an analyst at Natexis Capital. "But it doesn't answer the problem of their investment banking weakness." (UBS reportedly had a plan to address that weakness, according to Bloomberg. The firm held talks with Lehman Brothers in early 2000 to combine UBS Warburg and Lehman into a securities firm co-owned by the two parents.) However, other observers felt the new firm's increased distribution capabilities will allow for natural growth in I-banking. HSBC Holdings analyst Derek Chambers told *The Daily Deal* that the PaineWebber acquisition "will give [UBS Warburg] a very substantial amount of placing power. It is by having placing power that Merrill Lynch was able to move up the league tables in corporate banking," Chambers pointed out. One potential pitfall for the merger is talent defection, an issue UBS addressed when it reportedly set aside $875 million in incentives for PaineWebber employees; $75 million was reserved for six top executives, including the firm's president. Additionally, according to *The Daily Deal*, PaineWebber CEO Donald Marron signed a separate contract extension with UBS.

Best at M&A

UBS Warburg's strength is its M&A advisory practice. According to Thomson Financial Securities Data, the firm ranked ninth in announced U.S. M&A in 1999, advising on 77 deals worth $178.7 billion. In completed worldwide M&A, UBS Warburg finished 10th, advising on 268 deals worth $146.3 billion. M&A assignments include advising Vodafone AirTouch on its $33 billion merger with Mannesmann. The firm has also lead managed a handful of IPOs as well, including Genomic Solutions' $56 million deal in May 2000 and Cepheid's $30 million offering in June 2000.

The firm is also making a play in the debt markets. UBS Warburg had great success in high yield underwriting in the first quarter of 2000, thanks in large part to a $275 million offering from Mexican retailer Grupo Elektra SA de CV. According to Bloomberg News, UBS Warburg won the Elektra deal by promising to buy any leftover bonds. "That's not something Wall Street is always ready to do," an Elektra executive told Bloomberg News.

GETTING HIRED

UBS Warburg posts recruiting schedules on its web site, www.ubswarburg.com. The firm has recently instituted a snazzy online application procedure that is required for all candidates outside of the U.S. and Switzerland.

Associates at UBS Warburg have in the past warned that a business degree doesn't carry the same weight at UBS Warburg as it does at most American banks, especially in sales and trading. However, the firm is taking steps to emphasize the MBA. For example, the firm has changed its training program to separate undergrads from MBAs in corporate finance, and to initiate undergrads in S&T with a three-week "core training" program before they join the MBAs for training (rather than have undergrads and MBAs go through the exact same program, as they had in the past).

On the other side of the coin, insiders note, the firm provides greater opportunity for undergrads. Says one contact: "For undergrads in the analyst position, it's a fantastic place. If you're a Wharton undergrad, it's really ideal. They really love that profile, the really hungry young person." Says one corporate finance analyst, "I worked on a divestiture where I did all the plant tours in addition to the management presentation. On the other side, the most junior person I saw was an associate. That's the opportunity. On the other hand, if you're looking for structure, it's probably not the best place for you."

Hungry for more inside scoop? Join Vault.com's popular online community for finance and banking — www.vault.com

VAULT.COM   **393**

OUR SURVEY SAYS

Merger bumps? Depends who you are

For UBS Warburg in the U.S., all sales and trading and operations employees are housed in Stamford, Connecticut, while corporate finance and research departments are located in offices on Park Avenue in midtown Manhattan. How the merger between SBC Warburg Dillon Read and UBS in 1998 affected the firm depended to a large extent on the location: the firm's sales and trading force saw considerably more turmoil than its I-banking colleagues. For example, there was a brief flurry of policy changes instituted by UBS (as one contact put it, "No more jeans, no more sneakers, no more this and that") that were "beaten back down." "Up until the merger with UBS, the SBC part was like a lot of mini-firms, strung together with a huge balance sheet," explains one insider.

In corporate finance and in London, it's something of a different story. "It's basically a lot of old Warburg people running the show," according to one contact in London. "It's very much of a U.K. British culture — it's a bit stodgy." Also, sources in New York report being not as affected by the merger with UBS as those in Stamford. "We definitely added some people in some areas, like some good research analysts, but culturally I didn't think that it was that much different," reports one corporate finance insider. "There's maybe more of a London presence — it's the small things, like you'll get e-mails every day from overseas, and they'll use British spelling and British language." Says another insider, "Coming from Dillon Read to Swiss Bank and then UBS, and being absorbed into a larger organization, there are more Swiss-like forms — it's just a little more bureaucratic, but I think the mergers have gone pretty well."

As for the actual offices, Stamford, Connecticut, the American headquarters and site of sales and trading, is a New York suburb in wealthy Fairfield County. The firm's offices are located across the street from the Metro North train station in Stamford. Reports one banker in Stamford: "The younger people tend to all live in New York. People with families tend to live in Connecticut — for them, it's an ideal situation. Anyone who doesn't live in Connecticut better think twice [about joining UBS Warburg]."

Relaxed culture, but issues with senior bankers

"It's hard to make blanket statements for hundreds of people, but overall, in a relative sense, I think this firm has a looser culture than other investment banks," reports one insider about UBS Warburg. Says a contact in Asia: "I would describe the culture at UBS Warburg as relatively loose compared to the U.S. banks." At least one former employee blasts the firm's senior bankers, saying "When you go to Wall Street you assume you'll be working with the cream of the crop. I was bluntly shocked to see how such low-quality people could occupy high posts at a Wall Street firm. Instead of them teaching us, I was in a position where I wound up editing senior people's text [and] explaining basic concepts."

Insiders appreciate the current aggressiveness the firm is displaying in I-banking, as it means more opportunity personally. "I think that generally, people sense there's a lot more opportunity as far as upward mobility is concerned when compared to other firms," reports one insider, "because we're trying to grow fast." Of course, part of the drive to grow fast means eye-popping salaries to lure lateral bankers, but this doesn't mean UBS Warburg is above the curve at all levels. "If you look at what the average ranges are like, I would say that we are basically smack dab in the middle," reports one insider.

Hungry for more inside scoop? Join Vault.com's popular online community for finance and banking — www.vault.com

VAULT.com 395

U.S. Bancorp Piper Jaffray

U.S. Bancorp Center
800 Nicollet Mall
Suite 800
Minneapolis, MN 55402
(612) 303-6000
Fax: (612) 303-6996
www.piperjaffray.com

LOCATIONS

Minneapolis (HQ)
Chicago
Menlo Park
New York
San Francisco
Seattle
London
Over 100 additional brokerage offices

DEPARTMENTS

Equity Capital Markets

- Equity Research
- Investment Banking
- Institutional Equity Sales
  and Trading
- Corporate Client Services
- Capital Markets

Fixed Income Capital Markets

- Public Finance Group
- General Capital Markets Group
- Individual Investor Expertise

Individual Investor Services

- Venture Capital

THE STATS

Chairman & CEO: Andrew Duff
Employer Type:
Subsidiary of U.S. Bancorp
No. of Employees: 3,133
No. of Offices: 100+

UPPERS

- Friendly corporate culture
- Low cost of living in Minnesota

DOWNERS

- Headquarters removed from
  financial hot spots
- Poor diversity

KEY COMPETITORS

Banc of America Securities
CIBC World Markets
Deutsche Bank
Legg Mason
Robertson Stephens

EMPLOYMENT CONTACT

Human Resources
800 Nicollet Mall
Suite 800
Minneapolis, MN 55402
(612) 303-6000
Fax: (612) 303-6996

THE SCOOP

The Twin Cities I-bank

U.S. Bancorp Piper Jaffray is the investment banking arm of U.S. Bancorp, the Minnesota-based commercial bank. Piper Jaffray offers clients typical I-banking services, including underwriting, research, sales, and trading. The firm also has a respected venture capital arm. One of the firm's biggest strengths is fixed income investment banking and Piper Jaffray is the established leader in Midwestern municipal bond underwriting.

Piper Jaffray was founded in 1913 by C.P. Jaffray and H.C. Piper, Sr. (grandfather of former CEO and current chairman Addison Piper). Five years after its formation, the firm merged with George B. Lane & Co. Both firms specialized in corporate lending and didn't begin underwriting activities until the 1920s. The company acquired Hopwood & Co. (and with it, a seat on the New York Stock Exchange) in December 1931. In 1971 the firm went public. In May 1998, Piper Jaffray was purchased by U.S. Bancorp for $730 million.

Meet the new boss

The firm has recently experienced some notable changes. Addison Piper stepped down as CEO in December 1999. Piper, who remains chairman, had led the firm since 1983, when he took over for his father, Harry Piper, Jr. Andrew Duff, who had been president of Piper Jaffray, succeeded Addison. Duff is the first non-Piper to lead the firm.

Duff's first challenge as CEO came in May 2000 when three female brokers filed a discrimination suit against the firm. The three brokers, based in the San Francisco office, claimed that Piper Jaffray failed to promote qualified women and retaliated against those who filed complaints. The three women (one of whom still works at the firm) have sought class-action status for the approximately 150 female brokers working at Piper Jaffray.

In May 2000, the firm moved its headquarters to U.S. Bancorp Center, a move necessitated by the firm's rapid growth. In March 2000, the firm also moved into new quarters in San Francisco. The new office houses 80 investment banking professionals, up from the five that opened the original San Francisco office in 1996. The San Francisco outpost added a new trading floor in May 2000, described by the firm as "state-of-the-art."

Healthy deals

Piper Jaffray's investment banking operations may not be bulge bracket but are nonetheless healthy. The firm set records in both the number and the value of investment banking transactions completed for the fifth consecutive year in 1999. The company completed 203 total transactions for a combined value of $19.4 billion. Piper Jaffray worked on 63 IPOs (mainly as a co-manager) in 1999 (a 270 percent increase from 1998), raising $3.9 billion. In 1999 the company lead managed six IPOs for companies such as Internet.com, BioMarin Pharmaceutical, and Interspeed. Recent lead-managed deals include IPOs for Eloquent and Antigenics in February 2000. As a co-manager, the firm was involved in Therapeutic Systems' $230 million offering and Buy.com's $209 million IPO in February 2000, GoAmerica's April 2000 offering worth $160 million, and the June 2000 offerings of Handspring ($200 million) and Charles River Laboratories ($224 million). Piper Jaffray also participated in 35 follow-on offerings worth $6.5 billion.

Mergers and acquisitions advisory is also climbing for Piper Jaffray; the firm advised on 92 deals worth $10.4 billion in 1999, up from 67 transactions worth $4.9 billion in 1998. Recent M&A work includes advising Small Planet Foods in January 2000 on its sale to General Mills, DreamWorks Interactive on its February 2000 sale to Electronic Arts, and Naviant on its April 2000 purchase of Softbank Marketing Solutions.

Even with respectable numbers in equity and M&A, the firm's strength is clearly in the fixed-income markets, specifically municipal offerings. The bank underwrote 537 municipal offerings in 1999, with a total value of $5.1 billion. Piper Jaffray ranked first in underwriting in the Midwest for the ninth consecutive year and ranked first among municipal underwriters in Iowa and Minnesota.

The bank has also developed a notable venture capital practice. Piper Jaffray has four funds, three of which invest primarily in health care companies; the other invests in technology firms. Investments include CV Therapeutics, Vision 21, and AdminiQuest in health care, and Applicast and Pluris in technology.

Hungry for more inside scoop? Join Vault.com's popular online community for finance and banking — www.vault.com

VAULT.com   **399**

GETTING HIRED

U.S. Bancorp Piper Jaffray's web site, www.piperjaffray.com, provides a listing of current job opportunities and contact addresses. Applicants can submit their résumés to the Employment Department at the company's corporate headquarters. Most new employees in the investment banking department are assigned to industry groups based on preference or previous experience. They also have the latitude to pursue other specialties in the event they wish to change focus.

In investment banking, Piper's analyst recruiting covers about 50 major colleges and universities with actual campus visits at about six schools. Associate recruiting has been focused on the top-10 business schools for the past 15 years. In the last five years, the firm has formalized the associate recruiting process to include on-campus presentations and interviews with dinners for pre-selected candidates. "They definitely recruit from the top five schools — they draw a lot from Chicago and Northwestern because they're in the Midwest, but they have a lot of Harvard Business School people," reports one insider. "Also, they opened an office in Menlo Park and San Francisco and are hiring a lot [more] from Stanford, too."

Unlike other I-banks, U.S. Bancorp Piper Jaffray doesn't offer I-banking summer programs. As one insider explains: "People who want to do I-banking don't necessarily want to do a summer in Minnesota." "They want to get the best candidates they can, but they don't want them to leave six months later, either. I think they try to hire people who have Piper Jaffray as their first or second choice."

OUR SURVEY SAYS

High-level

U.S Bancorp Piper Jaffray employees call the firm's work environment a "superb" place to begin a career, thanks to an "interactive" atmosphere and "genial" colleagues who help new hires "learn the subtleties of the business." Explains one insider: "Traditionally they've been a very top-heavy firm. They don't win deals based on their name recognition. They win based on research, and because the companies that work with them know they're going to get senior-level attention. So they don't leverage analysts as much as other firms do — senior people need to be more involved." This means, in part, that moving up the ladder at the firm is somewhat easier than at larger firms. In fact, promotions can happen rapidly; one source says that associates can move up to the VP level in two years. Some insiders report a conservative environment. "The corporate culture is a bit stuffy and prone to micro-management," says one employee. "There is a lot of red tape," concurs another contact.

The firm is also unique when it comes to job responsibilities for junior bankers. "Associates don't do any modeling, analysts do all the modeling. You could literally never do a model there if you're an associate," reports one insider. "It's great for an analyst because you do all the models, including the complex ones. The associates get a lot of client time; they're always included in the meetings." I-banking analysts can stay on for a third year, and in rare instances, be promoted to associate without getting an MBA.

How has Piper Jaffray's recent acquisition affected life at the bank? "It is affecting morale, though not as much in the investment banking division." Says one I-banking insider: "It's still run the same as a wholly owned subsidiary — and they haven't affected compensation."

Good pay (especially for MN)

The firm offers "healthy salaries" that tend to vary with the performance of the stock market and "some of the best employee benefits" in the industry, including an "unbeatable" employee stock ownership program. When it comes to starting pay, the firm isn't all that different from the big boys back East. According to one insider, "First-year associates can get paid close to what they get paid in New York. Where it gets skewed after four or five years. Here, people make a million dollars but it's not the rule. But here, people can buy a huge house for $250,000 10 minutes out of town."

Location hurts diversity

Insiders comment that "Piper, like Minnesota itself, is homogenous, with few minorities," though "it is an open environment and the only criteria for advancement is hard work." Says another insider: "I think Minnesota in general doesn't have a strong mix of ethnicity. If you wanted strong cultural diversity, you'd be somewhere else." However, says that I-banking contact: "I think they're very good with the male/female ratio. They're not 50/50 at the top, but they definitely have some strong women there."

Hungry for more inside scoop? Join Vault.com's popular online community for finance and banking — www.vault.com

VAULT.com   **401**

Because of Piper Jaffray's Midwestern location, employees usually start the day early in order to be open during East Coast market hours. For I-bankers, "the hours are extreme, 12 to 14 hours a day, plus weekends for bankers, though it's still not quite as bad as New York." Says one former analyst: "You work hard, but they allow you to have a life. Workweeks are in the range of 70 to 80 [hours]. You do work on weekends but it's not all weekend. You work hard, but it's not like New York. If you have a birthday party, or concert tickets, you can get away. A lot of times you have to cancel, but it's not like other places. Here they're more lenient — it's the Midwestern values."

"The corporate culture is a bit stuffy and prone to micromanagement."

— *U.S. Bancorp Piper Jaffray Insider*

Wasserstein Perella & Co.

31 West 52nd Street
New York, NY 10019
Phone: (212) 969-2700
Fax: (212) 969-7836
www.wassersteinperella.com

LOCATIONS

New York (HQ)
Boston
Chicago
Dallas
Houston
Los Angeles
San Francisco

Frankfurt
London
Paris
Tokyo

DEPARTMENTS

Capital Markets
Investment Banking
Merchant Banking
Restructuring

THE STATS

Chairman & CEO:
Bruce Wasserstein
Employer Type: Private Company
No. of Employees: 500
No. of Offices: 10

UPPERS

• Relaxed culture
• Working with top-notch talent

DOWNERS

• Long hours in M&A
• Weak sales force

Note: Wasserstein Perella Group owns American Lawyer Media which holds an investment in Vault.com

KEY COMPETITORS

Goldman Sachs
Lazard
Morgan Stanley Dean Witter

EMPLOYMENT CONTACT

Domestic

Frances A. Lyman
Vice President — Recruiting
Wasserstein Perella & Co.
31 West 52nd Street
New York, NY 10019
(212) 969-2649
Fax: (212) 969-7977
E-mail: fran_lyman@wasserella.com

Ziki Slav
Vice President
Grantchester Securities
Wasserstein Perella Securities, Inc.
31 West 52nd Street
New York, NY 10019
(212) 903-2150
Fax: (212) 969-7965
E-mail: zvi_slav@wasserella.com

European

Charlotte Knight
Recruiting Coordinator
Wasserstein Perella & Co. Limited
Cassini House
57 St. James' Street
London, SW1A 1LD
44-171-446-8000
Fax: 44-171-494-2053
E-mail:
charlotte_knight@wasserella.com

THE SCOOP

M&A shop

Wasserstein Perella & Co. represents the investment banking operations of the Wasserstein Perella Group. The Group owns several media properties, including American Lawyer Media, and has investments in other Internet content firms. The investment banking arm, while it offers I-banking services such as debt and equity underwriting and investment management, specializes in mergers and acquisitions advisory. The firm doesn't transact the same volume of deals as some of its bulge-bracket competitors, but it has advised on some major deals, most notably the Time Warner/America Online merger, announced in January 2000. The Grantchester Securities division of the firm focuses on fixed income sales, trading and research. The primary groups in this division are high yield, distressed securities, and private debt.

Talent at the top

Wasserstein Perella was founded in 1988 by Bruce Wasserstein and Joseph Perella, both refugees from the former First Boston (now known as Credit Suisse First Boston). According to firm lore, in the early 1970s Wasserstein was an attorney with super-prestigious law firm Cravath, Swaine & Moore, while Perella was head of First Boston's M&A group. Perella was so impressed after working with young Wasserstein (who had entered Harvard Law School at 19) that he requested the Harvard JD/MBA work on all transactions for First Boston. That request didn't sit too well with Cravath's partners, who favored a structured assignment system. Perella decided the best way to get his hands on Wasserstein was to hire him away.

After building First Boston's M&A business for over 10 years, Wasserstein and Perella founded their own firm. In 1993, after five years out on his own, Perella headed back to the safety of a large investment bank; he now serves as head of investment banking at Morgan Stanley Dean Witter. The always-enterprising Wasserstein was left to run the firm on his own, which industry observers concede he has done admirably. (Literary buffs should note that Bruce is the brother of award-winning playwright Wendy Wasserstein.)

In the late 1990s, the firm was reportedly looking at partaking in a merger itself. The firm was linked to international M&A powerhouse Lazard (then known as Lazard Frères & Co.) in 1997. Two years later,

Schroder & Co., the U.S. operations of Britain's Schroders Plc, was rumored to be interested in buying out Wasserstein Perella. The speculation, however, did not lead to any deals and the company remains a private organization.

Now growing

After rejecting merger overtures, the firm has expanded recently, opening a Boston office in March 2000 with six equity sales professionals. Additionally, the firm added Edward Necarsulmer III as a managing director and the head of the firm's equities division. Prior to joining Wasserstein Perella, Necarsulmer was the head of the North American equities business of Deutsche Bank. Wasserstein Perella is no stranger to luring top talent from other banks. In 1997 Kenneth Tuchman, former co-head of M&A at Lehman, joined the firm as vice chairman. A few years earlier, the firm lured Frederic Seegal, then a managing director and co-head of domestic corporate finance at Salomon Brothers, into the fold. Seegal now serves as president of the company.

In addition to advising Time Warner on its $165 billion merger with America Online (one of the most high-profile deals in merger history), Wasserstein Perella has been a part of several other big-name transactions. The firm advised Geocities on its $4.8 billion purchase by Yahoo! and SunAmerica on its acquisition by American International Group. More recently, the bank counseled Wal-Mart Stores on its purchase of Asda Group for $11.7 billion in June 1999, SlimFast Foods on its $2.3 billion April 2000 sale to Unilever, and Philip Morris on its $14.9 billion pending acquisition of Nabisco. While equity underwriting isn't the bank's specialty, it has participated in a handful of deals. For example, Wasserstein Perella co-managed the $154 million Universal Compression Holdings IPO in May 2000.

GETTING HIRED

Meeting the man himself

Wasserstein Perella posts a schedule of its on-campus recruiting visits (which at some schools includes a talk by Bruce Wasserstein) and interviewing schedule on its web site, www.wassersteinperella.com.

Hungry for more inside scoop? Join Vault.com's popular online community for finance and banking — www.vault.com

VAULT.com **407**

During on-campus school visits, the firm reportedly prefers to conduct two-on-one interviews. The candidate then makes a visit to the New York office. For analysts, the interviews last "all morning, with a lunch afterward." Candidates should know that "[the firm will] get back to them very shortly."

More than other I-banks, Wasserstein Perella reportedly recruits candidates with legal backgrounds, as legal training comes in very handy for M&A work. "There's a fair push to get either laterals [from law firms] or people at the top law schools," reports one insider. Bruce Wasserstein is reportedly "closer to [Harvard] Law School" than he is to Harvard Business School. In part because of Wasserstein's history with Cravath, Swaine & Moore, sources report that "Wasserstein Perella actually has a lot of Cravath people."

Wasserstein Perella offers a "limited" number of 12-week summer analyst and summer associate positions. These summer hires aren't necessarily guaranteed a full-time spot, insiders say: "It really depends on the quality of the summer associates — some may get offers, some may not."

Our contacts give advice on what Wasserstein is looking for in its applicants. "It obviously helps to know about the recent deals and that sort of stuff," reports one banker, but more importantly, "you definitely want to have someone who knows what they're getting into. I don't think its advisable to say 'I'm looking at all the bulge-bracket firms — plus Wasserstein.' You want to see people who are very focused." Another adds, "They prefer a good schooling background, but their definition of pedigree is much wider." That insider continues, "They are far more interested in fit than the bulge bracket is."

OUR SURVEY SAYS

Small firm mentality

Wasserstein Perella is known for working its bankers hard, but insiders report that the workload is better characterized by periods of intense work with some lulls. "The nature of M&A is more cyclical than anything. Sometimes, you could be working until four or five in the morning fairly constantly," reports one Wasserstein source. "But other times, there may not be anything to do." Another contact agrees: "For all the long hours, much of the day is spent waiting for work to trickle down." Staffing issues have also led to increased workload, at least in equity research. One associate in that department says, "It's a bit of a sweatshop now because we're understaffed. They're really being cautious because they don't want to hire a ton of people and then fire [them]" in the event of a market slowdown.

Wasserstein candidates should be prepared for all-nighters. According to one employee: "They're definitely looking for people who can work the late hours, people who understand the differences between the small firm and a large firm. It's not a firm where you can sort of hide in the corner and do one small part of a deal."

Good training

Unlike other mid-sized firms, Wasserstein Perella has a well-developed training program for new hires which lasts "about a month." The first two weeks include classes taught by an accounting professor and a finance professor. The other two weeks feature modules, M&A training, and valuation techniques. The firm also brings in outside speakers. For example, the bank invites a partner from Cravath, Swaine & Moore to talk about legal issues involved in M&A. All analysts and associates take part in the training.

Get to know the superstars

As with other smaller firms, insiders at Wasserstein report that "the best thing about the firm is you work with very senior members." "What Wasserstein has done is picked up very senior members of these bulge-bracket firms," explains another contact. "They're giving them a lot more flexibility — and of course, they're getting more compensation." As for Bruce himself? "He's obviously a very, very bright guy," reports one banker who has worked with him. "He can be in a room, and he doesn't have to say a whole lot. But when he does speak, the whole room will listen to him. He's very, very good on the sell-side — no one else in the room is on the same level. He's very, very good at getting to the point quickly."

The friendly, white shoe firm

Wasserstein insiders report that the firm is a pretty chummy place, though not a party. "People will typically eat together or watch TV in a conference room," says one former analyst. "People dress down, go

Hungry for more inside scoop? Join Vault.com's popular online community for finance and banking — www.vault.com

VAULT.com **409**

to the gym for half an hour or an hour together. At night, it's a different firm — everyone knows everyone. You're very close with the analyst class." Says another: "It's almost always quiet. People work really hard. But the guys are just generally nice. They're friendly and jovial, but it's not a party atmosphere." A source in the equity research department says, "On the investment banking side, Wasserstein is pretty eclectic [and] incredibly white shoe." That contact also blasts the sales force, calling it "pretty weak" though improving. As for his own department, "Equity research is still pretty much in the starter phase. Really only in the last 18 months has the equity effort been a major push at the firm." He reports the firm gives its equity analysts "a lot of leeway in what you write."

German aggression

Wasserstein Perella's New York headquarters are currently located in the same building as the Museum of Modern Art museum shop, in midtown Manhattan. "[Wasserstein] rents offices from Deutsche Bank, and Deutsche Bank really wants to kick them out," says one banker. "But Wasserstein, he's got this thing about where he wants the office to be. There are only about six blocks that he wants, and therefore we have to stay." Dining choices in Midtown tend to be somewhat limited. "There's a cafeteria in the building, [but] it's Deutsche Bank's. Nobody's really encouraged to go there," says one insider. "Most people go out — there's a salad place across the street where lots of people go." The firm says, however, that it plans to move offices in November 2000. Reportedly, the new digs are just across the street from the firm's current location.

A river of free liquid

"All in all, the benefits outweigh the detriments," says one Wasserestein employee. "And we get free sodas." Another source also enjoys the free liquids: "On every floor they've got a pantry. It's stocked with drinks — soda, cranberry juice, lemonade, apple juice." Reports one contact: "If you work past 8:30 at night you get a car service home, which is standard." Late nights also get bankers a free dinner, and "you get free meals for weekend work." Wasserstein also offers a "401(k) with match. The firm will even pay for your GMAT course at Kaplan."

"They're definitely looking for people who can work the late hours, people who understand the differences between the small firm and the large firm. It's not a firm where you can sort of hide in the corner and do one small part of a deal."

— Wasserstein Perella Insider

Wit SoundView

826 Broadway
6th Floor
New York, NY 10003
(212) 253-4400
Fax: (212) 253-4428
www.witsoundview.com

LOCATIONS

New York (HQ)
San Francisco
Stamford

Dublin
London
Tokyo

DEPARTMENTS

Investment Banking
Research
Venture Capital

THE STATS

CEO: Robert H. Lessin
Employer Type: Public Company
Stock Symbol: WITC (Nasdaq)
1999 Revenue: $48.6 million
1999 Net Loss: $20.9 million
No. of Employees: 437

UPPERS

- Culture light years away from traditional I-banking
- Growing firm
- Lots of responsibility for junior bankers

DOWNERS

- Low pay unless/until the stock price takes off
- Start-up infrastructure
- Uncertainty after recent mergers

KEY COMPETITORS

Chase H&Q
Robertson Stephens
Thomas Weisel Partners

EMPLOYMENT CONTACT

Tiffany Wells
826 Broadway
6th Floor
New York, NY 10003

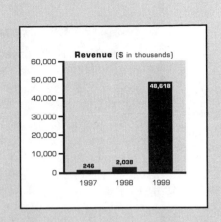

THE SCOOP

Leading the IPO craze

Wit SoundView is the investment banking arm of Wit SoundView Group. Wit Capital, the predecessor firm to Wit SoundView, was founded in 1996 by Andrew Klein, now vice chairman and chief strategist at the New York-based investment bank. Klein, a Harvard Law graduate, had previously founded Spring Street Brewing Company after a six-year stint in corporate law. Spring Street claims the distinction of being the first firm to complete a public offering via the Internet. The brewery created the first Web-based trading platform for the company's shares, essentially a pair of bulletin boards where buy and sell orders were posted. Initially, the Securities and Exchange Commission expressed concerns over the bulletin boards, which Klein dubbed Wit-Trade, but allowed the company to continue electronic trading after small regulatory concessions were made.

Klein managed to sell the success of his experiences and win some seed money to form Wit Capital in September 1997. Wit-Trade's philosophy concerning IPOs remained intact at Wit Capital, an online investment bank. Wit professes a "first-come, first-serve" approach to public offerings, and any Wit customer with $2,000 in his/her account is eligible to participate in IPOs. Traditionally, investment banks had given preferential treatment to wealthier customers, with some banks requiring as much as $1 million in an individual account before granting access to IPOs. While the public offering process still isn't completely democratic, Wit's strategy gave investors access to hot IPOs they normally couldn't touch. Wit leads all other banks in online distribution of IPOs, participating in 36 deals in the first quarter of 2000 alone. Some of Wit's hits included Palm, Inc., Cobalt Networks, Goldman Sachs, and MiningCo.com (now known as About.com). Wit reported its first profitable quarter in April 2000. For the quarter ended March 31, 2000, the company posted record revenues of $106.6 million and $7.5 million in net income.

New blood at the top

The company got some much-needed muscle in the spring of 1998. In late April, Robert Lessin resigned as vice chairman at Salomon Smith Barney to become Wit's chairman. Lessin brought immediate stature to the firm, but he also retooled the organization, eliminating Klein's idea of public venture capital and essentially restarting the company from the beginning. An April 1998 *Industry Standard* article, which was disputed by Klein, claimed Lessin purchased a controlling stake in Wit. In his dispute of the article, Klein said he, not Lessin, was the largest individual shareholder. Whether that was true at the time or not, Wit's 1999 proxy said that Lessin owned 6.1 percent to Klein's 5.6 percent, not counting 200,000 options Lessin had been granted but had not yet vested.

In June 1998, Ronald Readmond, formerly vice chairman at online brokerage Charles Schwab & Co., joined as president and COO. The deck was reshuffled in March 1999 when Lessin and Readmond were named co-CEOs. Lessin and Readmond also retained chairman and vice chairman titles, respectively. Readmond's tenure, however, was brief. In June 2000, he announced his resignation from the firm. "It was the right time to transition to the next generation of leaders," Readmond explained in a company press release. Lessin assumed the CEO role, and Russell Crabs and Mark Loehr, who had previously served as co-heads of Wit SoundView, were named co-presidents of the parent firm.

Wit also scored a major coup in February 1999 when Jonathon Cohen joined the firm as director of research. Cohen joined Wit from Merrill Lynch, where he had headed up the Internet research department. He was a fixture on *Institutional Investor*'s "All-American Research Team," the annual listing of the best research analysts in the industry, from 1996 to 1998. Cohen's arrival immediately boosted Wit's research department. In March 2000, Wit poached Mack Rossoff, an 18-year investment banking veteran, from J.P. Morgan. Rossoff, the head of media and entertainment investment banking at his former firm, joined Wit as head of M&A.

Some deals of their own

Wit received another boost to its credibility in March 1999 when venerable investment bank Goldman Sachs purchased a 22 percent stake in Wit for about $20 million. Goldman expanded its distribution channels, allowing Wit customers the chance to get in on deals underwritten by Goldman. In the spring and summer of 1999, the Internet IPO market was booming. Wit, a proponent of the Internet IPO, saw the perfect opportunity to make a public offering of its own.

Hungry for more inside scoop? Join Vault.com's popular online community for finance and banking — www.vault.com

VAULT.com **415**

The company raised $70 million in its offering, and the stock price rose over 63 percent on the first day.

In January 2000, Wit acquired SoundView Technology Group, a Stamford, Connecticut-based boutique firm, for approximately $310 million. The merger added 23 investment bankers to Wit's staff, increasing the total to 58. Wit's research team numbered 44 after the merger, up from 14. (Wit reportedly gave SoundView staffers $25 million in stock to convince them to stick around.) SoundView had co-managed 31 IPOs in 1999 and had $16 million in profits in 1998 (unlike Wit, which lost $20.9 million on $48.6 million in revenues in 1999). Most importantly, though, SoundView added a truckload of support staff necessary for a serious underwriting presence. For example, SoundView had an experienced team of market makers, the salespeople who create interest for a company stock. "[SoundView] takes us to the next level of the capital formation process," Ron Readmond, Wit's co-CEO at the time, told *Red Herring*. Wit's investment banking operations were renamed Wit SoundView. The parent company (formerly known as Wit Capital Group) officially changed its name to Wit SoundView Group in June 2000.

Capturing the lion's share of shares

In May 2000, Wit altered its strategy somewhat when the company entered into a strategic alliance with E*Trade. Essentially, Wit acquired E*Trade's underwriting unit, E*Offering, in a $328 million stock-for-stock deal. E*Trade shareholders were allocated 32 million shares of Wit. As part of the deal, E*Trade absorbed Wit's retail brokerage accounts. Approximately 100,000 accounts with an average balance of $10,000 each were transferred. Under the terms of the transaction, Wit will act as the exclusive provider of equity shares for all E*Trade customers.

Typically, Wit has been co-manager on IPOs. (In fact, Wit wasn't even lead manager of its own IPO. That honor went to Bear Stearns.) Wit Capital co-managed 57 deals in 1999 and participated in the syndicate group for another 71. However, as a co-manager the firm receives a minimal number of shares. The lead manager of the transaction typically takes the bulk of the shares and distributes a smaller percentage to the co-managers. With an increased army of bankers, research analysts, support staff, and an expanded retail customer base in which to distribute more shares, Wit SoundView now hopes to become a lead-managing powerhouse. "The E*Offering acquisition and our exclusive strategic alliance with E*Trade is another step in the evolution of our corporate strategy," Readmond said in a press release at the time of the deal. "It represents an aggressive move, catapulting Wit SoundView to the next level and positioning us to compete successfully for lead manager roles in Internet and new technology offerings."

Wit has also expanded internationally. In October 1999, the company announced an alliance with Enba, a Dublin-based financial services firm, to create Wit Capital Europe, an Internet investment bank headquartered in Ireland. Wit will own a 55 percent stake in the venture, which will initially focus on business in the U.K., France and Germany. Edward Annunziato, formerly co-head of investment banking in Europe, the Middle East, and Africa for Merrill Lynch, was named CEO of the European venture. Wit also exchanged about $31 million in stock for a 12 percent stake in Enba. Finally, the firm has established a Japanese investment bank, creatively dubbed Wit Capital Japan. WC Japan has raised over $40 million in financing in two rounds of venture capital financing.

Whoops!: an IPO glitch

In late March 2000, approximately 20,000 Wit customers received an e-mail notification informing them that they had been allocated shares in Telocity's IPO. (Telocity is a Cupertino, CA-based maker of Internet devices.) A human error led almost everyone who had initially expressed interest in the offering to believe they had been granted shares. Some customers received more than they asked for, while others had never confirmed their order with Wit. It turns out only 2,000 customers received shares, and Wit suffered a minor embarrassment. (The remaining 18,000 didn't miss out on much: Telocity's stock closed at $13.25 at the close of the first day, up $1.25 from the $12 offering price.)

More than IPOs

The firm is not planning to focus only on equity underwriting. Wit has mimicked large banks by jumping into the venture capital arena. Wit contributed $39 million to VC firm Arista Capital Partners in August 1999 to invest in private Internet businesses. The firm furthered its VC cause by hiring the management team of Dawntreader Fund I LP to manage Wit's Venture Capital Fund Group. The firm was renamed Wit SoundView Ventures in early 2000. (The selection of Dawntreader was

Hungry for more inside scoop? Join Vault.com's popular online community for finance and banking — www.vault.com

VAULT.com **417**

no coincidence, by the way. Wit chairman and co-CEO Lessin co-founded the firm in 1998.) Industry analysts, for the most part, embraced the move, saying that Wit's expansion into venture capital would give it a leg up when it comes time to underwrite deals. The company has also stepped up its efforts in the M&A advisory business and fund management in order to avoid too much dependence on the fickle equity markets.

GETTING HIRED

Hello, everyone

According to insiders, Wit recruits mostly from "Ivy League and top-20" schools. Contacts report that the San Francisco office employs a number of UC Berkeley and Stanford alumni. While the company has offices in London, Tokyo, and Dublin, it generally only hires experienced professionals for those international posts. The firm also engages in a fair amount of lateral and off-cycle hiring.

The interview process is typical for the industry. There are "two rounds with four to six interviews each round," according to one contact. "You will meet everyone who is in the office on your day," says another source.

The interviews themselves are described as informal and unstructured, with "emphasis on experience, intelligence and cultural fit." One banker says the questions are "not too technically challenging, but this depends on the level of financial experience the candidate has." The firm, though growing, can be fairly selective. "It really depends on the fit of the individual with the firm," says one insider. "We have had candidates get offers from larger bulge-bracket firms who we did not feel were a good fit."

OUR SURVEY SAYS

No deals with Satan

Wit SoundView's culture, by design, is different from that of most banks. "We are a dot-com operating within the investment banking world," explains one source. "Most people [here] are risk-takers and are confident in their ability to succeed." Insiders say the firm is "very exciting and entrepreneurial." One banker explains, "It's like doing traditional banking without selling your soul."

The Wit Capital/SoundView merger has resulted in some change. "The combined firm of Wit SoundView is still merging its culture," according to one banker. "Wit tends to be more laid back and relaxed while SoundView is a little more like a traditional I-bank. The culture seems to be meeting in the middle."

The culture is so attractive, it has became a selling point for the bank. "This is why we all joined Wit," says one banker. "We want to change the way banking is done." "If you think you're a master of the universe at 22," warns another Wit insider, "you better apply to Goldman or Morgan." While long hours and stress can't be avoided in investment banking, the firm does the little things that make the work more enjoyable. The offices have ping-pong and foosball tables, as well as free snacks. Dress is casual every day, which is a plus for most. One source, however, complains: "[I have] a closet full of suits I can't wear anymore."

Great expectations

Of course, the firm expects great results for all its quality-of-life efforts. "One time, we [the analysts] had a large project on top of our everyday work," according to one source. "We worked from 8 a.m. to 11 p.m. every day on our normal work and worked until 4 a.m. on this project every day for a couple of weeks. We were called into a meeting where we were all told that we were not working hard enough." Another source says that while the majority of the senior bankers treat juniors well, "some are more traditional in that they expect you to put in the years regardless of your level of relevant work experience."

"The firm probably pays a little on the low side compared to recent increases in investment banking compensation and given the under-performance of the stock," says one banker. Though insiders concede the bank tries to pay near the industry average, the firm offers more compensation based on firm performance. Wit offers private equity investment opportunities to employees who are also accredited investors. Most junior bankers do not qualify. Additionally, since the company is so much like an Internet startup, compensation includes more stock options than at most I-banks. "The options vest on a four-year/quarterly schedule (1/16th per quarter) so you don't have to wait forever for your options to vest," according to one insider.

Hungry for more inside scoop? Join Vault.com's popular online
community for finance and banking — www.vault.com

VAULT.com **419**

The perks at Wit are "nothing out of the ordinary, but people are well taken care of in general — meals when staying late, cabs or cars home, business class on transcontinental flights, cell phones that can be used for personal [calls] as long as they are not abused." The bank also offers laptops, Blackberry pagers, sponsored trips (including whitewater rafting), and social events.

Manageable hours

The hours at Wit SoundView are more or less typical of the industry: "Compared to other investment banks, the hours are manageable but nevertheless numerous and unpredictable." For example, one source explains, "Right now, it is totally fine. Before, when the markets were roaring, it was overwhelming." In any case, contacts report "very little face time at Wit SoundView. Quality, not quantity, is emphasized."

Since Wit is a smaller company, bankers can expect more access to deals and clients than at a bulge-bracket firm. "Analysts can take on a lot of responsibility and work on a lot of deals when the market is busy," says one source. Another insider boasts, "We can work on more transactions per banker because there is less nonsense keeping you in the office late." Says one source, "Most if not all of our meetings are with the CEO or CFO." That may be a function of the type of companies Wit services. "Most clients are Internet companies that don't need to talk to older bankers to feel that they are being properly serviced," according to one banker. One junior banker expresses the high level of resposibility with delight: "On some transactions I will be the sole representative of Wit SoundView." Another brags, "From the first day I came in, I was in front of and on the phone with clients."

Training by fire

Since Wit SoundView has many lateral hires, there is little emphasis on training. Insiders spout the usual clichés when it comes to formal training. One banker describes it as "trial by fire" while another calls it "more baptism by fire than actual training." However they set you on fire, you'd better be ready to work with a minimum of training. Some insiders believe that may change as the firm grows and does more campus recruiting, requiring more formal structure in the training program. Others swear that informal training is better, as many senior Wit bankers are bulge-bracket veterans. "[Senior bankers] are exceptionally knowledgeable regarding the Internet and technology space," says one young contact.

The one area where Wit's start-up status shows most is its offices. One insider calls the space "startupish" while others complain the New York digs "lack appropriate file space." Also, the "cubicles are great but a little too small." Insiders report the San Francisco offices are new and "not overdone but very practical." The number of support staff personnel is also smaller than that of larger banks. One source claims this is because Wit is "too small for a lot of support." The staff that does exist is described as "very hardworking and supportive."

Hungry for more inside scoop? Join Vault.com's popular online
community for finance and banking — www.vault.com

VAULT.COM 421

GLOSSARY

Agency bonds: Agencies represent all bonds issued by the federal government, except for those issued by the Treasury (i.e. bonds issued by other agencies of the federal government). Examples include the Federal National Mortgage Association (FNMA), and the Guaranteed National Mortgage Association (GNMA).

Arbitrage: The trading of securities (stocks, bonds, derivatives, currencies, and other securities) to profit from a temporary difference between the price of security in one market and the price in another (also called risk-free arbitrage). This temporary difference is often called a market inefficiency. Distinguish from risk arbitrage (see below).

Asset management: Basically, this is exactly what it sounds like. Investment banks take money given to them by pension funds and individual investors and invest it. For wealthy individuals (private clients), the investment bank will set up an individual account and manage the account; for the less well-endowed, the bank will offer mutual funds. Investment banks are compensated for asset management primarily by taking a percentage each year from the total assets managed. (They may also charge an upfront load, or commission, or a few percent of the initial money invested.) Asset management is considered a less volatile business than trading or investment banking, providing a steadier source of revenues.

Beauty contest: The informal term for the process by which clients choose an investment bank. Some of the typical selling points when competing with other investment banks for a deal are: "Look how strong our research department is in this industry. Our analyst in the industry is a real market mover, so if you go public with us, you'll be sure to get a lot of attention from her." Or: "We are the top-ranking firm in this type of issuance, as you will see by these league tables."

Bloomberg: Computer terminals providing real time quotes, news, and analytical tools, often used by traders and investment bankers.

Bond spreads: The difference between the yield of a corporate bond and a U.S. Treasury security of similar time to maturity.

Bulge bracket: The largest and most prestigious firms on Wall Street (including Goldman Sachs, Morgan Stanley Dean Witter, Merrill Lynch, Salomon Smith Barney, Lehman Brothers, Credit Suisse First Boston, and Donaldson, Lufkin & Jenrette).

Hungry for more inside scoop? Join Vault.com's popular online community for finance and banking — www.vault.com

VAULT.com **425**

Buy-side: The clients of investment banks (mutual funds, pension funds) that buy the stocks, bonds and securities sold by the investment banks. (The investment banks that sell these products to investors are known as the sell-side.)

Commercial bank: A bank that lends, rather than raises money. For example, if a company wants $30 million to open a new production plant, it can approach a commercial bank for a loan.

Commercial paper: Short-term corporate debt, typically maturing in nine months or less.

Commodities: Assets (usually agricultural products or metals) that are generally interchangeable with one another and therefore share a common price. For example, corn, wheat, and rubber generally trade at one price on commodity markets worldwide.

Common stock: Also called common equity, common stock represents an ownership interest in a company. (As opposed to preferred stock, see below.) The vast majority of stock traded in the markets today is common, as common stock enables investors to vote on company matters. An individual with 51 percent or more of shares owned controls a company's decisions and can appoint anyone he/she wishes to the board of directors or to the management team.

Comparable company analysis (Comps): The primary tool of the corporate finance analyst. Comps include a list of financial data, valuation data and ratio data on a set of companies in an industry. Comps are used to value private companies or better understand a how the market values and industry or particular player in the industry.

Consumer Price Index: The CPI measure the percentage increase in a standard basket of goods and services. CPI is a measure of inflation for consumers.

Convertible preferred stock: This is a relatively uncommon type of equity issued by a company; convertible preferred stock is often issued when it cannot successfully sell either straight common stock or straight debt. Preferred stock pays a dividend, similar to how a bond pays coupon payments, but ultimately converts to common stock after a period of time. It is essentially a mix of debt and equity, and most often used as a means for a risky company to obtain capital when neither debt nor equity works.

Non-convertible preferred stock: Sometimes companies issue non-convertible preferred stock, which remains outstanding in perpetuity and trades like stocks. Utilities represent the best example of non-convertible preferred stock issuers.

Convertible bonds: Bonds that can be converted into a specified number of shares of stock.

Derivatives: An asset whose value is derived from the price of another asset. Examples include call options, put options, futures, and interest-rate swaps.

Discount rate: A widely followed short-term interest rate, set by the Federal Reserve to cause market interest rates to rise or fall, thereby causing the U.S. economy to grow more quickly or less quickly. (More technically, the discount rate is the rate at which federal banks lend money to each other on overnight loans.) Today, the discount rate can be directly moved by the Fed, but maintains a largely symbolic role.

Dividend: A payment by a company to shareholders of its stock, usually as a way to distribute profits to shareholders.

Equity: In short, stock. Equity means ownership in a company that is usually represented by stock.

The Fed: The Federal Reserve, which gently (or sometimes roughly), manages the country's economy by setting interest rates.

Federal funds rate: The rate domestic banks charge one another on overnight loans to meet federal reserve requirements. This rate tracks very closely to the discount rate, but is usually slightly higher.

Fixed income: Bonds and other securities that earn a fixed rate of return. Bonds are typically issued by governments, corporations and municipalities.

Float: The number of shares available for trade in the market times the price. Generally speaking, the bigger the float, the greater the stock's liquidity.

Floating rate: An interest rate that is benchmarked to other rates (such as the rate paid on U.S. Treasuries), allowing the interest rate to change as market conditions change.

Hungry for more inside scoop? Join Vault.com's popular online community for finance and banking — www.vault.com

VAULT.com **427**

Floor traders: Traders for an investment bank located in the firm's offices. Floor traders spend most of the day seated at their desks observing market action on their computer screens.

Glass-Steagall Act: Part of the legislation passed during the Depression (Glass-Steagall was passed in 1933) designed to help prevent future bank failure — the establishment of the F.D.I.C. was also part of this movement. The Glass-Steagall Act split America's investment banking (issuing and trading securities) operations from commercial banking (lending). For example, J.P. Morgan was forced to spin off its securities unit as Morgan Stanley. Since the late 1980s, the Federal Reserve has steadily weakened the act, allowing commercial banks such as NationsBank and Bank of America to buy investment banks like Montgomery Securities and Robertson Stephens. In 1999, Glass-Steagall was effectively repealed by the Graham-Leach-Bliley Act.

Graham-Leach-Bliley Act: Also known as the Financial Services Modernization Act of 1999. Essentially repealed many of the restrictions of the Glass-Steagall Act and made possible the current trend of consolidation in the financial services industry. Allows commercial banks, investment banks, and insurance companies to affiliate under a holding company structure.

Gross Domestic Product: GDP measures the total domestic output of goods and services in the United States. For reference, the GDP grew at a 4.2 percent rate in 1999. Generally, when the GDP grows at a rate of less than 2 percent, the economy is considered to be in recession.

Hedge: To balance a position in the market in order to reduce risk. Hedges work like insurance: a small position pays off large amounts with a slight move in the market.

High grade corporate bond: A corporate bond with a rating above BB. Also called investment grade debt.

High yield debt (a.k.a. Junk bonds): Corporate bonds that pay high interest rates (to compensate investors for high risk of default). Credit rating agencies such as Standard & Poor's rate a company's (or a municipality's) bonds based on default risk. Junk bonds rate below BB.

Initial Public Offering (IPO): The dream of every entrepreneur, the IPO is the first time a company issues stock to the public. Going public means more than raising money for the company: By agreeing to take on public shareholders, a company enters a whole world of required

SEC filings and quarterly revenue and earnings reports, not to mention possible shareholder lawsuits.

Institutional clients or investors: Large investors, such as pension funds or municipalities (as opposed to retail investors or individual investors).

Lead manager: The primary investment bank managing a securities offering. (An investment bank may share this responsibility with one or more co-managers.)

League tables: Tables that rank investment banks based on underwriting volume in numerous categories, such as stocks, bonds, high yield debt, convertible debt, etc. High rankings in league tables are key selling points used by investment banks when trying to land a client engagement.

Leveraged Buyout (LBO): The buyout of a company with borrowed money, often using that company's own assets as collateral. LBOs were the order of the day in the heady 1980s, when successful LBO firms such as Kohlberg Kravis Roberts made a practice of buying up companies, restructuring them, and reselling them or taking them public at a significant profit

LIBOR: London Inter-bank Offered Rate. A widely short-term interest rate. LIBOR represents the rate banks in England charge one another on overnight loans or loans up to five years. LIBOR is often used by banks to quote floating rate loan interest rates. Typically the benchmark LIBOR is the three-month rate.

Liquidity: The amount of a particular stock or bond available for trading in the market. For commonly traded securities, such as big cap stocks and U.S. government bonds, they are said to be highly liquid instruments. Small cap stocks and smaller fixed income issues often are called illiquid (as they are not actively traded) and suffer a liquidity discount, i.e. they trade at lower valuations to similar, but more liquid, securities.

The Long Bond: The 30-year U.S. Treasury bond. Treasury bonds are used as the starting point for pricing many other bonds, because Treasury bonds are assumed to have zero credit risk taking into account factors such as inflation. For example, a company will issue a bond that trades "40 over Treasuries." The 40 refers to 40 basis points (100 basis points = 1 percentage point).

Hungry for more inside scoop? Join Vault.com's popular online community for finance and banking — www.vault.com

VAULT.com **429**

Making markets: A function performed by investment banks to provide liquidity for their clients in a particular security, often for a security that the investment bank has underwritten. (In others words, the investment bank stands willing to buy the security, if necessary, when the investor later decides to sell it.)

Market Cap(italization): The total value of a company in the stock market (total shares outstanding x price per share).

Merchant banking: The department within an investment bank that invests the firm's own money in other companies. Analogous to a venture capital arm.

Money market securities: This term is generally used to represent the market for securities maturing within one year. These include short-term CDs, repurchase agreements, commercial paper (low-risk corporate issues), among others. These are low risk, short-term securities that have yields similar to Treasuries.

Mortgage-backed bonds: Bonds collateralized by a pool of mortgages. Interest and principal payments are based on the individual homeowners making their mortgage payments. The more diverse the pool of mortgages backing the bond, the less risky they are.

Municipal bonds ("Munis"): Bonds issued by local and state governments, a.k.a. municipalities. Municipal bonds are structured as tax-free for the investor, which means investors in muni's earn interest payments without having to pay federal taxes. Sometimes investors are exempt from state and local taxes, too. Consequently, municipalities can pay lower interest rates on muni bonds than other bonds of similar risk.

Pitchbook: The book of exhibits, graphs, and initial recommendations presented by bankers to a prospective client when trying to land an engagement.

Pit traders: Traders who are positioned on the floor of stock and commodity exchanges (as opposed to floor traders, situated in investment bank offices).

P/E ratio: The price to earnings ratio. This is the ratio of a company's stock price to its earnings-per-share. The higher the P/E ratio, the more expensive a stock is (and also the faster investors believe the company will grow). Stocks in fast-growing industries tend to have higher P/E ratios.

Prime rate: The average rate U.S. banks charge to companies for loans.

Producer Price Index: The PPI measure the percentage increase in a standard basket of goods and services. PPI is a measure of inflation for producers and manufacturers.

Proprietary trading: Trading of the firm's own assets (as opposed to trading client assets).

Prospectus: A report issued by a company (filed with and approved by the SEC) that wishes to sell securities to investors. Distributed to prospective investors, the prospectus discloses the company's financial position, business description, and risk factors.

Red herring: Also known as a preliminary prospectus. A financial report printed by the issuer of a security that can be used to generate interest from prospective investors before the securities are legally available to be sold. Based on final SEC comments, the information reported in a red herring may change slightly by the time the securities are actually issued.

Retail clients: Individual investors (as opposed to institutional clients).

Return on equity: The ratio of a firm's profits to the value of its equity. Return on equity, or ROE, is a commonly used measure of how well an investment bank is doing, because it measures how efficiently and profitably the firm is using its capital.

Risk arbitrage: When an investment bank invests in the stock of a company it believes will be purchased in a merger or acquisition. (Distinguish from risk-free arbitrage.)

Risk-free arbitrage: When an investment bank buys a derivative or equity for a slightly lower price in one market and resells it in another. For example, if Dell stock were trading at 212 in the United States and 213 in Japan, buying it in the U.S. and reselling it in Japan would be risk-free. Risk-free arbitrage opportunities are infrequent and much more arcane than the example provided.

Roadshow: The series of presentations to investors that a company undergoing an IPO usually gives in the weeks preceding the offering. Here's how it works: Several weeks before the IPO is issued, the company and its investment bank will travel to major cities throughout the country. In each city, the company's top executives make a

Hungry for more inside scoop? Join Vault.com's popular online community for finance and banking — www.vault.com

VAULT.com **431**

presentation to analysts, mutual fund managers, and others attendees and also answer questions.

S-1: A type of legal document filed with the SEC for a private company aiming to go public. The S-1 is almost identical to the prospectus sent to potential investors. The SEC must approve the S-1 before the stock can be sold to investors.

S-2: A type of legal document filed with the SEC for a public company looking to sell additional shares in the market. The S-2 is almost identical to the prospectus sent to potential investors. The SEC must approve the S-2 before the stock is sold.

Sales memo: Short reports written by the corporate finance bankers and distributed to the bank's salespeople. The sales memo provides salespeople with points to emphasize when hawking the stocks and bonds the firm is underwriting.

Securities and Exchange Commission (SEC): A federal agency that, like the Glass-Steagall Act, was established as a result of the stock market crash of 1929 and the ensuing depression. The SEC monitors disclosure of financial information to stockholders, and protects against fraud. Publicly traded securities must first be approved by the SEC prior to trading.

Securitize: To convert an asset into a security that can then be sold to investors. Nearly any income-generating asset can be turned into a security. For example, a 20-year mortgage on a home can be packaged with other mortgages just like it, and shares in this pool of mortgages can then be sold to investors.

Short-term debt: A bond that matures in nine months or less. Also called commercial paper.

Syndicate: A group of investment banks that will together underwrite a particular stock or debt offering. Usually the lead manager will underwrite the bulk of a deal, while other members of the syndicate will each underwrite a small portion.

T-Bill Yields: The yield or internal rate of return an investor would receive at any given moment on a 90-120 government treasury bill.

Tax-exempt bonds: Municipal bonds (also known as munis). Munis are free from federal taxes and, sometimes, state and local taxes.

10K: An annual report filed by a public company with the Securities and Exchange Commission (SEC). Includes financial information, company information, risk factors, etc.

10Q: Similar to a 10K, but contains quarterly financial data on a company.

Tombstone: The advertisements that appear in publications like *Financial Times* or *The Wall Street Journal* announcing the issuance of a new security. The tombstone ad is placed by the investment bank to boast to the world that it has completed a major deal.

Treasury Securities: Securities issued by the U.S. government. These are divided into Treasury Bills (maturity of up to 2 years), Treasury Notes (from 2 years to 10 years maturity), and Treasury Bonds (10 years to 30 years). As they are government guaranteed, often treasuries are considered risk-free. In fact, while U.S. Treasuries have no default risk, they do have interest rate risk; if rates increase, then the price of UST's will decrease.

Underwrite: The function performed by investment banks when they help companies issue securities to investors. Technically, the investment bank buys the securities from the company and immediately resells the securities to investors for a slightly higher price, making money on the spread.

Yield: The annual return on investment. A high yield bond, for example, pays a high rate of interest.

Hungry for more inside scoop? Join Vault.com's popular online
community for finance and banking — www.vault.com

VAULT.com **433**

Recommended Reading

SUGGESTED TEXTS

- Burrough, Bryan and Helyar, John. *Barbarians at the Gate: The Fall of RJR Nabisco*. New York: Harper & Row, 1990.

- Endlich, Lisa. *Goldman Sachs: The Culture of Success*. New York: Alfred A. Knopf, 1999.

- Gordon, John Steele, *The Great Game: The Emergence of Wall Street As a World Power, 1653-2000*. New York: Scribner, 1999.

- Lewis, Michael. *Liar's Poker*. New York: Norton, 1989.

- Lewis, Michael. *The Money Culture*. New York: W. W. Norton, 1991.

- Rolfe, John and Traub, Peter. *Monkey Business: Swinging Through the Wall Street Jungle*. New York: Warner Books, 2000.

- Stewart, James Brewer. *Den of Thieves*. New York: Simon and Schuster, 1991.

SUGGESTED PERIODICALS

- American Banker
- Business Week
- The Daily Deal
- The Economist
- Forbes
- Fortune
- Institutional Investor
- Investment Dealers' Digest
- Investor's Business Daily
- Red Herring
- The Wall Street Journal

Hungry for more inside scoop? Join Vault.com's popular online
community for finance and banking — www.vault.com

VAULT.com **435**

About the Authors

Anita Kapadia is the Finance Editor at Vault.com. She graduated from New York University's Stern School of Business with a B.S. in Finance and holds an MFA from Columbia University in creative writing. Prior to joining Vault.com, Anita worked as an investment banking analyst at Merrill Lynch.

Chris Prior is a graduate of Queens College of the City University of New York. Before joining Vault.com as a finance writer, Chris was a staff reporter at *Treasury and Risk Management Magazine*, a financial trade publication based in New York.

Tom Lott, born in Dallas, Texas, graduated from Vanderbilt University in 1993. He started in the investment banking business upon graduation, joining Raymond James & Associates, an investment bank in St. Petersburg, Florida. His work experience includes a brief stint in research and four years in corporate finance. He obtained his MBA from the J.L. Kellogg Graduate School of Management (Northwestern), where he served as chairman of the investments club. He now works in fixed income trading at Merrill Lynch in New York City.

Hungry for more inside scoop? Join Vault.com's popular online
community for finance and banking — www.vault.com

VAULT.COM **437**